Cochise

Other books by Peter Aleshire

Warrior Woman

*The Fox and the Whirlwind: General George Crook
and Geronimo, A Paired Biography*

Reaping the Whirlwind: The Apache Wars

Cochise

The Life and Times of the Great Apache Chief

Peter Aleshire

CASTLE BOOKS

This edition published in 2005 by
CASTLE BOOKS ®
A division of Book Sales, Inc.
114 Northfield Avenue
Edison, NJ 08837

This edition published by arrangement with and permission of
John Wiley & Sons, Inc.
111 River Street
Hoboken, New Jersey 07030

Library of Congress Cataloging-in-Publication Data:

Aleshire, Peter.
Cochise: the life and times of the great Apache chief / Peter Aleshire.
    p. cm.
Includes bibliographical references and index.
1. Cochise, Apache chief, d. 1874. 2. Chiricahua Indians—Kings and rulers—Biography. 3. Chiricahua Indians—Wars. 4. Chiricahua Indians—History—19th century. 5. Apache Indians—Wars., 1872-1873. I. Title.

E99.A6 C569 2001
973'.04972'0092—dc21
[B]   2001022369

ISBN-13: 978-0-7858-2035-2
ISBN-10: 0-7858-2035-3

Printed in the United States of America

The End of the World

The old people used to tell us that when the end of the earth is coming, all the water will begin to dry up. For a long time there will be no rain. There will be only a few places, about three places, where there will be springs. At those three places the water will be dammed up and all the people will come in to those places and start fighting over the water. That's what old Nani used to tell us. Those old Indians found out somehow, I don't know how. And the way it looks, I believe it is the truth. Many old Chiricahua used to tell the same story. They said that in this way most of the people will kill each other off. Maybe there will be a few good people left.

When the new world comes after that the White people will be Indians and the Indians will be White people.

Contents

Preface

Imagine if you had to write a biography of George Washington using only accounts written by British soldiers and German mercenaries. Imagine if the only primary sources describing Julius Caesar were accounts by Gauls whose villages he destroyed. Imagine writing a psychological portrait of Marie Antoinette using only descriptions written by French revolutionaries with at least one family member who had been executed by the king.

These analogies roughly approximate the challenge of writing an emotionally, culturally, spiritually, and historically accurate biography of Cochise, perhaps the greatest war leader of a warrior people and arguably the only Native American leader to actually win his war with the United States of America. From his birth between 1800 and 1810 and his death in 1874, Cochise fought both the Americans and the Mexicans to a standstill. He battled almost continuously for half a century, sometimes leading small bands of raiders, sometimes leading hundreds of warriors who depopulated whole provinces. These war parties killed thousands of people and fought major pitched battles with both Mexican and American armies. He proved himself a master strategist, exercising unprecedented control over his fiercely independent warriors and setting ambushes so cleverly they became his terrifying trademark. He was outnumbered and outgunned, but fought on decade after decade after decade. In the end, he forced the United States government to cede to his people their own land—a reservation centered on the Dragoon and Chiricahua Mountains in southeastern Arizona. This great victory did not long survive him. The government discarded its promises to his people soon after he died, which spurred another decade of warfare and ruin—a tragedy for both the Apache and the Americans. This makes his life an epic of courage and loss.

It's almost impossible to do justice to the life of Cochise using conventional historiography. Neither Cochise nor his closest associates left any direct record of their thoughts or actions. His enemies, who lived in a time when Native Americans were considered subhuman savages, left the only firsthand descriptions we have of him. Those enemies were mostly interested in their unending war with him and so dwelled on the killings, torture, and genocidal fury the conflict inspired. As a result, this unending chronicle of raids and battles dominates most accounts of the life of Cochise. And although he was a spellbinding orator, we have only a handful of examples of his speeches—mostly recorded after translations from Apache to Spanish and then to English—at conferences with soldiers trying to convince him to surrender. These existing primary sources focus on warfare to the exclusion of almost everything else, which badly distorts Cochise's role as a religious, political, and moral leader.

The one-sided nature of the sources convinced me I could be true to the life of Cochise only by violating many of the rules of conventional biography. I was encouraged in this notion by the fact that Edwin Sweeney has already written an excellent, definitive, conventional biography of Cochise, published in 1991 by the University of Oklahoma Press. This book proved invaluable in my own research, and anyone who reads my book will find all sorts of treasures and a different perspective by turning to Sweeney's *Cochise*. However, the very thoroughness of that biography convinced me to try something different. My goal was to produce a biography that was both historically accurate and culturally authentic.

Fortunately, other historians and researchers have gathered wonderful material of which I made use. Anthropologist Morris Opler spent decades working with Apache informants in the early twentieth century and wrote two crucial books—*An Apache Life-Way: The Economic, Social, and Religious Institutions of the Chiricahua Indians* and *Myths and Tales of the Chiricahua Apache Indians*. In addition, anthropologist Keith Basso has provided a moving and absorbing glimpse into Apache philosophy and thought in his remarkable *Wisdom Sits in Places*, a humbling glimpse into a beleaguered culture of great beauty and insight. Anthropologist Grenville Goodwin also wrote with sympathy and insight into Apache culture, although he focused on the closely related White Mountain Apache. Moreover, we have some first-person Chiricahua and Chihenne Apache accounts gathered by historian Eve Ball. She wrote *Ideh* and *In the Days of Victorio*, which provide an invaluable sense of the Apache voice and view. Finally, we have some wonderful firsthand accounts by whites sympathetic to the Apache—notably the journal of Captain

Joseph Sladen, published recently as *Making Peace with Cochise*, and several accounts left by General Oliver Otis Howard. These vivid and insightful descriptions of Chiricahua culture and outlook gave me the courage to attempt a biography that remains true to both events and perspectives. In this, I was also inspired by Mari Sandoz's biography of Crazy Horse, which conveyed the life of this great war leader with a seemingly Sioux voice.

So this introduction is really something of a confession and a guide. I'm going to confess my sins against historiography here so you can take those trade-offs and presumptions into account in reading the ensuing pages.

I give myself the latitude to speculate on what Cochise was thinking and use a seminovelistic narration to convey it. I tried to base these excursions into his mind on historical events or descriptions of Apache attitudes and beliefs offered by people like Basso, Opler, and Ball and their Chiricahua Apache informants. I have included in the text most of the known direct quotations from Cochise, in each case using direct quotation marks. I have also borrowed from Opler's and Basso's works statements or myths or stories offered by their informants. You'll find these myths and stories scattered throughout the book, noted as to the source.[1] In some cases, I've taken the liberty of attributing these stories to Cochise or to other people, in each case noting when I've done so. This seemed the best way to give the story of Cochise's life the tenor and outlook of his culture.

I tried to give the biography a certain narrative momentum—which required another departure from convention. The accounts of the Apache Wars are full of contradictions and inconsistencies. The conventional way to deal with these contradictions would be to present them all, as Sweeney does in *Cochise*. But I wanted to present the story largely from an Apache viewpoint and so tried to limit the narration to what Cochise probably knew. In my *Fox and the Whirlwind*, a dual biography of General George Crook and Geronimo, I could present a complete picture by shifting back and forth from Geronimo to Crook. But in *Cochise* I stuck to an Apache view, although I did include more dates and numbers than would appear in a traditional Apache telling. I also used American and Mexican names for people and places, to avoid confusion with other accounts.

You will find a lot of the conventional historical approach in the notes, which play a crucial role in this biography. My notes list sources, indicate when I'm speculating as to thoughts and feelings, show where I've attributed stories and myths and beliefs, explain things that were happening offstage, and discuss other versions of the same events. Anyone who suffers a jittery withdrawal from conventional historiography can gain some measure of reassurance by reading all the notes—which account for about 10 percent of the total word count.

I want to also acknowledge the great support and assistance of many people. Kathy Koury was kind enough to edit the manuscript. She couldn't possibly have located all my mistakes—but she made me seem more coherent, careful, and insightful than I deserve. She also helped me figure out how to go about this biography by responding with wit, sympathy, and good sense to my ruminations and ramblings as I was writing. Hana Lane, my editor at Wiley, deserves great credit (or perhaps it is blame) for encouraging me in this attempt. She was my editor for *The Fox and the Whirlwind*. Far from restraining me, she encouraged the further development of this approach you hold in your hands. Of course, I am also deeply indebted to Sweeney, Basso, Opler, Ball, and the other historians and anthropologists who have worked so hard and long to gather up the materials and perspectives I wove together into this book. In addition, I am grateful for the support of Arizona State University West and my colleagues there, where I'm a senior lecturer in the Department of American Studies. Finally, I want to thank my wife, Elissa, for putting up with me—a not inconsiderable task—and for her long support and interest in my odd and seemingly inexhaustible obsession with this terrible, wonderful, triumphant, tragic time in our history. My sons—Noah, Seth, and Caleb—also deserve mention, both for needing the college money that spurred me on whenever this project seemed too ambitious and for being such considerate and likable fellows that I could actually write a book in a home office in the living room.

I also must apologize to my readers. I set out to tell the full truth—but I failed. It is of only modest comfort that I was doomed to failure, as are all historians. I doubt I could tell the full truth about my own life, so I know I haven't captured the undistorted "truth" about Cochise—especially given the limitations of the sources. However, even if Cochise and all his family and friends had left long autobiographies, I would still inevitably skew the story as a result of my own cultural biases. If Cochise could read this account, he would no doubt shake his head at the arrogance and hubris of the whites and point out that I have it all wrong.

My one slender hope is that he would conclude I was less wrong than many who have described his life. He might even concede that I tried to tell the truth and wrote with respect and humility.

I hope he would conclude I didn't do too badly—for a White Eye.

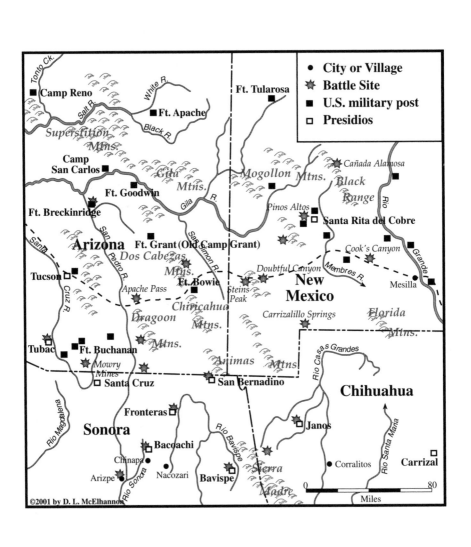

Legend
- ● City or Village
- ✸ Battle Site
- ■ U.S. military post
- □ Presidios

Torto Ck.

■ **Camp Reno**

White R.

Ft. Tularosa

Salt R.

■ **Ft. Apache**

Black R.

Superstition Mtns.

Camp San Carlos ■

Gila Mtns.

Mogollon Mtns.

Cañada Alamosa ✸

Black Range

Ft. Goodwin ■

Gila R.

Pinos Altos ✸

Rio Grande

Ft. Breckinridge ✸

■ **Santa Rita del Cobre** □

Arizona

San Pedro R.

Dos Cabezas Mtns.

San Simon R.

■ **Ft. Grant (Old Camp Grant)**

✸

Cook's Canyon ✸

Santa

Doubtful Canyon ✸

Membres R.

New Mexico

Tucson □

Apache Pass

■ **Ft. Bowie**

Cruz R.

Steins Peak ✸

Mesilla ●

Chiricahua

Dragoon Mtns.

Carrizalillo Springs ✸

Florida Mtns.

✸

Animas Mtns.

Tubac □

■ **Ft. Buchanan**

Rio Casas Grandes

Chihuahua

✸ *Mowry Mines*

✸

□ **Santa Cruz**

□ **San Bernadino**

Rio Magdalena

□ **Fronteras**

Rio Bavispe

✸ **Janos** ●

Sonora

✸ **Bacoachi** □

Rio Santa Maria

● Corralitos

Chinapa ●

Nacozari ●

Bavispe □

Sierra Madre

□ **Carrizal**

Arizpe ✸

Rio Sonora

0   80

Miles

©2001 by D. L. McElhannon

October 1869

He Turns to Fight

The Destruction of the Earth

The old world was destroyed by water, by a flood. There was
only one mountain at the time of this flood that was not entirely
covered by the water. And that mountain is called today "White-
Ringed Mountain." No human beings lived through this flood, but
there was a rooster that floated on the water and got on top of that
mountain. The water almost got to the top of that mountain, almost
covered it. Now you can see the mountain with the white ring at the
highest point the water reached. I think that mountain is in Old
Mexico.

It seems to me that it all goes to prove that the earth is just an old
world that has been cleaned up by a flood. The way the story goes,
there was a bad class of people before the flood; that's why Life Giver
brought the flood. It rained hard for a long while, I've heard, but they
don't say how long. Then after that Child-of-the-Water and White-
Painted Woman made human beings.

After the water had gone down, a bow and arrow and a gun were
put before two men. The man who had the first choice took the gun
and he became the White man. The other had to take the bow and he
became the Indian. If the second man had got the gun, he would have
been the White man, they say.

Cochise, the hard, scarred shield of his people, lay against the
rough skin of the rock and watched the yellow dog coyote pick his
way up the pine-picketed, boulder-studded slope toward silently
waiting death. He could almost hear the thoughts of the rock, long
and slow—like a woman who dreams while her baby sleeps at her
breast. The thoughts of the rock comforted him—although he knew
that the enemies who yearned so fiercely for his death were drawing

close now. Cochise watched with the motionless patience of the
heron as Merejildo Grijalva led the soldiers carefully up the slope
toward where more than 150 Chiricahua warriors waited in perfect
silence. They lay coiled all along the wall of boulders just below the
ridge, still as the rattlesnake in the moment before it lashes out with
its mouth agape. Cochise watched Grijalva come on with a heavy
mixture of satisfaction and sorrow. He cast his mind back across the
years to the day when his warriors had killed so many in that small
village deep in Mexico, and then scooped up the boy to become one
of the People. The warriors often took the children in payment for
the lives the Mexicans had in their turn gathered up and cast like
leaves on the fire of the hatred that burned always between the two
peoples. Cochise had sheltered the baby in his own wickiup and
raised him as a son, teaching the hard lessons of a warrior with
unflinching discipline. Grijalva had learned every lesson, thirsty as
the sand. But his heart had remained as false as a Mexican's, and so
when his chance came he ran away and joined the soldiers. He had
hunted the People now for these many months, running ahead like
a camp dog, panting and eager. Now Grijalva brought the soldiers up
this slope, using everything Cochise had taught him to cling to their
trail as the gila monster clings to the hand, poison dripping down its
teeth into the wound.[1]

Cochise looked down along the line of the boulders, satisfied
that he could not see his own warriors—although he knew where
each one lay in the embrace of the rocks. He closed his eyes for a
moment, listening for the whispering of his Power so he would know
what he should do. He wondered whether he had offended his
Power in some manner, for his people had dwindled like a spring in
a year without rain. He wondered whether he had misunderstood
his Power, in making war on the Whites, in running off the horse
herd from the fort, in attacking the miners clawing at the body of
the earth, and in staying here in the mountains where the rocks lent
him their Power. Perhaps he should have gone down into Mexico
until the soldiers grew tired of looking for him. Impatiently, he
shook off that thought, knowing that he must run down the mountain of his life without looking back, fated as the rain. His Power
had brought him safely through all of these years, when so many
others had died. Doubts could only weaken him now, like blood
seeping from a wound.

He opened his eyes and focused them on Grijalva and the five
men with him, moving up the slope like deer into a clearing.

Chiricahua rocks. The compressed volcanic ash of the Chiricahuas eroded into strange shapes and profiles that spurred rich myths and stories among the Apache. *(Peter Aleshire)*

Cochise wondered how long it would take the many soldiers down in the trees at the bottom of the slope to come up once the warriors had killed Grijalva. And he wondered whether other soldiers might already be coming down the canyon from the other end, or making their way up the slope on the other side of the ridge, or coming from each of the four directions—like wind to a ceremony. He wondered whether the women and children and the few warriors he could spare had made it safely to the hiding places, from which they would gather again when the battle had ended. So many uncertainties remained, like moving across ice that cracks and groans. He had thrown out his lookouts with his customary care, spreading them out like the splayed fingers of his hand. But the soldiers were everywhere these days, even here in the heart of the Chiricahua Mountains, where the rocks stood up like dancers and the Ga'an spirits drummed in the earth so that sometimes he could feel the thrumming when he pressed his cheek against the stone. He had been running from the soldiers for weeks, feinting like a knife fighter and then falling back and away when they lunged. Now, finally, he had turned, knowing he would not find better ground. He knew this ground as well as he knew the hollows of the body of his wife and had placed warriors overlooking every path, crack, and crevice up which the soldiers would have to come to get at them. He knew that the People had not won such a battle in many turnings of the leaves, but something had risen up in him. He had turned now to this fight as to a lover, long absent. He could only hope that it was his Power that turned him, not his pride or his anger.

He brought his long rifle to his shoulder, with the etched silver inlay sun-warmed against his skin, and sighted on Grijalva, stealing from one scrap of cover to another and scanning the slopes ahead with the ferocity of an eagle. Just as Cochise fired the shot that would start the fight, Grijalva pulled back from the bullet as though his own Power had whispered a warning. Instantly, shooting started all along the ridge, and several of the soldiers with Grijalva dropped to the ground, crying out. None of the bullets found Grijalva, although they all longed for him. Three of the five men went down, but Grijalva and the other one retreated down the slope to good cover. Down below, Cochise could see the movement of the soldiers through the trees, coming up quickly.

Cochise picked his shots carefully, knowing they had not much powder or bullets—their greatest weakness in this death fight with the soldiers, who had more bullets than the ants have sand. The stories said Usen had let Killer-of-Enemies—who loved the White Eyes—and Child-of-the-Water—who loved the People—choose gifts for the people they each favored. Child-of-the-Water had chosen the bow, the arrow, and all the best places for the People—so they could hunt and live free. Killer-of-Enemies had chosen for the Whites the gun, corn, and the ability to put all of their Power into metal—so they could make many clever things. Now it seemed the gifts of Killer-of-Enemies would grind down the People, like corn on a stone.

The soldiers were well led; they did not rush up the slope, which would have made them easier to kill. When Cochise saw the rush of the soldiers stop behind good cover, he felt his heart settle in his chest. In truth, he had known they would not come easily into the snare that he had concealed for them with such care. The *nantan* leader of these soldiers[2] had come from Fort Bowie, at the north end of the Chiricahuas, and had held to their trail and kept his head all the time he had chased them. Cochise knew he could not count on this one to make a great mistake. Several warriors showed themselves, hoping to taunt the soldiers so they would use up their ammunition or charge up the hill. But the soldiers held their discipline—the one thing they could do better than warriors. Cochise lay against the rock and waited, seeing the battle in his mind as though he was a red-tailed hawk floating above the mountain. He knew how the ridge would look down there where the *nantan* was squinting into the sun, trying to make his decision. Therefore, Cochise also knew that the *nantan* would send soldiers around to the right and around to the left, hoping to flank the strong position of the warriors above him.

Sure enough, in just the time Cochise had expected, he heard shooting on the left where he had placed Nahilzay and his warriors. He knew Nahilzay would hold the warriors in the palm of his own Power, waiting until the soldiers had come within one hundred feet before firing. Nahilzay was tightly bound to Cochise, having married the daughter of the chief. Nahilzay, a short, powerful man with the barrel chest of a bear and fierce dark eyes, had his own following of warriors. He could not be commanded, only consulted and urged. Nahilzay had many scars and his own strong Power and could not be patted into shape like wet mud by the Power of Cochise. Naturally, these things made him all the more valuable—for love and loyalty stronger than gunpowder and bullets could not be commanded, only earned and freely exchanged. Cochise listened until he was certain from the sound of the shooting the soldiers had been turned back. Then he rose into a half crouch and slipped along the line of rocks he had chosen before he took this firing position so that he could move to the other side, where he knew the soldiers would make their next probe.

And so the battle continued through the hours of daylight, the soldiers probing, the warriors rising from where they had been placed by the Power of Cochise, the soldiers tumbling back down the hill—shooting as they gave back the ground they had gained. Sometimes the warriors dashed after them, mocking them to show their courage, half drunk with the pride of standing in place and driving the soldiers back. Cochise moved everywhere among them, careful of his cover, but disdainful of the bullets. Every warrior who saw him felt his Power as he moved past, like the taste in the air that warns of approaching thunder.

Finally, near sunset, the exhausted soldiers began to retreat down the slope, as the warriors jeered and sent a few more hoarded bullets after them. Just as the sun was giving way reluctantly to the darkness—which that troublesome Coyote had let out of the sack in the beginning of times—one very brave soldier went up the hill toward the place where the bodies of the first soldiers killed lay twisted and still in the red light. Cochise admired the courage of the soldier who came up the hill after his friends, and saw that he had the markings of a *nantan* on his shoulder. Still, Cochise was glad when a bullet hit the man in the face, taking away his jaw.[3] Cochise could admire courage in his enemies—but knew also that those were the very men most in need of killing.

The warriors all gathered uneasily that night on the ridge caught between triumph and alarm. They had driven off the soldiers—not just a patrol, but a large force. This was a powerful thing, and the few who had begun to wonder whether Cochise's Power still spoke to him because of the losses they had suffered in these past few weeks felt reassured. They talked among themselves, each recalling other fights they had been in, each trying to remember the last time the People had stood their ground and driven the soldiers away. Only Cochise could have done such a thing, they said quietly one to the other. And yet, they had also lost good men that day. Not many—but they all knew that a warrior was like a great, yellow-barked pine that once felled leaves an empty space for many years. But killing soldiers was like cutting grass that would return in a week. They knew that the word must already have hurried back to the soldier forts and to the roving columns that sought them always in the land that had once been theirs. The soldiers would come out of their ant-hills, converging on this spot as to a broken honeycomb.

And yet, Cochise did not gather the warriors and fling them south, toward Mexico, where the soldiers would not follow.

Instead, they moved a little north in the darkness—back toward Fort Bowie, keeping to the protection of the stone pillars and hiding places among the rocks standing upright, watching the sky like the first people turned to stone.

Cochise remained apart, circling some great question like a knife fighter, the point of his blade tracing the shape of it in the darkness. How had he come to this place—where he could win such a battle, but still have so little hope?

He had fought all of his life, killing so many enemies with his own hand that he could not remember them all even if he spent the night in counting them. He had walked in the footsteps of Child-of-the-Water—as his father had urged him to do from the first exhortation of his Moccasin Ceremony when he could not cover the track of a badger with his foot. His Power had favored him and guided him and protected his people. He had killed ten of his enemies for every death that had fallen on him as an obligation to avenge. He had drawn back even strong leaders like a single bow and led more warriors than even his father, whose name had been great for many years, before the Mexicans killed him by treachery. He had prayed and danced and done right in all things. But now he seemed helpless against the pitiless numbers, pack trains of bullets, and soulless greed of these Whites. Turn any White loose alone and he would die of thirst. But bring them all together, and they seemed as irresistible as the front edge of a sand dune. The harder he fought, the more death he drew to him—like lightning seeking a foolish man in a red shirt. What had he done to bring this down on the people who had been given into his hands to protect? What prayer had he neglected? What offense had the People committed that the gifts of Child-of-the-Water should be taken from their bleeding hands now?

Cochise, who all other men feared, prayed and sang and waited for his Power to move him to the place he must go, seeking some solution to the riddle of his life. Could it be that all his life, all his deaths, all his loss, all his struggle had only put off the inevitable surrender?

Had it come to him now to turn his palms upward and let the White Eyes take from him everything that had belonged to the People, excepting only their lives?

So Cochise passed the long night, casting his mind back through his life—seeking the answer to that one, deadly question.

2

In the Beginning

Two Women Play Dead and Escape from the Giant

The Giant used to kill people. There were two women hunting for wild berries. The Giant came along. They saw that they couldn't get away. But they knew that he wouldn't eat anything dead that he had not killed himself, so they took off their clothes and lay down as if dead. Giant came along and saw them. He took a stick and poked their nipples. He played for a while and then got tired and left them. When he was gone they got up and ran away.

No man's life starts with his own birth, for every man walks along the path of those who came before. Every warrior's life starts with Child-of-the-Water, who came down onto the earth in the beginning times—before the first people, when the animals and the Powers were intermingled, talking one to the other. Each one was both like a person and like a Power, like an individual and like all of the qualities of that individual, like a brave man and like Courage itself, all aspects of one another.[1]

At the first was only White-Painted Woman—who was herself an aspect of Power. But the world was full of monsters and Powers and the animals who were Power and who used Power. Human beings could not live in the world at the beginning times, because the monsters would devour them—even the children of White-Painted Woman. For a Giant lived near her camp and he would come to eat her children whenever she had them.[2]

But then a Spirit came to her one day and told her to take off her clothes and go out into the open under the sky and lie down there with her legs open. She did as the Spirit had told her and a great cloud came over her. Thunder sounded and the rain fell on her and seeped into her. The Spirit told her that she would have twins, the children of Water and Thunder. The Spirit said she must

8

hide her children under the fire, so the Giant would not find them and eat them. But when the boys were old enough to fire a bow, she should give them a bow and let them go out hunting.

White-Painted Woman did everything she had been told. But sometimes she let her children out from under the fire to sing to them and nurse them and watch them play in the sunlight. One time, the Giant heard them crying and hurried to her. But she felt him coming and hid her children under the fire. When the Giant questioned her, she said she was lonely for children and so had made the noise like a baby crying. Then another time the Giant came again and found the piece of cloth she had used to wipe their bottoms. But again she said she was lonely for children and had taken honeycomb that bees had left in a yucca stalk and smeared it on the cloth so that she could imagine that she still had children. Then another time the Giant came again and found the children's footprints in the dust around her campfire, but she said she had made the footprints herself. The Giant did not believe her, but she made the footprints with the edge of her hand and the tips of her fingers and he went away satisfied with her story.

When the two boys were old enough, White-Painted Woman gave them bows and arrows as the Spirit had instructed. One time after that, Child-of-the-Water wanted to go out. It was raining and lightning. His mother didn't want the boy to go. "It is dangerous to go out now," she said.[3]

"But I can go. I am the son of Lightning," Child-of-the-Water told her.

Then White-Painted Woman said, "This is your son."

"I do not believe he is my son, but I will test him," Lightning said.

Lightning tested him. Child-of-the-Water stood to the east and black lightning struck him. But it did not harm him. Then he stood to the south and blue lightning struck him. Then he stood to the west and yellow lightning struck him. Finally he stood to the north, where white lightning struck him. He was not injured at all.

Then Lightning said, "Now I know he is my son."

Killer-of-Enemies was the brother of Child-of-the-Water. He was the son of White-Painted Woman, too. Child-of-the-Water didn't want his brother to accompany him on the hunt, but he came. Child-of-the-Water wanted to send him back, but he came, anyway.

Child-of-the-Water decided to go out to kill Eagle. His mother told him it was dangerous and tried to keep him from it, but he said he would go, anyway. He killed a horse or a cow, filled the gut with blood, and wrapped this around himself.

Eagle picked him up and dropped him on a sharp rock. The blood from the entrails came out and Eagle thought he was dead and took him to the nest. The Eagles had three little ones in the nest. The old Eagles went out to look for more food.

Then Child-of-the-Water asked, "When will your father come home?"

"When the clouds gather and it looks like rain."

"And where will he alight?"

"On that rock sticking up there."

When the father Eagle came, Child-of-the-Water was ready for him. When Eagle beat his wings just before settling down, Child-of-the-Water hit him with his war club and threw him over the cliff. Then he asked when their mother would come back.

"A little later when it gets very cold," he was told.

Soon she came and Child-of-the-Water killed her in the same manner.

Then Child-of-the-Water asked which of the eaglets could fly farthest toward the ground. They said the smallest one could. So he killed the others. He got on the smallest one and rode to the ground. Then he also killed that one with his war club and plucked out the feathers. As he threw the feathers into the air, he called the names of the birds and each feather became a bird we know today.

Killer-of-Enemies had been going out hunting, but every time he killed something the Giant would come along and take the meat away from him. Killer-of-Enemies always cried, but it did him no good. He was afraid of the Giant.

On one particular occasion Killer-of-Enemies was afraid to go hunting. But his brother, Child-of-the-Water, wanted him to go hunting with him. His mother didn't want Child-of-the-Water to go. "You are too small. You couldn't do anything against that big Giant," she told him.

"I'm big, too," he said. He had an arrow of grama grass. Four times Child-of-the-Water asked his mother to let him go. She refused three times, but the fourth time she smiled a little and let him go.

The two brothers went out. Soon they killed a deer. They began to cut it up and to prepare a fire over which to cook some of the meat.

"Maybe Giant will come and take this away from us," said Killer-of-Enemies.

"I hope he does come," Child-of-the-Water replied.

"Don't say such things. He is big and strong and kills people."

"I'm strong, too."

Just as he said this, Giant came. He looked at the roasted meat lying near the boys. He picked it up and put it near himself. Child-of-the-Water got up and brought it back. The meat went back and forth like this four times.

By this time the Giant was very angry. "What can you do?" he asked Child-of-the-Water.

"I don't care how big you are. We are going to eat that meat."

Killer-of-Enemies was afraid and said nothing. Child-of-the-Water told him to eat.

Then the Giant said, "You're too small to fight me. Look at my arrow." His arrow was a big pine tree. It is not said what sort of wood he used for a bow.

Child-of-the-Water showed his arrows of grama grass. Giant took them and rubbed them along his anus. Child-of-the-Water could not lift the Giant's arrows, so he sat down on them and rubbed himself against them. Now they were going to fight. Each agreed to shoot four arrows. Giant said, "I'll shoot at you first," and Child-of-the-Water agreed.

When the Giant was about to shoot the first arrow, Child-of-the-Water stood facing east. The Giant shot his first arrow. As it came toward his breast, Child-of-the-Water said, "Phoo!" There was nothing in his mouth, but the pine tree broke into pieces as though lightning had struck it. Each time the Giant shot another arrow, Child-of-the-Water turned clockwise to another direction. Each time he said the same thing and the arrow was shattered. Because Child-of-the-Water turned clockwise at this time, the Chiricahua do so today.

When the Giant's four arrows were used up, he had to stand and let Child-of-the-Water shoot at him. He tried to make the same noise as Child-of-the-Water, and he turned just as Child-of-the-Water had done. But it did him no good. The Giant was dressed in four jackets of flint, and each time Child-of-the-Water shot, one of these jackets fell to the ground. Before the last shot the brothers could see the Giant's heart beating beneath the jacket, and when Child-of-the-Water shot the last arrow, the jacket was pierced and the Giant was killed.

And then Killer-of-Enemies was glad. They went over there and ate the meat they had cooked. They took a piece of meat on their backs and took it to White-Painted Woman, their mother.

White-Painted Woman had been worrying about the two boys. Then she saw them coming with the meat. She was so happy that she sang for those boys. She was dancing. This is the song she sang:

What a happy day it is
To be bringing in such good news.[4]

After this, Child-of-the-Water killed each of the other monsters that made it impossible for people to live in the world. He killed Buffalo, who breathed fire and trampled anyone he saw on the open prairie. He killed Buffalo with the help of Gopher, who dug a hole beneath Buffalo so that Child-of-the-Water could shoot him in the heart as he lay down. Then Child-of-the-Water killed Antelope, who killed with his eyes. This time he had the help of Lizard, who showed Child-of-the-Water the trick to making himself the same color as the ground to become invisible. When he had killed the Giant, and Eagles, and Buffalo and Antelope, people could live in the world. And they could follow the path of Child-of-the-Water, putting their own feet in his footprints so they could live rightly. Everyone learned that path, from the time they were babies in their cradleboards. The father of Cochise and the mother of Cochise stretched his head and his heart over the frame of the stories, like the wet leather over the ash staves of a cradleboard. In this way, he learned that even a boy may kill a Giant, if Power favors him and if he does right and thinks right. He learned that people can only survive with the help of Gopher and Lizard and all of the other aspects of Power. In this way he learned that a warrior must use his wits as much as his courage or his lungs or his legs, and that an enemy that seems too strong to kill can nonetheless be defeated through cleverness. In this way he learned the duties of a warrior—to protect the women and the children and to face danger and duty and death without complaint or fear. So in this way he learned that the smallest breath of Power can shatter even an arrow as large as a tree and that an arrow made of reed may be enough to triumph in the hands of a warrior with courage and intelligence and the respect of his Power.

Of course, Cochise learned many other lessons in his growing up, for he was born[5] into a powerful and respected family in a peaceful time on the brink of change—when the flood of changes rearranged the world like sandbars on a great river in the spring.

He was Chokonen, one of the four divisions of the Chiricahua, who were the strongest fighting people. The Chokonen lived mostly in the Dragoon and Chiricahua Mountains, but ranged freely over a large territory and spent much of the year living in Mexico—sometimes camping near friendly towns but mostly staying in the Sierra Madre and other mountain ranges, where the rocks, their friends, would protect them. The Chokonen were close friends and allies of the Bedonkohe, who lived just to the northeast, and the Chihenne,[6] who lived in the mountain ranges to the east.[7] The Chokonen also often raided with and married into the bands of the Nednhis,[8] who lived down in Mexico, oftentimes near the Mexican town of Janos and in the fortress of the Sierra Madre. Other bands lived alongside the territory of the Chiricahua, including the Tonto and the White Mountain bands to the west and north. But even though those bands spoke the same language, the Chiricahua often fought them. The Navajo[9] lived to the north, but they also were more likely to fight the Chiricahua than to join them in fighting.

Cochise was born into a peaceful time, but their world was like a cracked rock on a cliff edge waiting for the weight of an unwary foot.

Once the People had lived quietly, moving with the seasons like the bluebird. In the summer, they lived high in the mountains. In the winter, they lived down in the valleys. They scattered seeds here and there, so they would have corn and squash when they came back in the spring or in the summer. But mostly they moved as easily as the animals, first to harvest the mescal, then to gather the acorns, then to wait for the elk, then to harvest the fruit of the saguaro. They carried only a few things with them and listened to the drumming of the Ga'an in the mountains, in the rocks, in the deep canyons. They lived in small bands—hunting and dancing and singing—with few enemies. Sometimes when times were hard and they had not enough food, they went down into the river valleys where the bean eaters lived—the Papago and the Pima. Sometimes they would carry baskets of corn and seed away from the storehouses of the farming people. But more often they traded with them. Sometimes they fought the Yaqui, who lived in the valleys in Mexico. But mostly they stayed to themselves in the mountains, giving thanks for the gifts of Child-of-the-Water.

Then the first of the pale strangers had come from the south—
fierce, bearded men in steel shirts. They fell upon the valley people,
with steel swords and lances, and made them into slaves. More
important, they brought with them horses and cattle. The People
watched them come on, burning through the valleys and consuming
the stay-at-home people who lived along the rivers and depended
on their ripening corn to survive. They depended on their corn and
so could not get out of the way of the newcomers, who had hair on
their faces like bears and a seemingly relentless hatred for all other
people. The Pima resisted at the first, but they were no match for
the steel swords and steel shirts and wonderful horses of the
invaders. The river people surrendered and became the creatures of
the pale invaders, who built small towns and began farming, and
sent the broken river people as slaves into holes in the earth. The
invaders—the Spanish—had a kind of madness for gold and silver—
soft, shining metals that Usen had forbidden to the People. They
could not have enough of it, although gold and silver were good
only for jewelry, as they were too soft to be tools or any other useful thing. The villages of the river Pima and the Papago became
camps of the Spanish, who rewarded them with sheep and cattle
and horses.

The warriors of the People quickly understood the value of
horses and of cattle. They took these animals from the Spanish and
from the Papago and from the Pima. Before the Spanish came,
there was not much use in raiding the river people. How much grain
could a warrior carry away on his back, pursued all the while by the
Pima? How much turquoise or shell did a warrior need? So they did
not bother much with the Pima—except when the acorns failed or
the deer hid themselves so well they needed a little food from their
storehouses. But everything changed when the Spanish brought
their horses and their cattle. Now a raiding party could travel a
thousand miles on a single raid. Now they could round up horses
and cattle and sheep and drive them back to their camps. Now they
could load mules with things worth taking. Now a skilled warrior
could bring back enough wealth to pay the bride-price for a wife or
host his family and his clan and his friends at the coming-of-age
Sunrise Ceremony for his daughter or at the Moccasin Ceremony for
his son. Now the leading warriors could grow in influence and
respect by bringing back things they could share with their wives'
families, and the young warriors and the old people and the widows.

Of course, the Spanish and the Pima got mad when the warriors took their horses and their cattle. The Pima had always been good fighters when defending their towns and sometimes chased raiding parties a long way. But the Spanish were altogether different. They had men who did nothing but fight. They organized expeditions that chased raiding parties for a long time. They sent messages from one village to another. They made alliances with other people, even the warlike Comanche who lived to the east, so they could attack the People from many directions at once. They struck back whenever they lost a single horse—and they did not worry too much about finding the man who had taken the horse. They seemed happy to kill any warrior they could find—and oftentimes any woman or child. Often they put chains on the women and children and sent them to work in the mines, which was worse than simply killing them.

The arrival of the Spanish changed everything, and made the People into warriors first and foremost. Child-of-the-Water had made it clear to the first people that they must fight when they were threatened. No true man would stand by when a relative had been killed. No leader could accept the loss of one of his men without a response. This had always been essential to right living. A warrior must think carefully before doing harm to any one of the People, because all of his relatives and friends would seek revenge. Sometimes, this caused many years of bad blood between different bands, with each death calling for another. But usually it contained the conflict, because everyone knew the consequences of starting the first stone rolling down the loose slope. The obligation of revenge also for a long time kept the scattered bands of the People safe from their enemies. All of their enemies knew that killing any one of the People would call down the lightning. If a raiding party went to get horses and cattle from others too weak to keep them, they would go quietly to get what they wanted, harming no one. But if someone fought back and killed one of the warriors who had come for the horses, everything changed. Then the warriors went back to their band, shamed by their loss. The relatives of the dead man cut off their hair and wept and gashed their arms and burned all of his things—and then called upon others to help them seek revenge. The closest women relatives of the dead man would go about the camp, weeping and angry, calling their relatives to their sacred duty. They went to the band leader as well. And they called on their relatives in other bands. In this way, they would gather one or two hundred warriors—each free to choose whether he would go along. Then these warriors would go and kill anyone connected to the one who had killed the warrior. They came not quietly, but as the fire. They killed as many people as they could, so that the lesson could not be mistaken.

At first, the Spanish did much the same. They also gathered up hundreds of men and set out for revenge. They also killed anyone they encountered. The great difference was that the towns of the Spanish were easy to find, their horses easy to steal, their crops easy to burn. But the camps of the People moved often, and the Spanish could not come into their country without the word going out for a long time before they arrived. Still, the fight went on for whole life-times. The Spanish built great walled forts in the most important towns and kept soldiers posted in them, but the warriors of the People moved about freely between the presidios. Once six hundred warriors gathered together to attack Tucson, taking all of the horses and burning the houses and the crops outside of the walled presidio where the soldiers hid.[10]

Sometimes, the soldiers would surprise a camp and kill everyone in it. More often, the allies of the Spanish, like the Comanche, would sweep in and kill many people. But those blows fell mostly on the Chihenne and the Mescalero—who lived to the east. The Choko-nen lived in the Dragoon and the Chiricahua Mountains, a long way from the presidios or the Comanche or the fierce Yaqui. Only rarely did the Spanish dare to send an army that far to chastise them, but usually the warriors watched the soldiers from their high places and laughed. Nonetheless, the years of warfare made many widows and many fatherless children. And even though the warriors gained re-nown and wealth and respect, the never-ending war wore them down and made the keening of grief as common as a sunrise prayer in the camps of the People.

Still they fought on, going with fierce joy in the footsteps of Child-of-the-Water. And because they did not flinch, and because they kept faith with Usen, and because they had respect for Power, and because they lived rightly and thought rightly and remembered all the prayers, the Spanish finally surrendered. They sent messen-gers to the People and begged for peace. They offered up cattle and horses and corn and goods as payment to the People for land along the rivers where they could grow their corn. They agreed to stop stirring up other Indians against them, and to give supplies to the bands several times every year. Many bands of the People then settled near the towns of the Spanish, where they could easily get the tribute of food and supplies—including guns and the quick and potent liquor of the Spanish. Some of the leaders said the Spanish gave them only inferior guns that needed repair to make them dependent. Other leaders said the liquor of the Spanish was like a poison, which caused fights and grudges and shameful behavior. They said it was not like tizwin, the sweet, weak, quickly spoiling fermented corn drink the People made and drank in great quantities for certain ceremonies and celebrations.[11]

An uneasy peace settled between the Spanish and the People that lasted for a lifetime.[12]

Cochise[13] was born into the thin, frayed end of this time of peace,[14] although that only became clear later, when the world had cracked open and spouted flames like a fire that has smoldered all night. Some people later wondered whether he had been born into those times, at just the proper time to grip the lance of his people.

He was born into the Chiricahua Mountains—the Mountain of Wild Turkeys[15] and the land of rocks standing up, where the stone spires stood sentry.

He was the son of Pisago Cabezón,[16] the leading man of the Chokonen. Of course, the son of such a man could not inherit leadership any more than he would keep the things that had belonged to a dead man. Among the People, leadership had to be continually earned. Every warrior followed his own heart and the urgings of his own Power. They followed men of good character, usually those who had Power in war. No man could command others even in his own right, and certainly no man could bind others to follow his son. Nonetheless, the sons and daughters of leading men and leading families were watched carefully. People looked for signs of Power and of favor. Such a man would train his sons and his daughters with care to keep them out of mischief and to make sure they were respectful. They could not resent things easily. They could not quarrel, which was beneath them. Above all, they were taught respect. They were taught to never steal, to treat their playmates with kindness and respect. They learned that if they were kind, then others would love them and follow them.[17]

From the beginning, his parents took care to guide Cochise on the correct path, using all of the old rituals to help his feet into the footprints of Child-of-the-Water. When the baby was born, they took him up and showed him to Usen and to Child-of-the-Water and to the Sun and to the Sky. Then they took him and rolled him in the dirt—once to the east, once toward the west, once toward the south, and once toward the north. All of his life, when he came back to that place, Cochise would put aside his gun and lie down on the ground to roll four times, once in each direction, so that the earth which had protected him would remember him and know that he also remembered.

His parents took great care also in making the cradleboard in which he remained for the first half year of his life. They hired a shaman who had Power in such matters. They found perfect, strong-grained branches of oak for the frame and sotol stalk[18] for the cross-pieces that formed the back. They made a canopy of the stems of red-barked dogwood, with a footrest of oak. They put in a soft bedding of wild mustard. Then they covered the frame with buckskin, into which they cut designs—crosses and four parallel slits. They hung the canopy and frame with amulets and charms, to bring him luck and amuse his eyes and seek the favor of Power. They hung a bag of sacred pollen, taken from the tule rushes. They hung turquoise beads, one of the four sacred stones, one of the four sacred colors. They hung a piece of wood from a lightning-splintered tree, for lightning was the father of Child-of-the-Water and still a great Power that must be treated and entreated with respect. The shaman spent many days making the cradleboard and sang many songs, soothing and flattering and respecting his Power on behalf of the baby and his family.

And when the cradleboard was finally ready and blessed and beautiful, Pisago Cabezón held a feast for all of his family and their relations and his followers and their relations and his allies in other bands and their relations. Many people gathered for four days of feasting and dancing and singing, to welcome the son of Pisago Cabezón into the band—so many it would take a whole season of raiding with the help of his maternal relatives to support the ceremony. The shaman conducted the long and careful ceremony, marking the child with sacred pollen and specular iron ore. He placed four dots of pollen on the face of the baby as he prayed and held him to the four directions as he sang, imploring Power that the baby might live long enough to outgrow the cradleboard—and for the years after that.

His parents understood the need for such prayers, knowing that life perches on the cliff above death. They knew that Usen had favored the People above all others, giving them the gifts which Child-of-the-Water and White-Painted Woman had sought for them. But then Usen had gone off somewhere and Child-of-the-Water and White-Painted Woman had gone off as well, climbing up the rainbow or perhaps going along the glowing path of stars each one must follow in the end. They had given the People great gifts and told them how to gain the favor and support of the Powers that remained the force behind all things—the wind, the sun, the deer, the acorns, the rocks and the springs. They also had left behind the Ga'an, dancing in the heart of the Earth inside the sacred peaks.

But the great spirits who had ordered the world no longer paid attention to the small concerns of human beings. Many of the jealous and spiteful and angry and malicious Powers and spirits they had left behind disliked human beings, who had been so favored by Usen. These Powers looked for opportunities to make mischief. It was easy to fall into the path of these malicious spirits, who liked to meddle. Good people understood this, and so never neglected their prayers and strove to make peace with friendly Powers who could protect them. Most of all, they did not fail in their obligation to live in a good way, showing respect, courage, and generosity. They performed the ceremonies connected with the cradleboard with great care. They taught their children to be strong and respectful and never to misuse words, which were like arrows. Such children must never step on the track of a coyote, or wear red in a thunderstorm, or speak disrespectfully of bear, or have anything to do with snakes or fish that came up out of the earth. The world remained a dangerous and uncertain place, fraught with dangers—like the bears and mountain lions and monsters and spirits that guarded the path to the Happy Place.

The parents of Cochise did not neglect their duties to him. They pierced his earlobes with a long thorn, so that he would hear clearly and learn the things necessary. And when he had left the cradleboard and grown old enough to walk, they held his Moccasin Ceremony with great celebration.[19] They made a shirt and moccasins for him out of flawless buckskin, the toes of the moccasins turned up to protect against rocks and thorns in the distinctive Chiricahua fashion. People gathered from all around in the joyous fashion of the People, so that Pisago Cabezón could renew his ties with his allies and relatives and demonstrate to everyone his generosity and his strength—which was the surest way for a man to gain influence and respect. The men gathered throughout the long, joyful day, going aside to the leveled place where they would play hoop and pole, rolling the hoop and throwing the elaborately marked pole after it. People bet recklessly, laughing, to see whose pole would come to rest lying across the hoop, with the markings within the circle determining the winner. The People loved wagering—and saw also the way in which it contributed to social harmony, because in the betting possessions passed freely back and forth so no one would become too proud or put too much weight on having many things. Some people had Power in the hoop and pole, which was a game Child-of-the-Water had taught the first people. But even people who won often eventually lost on some bet—on racing horses or footraces or the next wobble of the hoop. People prayed and sang and laughed and drank tizwin and did not worry too much about who had what things, for they mostly loved the excitement of the betting and the moment the pole hung in the air. They did not much value the things they had, for they could not carry much in their constant motion. They judged a man more by how much he could give away than by how much he could keep.

No woman could approach when the men were playing hoop and pole, for it was bad medicine. But the women went aside themselves and played the stave game, remembering ceremonially the first people who lived with the animals when they could all talk freely to one another. They chatted and exclaimed over their children and laughed at their antics—betting in their turn and laughing just as loudly as the men.

At sunrise, they all gathered for the Moccasin Ceremony of Cochise, chanting and repeating the chorus and drumming, and crying out as the shaman lifted the boy to the east just as the first rays of the sun hurried toward them. Then with sacred pollen the shaman re-created the footsteps of Child-of-the-Water, when he had gone out to kill the Giant, and Eagle and Antelope and Buffalo. He sang a different prayer about Child-of-the-Water for each step the boy took, somber and proud and a little bewildered that so many people had gathered to watch him now. The shaman sang "May he have good fortune" with each step. The boy walked four steps by himself, then turned and walked back four steps. Four times he did this, one time in each direction, as the shaman sang songs about Child-of-the-Water. And every time the shaman mentioned the name of Child-of-the-Water, the women all uttered the piercing trilling of applause with which White-Painted Woman had greeted Child-of-the-Water when he came back from killing the Giant.

Then the boy sat down and the shaman sang other songs, which were prayers that the boy should walk in the path of Child-of-the-Water and make his life a blessing to his people that would earn the favor of Power on their behalf.

The shaman told the story about how Child-of-the-Water had killed Buffalo, with the help of Gopher.[20] That bull was right in the center of an open prairie. He stood in that place all day long. He was always looking for humans or the smoke of their fires. Child-of-the-Water went out to get Buffalo, and he was trying to creep up on him. Child-of-the-Water was sitting in a low hollow. He wondered how he was ever going to get up to Buffalo to kill it. He was sitting there just as lonely as he could be and crying.

Soon little Gopher came digging out of the ground. He came up to Child-of-the-Water and asked, "What are you crying about, friend?"

"I've been sitting here all this time trying to think how I'm going to get that buffalo."

Gopher told him, "If Buffalo goes that way, you run right to that little hollow and lie flat. When you see Buffalo running out that way, just run as fast as you can to the place where Buffalo is now and lie flat in some little hollow."

That was done four different times. Each time Child-of-the-Water got nearer to Buffalo. Then Gopher came back again. Child-of-the-Water was very near Buffalo.

Gopher told him, "Now I'm going to help you to get Buffalo, and you must do exactly what I'm going to tell you. I'm going to make my first tunnel right from here to the spot under the heart of Buffalo, and the second tunnel I shall dig deeper down, and the third and fourth under these."

Buffalo was lying there looking around.

"The first tunnel will come out right at the heart of Buffalo, and you will be able to see his heart beating. Then you can shoot him right in the heart. After you shoot, you must follow this tunnel back this way and get to the second tunnel, for he will follow you. Then go to the third tunnel, and then to the fourth, for he is going to keep on digging for you with his horns. Now the tunnel is ready for you. Get in." Gopher told him to be sure to shoot Buffalo through the heart. Buffalo did not know Gopher was making a tunnel.

Then Child-of-the-Water went in. There was Buffalo lying right there. He could see the heart beating. Child-of-the-Water shot that Buffalo right through the heart. Then Buffalo was furious and began to dig into that tunnel. And Child-of-the-Water just crawled and crawled and jumped into the second tunnel. And Buffalo saw nothing in the first tunnel and kept digging to the second tunnel. And Child-of-the-Water kept going and got to the third tunnel. Then Buffalo followed, and Child-of-the-Water went to the fourth tunnel. Buffalo got through the third tunnel and started for the fourth. Child-of-the-Water got in the fourth and had no other tunnel to go to. Buffalo came after him and was very nearly upon him when he suddenly fell dead.

And so Cochise listened to that story, with all of his relatives signing and giving the trilling of applause at the name of Child-of-the-Water. That way, the story would begin to work on him. That was why they told stories like that to the children, so that the stories would change them and teach them. For once a story has started working, it just goes on working. In years to come, when Cochise led warriors in battle, that story worked on him and reminded him that he must always have four tunnels ready for his escape. And when he faced enemies that seemed as great and impossible to approach as Buffalo, the story reminded him to seek the hollows nearby and to use stealth and courage and a single arrow, well placed. And when in years to come he was tempted by pride and arrogance, that story worked on him and reminded him that even Child-of-the-Water would have been destroyed but for the help of tiny Gopher, who eats roots and digs in the ground and is the most humble of creatures.

When the shaman had finished telling the stories about how the earth was made, and how the fruit grew, and how Child-of-the-Water was born and lived under the fire and killed the monsters, everyone cried out in joy and respect. Then the boy got up to his small feet again to dance, everyone rising up to dance with him. The shaman then picked up the moccasins that had been made with prayer and ceremony and put sacred pollen on them and showed them to the four directions, to the Power that had gathered, to the Spirits that watched over them. Then he put pollen on the boy's feet—each foot in its turn—and then put on the moccasins, first the right foot, then the left, singing "Now you can run," knowing the best friends any warrior has are his feet and his legs.

Everyone rejoiced at the ceremony and commented to one another that the boy seemed serious and strong and respectful. Some people were already saying he would make a good leader to follow after Pisago Cabezón, who was feared and respected by all of his band, and who had strong Power on which they all relied.

Pisago Cabezón took great care in the training of his children. Cochise had two brothers who were his playmates and best friends—for brothers must protect and support one another all of their lives. He learned he could not count on anyone else like a brother, who would not leave him to his enemies and who would carry him on his back across a dozen mountains. Cochise was the oldest and strongest. He was a serious boy, hard on himself and others—and so prone to flashes of temper, which made all the other boys careful of offending him. Coyuntura was his long shadow,[21] both fearless and shrewd. He was careless of pain, tireless and fierce—but full of laughter. Others liked and respected him, but feared him a little. The two of them went everywhere together, growing up quickly and strong, always ready to join in one another's pranks or fights. Any boy foolish enough to taunt or strike out at Cochise had to stop and remember that mocking Cochise was the same thing as mocking Coyuntura, who felt less need to restrain his anger, even when they were boys. The third brother was Juan, who was pampered by his brothers. He also was fearless and strong, but reckless and full of mischief. He had not the serious temperament of Cochise nor the shrewd strength of Coyuntura. He loved to play jokes on his brothers, tell funny stories, and loll about laughing with his friends. But he was also indifferent to pain, laughed at hardship, ran always in the front of any pack of boys, and would pounce into the middle of a fight as sudden as a cougar in support of his brothers.

And because Pisago Cabezón was a leading man of the Chokonen, he took other wives as well. In the older times, few men had more than one wife. But when their enemies all turned together against the People, many women cut their hair and gashed their arms and mourned for the men who did not return, and many children looked around for the fathers they could not find. So as the peaceful times dwindled and the fights increased, leading men like Pisago Cabezón took second wives or third wives—often the wives of their brothers who had been killed. Pisago Cabezón had other children by his second wife.[22] Chirumpe was a playful and cheerful boy whom everyone doted upon. He tagged along after his brothers like the shadow of a hummingbird. He ran about the camp confident as Usen himself, for his older brothers protected him like a pack of wolves.[23] Chato also was born in these good times. Although he had a different mother, he had the same father—and so Cochise was rich in brothers. Now the sons of Pisago Cabezón felt that they were a tribe themselves, each the strong ally of the other in the rough-and-tumble of childhood.

Pisago Cabezón taught them always to help one another, for he was a leader with Power over men who had created alliances between different bands. He understood the nature of leadership and of the need to bind together the scattered bands so that they could not be killed off weak and separated, like elk scattered by a wolf pack.

Pisago Cabezón schooled his sons carefully. "Do not use a bad word that you wouldn't like to be used to you," he instructed.[24] "Do not feel that you are anyone's enemy. In playing with children, remember this: Do not take anything from another child. Don't take arrows away from another boy just because you are bigger than he is. Don't steal from your own friend. Don't be unkind to your play-mates. When you go to the creek and swim, don't dunk anyone's children. Don't ever fight a girl when you're playing with other children. Girls are weaker than boys. If you fight with them, that will cause us trouble with our neighbors. Don't laugh at feeble old men and women. That's the worst thing you can do. Don't criticize them and make fun of them. Don't laugh at anybody or make fun of any-body. This is your camp. What little we have here is for you to eat. Don't go to another camp with other children for a meal. Come back to your own camp when you are hungry and then go out and play again. When you start to eat, act like a grown person. Just wait until things are served to you. Do not take bread or a drink, or a piece of meat, before the rest start to eat. Don't ask before the meal for things that are still cooking, as many children do. Don't try to eat more than you want. Try to be just as polite as you can; sit still while you eat. Do not step over another person, going around and reaching for something. Don't run into another person's camp as though it was your own. Don't run around anyone's camp. When you go to another person's wickiup, don't stand at the door. Go right in and sit down like a grown person. Don't get into their drinking water. Don't go out and catch or hobble horses and ride them as if they belonged to you the way some people do."

He offered them many lessons such as this, for there are many rules that make it possible for people to live together. No one would make a person follow such rules. Even a chief could not make peo-ple do things. His judgment was respected and so people came to him to settle disputes, but he had only the weight of his words to enforce his judgments. If a man killed someone, it fell to the dead man's family to take their revenge on the killer and his family. There was no judge, no soldiers, and no law to make people behave.

The Spanish needed such things, because they did not know how to behave and had no shame—so someone always had to make them act in a certain way. But the People behaved in a right way because of the stories that worked on them. They behaved in a right way because they could not bear to be shamed in front of their families and friends, who lived close at hand without walls and so knew everything. Shame was the strongest force in teaching a child. Blows would not work, for every one of the People learned from the beginning that pain is meaningless—only a test of strength and character, almost purification. Little boys learned to light a sprig of sage on their arms, standing without flinching as it burned down into the skin. Pain was only a test, a ceremony—of no use at all in teaching a child. But the boys all dreaded a disapproving silence, a public criticism—especially the sons of Pisago Cabezón, who was held so high in the esteem of his people that his disapproval was like a rock dropped from a high place.

Pisago Cabezón also used stories to work on his sons. Some of the stories taught them respect. Cochise loved best the Coyote stories, full of fun, courage, and bad behavior. Some things you could not say at all in normal conversation were perfectly all right in stories about the trickster who had done great good and great harm in remaining always true to his own irrepressible nature. In later years, Cochise understood that the People were like Coyote, their strengths and weakness all mixed together—impossible to quench or contain or control, willful and powerful and sacred and irreverent.

One Coyote story his father told him worked on Cochise all of his life. He listened to the story over, to memorize it in his turn so he could tell it to his children and the children of his children—with their fascinated, owl eyes in the firelight.

Coyote met two other coyotes. Those two coyotes were standing near a great rock.[25]

He asked those coyotes, "What is that rock?"

They said, "That is a living rock. It walks slowly, and it runs fast; you can't outrun it. We've heard about you. You are a pretty bad man. You'd better be careful about that rock. If you ever do anything to this rock, it will surely run you down. You'd better be careful around that rock."

But Coyote told the others, "Where did you ever hear of a rock that runs! There is no such thing!"

So they said, "All right, go ahead and do what you want to about it."

So he defecated on the rock. Then he started to walk away.

At once that rock rolled after him. He went a little faster. The rock followed behind him. The faster he went, the faster the rock rolled. He talked to the rock. "Did you ever see my full speed?" he asked and went off at full speed. He was fast all right, but the rock was a little faster. It gained on him. Then he saw that running would do no good and that he would have to apologize.

The rock made him clean it off. Then that rock rolled back to the place where it came from.

That story got inside of Cochise when he was a little boy, and worked on him. After he heard that story, he knew that he must never defecate on any such rock. At first, he thought a rock might come rolling right after him. When he had to defecate, he would walk a mile from the camp as his father had taught him and make a hole, careful to avoid any rocks. But then he would worry that maybe there were rocks down there under the dirt where he didn't see them. He worried the rocks would get angry, even though he had intended no disrespect. But when he was older and understood the way those stories worked on you, he understood the story was teaching him about respect and the Power that lay coiled up inside of everything—even the rocks dreaming in the earth without visible change for all the years of a man's life. Later, he realized that a rock need not roll after you to punish you for disrespect. Did they not hide him from his enemies? Did they not take in the women and the children and shelter them in arms bullets could not break? Did they not sing with the Ga'an, thrumming against his cheek in the stillness of night?

Cochise learned early on that everything was alive, humming with the Life Force. Everything had this force—the wind, the rocks, the trees, the earth itself—all of them dreamed and spoke to anyone quiet enough to listen. This was the most important lesson, for it demonstrated the need to maintain reverence for all things—to walk and talk and think in a right manner. The world and everything in it was alive and so speaks to people. And the Power that was the expression of that Life Force would heal, and warn, and guard a person who lived in a good way. Everything that sustained a person was a gift of Power and of the earth—even the nourishment in roots and acorns and venison.

Others stories worked on him too—the place stories. He often went with his father, hunting or just rambling about, trotting eagerly

at his heels, or riding behind him on the horse. As he rode, his
father would tell him the story about this place or that. For the People had come to the Chiricahuas and the Dragoons in the beginning
times. They had named each important place, usually because of
something that had happened there.[26] Sometimes, they put the stories in the name. But usually they described the place with the
name, so that you would recognize it when you saw it. So they
would name a place White Rocks Coming Down the Hill Like Corn,
or Two Cottonwoods Leaning Far Over, or Juniper Tree Stands
Alone, or Green Rocks Side by Side Jut Down into the Water, or
Whiteness Spreads Out Descending to Water, or Trail Extends Across
Scorched Rocks.

Every place had a story of its naming, which Pisago Cabezón
repeated to his sons whenever he passed by those places. Those stories always had a message so that his sons would learn right behavior. For instance, he remembered the story about what happened at
Coarse-Textured Rocks Lie Above in a Compact Cluster (Tsee Chi-
izh Dah Sidile).[27] Listening carefully each time his father told him
the story, Cochise soon could recite it himself.

Long ago, a man became sexually attracted to his stepdaughter.
He was living below Coarse-Textured Rocks Lie Above in a Compact
Cluster with his stepdaughter and her mother. Waiting until no one
else was present, and sitting alone with her, he started to molest her.
The girl's maternal uncle happened to come by and he killed the
man with a rock. The man's skull was cracked open. It was raining.
The girl's maternal uncle dragged the man's body up to Coarse-
Textured Rocks Lie Above in a Compact Cluster and placed it there
in a storage pit. The girl's mother came home and was told by her
daughter of all that had happened. The people who owned the storage pit removed the man's body and put it somewhere else. The
people never had a ceremony for the dead man's body.

It happened at Coarse-Textured Rocks Lie Above in a Compact
Cluster.

Every time after he first heard the story that Cochise passed by that
place, he remembered the story and the consequence of failing to protect the people in your family—even the daughter of another man.

And Cochise also remembered the story of Big Cottonwood
Trees Stand Alone Here and There (T'iis Cho Naasikaade).

Long ago the Pima and the People were fighting. The Pima were carrying long clubs made from mesquite wood; they were also heavy and hard. Before dawn the Pima arrived and attacked the People. The Pima attacked when the People were still asleep. The Pima killed the People with their clubs. An old woman woke up. She heard the Apache crying out. The old woman thought it was her son-in-law because he often picked on her daughter. The old woman cried out: "You pick on my child a lot. You should act pleasantly toward her." Because the old woman cried out, the Pima learned where she was. The Pima came running to the old woman's camp and killed her with their clubs. A young girl ran away from there and hid beneath some bushes. She alone survived.

It happened at Big Cottonwood Trees Stand Alone Here and There.

Cochise remembered that story each time he passed by that place, so he would not forget the trouble dissension in the family could cause, or the importance of knowing what was happening before you spoke.

For a long time, he did not fully understand why his father told him these stories so carefully every time they passed those places, although he loved the sound of his father's voice and the flourishes his father made when he told them. His father was a good storyteller, like most of the leaders—because the stories were essential to leading. He changed his voice and he danced and he made gestures more eloquent than words so everyone turned and fell silent to listen. But at the first, Cochise thought these were only stories to help you remember the places.

But then he noticed that the places were working on him, just like the Coyote stories told around the campfire in the long nights of winter. He found that the story would repeat itself in his mind every time he went by that place. He found that he would remember the story of Big Cottonwood Trees Stand Alone Here and There whenever he came to a place with trees like that. And every time the story worked on him, the lesson would seep down further into him until it became a part of him—the way water seeps into the sand of a wash until it made a pool in the sand under the surface.

As he grew older, Cochise learned to listen to the grown-ups talking, and soon saw that they used the places and the stories to talk to one another without giving offense. They said those places stalked you, to correct bad thinking. If someone had been doing wrong and thinking wrong, people who were worried about that person would have a conversation and mention certain places. If someone noticed a man was paying too much attention to his stepdaughter, they would find a way to mention Coarse-Textured Rocks Lie Above in a Compact Cluster. And if a man argued too much with his wife, or an old woman talked too much, people would mention Big Cottonwood Trees Stand Alone Here and There. In this way, people could help put others back on the path without shaming them and without getting into a fight that would shed bad blood. So people talked in places.

After he had learned many place-names, the stories would rise up in his mind like spring water whenever he traveled through those places. He began to see that the places knew those stories as well. Sometimes he could hear the places whispering to him as he went past them, as though to shape him. In time, he came to understand that these places cared for him just as his father did, and told him stories to guard him and to pull him back from bad behavior.

When he had begun to understand the importance of talking in places, Cochise spoke to his father about this. And his father spoke in this manner.

"The trail of wisdom—that is what I'm going to talk about.[28] Do you want a long life? Well, you will need wisdom. You will need to think about your own mind. You will need to work on it. You should start doing this now. You must make your mind smooth. You must make your mind steady. You must make your mind resilient.

"Your life is like a trial. You must be watched as you go. Wherever you go there is some kind of danger waiting to happen. You must be able to see it before it happens. You must always be watchful and alert. You must see danger in your mind before it happens.

"If your mind is not smooth, you will fail to see danger. You will trust your eyes, but they will deceive you. You will be easily tricked and fooled. Then there will be nothing but trouble for you. You must make your mind smooth.

"If your mind is not resilient, you will be easily startled. You will be easily frightened. You will try to think quickly, but you won't think clearly. You yourself will stand in the way of your own mind. You yourself will block it. Then there will be trouble for you. You must make your mind resilient.

"If your mind is not steady, you will be easily angered and upset. You will be arrogant and proud. You will look down on other people.

You will envy them and desire their possessions. You will speak about them without thinking. You will complain about them, gossip about them, criticize them. You will lust after their women. People will come to despise you. They will pay someone to use his Power on you. They will want to kill you. Then there will be nothing but trouble for you. You must make your mind steady. You must learn to forget about yourself.

"If you make your mind smooth, you will have a long life. Your trail will extend a long way. You will be prepared for danger wherever you go. You will see it in your mind before it happens.

"How will you walk along this trail of wisdom? Well, you will go to many places. You must look at them closely. You must remember all of them. Your relatives will talk to you about them. You must remember everything they tell you. You must think about it, and keep on thinking about it, and keep on thinking about it. You must do this because no one can help you but yourself. If you do this, your mind will become smooth. It will become steady and resilient. You will stay away from trouble. You will walk a long way and live a long time.

"Wisdom sits in places. It's like water that never dries up. You need to drink water to stay alive, don't you? Well, you also need to drink from places. You must remember everything about them. You must learn their names. You must remember what happened at them long ago. You must think about it and keep on thinking about it. Then your mind will become smoother and smoother. Then you will see danger before it happens. You will walk a long way and live a long time. You will be wise. People will respect you."

In listening to the stories of the father he worshiped, Cochise learned that the People could not be separated from the places that cared for them. It was not merely that the peaks of the Dragoons and the Chiricahuas held them up against the sky, so they could see their enemies approach from a day's ride away. It was not merely because the rocks stood up straight and caught the bullets of their enemies. It was not merely that the mountains offered acorns in the winter and mescal in the spring and saguaro fruit in the summer. It was not merely that they knew all of the hiding places, and the hidden springs, and the secret ways through the mountains. It was that the places themselves smoothed the mind, and harbored wisdom so the people would remain in harmony with the Powers that held their fate in cupped hands. The People might breathe and dance

Chiricahua rocks. The Apache believe that wisdom "sits in places" and that the long, quiet contemplation of such places made the mind steady, smooth, and resilient, thereby conferring wisdom and virtue. *(Peter Aleshire)*

and eat and defecate, and live in another place—but they could not remain themselves in another place. All these things Cochise learned slowly, the light spreading like dawn to a dark sky, as he rode behind his father over the land that had made them both, listening to his stories. The places molded and shaped him, even helping him in his ongoing struggle to master himself and the anger that flared up in him sometimes. Cochise walked along a high ridge in his anger, trying to keep his balance. On the one hand, he knew anger could bend others to his will. On the other hand, he knew people would lose respect for a man who could not master himself, whose mind was not smooth.

Nor did Pisago Cabezón neglect the physical training of his sons, for they knew from the beginning that they would be warriors and responsible for their people. They vied with one another to see who could run farthest and fastest. When they were five, they learned to climb up onto a horse by stepping on the leg and pulling themselves up with a handful of the mane. By the time they were eight, they had begun their hard physical training. They rose every morning before the sun, so they could pray to the sun in gratitude and then begin running. They would run to the top of a mountain near their camp and then run back again before eating. They learned to run with a mouthful of water, which they would spit out when they returned to show they had the discipline not to swallow that water. In the winter, their father would take them to a frozen stream and break the ice, and they would go into the water until he said they could leave it and then stand beside him without complaint. He would send them back into the water again, until they had learned that pain and discomfort were unimportant. Then he would set them to rolling snowballs.

They ran constantly, taking care to smear grease on their legs to feed them. Oftentimes, the men who were in charge of the training would round up all of the boys and set out with them on a run. Sometimes one of the men would run at the back of the group and use a switch to whip the boy who ran last. And sometimes Cochise or Coyuntura would drop to the back of the group, going slower and slower, as the man lashed them with the stick. Then when the other boys had gotten well ahead, they would suddenly tackle the man with the switch, so that they tumbled down in the dust. Then Cochise would jump up and run on, staying ahead of the man with the switch, who was now too far behind to bother the other boys.[29]

Often, the young boys yearned for the time when they could be warriors and would be set to fighting one another. Sometimes they would set a small boy against a much bigger boy, and push that big boy to fight hard. They did this because Child-of-the-Water had been only a boy when he killed the Giant, so that a warrior should understand that he must fight a great enemy, even when he had no hope of winning. Sometimes they would fight with slings and stones that could inflict serious injury, but they learned in that manner to dodge stones as they sailed through the air. They played endless games with arrows, practicing incessantly. They had many games that involved shooting, and often the winner would take the arrows of the loser. Cochise quickly became one of the best shots with a bow, and after many hours of practice, he could shoot at a target and put two more arrows in the air before the first one hit. Often, the boys would shoot at one another, to learn to dodge arrows. One boy lost his eye when he was too slow, and many boys were hurt in these games. But the men only nodded and urged them on, knowing these lessons were better learned here in games with other boys than on a raid in the gunsights of their enemies.

Cochise understood that the physical training was just another way to train his mind—to make his mind smooth and resilient and steady. The places worked on him, and the running, and the release of fear when the other boys shot arrows, and the release of pain when the switch fell across his naked back. He knew that the warriors and the other boys were all watching one another. He never faltered. He never complained. He even sought pain, knowing that it was also a teacher. He yearned to win the respect of the warriors, as his father had done.

He learned early how to hunt and soon had a reputation as perhaps the leading hunter among the boys. He learned to make the deer head mask and the leaf whistle to call the curious deer in closer. He learned to fast before each hunt, so that Usen would have pity on his hunger and grant him success in the hunt. He learned the prayers and songs for the raven, which was associated with the hunt and who hid the animals from the hunters. Cochise also learned about the obligation of the hunter. "You must not show yourself selfish in any way," admonished his father, for Deer Power would never favor a selfish man.[30] He learned that if he shot a deer he must offer that deer to the first man who came up to him while he was butchering it. Usually, that man would only take a token piece of meat—but he might have a great need and take the whole kill for his family. "You say to him, 'Go ahead, help yourself. Leave what you want for me,'" said Pisago Cabezón. "He can leave half or take most and leave you a little. You can't say anything. He can take the skin and all. If you have already butchered a deer and have it on your horse carrying it into camp and meet someone, that is different. Then you give him whatever you want to. It's up to you."[31]

Cochise finally began his training as a warrior at fifteen. Each boy had to serve an apprenticeship of four raids. His father prepared him carefully for the first raid of his apprenticeship, an expedition to get horses from a Mexican village a long way off. He asked a shaman with Power in such things to prepare for Cochise a shirt that would help protect him from bullets. And the shaman gave the boy a charm with goose feathers, so that he would have access to the endurance of Goose. Of course, the war leader in charge of the raiding party would be careful not to expose the apprentices to danger. They would usually wait at a distance from the fighting. They would go along to hold the horses, make meals, gather wood, make bedding, stand guard, and serve any of the needs of the warriors. And the warriors, in turn, called the apprentice Child-of-the-Water and treated him with reverence. Cochise had learned the many rules he must follow. He must drink only through a tube, wear a certain hat, and scratch only with a scratching stick—each thing made by a shaman with much prayer and ceremony. If he did not drink through a tube, it would make it rain and spoil the raid. If he scratched with his fingers, he would grow whiskers faster and have soft skin. He must not have intercourse and remember to speak respectfully and carefully about women. He must not gaze upward or stand up quickly. He must remain awake until given permission to lie down, or he would cause the entire party to grow drowsy. He could not laugh or look over his shoulder. He could eat only a little and never anything from the entrails or head. Mostly, he would eat only the tough neck cuts of animals killed on the raid—for he could not eat anything from the inside of the animal except the lungs.

He used only the raiding language, with its own vocabulary. Perhaps eighty words that they used at home could not be spoken on a raid. Instead of saying "owl" he would say, "He who wanders by night." And instead of saying "pollen" he would say, "That which is becoming life." And instead of saying "heart" he would say, "That by means of which I live."[32] This showed respect and avoided making bad luck for the raiding party. It also made raiding seem like a ceremony, and for all of his life thereafter Cochise loved the language of the warpath, so like a prayer.

Cochise remembered everything his father told him, mindful that his behavior in his apprenticeship would determine his nature for the rest of his life. His father had told him, "Don't be a coward, don't be untruthful, don't eat too much when you come back to camp between raids, or that will be your nature."[33] He also began the lifelong task of learning the instincts and habits that would protect him through a long, violent life. He learned never to travel across open spaces in the daylight, when the dust of his passing would send a message to his enemies for many miles around. He learned to find water by climbing to a high place and marking the telltale bits of green. He learned never to approach water sources in the daylight, but to wait for the protection of night. He learned to always rest and always sleep in places where he could find good cover quickly—but not in deep shade, where his enemies would look for him. Instead, the warriors would rest in a hollow of the ground, behind a bush, in some place where no one would think that a man might conceal himself. And if he were caught in the open, he learned to lie still like the antelope fawn and perhaps very slowly pull a bit of brush in front of himself to break up his form—the way a jaguar's spots make him invisible. He learned never to run toward the sound of shooting, but to circle around and investigate before showing himself. He learned that when he saw someone following, he should make a small fire with smoke and then go off a ways to see who came to the fire. He learned how to read tracks, so that he could recognize the individual print of the horse of each warrior in the tribe, or determine whether a horse had a rider. He learned to break apart the leavings of a horse and know by that whether the horse carried a Mexican or a warrior—and how long it had been since the horse of a Mexican was at home eating oats. He learned to identify what band a man had come from by the print of his moccasin. He learned the subtle arrangements of stones and twigs by which a warrior could leave a message for any members of his band, so that they could find him again or be warned about dangers up ahead or coming on behind.

Cochise covered himself with honor in completing the four raids of his apprenticeship. The warriors spoke well of him. And so he came into manhood, and now could marry and attend counsel, and step forward into the firelight when war leaders sought warriors to accompany them on raids.

It was good and right that he should have completed his training. For as he learned his calling as a warrior, the world had changed. The storm had been gathering like the thunderheads of summer, black and bursting with wind and thunder.

Cochise ran eagerly toward the sound of thunder, glad that he could distinguish himself as a warrior after all the quiet times that had gone before. But he was a young man then who did not understand death or weeping.

He would learn that later.

And ponder it all his life.

3

The Peace Unravels

Usen Gives Corn to Killer-of-Enemies

Usen told Child-of-the-Water and Killer-of-Enemies to separate.
Usen told Killer-of-Enemies, "You go out this way and take one grain
of corn and put it in the ground. You will live from that." So they gave
this corn to Killer-of-Enemies and Usen said, "You shall live happily
on this grain of corn."

Child-of-the-Water and White-Painted Woman were on the side of
the Chiricahua. Usen told them, "You must live on yucca fruit, piñon
nuts, and all the other wild plants."

Pisago Cabezón and the other leaders of the Chiricahua saw the
signs accumulating, buzzing like cicadas before the monsoons. They
had lived peacefully a long while near the Spanish presidios, accepting the supplies the bearded ones provided and holding their young
men back from raiding the settlements around that area. Sometimes,
small raiding parties would go out and raid at other towns with which
they were not at peace, but mostly life was quiet. Pisago Cabezón
was the leading man of the Chokonen bands staying near Janos
while Juan José Compá led the Chihenne bands. Perhaps 1,400 people lived near Janos and the other towns in Chihuahua, which was
one of the two great tribes of the Spanish. Other bands lived in
Sonora, which was not so friendly to the People as Chihuahua.[1] To
the north, Fuerte and Mano Mocaha led the Chihenne bands that
lived near Santa Rita, where the Spanish and their slaves burrowed
in the earth after gold and silver. Some of the shamans warned this
would bring bad luck to everyone, but most of the leaders accepted
the mines as necessary to placate the Spanish, who were all like
drunks when it came to those metals.

But gradually changes began to mount up. Many of the Spanish soldiers gathered up their horses and their weapons and marched away from the presidios.[2] Pisago Cabezón took care to talk to friendly settlers, trying to find out why the Spanish had withdrawn their soldiers. Many of the men that remained—or the new men that came—were of a different sort. They did not have as much discipline. They did not pay so much attention to their duties, and you could not be sure about what they might do. Many of them were drunk most of the time. Pisago Cabezón heard rumors the bearded ones were fighting a war among themselves or with the Indians to the south or with other people living down there. As the soldiers bled away from the forts, the supplies also began to dwindle. Soon they had barely enough food to feed their families—when rations came at all. Naturally, the young warriors set on raids, to bring back cattle and sheep and grain to feed their families. Once, the People had gotten everything they needed from the earth and the deer and the elk and the antelope and the rabbits. But they had lived a long time near the presidios and their numbers had grown on the easy food and the settled times. Besides, they lived now so close together that there wasn't enough game to feed them. Now when the food stopped coming, the children quickly grew hungry.

Then a deadly sickness ran through the Chokonen camps. Many people had the coughing sickness. Many others had the spotted sickness. People said the Spanish had made these plagues, because the Spanish had these things as well, but did not die in such numbers. The Chokonen left Janos, returning to the Chiricahua Mountains. The young warriors, eager to prove themselves, set out in bands to raid in Sonora and bring back the cattle and horses and food of which their families now had such need. The Sonorans countered, sending out patrols and expeditions to try to follow the raiders. They did not have much success, but they sometimes caught up to a raiding party and killed one or two warriors. Of course, the women relatives of the dead went around camp calling on other warriors to avenge the ones now missing. Then larger revenge war parties would set out and kill anyone they could find near the Sonoran town that had sent out the soldiers.

Pisago Cabezón saw the first rocks of the avalanche bounding down the hill of these raids, and thought what he might do to stop it. His Chokonen remained in the Chiricahuas for several seasons,

then went cautiously back to Janos, in Chihuahua, with whom the
Chokonen were still at peace. But it seemed that the Spanish had
gone. Perhaps they had lost their war. Now he had to deal with the
Mexicans, who seemed more confused and suspicious. They said
they had very little to offer as rations. Pisago Cabezón asked for
farm tools, an interpreter, and more rations. The Mexicans gave
them a few tools and Pisago Cabezón urged his people to farm a little bit to see if they could feed themselves without rations. They
lived near the Chihenne band of Juan Diego and tried to keep the
peace. But finally the rations stopped coming and the spotted sickness returned—so they again fled Janos.[3]

The People resumed a life of raiding and warfare just as Cochise,
and Coyuntura, and Juan came into their maturity. Their strength as
warriors gave Pisago Cabezón added influence and he took them
into his counsels. Cochise quickly began to accumulate a personal
following, so that even older and more experienced warriors would
step into the firelight when he danced out to the drumbeat to accumulate a raiding party.

Cochise by then already had a commanding presence. He was
taller than most warriors, standing nearly six feet tall. He was
upright as a pine, with the lithe grace of a lion. He had broad shoulders, a deep chest, long muscular arms, a tapered waist, and long,
graceful legs with muscles like corded sinew. Women nudged one
another and lowered their eyes when he passed, for he was striking
to watch. He had strong angular features, with a handsome, prominent nose. This nose and the angles of his face gave him the aspect
of an eagle, fierce and alert and intimidating. His eyes bespoke
Power—careful, deliberate, deep, and glinting with intelligence. He
watched everything with grave attention and a glimmer of calculation—so he could strip a man down to the bone and examine his
joints with his intent, wary gaze. But normally his eyes seemed kind
and careful, with a wavering of humor behind them, like heat shim-
mers rising off coals. He had learned to tether his coiled temper to
the perch of his duty, but it still lunged sometimes against the cord
of will that bound it when he was treated with disrespect or when
someone's laziness or carelessness put others at risk. The other warriors learned to have care around him—excepting only Coyuntura
and Juan and his other brothers, who teased and roughhoused with
him. Most warriors love to play small pranks on one another, smug-
gling nettles into the bedding, loosening a saddle cinch, putting pine

pitch on the notch of an arrow, rolling their eyes and making crude jokes when a certain man turns his back so that everyone else will laugh. Everyone laughs at such jokes, and loves to tell the stories later. But something in Cochise did not invite such mockery. He took it in good face, but even when he was a young warrior and all the others were spilling pranks like a cracked olla, Cochise maintained a certain detachment—a dignity that the horseplay could not penetrate. Save with his brothers, who delighted in pulling his tail—especially when others were watching.

He learned the lessons of leadership from his father, understanding that a leader must dedicate himself to the welfare of his people. His father told him that a leader must be sympathetic and by word and example help the People know how they should live. He must be generous, giving everything to those in need. A leader may have command in war, so that warriors will obey him, but in camp he only advises. He must help the unfortunate and those whose luck was bad. He must strive to avoid quarrels and settle disagreements within the group to maintain harmony. But he was just like everyone else, except he had proven by his wisdom and his conduct that his words had merit.[4]

From the sanctuary of the Dragoons and Chiricahuas, the Chokonen sent many raiding parties into Sonora, while mostly leaving Chihuahua alone. The Sonorans raised an army of four hundred men, which they sent after the raiders. But the slow-moving force of poorly trained soldiers could not catch up to a raiding party. They had to stumble over a careless raiding party in its camp to do any damage, and they did not dare make an expedition to the Chiricahua Mountains to strike at the camps the raiding parties left behind.

The war went back and forth, with the deaths mounting on both sides. Chokonen raiding parties ran off the horse herd from Fronteras and attacked the mail coach near Bavispe, striking and then retreating. Then the Sonorans surprised a camp near the Gila River south of the Mogollon Mountains, killing many people. So Pisago Cabezón, a rising young Chihenne war leader named Mangas Coloradas,[5] and Mano Mocha gathered up about three hundred warriors to seek revenge. Cochise rode with his father,[6] believing in his youth that no one could stand against so great a force of warriors. But they encountered a smaller Sonoran army and entered into a battle that went all day. Because they had so many warriors, they fought the Sonorans openly—charging in with their lances and bows,

showing their reckless courage. But the Sonorans held their discipline, charging up against the disorganized mass of warriors from
many bands. The Sonorans also had guns and lots of ammunition,
while only a few of the warriors had guns. At the end of the day, the
warriors retreated in confusion. They had lost many men, but had
killed only a few of the Sonorans.[7] The war party broke up in anger
and confusion and the shattered pieces of it made their way back to
the scattered camps of their women and children. Cochise made
careful note of this great loss. He saw that the battle had revealed a
great weakness of the People and a great strength of the Mexicans.
Certainly, the guns and horses of the Sonorans had made a difference. But more important was the way they had held their discipline, working as well together as a small raiding party. By contrast,
the warriors had each followed his own band's leader, or had acted
entirely on his own. This was the beginning of the long hard lesson
of his life, gained in death and blood.

Soon, a Sonoran army surprised a large encampment in Arivaipa Canyon, not far from the Chiricahua Mountains themselves.
In that fight, the Sonorans killed more than seventy people, and
suffered little loss. These losses convinced some of the leaders they
should make peace with the Sonorans after all, even if they could
not get rations. About twenty-nine leaders, including Juan José
Compá and Mangas Coloradas, went back down to Janos to make
peace again.[8]

For most of his life, Juan José Compá pushed hard for peace
with the Mexicans. He had been captured by the Mexicans as a boy
and raised first as a slave, then in a family, and then trained to be
one of the priests. But he had eventually gone back to his own people, using the things he had learned to try to stop the fighting and
negotiate a peace. In the negotiations, they relied, in part, for translation on a man who would soon cast a long shadow across the Chokonen. He was a new kind of man—very pale with a bushy beard
like an animal and vivid eyes all white around the pupil. His name
was James Kirker and he was an American, which was a tribe like
the Mexicans living far to the east. Some of them had been passing quietly through the Chokonen territory for years now, mostly
going along the streams to trap beaver. They would just throw the
meat aside and take the skins, which seemed in keeping with the
strange behavior of these White Eyes. Most of the leaders saw no
harm in them and urged their warriors to let them alone. They did
not know what sort of people these Americans might be, so they

thought it best not to start a war, as they had plenty to do in killing the Mexicans.

Other White Eyes came along in the seasons that followed, including Kirker and another man—Robert McKnight. They weren't interested in beaver. Instead, McKnight began running the copper mines at Santa Rita del Cobre, which was in the heart of the Chihenne territory. The Spanish had started the mine and the Mexicans kept it up, but then McKnight took it over. The Chihenne had tolerated this settlement in the heart of their land with misgivings, but they found they could trade meat and skins and things they'd taken in raids in Sonora with the miners and with McKnight, and with James Kirker, who often went there. Kirker was a good talker. People said he could talk faster than Coyote, who had convinced all the prairie dogs to dance all night by the fire while he clubbed them over the head, one by one. More important, Kirker had guns and powder, which he loaded onto mules and brought to the camps of the People. He traded the guns and powder for horses, cattle, and the gold and silver and money the warriors brought back from their raids. Before Kirker and men like him came around, the warriors didn't even bother to bring those things back because the coins were only good for ornaments, the paper only good for burning, and the gold only good for making ear hoops. But after the warriors discovered that Kirker would trade good guns for these things, they went through the packs and pockets of the people they killed to get some of it. Kirker went freely from camp to camp, sometimes staying a while. He even learned the tongue of the People, so he could translate for them when they talked to the Mexicans.

But the peace that Juan José Compá made with Janos only lasted for one full round of seasons, partly because he could not control the raiding by other bands—especially the Chokonen. Pisago Cabezón and his sons stayed out, and Cochise raided right to the outskirts of Janos, running off the soldiers' horses. The Chihenne living near Janos protested that they had nothing to do with this raid, although some of the more headstrong Chihenne warriors were raiding with the Chokonen. Juan José Compá explained that he could not command warriors, only urge them to remain at peace. But the Mexicans could not seem to understand this, and the continued raids caused bad feeling that broke the peace. Soon the war broke out again, and the Chihenne ran away from Janos.

Now the fighting grew stronger than ever. The Chokonen did not count everything like the Mexicans, but they killed maybe two hundred people in Sonora and Chihuahua in the next round of seasons. Pisago Cabezón and Relles, who also led a large faction of the Chokonen, ran off the Fronteras horse herd, riding to within bowshot of the walls of the town to taunt the soldiers.[9] The soldiers chased them, but this time Pisago Cabezón set a trap, killing their leader and three soldiers. After that, the warriors rode right into Chinapa and took everything they wanted because the soldiers were frightened and scattered and could do nothing.

Then the warriors returned to the Chiricahuas to celebrate their great victory, with many days of dancing in which they acted out their battles and their victories. They invited some friends and relatives among the White Mountain People to come down for that, and this led to a joint raid by the Chokonen and the White Mountain warriors on Tucson and Tubac, which were the closest Mexican settlements to the strongholds of the Chokonen. They routed the small force of soldiers who resisted them and killed anyone they found outside the protection of the city itself.

Of course the Sonorans fought back, as blood always calls for blood. An army of more than 400 Sonorans guided by Opata Indians, who had long been enemies of the People, and also some warriors from other bands, went deep into Chiricahua territory. In Apache Pass,[10] they surprised a band in the Mogollon Mountains led by Tutije, who was a friend and ally of Pisago Cabezón.[11] The Mexicans took Tutije back and paraded him through the streets of Arizpe to shame him. He gave them no satisfaction, looking about curiously with no show of distress. Then they took him into the town square to hang him, so his neck would be bent and stretched in the afterlife and he would be shamed by this. Still he said nothing as they hanged him, only watched the jeering crowd, his dark eyes flashing with contempt. When Cochise heard this he gathered up warriors and led them down into Sonora toward Arizpe to kill as many people as possible.

By this time, it was clear to the warriors that Power had spoken to Cochise.[12] They did not ask him directly, for one does not speak directly about Power. They knew this because Cochise had a reckless courage that would have been foolish if his Power had not given him protection from bullets. Moreover, People said Cochise understood his enemies' plans, as though Power had warned him before the battle. But no one was sure as to the nature of Cochise's Power. Certainly, Pisago Cabezón had Power—everyone could see that. And they knew he was grooming Cochise for leadership, so everyone assumed he had given Cochise his ceremonies.

Of course, Power must make the first approach. Power resides in everything, and each Power expresses itself through the things that partake of its aspect. Goose Power moves through the world and everything that expresses an aspect of its essential nature provides some connection to Goose Power—which confers great endurance. Power has feelings and needs, just like human beings. Power wants to talk to people. It wants someone to learn its ceremonies, as a man wants to teach his son. Power is always looking around for people that might suit it—especially people whose minds are smooth and resilient and steady. You cannot gain the help of Power simply by learning the ceremonies, because if Power does not want you then, you'll always do the ceremonies a little bit wrong and they won't work at all. Usually Power comes first to you, using flattery to win you over. Power says, "I can't find a better man than you are. I like your ways. There are many men here, but I can't find a better one. You are the very person for me. I want to give you something to live by through this world, because you will meet many difficulties."[13]

Sometimes people learn ceremonies from someone who has already made friends with a certain Power so they will have a better chance of attracting the attention of Power. This can pose a danger also. You can flatter Power by learning its ceremony and performing that ceremony with skill and respect, but if you make mistakes, you can also anger Power. Then maybe Power will turn its gifts around or tell you things that aren't true to humble you or even get you killed. That is why some people don't listen to Power, even when Power wants to teach them its ceremonies. After all, Power can trick you and use you and make people talk about you. Sometimes Power tests you, making you give up your friends and your family to it to prove your loyalty. Or sometimes Power tempts people to become witches. Sometimes Power will even tempt you, saying you can live a long time if you give it the lives of your wife and your children. Sometimes people say to that Power, "I'm a poor fellow, and there are many other people here good enough for that. Let me alone. I don't want your ceremony."[14] Of course, you have to be careful in doing this as well, so that you don't anger Power. Maybe Power will arrange for something bad to happen to you. Or maybe that Power will go to someone else who knows its ceremonies and get them to witch you.

Witchcraft was the dark underside of Power. Most people used Power for good—but sometimes bad people would use Power for evil. No one talked about witches, for they did not want to attract the attention of a witch. But they kept their eyes out for it. Witches would use someone's hair or clothing or a bit of bone to direct bad luck or illness or some disaster onto someone who had angered them. That was why everyone paid attention if two fellows had a big fight and then one of them died soon after in a way that suggested witchcraft. Whenever anyone got sick or had a lot of bad luck, that person would try to think who he might have offended. Had he refused to share his food? Maybe someone had come up and admired a beautiful Navajo rug in his wickiup and he had been greedy and selfish and refused to give that rug to the visitor—then that person might have witched him. That was one reason there was no use in grabbing hold of lots of things, for this only caused resentment and stirred up witches against others. Then a witch might give a person a stomachache or some other problem, using his own Power—which sometimes communicated with him through his sexual organ or even his own flatulence. On this account, people looked for signs that someone was a witch—strange ceremonies, little pouches with bones, leaving camp at strange times, running around naked and handling his or her sexual organs, wearing dirty clothes, or smelling of rotten meat. One of the surest signs of witchcraft was incest or sexual desire for a close relative. If the People caught a witch they would make that witch confess and explain whom they had hurt. Then they burned that witch alive. Of course, this was also a dangerous thing to do, for some of those witches were strong. Pisago Cabezón told Cochise about one case in which a woman and her husband were suspected of being witches. They ran away when they heard people talking about them, but those people followed them and caught the woman and her baby. She admitted she practiced witchcraft, although she didn't have bones or pieces of hair or other things to invoke her Power. However, she said she had caused the death of two good men in battle. Those people didn't believe that she didn't have any objects with Power in them through which she cast her spells, and offered to spare her if she gave them those objects—but she said she didn't have anything. They tied her up by her wrists and lit a fire under her and burned her up—although she took a long while to burn. All the time she was burning, she didn't make a sound. In the end, they threw that baby in the fire also, although they hated to do that. Later, all of the leaders of that band and most of the people who were there for the burning all died, for the witch had doomed them in her own dying.[15]

But despite the dangers of witchcraft, the wise and responsible exercise of Power remained essential to leadership among the People. Few warriors will follow a leader who does not have Power, for war is much too dangerous to go out without any help. The great leaders of the People all had Power over men, to guide their decisions, bolster their eloquence, and bend the wills of other men. How else could anyone lead the People, who treasure their independence more than do the lions? From the time he was a boy, Cochise longed for Power. He searched through his dreams for signs. He went out alone among the rocks and trees to pray. He listened carefully to any mention of Power. He looked for charms, to carry with him in a pouch on his belt. He made his mind steady, resilient, and smooth. And when Power finally did come to him, he listened long and carefully. He did not run after it like a dog to meat, but he spoke respectfully to it, as to his father. In return, Power gave him great gifts in war—protection against bullets, far seeing, the forewarning of danger, the endurance of Goose, the cleverness of Coyote. Power gave him also gifts of leadership—eloquence in speech, force of will, and a long shadow to cast out over others.[16] And with the Power came the responsibility to lead his people through the dangerous times that lay ahead, like the sunlit crossing of the desert.

In the flush of his Power, Cochise was hungry for war. The Mexicans seemed weak and helpless, the soldiers they sent out easy to evade. Cochise and Coyuntura and Juan pushed always to the front of a raiding party, gathering glory for themselves and respect for their father. Being young and full of anger and convinced of their Power, they did not understand why some of the old men spoke longingly of peace. Every now and then, some Chihenne warrior from the camp of Juan José Compá would find Pisago Cabezón with a message urging the Chokonen to make peace with Janos and with Santa Rita del Cobre. Juan José Compá said that James Kirker and others at Santa Rita del Cobre were friendly, and would provide plenty of goods—guns, ammunition, and supplies. He said peace would favor them all. Pisago Cabezón always listened respectfully, for Juan José Compá was a strong ally, but he never agreed to come in, and his sons and the other war leaders of the Chokonen continued to raid.

The Sonorans fought back as best they could. They grew stronger after they made a new general, José María Elías González. People said he was a good fighter and not as greedy as the man who had been the commander before. He raised an army of four hundred soldiers and sent them into the Chokonen territory, but Pisago Cabezón stepped out of their path.

Then word began filtering back that the Mexicans had a new tactic. Cochise noticed it first in great puzzlement when he began to find the stray bodies of people, each with the hair cut off. Many were from bands that had been trying to live peacefully near Mexican towns. But many of them were Mexicans as well, people living in out-of-the-way places. The People did not take the hair of human beings. That would invite the Chindi ghost spirits of the dead ones to follow around after them and do mischief. The People had as little to do with the dead as possible, burying their own dead quickly and then ever afterward not even mentioning their names, so they did not invite the attention of the Chindi or disturb the loved one in the Happy Place. When someone died, they took all of his things, piled them up in his wickiup, and burned everything—partly as a gesture of respect and partly so the things the person had loved would draw him back from the Happy Place. So the idea of cutting off the hair of a dead person and carrying it around as a trophy was repulsive to the People. When he first started finding people without their hair, Cochise studied the nearby tracks. Mostly the killers seemed to be groups of well-armed men—not soldiers. He began asking people he captured about the killings. Finally, he learned that the Sonorans had promised to pay money to anyone who could kill any of the People and bring the hair back as proof. The Sonorans paid 100 pesos for the hair of a warrior, 50 pesos for the hair of a woman, and 25 pesos for the hair of a child.[17] When the warriors learned about the bounty for even the hair of their children, anger rose up in them like flames into the great logs when the Ga'an dancers whirl. After that, they sometimes cut off a piece of the hair of Sonorans they killed, usually throwing the hair back down on the body in disgust. Sometimes they cut out the heart and left it there on the stomach as well, so that the person would walk around that way in the afterlife—just as their friends and relatives must walk around in the Happy Place without their hair.

Then, during the season the Earth Is Reddish Brown,[18] James Kirker found the camp of Pisago Cabezón, bringing with him supplies for trading. Pisago Cabezón held a feast for Kirker, impressed that the White Eye spoke as the People, and seemed so willing to help them against the Mexicans. He began to think that Juan José Compá was right, and that they should at least make peace with Santa Rita del Cobre so they could bind up their greatest weakness in this long fight with Sonora—their lack of guns and ammunition. But after the feast, when everyone was sleeping off the tizwin and the great quantities of whiskey Kirker had brought, the Sonorans under Elías González attacked the unprepared camp. They were nearly in among the wickiups before the first warriors saw them, and in the first few minutes of the fighting they had killed ten warriors. Among the dead was Chirumpe, the little brother whom Cochise loved so dearly.[19] Kirker jumped up with the warriors when the Mexican attack began and himself rallied one group of warriors behind some good cover, showing them how to fire in volleys so that the shooting would have more impact. This stand by several groups of warriors stopped the first rush of the soldiers so the women and children could jump up and run away. Fortunately, Pisago Cabezón had selected the camp with his customary care, so the women and children had a safe route of escape and the warriors could hold back the soldiers, giving ground from cover to cover.

After that, Cochise went to raid even more, living almost constantly on the warpath and killing as many Sonorans as possible, trying to ease the fury of his heart for the brother whose name he no longer spoke. But the death of his son seemed to work a change in Pisago Cabezón. He cut off his hair and grieved for a long while, going off alone to speak with his Power. At first, he talked about seeking his revenge. He sent out runners to allied bands—and also to the Navajo and the Ute—who were often enemy people. And for a while, the runners went back and forth, so it seemed many people would join together to inflict a terrible punishment on the Sonorans. But the great plan soon began to fall apart—perhaps because so much blood lay between the People and the Navajo and the Ute. Or perhaps because the Power of Pisago Cabezón decided not to help him do this thing. After that, Pisago Cabezón began to talk more about Santa Rita del Cobre and Juan José Compá. Often he would remember how James Kirker had fought with them against the Mexicans, even rallying the warriors to protect the women and children. He said that James Kirker and the other White Eyes at Santa Rita del Cobre might make good friends. He said Santa Rita del Cobre was part of Chihuahua, which was a different tribe from Sonora. Perhaps they should make friends again with Chihuahua, but continue to raid Sonora. Cochise was worried about the change in his father, for he did not altogether trust Kirker. There was something cunning and dangerous about the man. So Cochise mostly remained out raiding with the warriors who now comprised his personal following. But when he came home, he listened to his father's talk about peace with a troubled mind.

In the season of Many Leaves,[20] Pisago Cabezón took his personal following to Santa Rita del Cobre and talked to the commander there about settling nearby and living in peace. The *nantan* there said the Chokonen must make peace with Sonora as well, but that perhaps Elías González would listen to them. A little bit later some of the Chihenne and Chokonen leaders, including Relles, Matías, and Miguel Narbona, met with Elías González at Arizpe—the very place where the Sonorans had hung Tutije. Elías González said he wanted peace with the People and would give them rations if they settled near the presidios.

Pisago Cabezón and his sons did not go, for they were still camped near Santa Rita del Cobre and did not trust the Sonorans. But then the Mexicans in Santa Rita del Cobre one day beat, stabbed, speared, and shot a woman and two men—all relatives of Pisago Cabezón—for no reason anyone understood. So the band left the area. Cochise said they should avenge the deaths and kill anyone they could find near Santa Rita del Cobre. But Pisago Cabezón said they should go as quickly as possible away from that place. A messenger from Relles said that now Sonora wanted peace, and although Cochise urged his father not to trust Elías González, Pisago Cabezón seemed determined to end the fighting. He went to Fronteras, the chief city of Sonora, to meet with Elías González. He was impressed with Elías González, who seemed an honorable man and a good enemy—but perhaps a better friend. Pisago Cabezón agreed to go back to Santa Rita del Cobre to talk about a grand peace that would include both Sonora and Chihuahua.

But the peace did not work out. The Chihuahuans did not agree to it and would not provide rations. The Chokonen and the Chihenne settled in Sonora, but continued to raid settlements in Chihuahua. After a while, even the peace with Sonora broke apart, as Pisago Cabezón and Juan José Compá could not control raiding by other bands, or even their own warriors.

Still, Pisago Cabezón remained alert to the possibility of peace. He could remember the peaceful times, when a man would sleep through the night and not start up four times holding his bow because an owl made a noise in a tree. Now he had been fighting for many years. He had lost his son and his relatives and many warriors—and still the Mexicans seemed as numerous as ever. The size of his raiding parties had dwindled. Once he had led three hundred warriors in the great battle against the Mexicans, but now he could rarely raise more than a few dozen. They had little hope anymore of winning great battles, but had to go with a few warriors and pick their fights carefully. So he looked for some opportunity to make peace.

Then in the season of Little Eagles,[21] Juan José Compá's Chihenne and Nednhis were camped in the Animas Mountains[22] when the sentries reported the approach of John Johnson, a White Eye trader who, like Kirker, had kept the Chihenne and the Nednhis supplied with guns and powder. He had with him seventeen White Eyes and five Mexicans, and supplies for trading, so Juan José welcomed them. The sentries said Johnson had two strange metal tubes on wheels with him, but Juan José did not worry too much about that—and his Power remained silent.

The warriors feasted and danced with the White Eyes for the next two days, the boisterous mood of celebration greatly improved by the potent liquor Johnson brought. The liquor of the Mexicans was stronger than tizwin, and did not spoil, so a man could stay drunk for days at a time. The People would stay in their own camp, but then go to Johnson's camp to trade and gamble and joke with the White Eyes, who seemed hard-bitten men and well armed, but friendly and generous. On the second day, the warriors, with many of their wives and children, rode carelessly into camp. Johnson had made a big pile of presents in the middle of a clear space, so the women and children and warriors hurried toward the pile.

Suddenly, one of the White Eyes threw the covers off the metal tubes on wheels and all of the other White Eyes pulled out guns they had concealed. The metal tubes on wheels roared, spitting out bullets like a swarm of bees. Immediately, everyone began running about in confusion. Juan José, thinking someone had made a terrible mistake, ran to Johnson, begging him to stop his men from shooting. But Johnson shot Juan José. In moments, twenty people lay dead on the ground.[23]

They would have killed even more, but some of the warriors rallied and began shooting back. Foremost among them was Mangas Coloradas, a giant warrior who stood six feet four inches and was already fierce in raiding. He had a head like a buffalo, and penetrating, careful, calculating, fierce eyes. He had so long a reach that few could survive for five minutes in a knife fight with him. In council, he could set fire to grass with his words, driving his opponents before him like antelope. He was shrewd and farseeing, sure of his own mind, so striking in appearance that women who had never seen him talked about him, a sought-after storyteller, and a terrible foe. Some said he was called Mangas Coloradas, "Red Sleeves," because of his fondness for colorful outfits—often taken from soldiers he had killed. Others said it was because his sleeves dripped the blood of his enemies. He had gained already a great reputation in war, distinguished more for the complexity and sophistication of his plans than for the sort of personal courage and headlong attack that had distinguished Cochise. He had long questioned Juan José Compá's strong embrace of peace and chafed under the restrictions the chief imposed on him and on his raiders. But he had gone along with his chief, bound by duty and family ties. He had come to the feast with the others, but he had not drunk any of Johnson's whiskey as he loitered on the edge of the festivities, with his dark, wary, cunning eyes moving constantly about. He had reacted quickly when he saw the guns coming out and dashed for cover, stopping only to gather up a baby who had fallen from the arms of a dying woman as he ran. Only later did Mangas Coloradas realize that the baby he had scooped up was his own son.

So died Juan José Compá, the strong ally of Pisago Cabezón, and the great advocate of peace with Chihuahua. And so rose Mangas Coloradas, whose life would soon loom up alongside that of Cochise, like two giant pines from the same root so tall that all others lived in their shade.

1838

The Death of Pisago Cabezón and the Rise of Cochise

Horned Toad Saves a Woman and a Boy from the Giant

The Giant caught a woman and a little boy when they were out picking berries. He put them in his basket. While he was carrying them, they defecated in the basket. Then, as they went under a tree, they caught on to a limb and got out.

Giant got tired and put the basket down. He saw that they were gone and saw the excrement there. He looked back and saw them, coming down from the tree. He started after them. They ran and cried, but he was gaining on them.

But as they ran they saw Horned Toad. "Pick me up," he called to them. "The Giant is afraid of me."

They stopped and picked up the horned toad and held it up. Sure enough, the Giant was afraid and ran and they were saved.

The Chokonen and the Chihenne and the Nednhis and the Bedonkohe now struck back at the Mexicans, both in Sonora and Chihuahua. They also struck back at the White Eyes, because the White Eyes had killed Juan José. Until then, war parties rarely molested the American traders, trappers, and miners that wandered through their territory, reasoning that they were of a different tribe from the Sonorans or the Chihuahuans and so not at war with the People. But now one war party killed a group of twenty-two American trappers and then twelve people on the wagon road from El Paso. Another war party attacked Ramos, first running off most of the horses and

cattle, then killing a judge and eight other people there. Seeing that
the war had returned and that the soldiers could not protect them,
the remaining people in Ramos abandoned the town.

Mangas Coloradas rose quickly to leadership among the Chihenne
and the Nednhis. He had a great Power over men. He could stalk
their minds, moving ahead to each place they might turn in an argument so that soon they would find themselves trotting along after
him like horses led into the corral at the end of a box canyon. He
also had great skill in bringing the leaders of different bands
together, braiding their hearts like a horsehair riding crop that fit
perfectly into his hand.

Now the death of Juan José and the rise of Mangas Coloradas
seemed to rejuvenate Pisago Cabezón, who returned to the warpath
with a vengeance. He called a council that drew many Chiricahua
bands. James Kirker came also, knowing they would need the guns
and ammunition he could trade. They formed two great war parties.
Tapilá would lead two hundred warriors into Sonora, accompanied
by Kirker, who knew many useful things about the tactics of the
Mexicans. Pisago Cabezón would lead the other toward Santa Rita
del Cobre, where he would lie in wait for the supply wagons that
nourished that isolated settlement. More than three hundred warriors went with him. Many of the younger warriors, seeing so great a
war party, said one to the other that they would surely now drive all
of the Mexicans out of Chiricahua territory. But Pisago Cabezón had
deeper plans, for he knew that any victory against the Mexicans
could not last. His hair was now as white as snow on pine branches,
and he could remember when the Mexicans had been weaker than
they were now and the People much stronger—and still they had not
driven the Mexicans out. But he thought perhaps this great show of
force would finally convince the Mexicans to come to terms, especially the ones living at Santa Rita del Cobre.

He set an ambush at Carrizalillo Springs for the wagons, which
at that place must go through a narrow pass. When the wagons came
into the pass, the warriors showed themselves and took up positions
around the spring, knowing that the horses pulling the wagons
could not continue unless they came to the water. But Pisago
Cabezón did not attack, and instead let the Mexicans think carefully
about their position through the night. The next day he sent out his
son Chato to propose a parlay.[1] One brave man among the Mexicans, Gabriel Zapata, who had been friendly with Pisago Cabezón

when he lived near Janos, said he would go alone to talk with Pisago Cabezón, although his friends said that the warriors would take him and torture him to death. Zapata walked alone to the warriors and said he believed Robert McKnight or the Mexican commander at Santa Rita del Cobre would make a peace with the Chiricahua. Zapata even offered to remain with Pisago Cabezón as a guarantee if the chief would let the wagons through to the settlement. Pisago Cabezón seemed willing to accept Zapata's plan, but other warriors reminded the other chiefs about the things the Mexicans had done— especially they way in which they had killed Juan José Compá. The wind of the council shifted until it was all Pisago Cabezón could do to convince them to let Zapata return safely to the wagons with an offer to spare their lives if they abandoned the supplies. The next day the Mexicans and the White Eyes left the wagons and turned back to Janos, taking with them only twenty-two horses and their lives.

After that, the great war party attacked the mines themselves. All of the divisions of the Chiricahua joined in the attack and Mangas Coloradas took the leading role. People said Mangas Coloradas seemed marked for great things, for you could see Power in him like the glare of a flame. He was ferocious in fighting—but all war leaders must win respect with their skill in fighting and the courage with which they went first into danger. The Power of Mangas Coloradas showed itself more in the way he could draw other men to him, giving them courage to fight and belief in the possibility of victory. Even so, when they attacked the mines they did not press the attack closely, for that would cost the lives of too many warriors.[2] But the attack served notice that the Chihenne would no longer tolerate this settlement in the heart of their territory and that their brothers the Chokonen and the Nednhis and the Bedonkohe would join with them. Some little while after that, the Mexicans and the White Eyes abandoned the mines.

After that, the war turned strongly against the Mexicans for a time, the way floodwaters overtop the sandbars in the river.[3] The People first drove the Mexicans out of the core territory of the Chihenne, where they had maintained their foothold for lifetimes of men. After that, they took the fight deep into Sonora, with Mangas Coloradas and Pisago Cabezón and other leaders leading long, bloody raids with more than one hundred warriors at a time.

The Sonorans retreated into their towns, garrisoned by soldiers, and again offered the bounty for the hair of warriors and women and children. Although the soldiers did not move far beyond the cities they struggled to protect, other lawless bands of White Eyes and Indians and Mexicans roamed around and killed anyone they could find for the bounty. One group took Pisago Cabezón's camp by surprise, killing ten warriors. But the roaming bands of scalp hunters were just as likely to kill Mexicans they found off by themselves because the government officials could not easily tell the difference between the hair of Mexicans and the hair of the People.[4]

But as the war dragged on, with mounting losses on both sides, Cochise and his father began to diverge, like two logs on a flooding river. Cochise drew closer to Mangas Coloradas, who burned like a great flame, consuming everyone near him. The two often raided together, slashing and burning across Sonora, extracting a full measure of revenge for his brother and all the others the Mexicans had killed. But Pisago Cabezón had grown weary of fighting and was troubled by dark dreams and the growing sense that the harder they fought the more death they drew toward them. To Cochise, it seemed that his father was now burning down into coals, while the Power of Mangas Coloradas climbed up into the great logs that would carry the fire through the night that pressed so close around the People. Cochise spent more and more time in the camp of Mangas Coloradas, where his own Power led him.

In the camp of Mangas Coloradas, Cochise turned his eyes more and more toward Dos-teh-seh, the beautiful and strong-willed daughter of Mangas Coloradas. Her face was perfectly proportioned and smooth, her body shapely but hard, so she could run all day and keep up with even a well-conditioned warrior. She had long, gleaming black hair, small, dexterous hands, and great dark eyes, careful and deep and intelligent. She missed nothing with her flashing, far-seeing eyes, which she raised up to meet the gaze of the fiercest warrior without apology or fear. Her name meant "Something Already Cooked by the Fire," for she was skilled in the arts of women, who worked steadily and hard and in their labor obtained most of the food the children ate and produced most of the goods that a family owned. That was why a hardworking and shrewd woman was sought after, and why women held great power among the People. They were the ones who remained at home to feed and protect and raise the children when the men went on their long raids. When a man married, he left his people and went to live with the people of his wife. He owed his protection and the bounty of his hunting and the proceeds of his raiding to her parents and to her family, not to the parents who had raised him. That is why daughters were prized by the People as much as sons, for they would bring new life and strength into the band, while most of the young men would eventually marry and go to join the bands of their wives. But even among women of the People, Dos-teh-seh was strong and respected and desired. Some women deferred to men, not speaking directly, not offering their opinions and advice, not meddling in the affairs of warriors. But Dos-teh-seh was open and sharp and interested in all things—even war and raiding. Her father had trained her in many ways like a warrior, so she could endure hardship, paid little attention to pain, and could trot all through the day and all through the night and into the next day, with only a little bit of water and a handful of mescal, the sweet, dried, nutritious heart of the agave that sustained the People when all other foods failed them. She liked to talk about war and listened eagerly to the stories of the raids and made shrewd suggestions and observations. People said she had Power, like her father, in farseeing and in strategies of war. Cochise turned his face toward her, watching her with admiration and a growing need.

He made excuses to go to the camp of Mangas Coloradas—especially when he heard that the Chihenne planned social dances. Because the People were chaste and shy, it was difficult for young men to speak openly with young women they favored. Everyone was always watching, for the People lived their lives openly among their relatives—so everyone knew the business of everyone else. The social dances were the best time for young people to gather openly, to exchange glances and fleeting touches and to feed the fire of their desires with the sticks of these contacts. Cochise brought presents for Dos-teh-seh, to give to her after they danced. And whenever he was not with her, the songs of the social dances ran through his head along with the image of her.

> I see that girl again,
>   Then I become like this,
> I see my own sweetheart again,
>   Then I become like this.
>
> Maiden, you talk kindly to me,
>   You, I shall surely remember it,
> I shall surely remember you alone,

Your words are so kind,
> You, I shall surely remember it.

My sweetheart, we surely could have gone home,
> But you were afraid!
When it was night, we surely could have gone home,
> But you were afraid.

Oh maiden, don't be afraid.
> They are already gossiping about us,
But don't be afraid
They who speak so chew rocks,
> Don't be afraid.[5]

Mangas Coloradas encouraged his interest. The chief was rich in daughters, and he soon put them in the path of men of Power and influence in other bands. He well understood how important his daughters could become to his plans. A son could lead raiding parties and extend the reach of his father. But daughters could become the cords binding one band to another. Mangas Coloradas saw that Cochise was growing in Power. He could see how his following of warriors had grown, and the absolute faith that those warriors placed in him. He could see that the leaders of the Chokonen had grown old, even Pisago Cabezón. Mangas Coloradas knew also that only a man with Power in war and the spirit of the wolf could lead Chokonen warriors, who were among the best of all fighters. He could see that soon Relles and Pisago Cabezón and the other Chokonen leaders must give way to Cochise and other younger men. Mangas Coloradas also saw that the bands of the Chiricahua must make a common cause to drive off the Mexicans. He encouraged the interest of Cochise in his daughter, and her interest in him. In the same way, Mangas Coloradas encouraged another daughter to marry Francisco, a great man of the White Mountain people. And he gave another daughter in marriage to one of the leading men of the Navajo. Another daughter married a leading man of the Mescalero. He knew that his daughters would create for him family ties to all these other bands, so he could make of them a single shield behind which his people might survive.

Cochise took Dos-teh-seh as his wife and made his home in the camp of Mangas Coloradas. He found in Dos-teh-seh a kindred spirit, as though two fires had burned through a forest to become a single fire. Partly this was because he also understood the importance of his marriage to the daughter of Mangas Coloradas. Even as Mangas Coloradas thought to bind Cochise, so Cochise sought to bind Mangas Coloradas. But more than this, Cochise found in Dos-teh-seh a strength to match his own. She was also held tightly in the grip of her duty to her People. She was quiet but strong. She made his home a good one, keeping food at hand, making him all the things he needed. But she spoke her mind and often when he did not know which path he should take, she helped him see things more clearly. He talked freely to her and valued her replies and her perceptions of this man or that man. She used her influence with her father and with the other leading men of the Chihenne to advance Cochise's position and told him everything that was happening in all of the wickiups, for women tell one another everything. She offered Cochise an invaluable source of information and shrewd advice and a safe place for him to work out his plans. She also offered Power of her own, to bolster his.

He stayed for nearly a full round of seasons in the camp of Mangas Coloradas. Most men would have lived out their lives in the camp of their father-in-law. But both Cochise and Mangas Coloradas knew that things would be different for him. Pisago Cabezón had led the Chokonen for a long while, but both Cochise and Mangas Coloradas knew that his will to fight had weakened and the younger warriors had grown restive and begun to drift toward other leaders. They knew Cochise would rise to leadership among the Chokonen and so must one day return to the camp of his father. And truly, this fit well into the plans of Mangas Coloradas—for Cochise would offer him more strength as an ally among the Chokonen than as a war leader in his own camp.

Soon Cochise heard that his father had decided to seek peace with Chihuahua at Janos. Pisago Cabezón and his longtime allies Ponce and Mano Mocha had all decided to test the willingness of the Mexicans to end the fighting, hoping that they also had wearied of the war. And indeed, they found the Chihuahuan governor Francisco García Conde was eager for peace. García Conde promised rations and gifts for anyone who would made a peace and settle near Janos. He said that if the People would return stock they had taken and prisoners they had kept, he would issue weekly rations of corn, tobacco, sugar, and meat. He said nothing about Sonora, so Pisago Cabezón reasoned that the younger warriors might continue to raid there and bring the plunder back to Janos to trade. Pisago Cabezón,

Ponce, and others signed the paper and agreed to the peace, and in the season of Large Fruit they made camp near Janos, with 30 warriors, 55 women, and 86 children. After a while, Cochise decided to join his father to see for himself whether the peace was a good one. He took Dos-teh-seh and his personal following of perhaps 10 warriors and their families and joined Pisago Cabezón near Janos. After a time living near Janos, Cochise sent word back to Mangas Coloradas that the Mexicans seemed willing to abide by the peace, and to supply rations and supplies.

Mangas Coloradas agreed to negotiate with Chihuahua and met with the peace commissioner in the season of the Ghost Dance[6] along with some of the leading war chiefs of the Chihenne, including Itán, Cuchillo Negro, and Teboca. He agreed to the same terms as Pisago Cabezón and even agreed to send some of the leading men of the Chihenne to offer the same terms to Sonora.

But, of course, Mangas Coloradas was right all along. You could not trust the Mexicans. Within a few months, some raiders came down from the White Mountains and ran off some stock from near Fronteras, where several Chokonen and Chihenne bands had settled to live peacefully. Seven Chokonen warriors agreed to lead the soldiers after the stolen stock and help them bring it back, to demonstrate that the Chokonen wanted the peace to be a strong one. But the Sonorans, for no reason at all, killed six of the seven warriors. Only one managed to escape to carry the word back to his band. Mangas Coloradas and Pisago Cabezón launched an attack on Fronteras in retaliation, and resumed the war against Sonora. However, many bands remained at peace with Janos.

Cochise assembled his personal following and resumed raiding against Sonora, not sorry to have ended the uneasy twilight of peace. Sometimes when he remained too long in camp, he could feel his Power pacing about like a lion in a pit, impatient to get loose. Sometimes he raided with his father or with Mangas Coloradas, leaving a bloody swath through Sonora. Sometimes he went with his own following, taking horses and cattle and supplies. When his warriors missed their families or grew weary of the discipline of the war trail, they would circle back to Janos, where they could trade the things they had taken from Sonora. Cochise was glad that they had made peace with Janos, for it seemed now a safe place to leave their families when they were off at war with Sonora. At first after they had married, Dos-teh-seh had come with him on raids, for he valued her instincts and her advice and her Power—and sought her out every night, comforted in her arms. But then she had begun to swell up with child, and after they had moved to Janos, she bore their first child. They named the baby Taza, for he was a strong, happy child. From the first, he rarely cried—so Cochise knew his son would grow into a fine warrior, strong and uncomplaining. Cochise then redoubled his efforts against the Sonorans, determined to punish them so severely that they would give up going at all into the territory of the Chihenne and the Chokonen. Only in this way could he ensure that his son would grow up the strong warrior of a free people.

Cochise was alarmed when the spotted sickness broke out among the camps of the people living near Janos. Even Chato was stricken, burning up with fever and talking as if in a dream before he died—despite the best efforts of the shamans, who had little Power against the diseases of the Mexicans. Almost all of the bands fled Janos then, so that the number of people who came for the rations declined in a few weeks from 800 to 120. Cochise quickly moved his family to a place near Galeana, for the diseases of the Mexicans were more relentless and deadly than the soldiers had ever been. He lived there for a time between raids with the families of Juan and Coyuntura nearby. Although he feared the disease and still did not trust the Mexicans, he began to see the wisdom in his father's plan—to make peace with Chihuahua so that they could continue their war against Sonora.

In the season of Many Leaves,[7] Cochise and Pisago Cabezón and Coyuntura and Juan went raiding again into Sonora, hoping that fighting alongside one another would ease the loss of Chato, whose death had grieved them so. Pisago Cabezón set a good trap for soldiers coming out from Fronteras and would have killed them all, but a young warrior eager to show his courage stood up and taunted the soldiers too soon. Cochise felt a fury rise in him and might have struck down that warrior, except the leadership of the raid belonged to his father and so he held his peace—seething and determined to enforce better discipline than that when he was leading the raid. A little later they met up with Mangas Coloradas and Relles and rode into Cuquiarachi and took the whole town. They took most of the people prisoner and told them to get all the cattle and horses and supplies they could to ransom the villagers. Next they rode to Santa Cruz, where Mangas Coloradas led a small party of warriors close by the town to lure the soldiers garrisoned there into giving chase.

Then he led them into a trap where Pisago Cabezón and the others were waiting. They surrounded the thirty soldiers and killed every one of them.

Cochise and the others did not know then that their raids had so angered the Sonorans that they decided to invade Chihuahua, which remained at peace with the People, who did not take anything that belonged to Chihuahua. Elías González, who had long been so strong an enemy, led a Sonoran army into Chihuahua while most of the men were away raiding. The Sonorans marched secretly to Janos and Corralitos in the season of Large Fruit,[8] and fell upon camps full of women and children at dawn. They killed eighty people—most of them women and children—and cut away their hair, and their ears, and even the private parts of the women as trophies. Everyone who survived fled from that place, making their way in small bands brimming with grief to the heartland of the Chokonen and the Chihenne. [9]

Mangas Coloradas convened a great council of the Chiricahua using the bonds he had braided with many bands and the eloquence of his Power to assemble a great war party to take revenge. He reminded them of the story of the boy and the woman who had escaped from the Giant with the help of Horned Toad, whose Power the Giant feared.[10] Fear was a powerful ally, he reminded them, stronger than guns or bullets or numbers. So they went down deep into Mexico, punishing Sonora and Chihuahua alike—as they believed that the two had been in league in the slaughter of so many women and children. In the raiding season following the massacre, they rode through Mexico as a fire moves through the trees. The People resumed their war with all of the Mexicans, and each side tried to get ahead in revenge, like a man who cannot stop eating because he cannot ever fill himself.

Cochise and Mangas Coloradas welcomed the war, insisting they could never trust the Mexicans and that it would be better to fight and die as warriors than to grow soft and dependent on the rations of the Mexicans. They had already driven the Mexicans out of Santa Rita del Cobre and made them like prisoners in Tucson, which was the closest town to the Dragoons and the Chiricahuas, whose sacred places and dreaming rocks provided the one sure refuge for the Chokonen. Could they not drive the Mexicans further south, so that they could live safely in the northern mountains and go raiding whenever they had need of food or guns or powder? But Pisago

Cabezón had grown gray and bent in the long war and his body was a patchwork of scars and bullet holes and wounds barely survived. He seemed more and more reluctant to lead war parties and still talked wistfully about the peaceful times, when a man had reason to hope that his son would in the fullness of time grow old and gray.

When Pisago Cabezón got word from James Kirker that Chihuahua wanted peace after all, he decided to test the news of his old friend—the only White Eye he knew. When Kirker sent runners saying he had with him fifty men and that he would guarantee their safe conduct to Galeana, Pisago Cabezón packed up his camp and moved south. Kirker promised he would help the Chokonen negotiate a peace, and provide them with lots of guns and bullets and supplies and whiskey besides. Some people were suspicious of the offer, and Cochise warned his father not to trust Kirker. Some people said he had turned into a scalp hunter, with his own army that had no pity on women or children—or even Mexicans, whose hair looked much like the People's. But Pisago Cabezón said Kirker had eaten his meat and slept in his wickiup and was perhaps the only friend the People had among the White Eyes. Had he not helped them fight the Mexicans? Had he not killed Mexicans with his own hand, on behalf of the People? Had he not grown rich from trading with the People, so he could come in perfect safety where no other White Eye and no other Mexican would dare to go? Pisago Cabezón insisted they should go to meet with Kirker and the Chihuahuans and see if they could put the peace back together whole.

They went down and made camp not far from Galeana. Kirker came with his men, very friendly. He gave them many things, making generous trades. He gave whiskey to any warrior who asked, saying they should celebrate the end of the war. Everyone was careful on the first day, keeping their weapons close at hand, keeping sentries out around the camp, and watching every one of the Mexicans carefully. But the Mexicans and Kirker and all of his men seemed interested only in celebrating the peace. After the second day, the warriors began to believe what Kirker had told them. Except Cochise. He remained apart. At first, he tried to sway his father against Kirker, but Pisago Cabezón said this was the last and best chance for peace—so that his grandchildren could grow up to become old men. Besides, Pisago Cabezón soon got drunk on happiness and hope and cheap whiskey.

Just at dawn on the third day, when almost everyone was laying about on the ground still drunk from the night before, Kirker and his men rose up and moved among them. They were armed with clubs and went from one person to the next—men and women and children—and cracked their heads open with their clubs.

When Kirker had finished, more than 130 Chiricahua lay dead, with their brains spattered out on the ground. Then Kirker's men cut away the bloodied scalps and carried them triumphantly into Galeana, where they spitted them on poles like decorations at a festival.

Pisago Cabezón and the mother of Cochise were among the dead. So were Relles and Yrigóllen, and all of the old-time leading war chiefs of the Chokonen.

And so passed Pisago Cabezón, who had taught Cochise all the ways of a warrior, who had carried him on his shoulders, who had taught him the names of the places to make his mind smooth and steady and resilient.

And in his death, Pisago Cabezón once again taught his son the hard lessons of a warrior.

So Cochise learned the People had no friends anywhere in the world.

So he learned the White Eyes were just as false as the Mexicans.

So he learned peace may be more deadly than war.

So he learned Power cannot save you, if you drink enough whiskey.

So he learned death will find you, no matter how fast you run, no matter how great your name, no matter how strong your will. And having learned all this, Cochise turned to vengeance like a starving man to a feast, resolved to take so many deaths in return that the Mexicans would curse the day they had paid their blood money to Kirker.

He thought that he had taken already the worst wound. But he was wrong. For all of his blood and loss and grief, the hard, bitter times of his life lay ahead. Later, he would look back on the long fight with the Mexicans as a strong, hopeful, victorious time—when all things seemed possible and the path ahead hopeful. He did not know it then, his hair cut jagged and short and his grief like a great stone on his chest, but his people were caught already between two fires.

They faced already the fire to the south—their long death fight with the Mexicans. They did not yet know that a hotter fire was burning toward them from the north—so distant they could not yet see the smoke, but so great that it would consume the world. For off to the north, far to the east, the Americans were coming already—so fierce in their greed and their Power that Kirker would later seem like but the first frost in the season of the Ghost Dance.

5

War to the Death: Cochise He Rises

Coyote Causes Death

Raven said that he didn't want death in this world. "I'll throw a stick in the river. If it sinks there is going to be death, but if not everything will be all right," he said.

Then Coyote came along and said, "I'll throw a rock in the river. If it sinks people will die. If it doesn't sink there will be no death."

Raven threw the sticks and they floated off. Then Coyote threw the rock and it sank. After that people began to die off.

The shattered bands of the Chokonen fled back to the Dragoons and the Chiricahuas, whose rocks had so long protected them from their enemies and whose places had taught them and smoothed them and steadied them for all the seasons of their children. Cochise had by now risen to leadership of his local band and other, younger warriors discontented with the leadership of their own bands had begun to seek him out, drawn by his reputation for Power and skill in fighting. The death of his father, whose name no one could now speak, had left a great gap in the canopy of leadership, like a giant tree that falls in the forest. The shadow of Mangas Coloradas now seemed longer across that clearing and more warriors made their camps near his. He dominated among the Chihenne, with the strong support of Cuchillo Negro. But leadership among the Chokonen had splintered, with Miguel Narbona occupying the most prominent position. Cochise sometimes raided with Miguel Narbona and sometimes with Mangas Coloradas, but more often alone with his own following. But the massacre at Galeana had discredited the leaders who advocated peace and strengthened the influence of the war leaders like Cochise and Mangas Coloradas, so that when they sent out runners to allied bands to mount a revenge raid against Galeana in the season when Earth Is Reddish Brown,[1] many warriors answered their call. So many of the People had died that every band labored under the obligation of revenge. The fury and Power of Cochise rose up in him, casting his shadow out over the other bands like the dancing flames of the campfire.

Cochise and Mangas Coloradas and Cuchillo Negro led more than 175 warriors back down to Galeana. They did not skulk about waiting for a few careless people, but rode into the city itself, killing anyone they encountered. The few soldiers and the terrified villagers fled as quickly as they could and the warriors sacked the town, taking anything useful and destroying everything else. After that, the warriors went here and there, falling upon anyone they encountered so the Mexicans would long remember the cost of their treachery. Cochise rode at the front of his warriors—always the first into danger—and yet he never forgot caution. He picked his camps with great care and always posted his sentries. He never needlessly risked the lives of his warriors, always picking the best ground for a fight. This habitual and instinctual caution—even when the fury of revenge had hold of him—helped draw warriors to him. No leader can win respect if he is fearful—but no one among the People respected reckless courage. The People had too great a need of the protection of the warriors to throw their lives away on a boast or a foolish risk. Leaders who were careless of the lives of their men quickly lost their following, for no one held the joyful victory dances for a raiding party that had suffered serious losses. Cochise's following grew because of the way he hoarded the lives of his men, because he only fought on ground to his advantage, because he seemed proof against surprise. Many people said this showed Power stood at his shoulder and whispered in his ear, to warn him concerning the movement of his enemies as though he had been a shadow at their councils.

After the raiding party had inflicted as much damage as possible around about Galeana and taken many horses and cattle, the warriors turned north to where they would be safe from the soldiers now swarming about like bees from a broken hive. Among the Chokonen, Yrigóllen was one of the leading men—brave but cautious, fierce and skillful in raiding but dubious about the value of large war parties designed to kill as many Mexicans as possible. He

argued that such expeditions would only stir up the Sonorans and
eventually provoke a large-scale response. Besides, such open fighting risked the lives of too many warriors. But many of the younger
warriors preferred to follow Miguel Narbona, who led the most warlike faction. The Chokonen had always been divided in this way,
between the warriors and the peacemakers. The Mexicans had captured Narbona when he was a boy, and he had been adopted into
the family of one of the leading men of the Mexicans—Antonio Narbona. He had lived with that family for ten seasons, learning all of
their ways so he could read, write, and speak their language, and
even knew their prayers and icons. He had in that time developed a
deep and abiding hatred for the Mexicans. Later they said the Mexicans treated him more like a slave than like a human being. Moreover, he saw their greed and ruthlessness—with the earth, with one
another, and with the People. Narbona listened to the way they
talked about the People and so came to understand that the Mexicans would not rest until they had exterminated or enslaved the
People—with no more compunction than when they killed rats in
their storehouses. When he was eighteen, Narbona ran away and
went to find the Chokonens once again. His knowledge of the Mexicans, fearless strength, and great Power helped him rise quickly in
the respect of the warriors—and the fierce and bloody war with the
Mexicans he advocated silenced anyone who might have questioned
his loyalty to the People. Perhaps Narbona understood better than
the others how great was the threat, for he said that only in fighting
as Child-of-the-Water had instructed them could the People remain
themselves, and stand as the tall peak of the sacred mountain in the
midst of the desert. He led the war faction and Cochise raided
alongside him.

And then the world changed once again, although Cochise only
realized it later—like a man who remembers the portents only after
death had found him. Into the land of the Chihenne came the
American soldiers. Up until then, only a few of the White Eyes had
wandered through their territory—trappers and miners and a few
ruthless and terrible men like James Kirker. They moved through
quickly and did not stay long and so seemed to pose little threat to
the People. But now a large band of soldiers, well mounted and well
armed, appeared in the territory of Mangas Coloradas. Some three
hundred soldiers came along with the careless arrogance of guns
and numbers, guided by Kit Carson, a mountain man friendly with

many of the bands. First they rode into Santa Fe and took it from the Mexicans. Then they set out traveling west, straight into Chihenne territory—shadowed by the warriors of Mangas Coloradas. At first it seemed that they intended to carry the war to the Chihenne, but then they received messages from the west which prompted two-thirds of the soldiers to return to Santa Fe.[2] The remaining hundred, guided still by Kit Carson, continued west. They rode as to war, but greeted the People in a friendly manner. Mangas Coloradas went to take their measure, while sending out runners to allied bands.

Mangas Coloradas met with the White Eye *nantan* at the abandoned mines of Santa Rita del Cobre, and learned that the Americans were at war with the Mexicans. Mangas Coloradas rejoiced to hear this and immediately offered to join with the Americans in their war. But their commander was careful with this offer, although he maintained the forms of courtesy. He thanked Mangas Coloradas for his offer of help, but said that just now the Americans needed no help against the Mexicans. They exchanged presents and the promise of friendship, then the Americans went on their way west.

Some while later, another force of more than 340 American soldiers came through the territory of the Chihenne and Chokonen. They were as well armed and mounted as the first, but did not dress so much in the same uniforms and did not seem so disciplined.[3] They went along peacefully enough, passing through Apache Pass and the heart of the Chokonen territory. Manuelito, Yrigóllen, Miguel Narbona, and Cochise all went to meet with them, wary of these new soldiers, but reassured by messages from Mangas Coloradas saying these White Eyes were the enemies of the enemies of the People. Cochise remained suspicious. Granted, it would change everything if the People and the Americans made an alliance against the Mexicans. Even if the Americans did no more than provide the People with guns and powder, they could surely drive the Mexicans far to the south. But Cochise did not trust these newcomers. After all, they were the same people as Kirker and Johnson—two of the worst killers and greatest liars who had ever lived. But the *nantan* of the American soldiers said Kirker and Johnson were bad men, renegades who had become Mexicans. He said the Americans wanted to be friends to the People. This seemed reassuring, but Cochise remained skeptical. The soldiers of the Americans seemed better armed and mounted and disciplined than the Mexicans, which might mean they were better fighters. Moreover, the appearance of these soldiers in the Chokonen heartland seemed dangerous. Cochise understood perfectly that the People would have lost their war with the Mexicans a long time ago if they had not been able to retreat to the relative safety of these northern mountains when the Sonorans and the Chihuahuans went on the warpath. Granted, the soldiers passed quickly through Apache Pass and said nothing about wanting to stay in the land of the Chokonen. But they represented a new and unpredictable force in the complicated dance of death in which the People and the Mexicans had engaged for as long as anyone could remember. First the Americans took Santa Fe and then Tucson, pulling down the flag of the Mexicans and putting up their own. And when most of them moved on west, they left many soldiers in Tucson and in Santa Fe.

In the meantime, the war parties took full advantage of the effect of the war with the Americans on the Mexicans, who had stripped the frontier of soldiers. Now Cochise and Mangas Coloradas and Narbona raided freely through Sonora and Chihuahua. In the season of Little Eagles,[4] Cochise and Narbona and Yrigóllen and others went down to Fronteras, still seeking revenge for the massacre at Galeana. They surprised a party of twenty Mexicans outside Fronteras, killing fourteen and capturing two. Then they waited for the soldiers to come to investigate, and ambushed them as well. Narbona said the soldiers were led by Antonio Narbona, a Mexican commander from the family that had raised Narbona and so earned his hatred. After that, the war party surprised another party of eleven Mexicans, killing ten. Among the dead were six young boys, who at another time the warriors might have taken back to raise as warriors. But they were intent on punishing Galeana, where Kirker's men had killed many women and children. The warriors hardened their hearts and killed everyone who fell into their hands, to make sure the Mexicans would not forget the lesson.

The leaders began to debate among themselves what to do next. Yrigóllen said perhaps the Mexicans would make a peace now, seeing that the warriors had inflicted such damage. Narbona agreed, but for different reasons. He hoped that by talking with the Mexicans he could gain information on the Mexican defenses and the war with the Americans. The war party returned to Fronteras, and Yrigóllen went in to talk with their old enemy Elías González. They agreed to stop fighting, but that peace didn't last long. Narbona and other warriors had only feigned peace, and they soon began raiding again, retreating back into the Chiricahuas as the leaves turned.

Antonio Narbona pursued them there, with a force of 120 men. He burned a deserted camp and the next day found a woman hiding in the rocks. The soldiers murdered her. A short time later, soldiers captured several beloved relatives of Yrigóllen, taking them as prisoners rather than killing them. Several leaders, including Miguel Narbona, then approached the soldiers to divert and delay them by promising peace. Eventually, the soldiers turned back south. Then Miguel Narbona and Cochise and the other war leaders held council, advocating a revenge raid to punish the Mexicans for coming so boldly into the heart of their territory. Many warriors joined them and then went back down to the village of Cuquiarachi, west of Fronteras, where Antonio Narbona lived on his ranch. In the season of the Ghost Dance, when the Mexicans did not expect raids, they stormed the village. They found Antonio Narbona on his own front porch and killed him there, Miguel Narbona in the forefront of the warriors. They killed many people in the town and took a half-dozen women prisoner and did so much damage the frightened survivors abandoned the village and moved to Fronteras. Another party of raiders led by Yrigóllen burned Chinapa to the ground, killing 12 Mexicans and capturing 42 prisoners he could trade for his relatives who were being held by the Mexicans. Often raids were intended to get prisoners after the Mexicans had captured someone of importance. Each side understood these prisoners could prove valuable— although the Mexicans most often sold their prisoners as slaves.

The war parties continued to maneuver through Fronteras. Cochise and Narbona fell into an ambush by Mexican soldiers, because some Mexicans they had failed to kill two days before warned the soldiers that were nearby. Cochise lost two men, but escaped. Then he set an ambush at a nearby spring, and captured five prisoners that he then ransomed for needed supplies.

The war party should have gone north then, for they had fallen already into one trap because Cochise's Power had faltered. But proud and angry, Cochise and Narbona continued raiding although all the countryside was roused against them. They blundered into another trap, this time set by many soldiers with one of the great guns on wheels, which scattered bullets like hornets. In a moment, Narbona was knocked off his horse and wounded in the leg. Cochise also was knocked from his horse and quickly surrounded by soldiers

who came out of their hidden positions.[5] Remembering that the
warriors held many hostages and that the Mexicans had taken captive the relatives of Yrigóllen, Cochise reluctantly lay down his rifle.
He was tempted to run through the Mexicans, trusting to his Power
to turn aside the bullets. But his Power had failed to warn him of
this ambush and there seemed little chance of going safely through
so many soldiers. Besides, the soldiers had gathered around him,
which gave the rest of the warriors time to escape. He remembered
his training so long ago, when he had dropped back to take the
blows of the switch so that the other boys could run on ahead.
Cochise stood, fierce and contemptuous in the middle of their soldiers—holding their attention for as long as he could.

The Mexicans took Cochise back to Fronteras, happy to have
captured so prominent a war chief. They put shackles on his hands
and feet, out of fear and hatred. They knew he could kill any one of
them—and they hoped to humble his pride, grinding it like corn on
a metate. But Cochise paid no attention to the shackles, and little
attention to the Mexicans. He walked where they instructed and sat
where they indicated, but held his angled face immobile—save for
the dangerous flashing of anger and contempt in his dark eyes. He
hoped the Mexicans might trade him for the many prisoners the war
party had taken, but expected instead that they would take him into
the middle of the town square and hang him—jeering and taunting
and throwing small stones as he dangled. Instead, they took him to
a small, filthy adobe building with bars on the tiny windows. He
could not see the sky, could not feel the breeze, could not see the
long, graceful line of the horizon. Perhaps they intended to break
his spirit before they killed him. Perhaps they hoped he would
throw himself at the walls or cry out and plead with them to let him
out to see the sky. He did none of these things, although he felt like
an eagle in a leg snare. Instead, he sat quietly in his dark, stinking
prison, working to smooth and steady his mind. He put himself back
in the Dragoons, making a journey in his mind from one place to
the next, telling the stories so that it seemed he was back in those
places learning once again their wisdom.[6] He also listened to the
talking of the Mexicans, gaining their language, and honing his
hatred for them. They seemed to him more and more like the sheep
that they herded, foolish and bunched together and always fearful.
He watched them passing back and forth, always needing the safety
of a group, treasuring useless things and understanding nothing.

The days slipped past, lengthening into weeks—until he began to despair of ever walking free in the sunlight again. He thought he would die in that walled grave, like a rabbit staked out for bait and then forgotten.

But many bands of Chokonen had made their camps perhaps five miles from Fronteras, determined to make the Mexicans release Cochise. The garrison at Fronteras totaled fifty-six soldiers, but so many were sick, or absent, or locked in the guardhouse that they had only thirty-one fighting men. So capturing Cochise had really made them prisoners in their own town, for the Chokonen who had gathered around the town could have killed so small a force of soldiers if they ventured outside the walls of the town. Perhaps that is why they didn't kill Cochise, although he was already so well known that many thirsted for his blood. They knew that so long as Cochise was alive, the Chokonen would hold back in hopes of winning his release. Meanwhile, Yrigóllen and Narbona sent out raiding parties to get more prisoners they could exchange for Cochise. They laid siege to Fronteras all of the time the soldiers held Cochise, allowing no one to enter or leave the town.

The soldiers in Fronteras held out for a long time, thinking reinforcements would soon arrive. Then word trickled in that the war had turned against the soldiers, so no help would be coming. The Chokonen had them trapped now, like horses in the end of a box canyon. Narbona then moved his camp to within a mile of the town's gates to cut off all supplies. Soon the people in Fronteras had only thin tortillas to eat. The captain there sent out a strong force of twenty-three men to bring back supplies, but Narbona ambushed them, killing all but one. Then the captain in Fronteras sent out a soldier the Chokonen knew and trusted and offered to trade Cochise for some of the people Narbona had captured. In the end, Narbona gave back five soldiers and six civilians for Cochise, who walked out of Fronteras after six weeks of captivity—more determined than ever now to wage a long and terrible war against Sonora. His Power had delivered him when he might so easily have died, so he knew he had also a debt to his Power and to his people. The gift of his life had been given him, so now he must use it in the service of his people, in respect for his Power.

A Mexican force from Sonora journeyed to the Chiricahuas, hoping to put the Chokonen on the defensive. But the soldiers mutinied and insisted on a return to Sonora. The Chiricahua harried them as they went, then gathered up a force to attack Tubac, near Tucson. They swept through the small settlement, killing nine people and forcing the abandonment of the town for a time.

The Mexicans could not do much in reply. Most of their soldiers were fighting the Americans. Many others deserted their posts and went to California, chasing rumors of gold. Stripped of soldiers and beset by warriors, the people of Bacoachi abandoned their town, which had been one of the first settlements of the Spanish in Sonora. Then a war party attacked Santa Cruz and stole most of the horse and cattle, so that many people abandoned Santa Cruz as well. The Chokonen began to hope that all of the Mexican settlements along the frontier would collapse, and the Mexicans would abandon that country to the People, who had earned it with their courage and their prayers.

The fighting mostly paused in the season of the Ghost Dance, as the Chokonen withdrew into the Dragoons and Chiricahuas to live quietly through the storytelling time on the supplies they had taken during the raiding season and the mescal and dried meat the women had prepared.

Cochise welcomed the long nights of winter and quiet days of winter, when they could loll about in their camps. Of course, he maintained a screen of sentries all around his camps—especially up on the high points, where the dust trace raised by even a single horseman could be seen from a day's ride distant. They camped at the base of the mountains in the winter, where the snow was rare and fleeting and the brown grass easy for the horses and cattle to reach. This was the great gift of the mountains, that the seasons flowered and fruited on their slopes all through the year. The People could live in comfort in the low places during the season of the Ghost Dance, hunting the deer and the elk that moved down out of the snow and feasting on the supplies accumulated in the raiding season. In the season of Large Leaves, they could move thousands of feet up the sides of the mountains to escape the heat and hardship of the desert, harvesting acorns and agave and hunting the deer and the elk through the forest. More important, the rocks of the Dragoons and the Chiricahuas and all of the deep, rocky canyons provided a sure fortress against their enemies. No one could surprise them, unless they neglected their sentries. And whenever a force of their enemies too large to fight drew near, they could easily retreat up the slopes or pass through a network of canyons, emerging on the far side of the mountain while their enemies were still seeking them on the wrong side. Cochise knew that only the mountains had made it possible for them to survive their long war with the termite mounds of the Mexicans. If they had lived along the rivers like the Pima or out on the flat grasslands like the Kiowa to the east, the Mexicans long ago would have hunted, caged, and killed them. But the People survived because the Ga'an danced still in the mountains, and the rocks held the People in their long slow thoughts, and Earth protected them in her embrace.

So in the winter Cochise and the other warriors could remain a long while in their camps, playing with the little ones, training the young boys, playing the hoop and pole game, gambling, telling stories, making new bows and arrows and shields, catching up on the gossip they had missed. Cochise also loved to go out hunting in the winter months, traveling for days at a time seeking game. Often, he climbed up to the edge of the snow or went out after a fresh snow, when the tracks would be easy to read and the elk would concentrate in places where they would push aside the snow to reach the grass underneath. He never failed to bring back game, with which he fed his growing circle of dependents, and which he distributed as well to the families whose husbands had died, leaving no one to hunt. Cochise understood that providing meat to the helpless was essential to leadership, and no one would respect a man whose family was fat while his neighbors starved. In this, Cochise could count on the help of Coyuntura and Juan, who had both grown in skill and respect as warriors, so that the three brothers had far more influence and a longer reach than any would have had alone.

Cochise and Dos-teh-seh by now had two sons, who continued to grow strong and independent. Taza was as serious and intent as his father, but Naiche was a beautiful baby and a charming, mischievous, and faintly lazy little boy. Everyone loved him for his quick intelligence and beaming smile and gentle nature. Cochise tried to be stern with him so that he would be as serious and responsible as his older brother, but Naiche would crawl up in his lap, or touch his face, so that Cochise could remain angry with him for but a moment. In addition, Cochise took into his camp some captive Mexican children, knowing that only by raising some of these children as warriors could the People replace their grievous losses. One of these children was Merejildo Grijalva, who had been taken in Sonora when the warriors had been gathering up captives

Taza. Cochise groomed his son Taza to take over as chief. Taza did lead a large faction of the Chiricahua after his father's death, but never had the stature or dominance of his father. He couldn't prevent the resumption of raiding and infighting and died—probably of pneumonia—on a trip to Washington, D.C. (*Arizona Historical Society*)

to ransom for Cochise. Cochise undertook the training of the little boy, so he would grow to become a full warrior of the people. Years later, he remembered the little boy with pain and regret and wondered what he had done that the boy who had eaten his food and listened to his stories had turned so skillfully against the People.

Perhaps the best part about the season of the Ghost Dance was the storytelling. Many stories—especially those involving snakes and bears—could only be told in the season of the Ghost Dance when the snakes and the bears were sleeping and not likely to be offended. Also, the season of the Ghost Dance was the time for the Coyote stories—the favorite of all the children and most of the storytellers as well. Every storyteller had his favorites, and his special embellishments and mannerisms. Usually the stories went clear through the night as the fire in the wickiup smoldered and flickered. The children all begged for a spot around the fire, but many then struggled through the long hours of storytelling to keep their great dark eyes open. The storytellers would tickle their noses with a piece of grass, or make fun of them when their attention wavered, to make sure everyone was listening. Sometimes the storytellers would pick out some person who was not paying much attention and whenever they reached a certain funny part of the story about some foolish person, they would wink and roll their eyes when that one person wasn't looking—which prompted everyone else to laugh. The storyteller would go on like that, the laughter growing every time until that person figured it out.[7]

Cochise loved best the Coyote stories, and many people came to hear him when he told them. Sometimes the stories explained good things Coyote had done—as when he stole fire from the birds so that the People could have it. He fooled the bird children into showing him the secret way up the bluff where the birds kept fire to themselves and then convinced the birds they had won a great victory and should have a celebration—so they would have a dance around the fire. He tied the soft bark of the juniper to his tail and danced close to the fire until it caught, then went running away with his tale aflame, setting fires as he went. Wasp made it rain before the fire burned everything, but Coyote gave it to Bumble Bee, who hid a few coals in the sotol stalk out of the rain. That explains why people have fire today, and also why the tip of Coyote's tail is burned black.

But mostly the Coyote stories were about foolishness and bad behavior, and the rightful punishment such behavior always brings. And even though Coyote was forever making trouble and acting foolish, people also had to admire his persistence and the cheerful way he accepted the consequences of his actions—irrepressible and inventive for all of his disasters. The Coyote stories also helped explain how things had come to be, and were like the place-name stories. Each Coyote story had a lesson about right behavior and that story would work on people every time they remembered it.

One story went like this:

Coyote went on his journey again.[8] He was very hungry and he found an insect, Tipping Beetle. Beetle was standing right on its head.

He walked up to Beetle. He told him, "I'm the person who eats nothing but fat."

Beetle still had his head down. He told Coyote, "Old man, you let me alone. I'm listening to what they are saying down there under the ground."

Coyote said, "Hurry and tell me, because as soon as you tell me what they say I'm going to eat you." Pretty soon he said again, "Hurry up and tell me what they say down there."

"All right," Beetle answered, "I'm going to tell you now what they say down there. They are talking down under the ground, and they are saying that they are going after a certain man who has been playing some tricks back up here. They say that the person who dirtied a rock along the trail is to be found and killed."

Then Coyote said, "I'm going over there; I forgot something. I'll be back." But he was scared. He never came back. He went back to clean off that rock.

Cochise had memorized this story so that it could work on him. Ever after that when he saw the tipping beetles, he thought of the Ga'an and the earth spirits and the protection and care of the rocks, his mind smooth and respectful and the thought itself like a prayer to the dawn. So that story worked on him, to steady his mind and teach him respect.

He also enjoyed telling the stories about things you couldn't say in normal conversation—although he was careful not to tell such a story in front of the close relatives on his wife's side before whom he had an obligation to be ashamed and must remain on his best behavior. Of course, this was easier for Cochise than for most warriors—for his wife had come to live with his band, while most men went to live in the bands of their wives, where they were surrounded by people in front of whom they had an obligation to be ashamed. Even feared and respected leaders like Cochise were careful to observe the proper respect in their relationships with their maternal relatives. A young warrior owed the family of his wife the proceeds of his raids, and the bounty of his hunting. This was only right, for women had responsibility for the children when the men were off raiding and so needed the support and assistance of their relatives. But when the husband was in camp, he must scrupulously avoid his wife's mother, to show respect, or he would shame his whole family. Whenever his wife's mother came to his wickiup, he must run away and stay away as long as she was there. Sometimes people smiled, to see how quickly some respected warrior scrambled to leave when he heard his wife's mother was coming. Sometimes to show additional respect, a warrior would decide to avoid his wife's sisters as well. Some mothers-in-law would abuse this custom, and come and stay with their daughters for many days—so that the husband would have to go live somewhere else for all that time. A man had to pay close attention to the obligations due to his relatives and to his relationships with each of them. It would be rude or disrespectful to discuss certain subjects or tell certain stories if anyone before whom you had an obligation to be ashamed was present. Sometimes you would not have to avoid the sister, or cousin, or uncle, or father of your wife, but you would nonetheless use polite forms of address and avoid certain subjects. A good storyteller would always say something before one of those stories, to give any people with such a relationship a chance to leave—otherwise, he could not with respect tell that story.

One of those stories went like this:

There was a bunch of pretty girls, prairie dogs, playing the stave game.[9] One of them was especially beautiful. Coyote came along and looked over the girls, and saw one that was very pretty.

This coyote went around to Gopher. He said, "You see that pretty girl sitting down there? Make a little hole right under her. I want to crawl right under that girl."

Gopher did just as Coyote said. Then Coyote crawled in there, right under that girl. He stuck his penis up directly under that girl. The girl felt something. She moved around.

"What's that? Something is under me!" she said.

Pretty soon she moved over and saw something sticking up. She picked up the big center rock used in the stave game against which you throw the sticks and hit Coyote's penis with it. That is the reason the foreskin goes back, people say.

There was another story like that one, which you could also not tell in front of people before whom you were ashamed. It went like this:

One time Coyote found a very pretty woman.[10] He tried to make love to her. He took her in the woods on a walk. He wanted to have intercourse with her and was just about to do so when he saw teeth in her vagina. He was afraid. When she wasn't looking, he got a stick and a long, slender rock.

First, instead of putting his penis in, he put in the stick, and it was ground up. Then he put the rock in, and the teeth were knocked off until her vagina became just as a woman's is now. After that, he had intercourse with her.

Then the woman said, "Hereafter I shall be worth a lot. I am worth horses and many things now."

That is why men give horses and different things when they marry a woman today.

Those Coyote stories had many lessons and many demonstrated the value of cleverness—a valuable reminder to a warrior who must spend his whole life fighting a more numerous and better-armed enemy.

Cochise especially liked this story:

This coyote had been doing a lot of mischief around a certain ranch, killing calves, or sheep, or goats, and these people went after him and ran him down and caught him. They took him home and they tied him up. Then along came another coyote and asked him, "What are you doing here with that rope on you, tied up?"

"Why, these people love me so much that they feed me well here and give me everything I want. They promise that they're going to give me the very prettiest girl they have tomorrow. These people really like me very much. If you want to, you can take my place. You can get that girl if you want to. She's supposed to be a very pretty girl," he said.

Really the people were going to skin the first coyote, take his hide off, and turn him loose. That was the plan of those people. They were going to do it the next day. But this second coyote believed the story about the girl and was very eager to be tied there.

"Well then, untie me." The second coyote untied the first and was tied there instead.

Some say that the people took this coyote's hide off. Others say that they put him in boiling water. Well, the second coyote got away from there after they had him skinned, and he went to another coyote camp. And he was red all over, and he was sitting there just as thin and cold as could be. Other coyotes looked at him. This was something new around their camps. And those coyotes yelled at him, "Hey, you with the red shirt!" He wouldn't look up. He was angry because they yelled about his red shirt. And they kept calling to him, "Hey, you with the red shirt!"

Then finally he looked at them, angry, half turning his head, and answered them. He said, "It's your father who has a red shirt!" He was angry and walked off.[11]

In this way, the People passed the season of the Ghost Dance, relying on their cached supplies and listening to all of the stories and songs that had always worked on them, smoothing and steadying their minds, teaching them right behavior. In just the same way,

Power shaped them and Places shaped them and Wind and Sun and Earth shaped them, so they would remain the People.

As soon as the season of the Little Eagles returned,[12] Cochise, Narbona, and the other war leaders once again held a dance to gather up a war party. First they danced out into the fire to act out the raid they hoped to mount and then waited to see which warriors would dance out to join them. Many warriors from allied bands danced out into the firelight, for Cochise and Narbona had great reputations and the warriors chafed against the long idleness of the Ghost Season and the supplies that had carried their families through the winter were gone. As the circle of women trilled their applause—as White-Painted Woman had greeted Child-of-the-Water—the warriors anxious for good stories to tell and the respect of their relatives danced out into the light to signal their willingness to follow Cochise and Narbona into Mexico.

Narbona led a hundred warriors to Banamichi and killed nine people on a ranch just a mile from the town. The warriors wounded five other men and captured ten women and four men with children. The men they generally killed quickly, unless they had need of hostages to exchange. Men were too much trouble, always looking for ways to escape. If they were riding to seek revenge for some killing, then sometimes they would turn the adult male prisoners over to the female relatives of the person the Mexicans had killed. Then these women beat the Mexican prisoners to death with sticks or cut them to pieces with knives, to satisfy the obligation of revenge. Sometimes they killed boys too old for training or women too old or too weak to work hard in the camps, or those who refused to learn the duties of a woman of the People. Sometimes these women would work almost as slaves, helping the wives of the warriors with difficult and laborious tasks. Often they were taken as wives and treated just like one of the People. Mangas Coloradas himself had married a beautiful Mexican woman, and though this had caused problems with the brothers of his first wife, Mangas Coloradas did as he pleased and favored his Mexican wife.[13] But everyone understood that the People were caught in a long war with no ending, and so they must use prisoners and captured children to replenish their numbers. As Narbona and Cochise raided once again through Sonora, they took many prisoners.

After several weeks, the war party grew so bold that it attacked Bavispe itself, killing 4 men and capturing 4 more children. Three weeks later Narbona, Yrigóllen, and Cochise attacked Santa Cruz, which had a population of perhaps 300. The people rallied and drove off the war party, but the next day the warriors ambushed workers going to their fields, killing 7. The people all fled into the village, and the warriors ran off most of the horses and cattle, laughing and calling out to one another. But they had grown too confident and lingered too long in the area. A force of 118 Mexicans took them by surprise nearby a month later—striking Yrigóllen's band and killing 10 people. Naturally enough, the Chokonen retaliated, raiding Bocoach to take prisoners and then trading those prisoners for warriors held captive at Bavispe. A month after that, a hundred warriors stormed Bacoachi, killing one man and taking another prisoner. But as the Sonorans gathered their soldiers, the spotted sickness of the Mexicans broke out in the camps of the Chokonen. The leaders decided to return to the Chiricahuas, where the Ga'an and the shamans and the gifts of the earth would help them defeat the sickness—which was, in truth, the strongest weapon the Mexicans possessed.

Elías González raised another Sonoran army to invade Chokonen territory. He moved north with several hundred men, but sickness broke out in his camp as well, and many men deserted, like blood seeping from a wound. He did not accomplish anything against the Chokonen, but his soldiers stumbled across a Nednhi camp and captured ten or fifteen warriors.

In the meantime, officials in Chihuahua, who had few soldiers to stop the constant raiding, again offered the scalp bounty—this time 200 pesos for the scalp of a warrior and 150 for a child's. Roving bands of cutthroats made it dangerous for any small party of the People to move about. Cochise avoided Chihuahua for a time, as the place was thick with well-armed scalp hunters who killed anyone they encountered.

Some bands began to get tired of the constant warfare, especially Chihenne bands whose home territory was not so far out of the reach of the Sonorans. Some Chihenne leaders opened up negotiations with Elías González and his Sonorans at Santa Rita del Cobre, seeking the return of people made captive. When a party of twenty-six White Eyes arrived in the middle of the negotiations, several hundred warriors surrounded them and made them prisoners. They then offered to trade the White Eyes for prisoners held by the Sonorans. But when they got word that the Sonorans had attacked another Chihenne encampment, an argument broke out among the Chihenne leaders. Some wanted to kill all of the White Eyes, but others said that the People were at war with the Mexicans, not the White Eyes. The two factions argued until fighting broke out. Angry warriors lanced seven of the prisoners to death, but other sympathetic warriors helped the remaining eighteen to escape, running bruised and naked back to the Mexicans.

Still, the Chokonen and the Chihenne had cause for satisfaction. Although the warriors had suffered many losses and the Mexicans remained huddled in scattered settlements, they had also forced the abandonment of many villages and the Sonorans had almost given up trying to invade the Dragoons and Chiricahuas and the sacred springs at Ojo Caliente. The Chokonen had not controlled so large a territory for many years, and the Mexicans were everywhere on the defensive. All of these gains had been possible because the Mexicans had been all this while fighting the Americans, so that most of their soldiers were off other places.

The People had not seen much of the Americans in the years since the two armies passed through their territory. The Americans had left a few soldiers at Doña Ana, north of Las Cruces. Some Chihenne warriors had captured two boys from a ranch near Doña Ana. When the Chihenne chief Itán found out about the raid, he set out for Doña Ana to negotiate the return of the boys, for he did not want to make enemies of the Americans. But the soldiers going out after the boys attacked Itán's party without waiting to talk. Itán sent word to his allies among the Chokonen, and Narbona and Cochise organized a raid on Doña Ana, driving off most of the stock and killing one man. The soldiers chased the raiders and wounded three of them. Then forty warriors surrounded a party of seven American soldiers, riding about boldly and challenging them to come out of the rocks in which they hid themselves. The Americans wisely decided not to fight, but retreated from that place as soon as they could. The warriors let them go, leery of their good guns and reluctant to do more to make enemies of the Americans. Cochise was impressed with the soldiers' discipline and their firepower, which stirred up the stewpot of his misgivings about the arrival of these new people in the land of the Chiricahua. But mostly the leaders of the Chihenne and Chokonen urged their warriors to avoid bothering the Americans, still hoping that the People and the Americans might make good allies against the Mexicans.

As usual, the councils of the People remained divided between peace and war. Some leaders said peace was the best idea. Even if they could drive the Mexicans out of Sonora altogether, where would they get guns and powder and horses and cattle? If they could make a peace that brought the resumption of rations and trade while keeping the Mexicans out of the heartland of the Chokonen and Chihenne, wouldn't that be better than this unending war and the roving bands of scalp hunters? Other leaders like Cochise and Mangas Coloradas and Narbona said that any peace was just cover for the Mexicans to stalk them all, and to weaken them with thin rations and bad whiskey.

Some bands went to Bacoachi to meet with Elías González in the season of Many Leaves.[14] When they met with a friendly reception and a promise of rations, Yrigóllen brought his band in to talk as well. The Sonorans wanted the bands to stop raiding and settle near the presidios, where it would be easy to provide rations. But Yrigóllen said last time they had done that, Kirker had killed 130 people in their sleep. Nonetheless, the leaders of the peace faction warily agreed to settle near the town in return for rations. Seeing this, many Chihenne groups also opened negotiations with Chihuahua and agreed to settle near Janos, where they could live peacefully and even trade supplies raiding parties brought back from Sonora, just as they had done years ago before the war had spread everywhere. Ponce, Itán, Delgadito, and Coleto Amarillo all brought their bands in to live near Janos, but Mangas Coloradas remained adamant against any peace with the Mexicans.

In the meantime, Mangas Coloradas, Narbona, and Cochise—fearful that many warriors would yield to the carefully concealed deadfall of peace—redoubled their raiding, partly to anger the Mexicans and spoil the peace talks. They ranged far south to the Yaquí River, killing people wherever they went. Everywhere, people abandoned their ranches and villages, heading south with many fearful glances over their shoulders. In one season of raiding, the war parties killed more than 111 people in Sonora, although they mostly avoided Chihuahua because of the peace between the Chihenne bands and Janos. Two war parties with more than 200 warriors went through Sonora like a brushfire before they turned and headed back toward the Chiricahuas, slowed by the 1,300 horses and cattle they drove along in front.

Sonoran captain Ignacio Pesqueira gathered up 100 soldiers and pursued the slowly retreating war party. Near Pozo Hediondo the warriors, led by Mangas Coloradas, Yrigóllen, Narbona, Cochise, and others, saw the soldiers coming up. One of the war leaders was a young Nednhi of great Power named Juh, a bear of a man with a stutter and so fierce a presence that his own warriors feared him. He was both tall and stocky, so that he was a mountain of muscle with a cold mind and a molten temper. He led a group of Nednhis who were desperate fighters, and so hard to govern that other bands called them "wild" and whose numbers included even exiles from other bands. But Juh was a shrewd fighter with a deep relationship with his Power, so he was welcomed in any raid. Cochise and a rear guard of fearless men formed up on high ground and waited, while the larger portion of the warriors concealed themselves. Pesqueira charged them, showing great courage.[15] The band of warriors on the high ground, who had really been left at the rear as bait, broke and ran from the Mexicans, looking back over their shoulders as though frightened. They made a great show of lashing their horses even as they held them back so the Mexicans would fill up with confidence and charge after them. It worked, and Cochise and the other decoys led the Mexicans into a narrow canyon, where 250 warriors awaited the command of Mangas Coloradas to spring the trap. The warriors closed in from all sides, killing many soldiers in the first shooting. Cochise turned and charged back toward the Mexicans, hoping they would panic and flee. He rode in among them, wielding his lance. No one could match Cochise with a lance, a long spear of wood to which he often lashed the broken blade of a soldier's sword. He could spear saguaro fruit on the ground riding at a full run, and drive a lance one-handed clear through a soldier's body. He could hurl a lance with deadly accuracy at great range. No one of his warriors could match him with a lance—which demonstrated both his great strength and his matchless horsemanship. He seemed so completely part of his horse when he rode people thought he must have Horse Power. When riding toward his enemies, he would hook his foot in the thin strap tied round the horse's middle and slip down so he could shoot from under the neck of his horse while presenting no target at all to the soldiers. Cochise rode right in among the fleeing soldiers, striking them down with vicious thrusts of his lance, disdainful of their bullets and their swords. Even so, the soldiers held their discipline and fought their way through to a place with good cover. The warriors then laid siege to them, trying to get to higher ground where they could shoot down at the trapped soldiers. The Mexicans fought bravely—standing off the attack though they were badly outnumbered, giving ground stubbornly from cover to cover. The warriors would form up behind leaders whose Power seemed strong and charged the Mexicans' positions, sometimes breaking before they could get close, sometimes overrunning the position of the Sonorans and killing some in hand-to-hand fighting. But the Sonorans would retreat to another position and continue fighting. The fight went on all afternoon, until the warriors had killed 26 soldiers and wounded 46. They ran off most of the soldiers' horses and left during the night, not willing to pay the cost in lives necessary to kill the rest. Even so, they suffered many losses—which muted the celebration of their victory.[16]

That loss so enraged the Sonorans that they resolved to strike back at the only people they could find—the bands living peacefully near Janos.[17] In the season of Little Eagles,[18] a Sonoran army went quietly to Janos, where several bands of Chihenne and Nednhis plus Yrigóllen's Chokonens had settled. The Sonorans surprised Yrigóllen's camp, killing twenty-one people—including the chief. They captured sixty-two others, whom they took back to Sonora to sell as slaves. But the attack did little to end the raiding, as it silenced one of the leading Chokonen advocates for negotiations. Some bands fled back to the Chiricahuas, others went to Fronteras hoping to make peace with the Sonorans there, others continued to raid. By the end of the raiding season, two hundred Sonorans had been killed—twice as many as the year before.

Then word came the Americans had returned with a small army with many horses and cows and well-armed White Eyes and Mexicans not in the soldier coats. They made their way to Santa Rita del Cobre and camped there, looking like they intended to stay for a time. Mangas Coloradas sent out subchiefs to find out what the White Eyes were doing there and how long they intended to stay. He also wondered whether this time he might make friends with the White Eyes. The soldiers seemed friendly and their *nantan*[19] gave the warriors presents, including a splendid soldier uniform with red pants and brilliantly ornamented shoulders. Mangas Coloradas had a great fondness for splendid and impressive clothes, so he wore the soldier uniform with the red pants proudly when he visited the soldiers. But he was also a proud and sensitive man, and sometimes it seemed to him that the soldiers smiled at his clothes, covering their mouths and turning away. He soon gambled away the new outfit, and watched the newcomers warily. To his dismay, he learned that the Americans had finished their war with the Mexicans and had taken much of the land that the Mexicans had claimed. This *nantan* had come to decide where the border should go between the Americans and the Mexicans. He said that now the Chihenne, the Chokonen, the Bedonkohe, the Mescalero, the White Mountain, and the Tonto people now all lived in the land of the Americans—and would be as the children of the Great White Father. Mangas Coloradas listened dubiously to this, wondering that the Americans could, by killing Mexicans, claim control of land the Mexicans had never controlled. But he did not argue with the Americans, for Mangas Coloradas was a subtle and careful man, one who could balance the needs and motivations of many men and look for ways to turn those needs to his own advantage. He thought things might work out to the advantage of the Chihenne. Perhaps the Americans would keep the Sonorans from chasing raiding parties all the way back to their homes. Perhaps the arrival of the Americans would give the People a sanctuary and a breathing space. There did not seem to be many Americans, just soldiers and trappers and traders and miners. And they did not seem as interested in staying as the Mexicans were, but mostly in passing safely through the desert to someplace in the west where they all wanted to go. Perhaps they could work things out with the Americans as they had in Janos, when they could live peacefully with Janos and raid in Sonora.

Mangas Coloradas insisted that his warriors respect everything that belonged to the Americans, even their horses, mules, and cows. Once, several warriors took some cattle—but as soon as Mangas Coloradas heard this he insisted the warriors turn over the livestock, his great, shrewd eyes glinting in dangerous anger. But the good feeling between the Chihenne and the Americans did not last long. After all, were these not the same people as Kirker and Johnson? First the Americans took away two boys, Mexican captives belonging to a respected warrior. Although Mangas Coloradas protested, the Americans refused to give the boys back to their owner. Then one of the Mexican packers killed a warrior for no reason at all. The Americans put chains on the hands of the Mexican and promised he would be punished according to their customs, but refused to hand him over to the Chihenne so they could be sure of their revenge. Finally, they offered to pay some horses and blankets to the family of the dead man—which was more of an insult than a recompense. Mangas Coloradas accepted this, unwilling to make the Americans his enemy. But he removed the injunction against taking the Americans' horses, and soon they had no horses left at all. They left after that, looking back anxiously over their shoulders. But some miners who had come with them stayed, and began digging again in the copper mines at Santa Rita del Cobre. Mangas Coloradas watched this with a grim foreboding. Word of the end of the war between the Mexicans and the Americans and the arrival of the soldiers and the miners spread quickly to the Chokonen. Cochise thought it dangerous news when he heard it, as a man who sees columns of dust both behind and ahead of him.

Meanwhile, the war with the Sonorans went on, from one round of seasons to the next. The Sonorans took an army of three hundred men into the Chiricahuas, pulling their heavy guns on wheels along behind. They killed more than twenty people and took prisoners, but most of the bands stepped out of their way. Some bands responded by going back down to Bavispe with prisoners of their own, seeking the return of the relatives. But an argument broke out and the soldiers killed the band leaders who had come into the town to negotiate. Cochise, seeing the Sonorans now had many well-armed soldiers, stayed out of their way by remaining in the Dragoons and Chiricahuas. But the Sonorans mounted another offensive the following season, returning to the mountains where the Chihenne and the Chokonen had been safe for many turnings of the leaves. When the Sonorans reached the Chiricahuas, Narbona, Cochise, and Coyuntura went out to parley, seeking to hold them in place with words while other bands gathered. When the Mexicans saw other warriors gathering, they broke off talks and moved into Bonita Canyon, seeking ground easy to defend should the gathering warriors attack. By dawn, more than three hundred warriors had gathered. Led by Narbona, Cochise, and the other war leaders, they attacked the Mexicans from all directions and drove them back, but lost ten warriors in a two-hour fight. Pressed closely, the Sonorans fell back through Apache Pass and retreated out of the Chokonen territory.

The Chokonen and the Chihenne had defended their territory, but they had suffered grievous losses. Yrigóllen was gone, who had the widest following since Pisago Cabezón. Many other important chiefs had been killed as well, so that no one could call on a large number of bands to raise a powerful force. Mangas Coloradas dominated the Chihenne, but the Chokonen were divided and splintered by their losses, for Cochise had not yet risen to fill as large a space as his father had left empty. The more warlike Chokonen leaders like Cochise and Narbona were drawn along behind Mangas Coloradas, as young stallions trot behind the leader.

Both Chokonen and Chihenne war parties invaded Sonora the next raiding season.[20] Chihenne raiders led by Mangas Coloradas swept past Fronteras, killed five boys herding sheep, and then ambushed the soldiers chasing them. Chokonen war parties totaling two hundred warriors moved down the Sonora River, then raided settlements along the western slopes of the Sierra Madre, killing scores of people and taking hundreds of cows. Mangas Coloradas spent most of his time leading warriors, going down through Sonora, his hatred for the Mexicans like an inexhaustible spring. The more peacefully inclined leaders who remained behind near Santa Rita del Cobre and the core territory of the Chihenne meanwhile signed treaties with the Americans, giving away land that was not theirs in return for vague and empty promises.

Cochise also spent much of his time raiding, pouring his hatred of the Mexicans into the broken pot of his anger. Sometimes his warriors joined up with Mangas Coloradas, but more often they moved alone through Sonora, as wolves move along the edge of an elk herd. They returned periodically to the Chiricahuas, where their families remained, ever on the lookout for the trail of dust of an approaching Mexican army. Sometimes warriors would bring their families along as they raided, hiding their wives and children on this mountain or that while the warriors fell like lightning on the villages and towns, or waited concealed along the wagon roads. Cochise ranged across a vast area, from the Gila River down through the Sierra Madre, riding 50 miles in a day and undertaking raids that would cover 1,500 miles before the weary warriors returned home. They picked their targets carefully, eluding the soldiers and falling on isolated ranchers and herders, miners and cowboys. They struck quickly, left no witnesses, and vanished again into the mountains before the soldiers could even find their trail.

Cochise gradually gained great authority over the warriors who sheltered under the wings of his Power. His raiding parties distinguished themselves for their tactics and their discipline. Most war leaders had only a little influence over their men, who jealously guarded their independence. Most war leaders led by personal example, running at the front of the attack so that the others would be ashamed to hang back. Sometimes they were so respected that others turned to them to settle disputes and pass judgment—but the leader had only the moral force of his reputation to enforce the decision. He could refuse to have an unreliable man join a war party, and so shame that man. But the leader could not give orders and impose punishment in the manner of the Mexicans. Often it was difficult even to set out sentries for a camp while the warriors slept, as no one had the authority to order another warrior to stand watch. That is why soldiers surprised so many camps at dawn, when the few warriors who had volunteered to stand watch decided they should sleep themselves.

But Cochise gradually accumulated far more authority than most war leaders among his followers. That was partly because the other warriors feared his anger. Usually, Cochise was quiet and thoughtful and tightly controlled; but sometimes when a warrior failed in his responsibilities to the band, Cochise would flare into white-hot rage. He had killed men in such a rage. Normally, anyone who killed a warrior would trigger a blood feud with the relatives of the dead man. But Cochise seemed unconcerned, and even close relatives of someone who had earned the rage of Cochise did not retaliate. His own family was too powerful—especially his brothers, who were feared and respected. And too many other powerful men owed him their loyalty—especially Mangas Coloradas, who was his father-in-law. Besides, the anger of Cochise was infrequent and righteous and people said to themselves that he had done the right thing. His influence and his authority also grew from the root of his Power and his success in leading raiding parties through the thickets of their enemies with few losses. Warriors moved as close to such Power as they could, knowing it would protect them. Besides, everyone knew that Cochise fought for his band and for the People. He could have been great in horses and cattle and wealth, but he kept only what he needed for himself and his family and gave everything else away. In his generosity and in his Power, he earned the loyalty of his followers. When Cochise selected a camp, no one dissented. When he told this man to camp here—to protect one approach—and this man to camp there—to protect the back way—no one complained. And when he set out sentries for the night or sent out his scouts to cover the front and back and flanks of the raiding party, everyone hurried to their places.

The Chokonen had little contact with the Americans, who left soldiers in Chihenne territory near Santa Rita del Cobre and near Mesilla, but only passed quickly through Chokonen territory on the way west.[21] One Chokonen band raided the horse herd kept by the soldiers near Mesilla, and the soldiers set out after them. The soldiers lost that trail, but kept on going and attacked the camp of El Cautivo, a Chokonen leader closely aligned with Cochise. The soldiers killed two of El Cautivo's relatives in that attack, which started a smolder of suspicion and hatred for the Americans in El Cautivo, who came to have a great influence over Cochise. El Cautivo had been captured as a boy by the Mexicans and made a slave for many years before he escaped. Now he nurtured an abiding hatred for the Mexicans, but had learned to speak their tongue so well that he could kill a Mexican cowboy, put on his clothes, and go into a village to gather information. He often acted as a translator for Cochise, who also spoke Spanish but preferred to pretend he could not when negotiating with the Mexicans. El Cautivo was a shrewd, angry, wary man of great Power and foresight, whose deep, glittering eyes smoked and burned like a branding iron. He nurtured his anger after the attack on his camp, and looked for the chance to even that score. Even so, Cochise told his warriors to stay clear of the White Eyes and avoid fights with them. He had enough trouble fighting the Mexicans; he did not want to start another fire close to his own home.

In the season of Many Leaves,[22] Mangas Coloradas called together a joint raid of the Chihenne and the Chokonen. One of the Chihenne leaders was a rising young war leader named Victorio, whose reputation for strategy and Power rivaled that of Cochise. He was perfectly formed, lithe and graceful as a lion with black, penetrating eyes that seemed to see past you. He was not as tall as Cochise, but powerfully built with a sense of coiled energy and a reputation for layered strategy. He also had an unfailing instinct for the movements of his enemies and a habitual caution in selecting his camps and directing his men that matched that of Cochise. Victorio was dignified and intense, for like Cochise he seemed aware from an early age of his responsibility to his people and to his Power. Many people said Victorio's Power came in part from his sister, Lozen. She often rode alongside him and had great Power in her own right. She had taken training as a warrior and had never married. Many people said Power had spoken to her after the four-day, coming-of-age Sunrise Ceremony, when she had become as White-Painted Woman. She had a ceremony in which she danced in front of the circle of warriors with her hands extended, palms up, as she prayed and turned slowly in a circle. When she faced in the direction of her enemies, her hands grew warm—or hot to the touch if her enemies were close. In this way, people said raiding parties led by Victorio and Lozen could not be taken by surprise. Cochise noted Victorio turned often to his sister for advice and counsel, even as Cochise turned to Dos-teh-seh.

Mangas Coloradas and Victorio and Cochise and Narbona and Delgadito and the other war leaders went on down into Sonora, determined to take horses and guns and ammunition and prisoners they could trade for people held captive by the Mexicans. They surrounded Bacerac, jeering at frightened people and running off all of the horses and cattle. They attacked Bavispe, killing several people and running off many horses. They nearly destroyed Chinapa, killing people too slow to flee. Warriors went door to door taking anything of value and killing those who tried to hide from them before setting the village on fire. Cochise marveled at all of the things the Mexicans had, most of them not worth carrying away. They seemed a strange and foolish people, shut up in their dark, stinking buildings as though they were afraid of the sky. They accumulated so many useless things they were tethered in one place, most of them weak and helpless and blind as moles to the wisdom of the wind and the thoughts of the rocks. After the warriors sacked Chinapa, the great war party spilt into different bands, which drove the captured horses and cattle back north, while Sonora bled and burned in their wake.

Cochise returned to the Chiricahuas, his warriors driving livestock loaded with enough supplies and ammunition to carry them safely through the season of the Ghost Dance. His followers made their camps in the Chiricahuas and the Dragoons, scattering into small family-based bands, so they would not overtax the game or the bounty of acorns or the supply of agave.

But Narbona remained restless and decided to go raiding again with a small group of followers. It seemed he could not get enough killing, as though his Power needed ever more wood on the fire of his hatred. He seemed only fully himself when they were raiding, but tired and sad when they remained long in camp. Cochise noted this with grave concern, for he believed that warfare remained of value only if it protected the camps of the People—where the women sat in small groups talking and laughing as the children tumbled over one another like puppies. But he knew also that war could consume a man, especially if his Power grew thirsty for blood and glory. Cochise had heard many stories about the demanding and sometimes blood-thirsty nature of Power. For instance, one war shaman consulted his Power before a battle and his Power told him that three of his men would die in the battle the next day—providing even their names. That war shaman argued with his Power, insisting that his Power tell him how to save the lives of those men. His Power became cross with him, insisting that He had protected the shaman and his men in many battles and now the shaman ought to give over the lives of the three men to Power. But that shaman wouldn't do it, saying that he didn't want Power if it meant he had to give up the lives of his men—and that his Power could just take back the ceremonies and give him no more help at all. Seeing that It had pushed too far, Power decided to soothe the shaman. They agreed that the war party would simply go home and not fight at all the next day.[23]

Cochise understood how difficult and complicated it was some-times for a great war leader like Narbona to deal with his Power and to know what he should do. Cochise said nothing when Narbona set off too soon and in a hard season with only a few warriors. One warrior did not question the decisions and the needs of another—certainly not one so great in Power and so great in the hearts of his people as Narbona.

The weeks slipped past without Narbona's return. For a long time, Cochise did not worry—for raids might easily last for weeks or even whole seasons. But as the cold time deepened long past a rea-sonable return, Cochise felt the knowledge of loss settle over him, like snow on the dead grass. And so Narbona, who had carried the fighting spirit of his people on his shoulders, vanished. They could only gather inconclusive rumors of his passing in the years to come. After many months, his family despaired of his return, and cut their hair off in grieving, and spoke his name no more.[24]

Now the Chokonen turned their faces all together toward Cochise. Pisago Cabezón was gone. Yrigóllen was gone. Narbona was gone. No one spoke their names thereafter. Cochise stood alone in the front of the Chokonen, as the only great tree left after a fire has consumed all the others.

Perhaps the Power that cared for the Chokonen had arranged things in just this manner. Perhaps the Ga'an who protected the People and danced in the sacred heart of the mountain reached out and turned events in just his direction, as a player with Power will change the course of the pole as it springs toward the hoop. For Cochise rose to undisputed leadership of the Chokonen just as the fire of the smoke that had been burning toward them from the east could be seen on the horizon.

Narbona had been a great leader for the long, bitter, war of no quarter with the Mexicans—for he understood them and hated them so that his Power had them always in mind. But for all of the death and victory and revenge and courage of the war between the People and the Mexicans, they did not pose the great riddle of the life of Cochise. As hard as things had been against the Mexicans, with their many guns and many soldiers and stubborn persistence, soon the warriors of the People would look back on that war as the last time of great hope and easy victory.

It was fortunate that the Powers who held the Chokonen dear brought Cochise to the height of his Power and cunning just as the White Eyes came swarming into the sky, like an irresistible swarm of grasshoppers. For the People now had need of the leadership, discipline, strategy, and courage of Child-of-the-Water, who stood unafraid in the deep shadow of the Giant.

They had a great and terrible need for Cochise.

1856

Storm from the East:
The White Eyes Arrive

It Happened at Tuzhj Yaahigaiye
(Whiteness Spreads Out Descending)

Long ago at that place there were lots of dead oak trees. There was
a woman living with her family not far away. "We're almost out of
firewood," she said to one of her daughters. "Go up there and bring
back some of that oak."

Then that girl went up there. She started to gather firewood.
It was very hot and she got tired fast. "I'm getting tired," she thought.
"I've already got enough firewood. I'll go back home."

Then she picked up as much firewood as she could carry.
She started walking down to her camp. She got careless. She stepped
on a thin, flat rock. It looked strong, but she forgot she was carrying
all that heavy oak. The rock broke when she stepped on it. She
stumbled and fell down. She hit her head on the ground. For a while
she was unconscious.

Then she came to and noticed that she was bleeding from cuts on
her cheek and chin. She walked unsteadily back to her camp. She told
her mother what had happened.

Then her mother talked to her. "You acted foolishly, but you're
going to be all right. You failed to see danger before it happened. You
could have fallen off the trail and gotten killed on those sharp rocks
below it. You were thinking only of yourself. That is why this
happened to you."

It happened at Whiteness Spreads Out Descending.

The dangerous rumors filtered slowly through to the Chokonen,
who remained preoccupied with their never-ending war with the
Sonorans. Cochise had established a network of sentries to watch

the approaches to the Dragoons and the Chiricahuas. He directed
the bands of trusted leaders to camp in certain passes on certain
ridges, so they would see anyone approach and hasten word to the
other bands. His lookouts informed him quickly when the American
soldiers made their way through the territory of the Chokonen to
Tucson and settled in there. And his scouts told him when the miners and settlers and soldiers returned to Tubac, which his raiding
parties had forced the Mexicans to abandon.

Moreover, he soon gathered disturbing news from runners sent
by Mangas Coloradas and word from Chokonen warriors who had
married Chihenne and Mescalero girls and so had gone to live with
their people. The White Eyes had started a war off to the east,
mostly with the Mescalero but sometimes with the Chihenne.[1]
Cochise did not give this news much weight, as his attention was
centered on binding together the Chokonen bands in the face of the
loss of Narbona. But it once again demonstrated the dangerous and
unpredictable nature of the White Eyes, and the importance of not
provoking them so the Chokonen would be hunted both in Mexico
and in their retreats in the Dragoons and Chiricahuas.

The Chihenne and other bands struggled to find sanctuary in
the new terrain created by the increasing aggressiveness of the
Americans. Everyone wondered how to balance the conflict between
the Americans and the Mexicans. Some Chihenne and Bedonkohe
leaders went back down to Janos, thinking perhaps Chihuahua
would offer better rations than the Americans. Chihenne leaders
like Itán did agree to a truce with Janos, and won the release of
some prisoners held there. But that peace did not last long and soon
tripped across unprovoked killings of several warriors by the Mexicans. Then a Sonoran army again came to Janos, but the Janos Mexicans managed to stop the Sonorans before they could attack the
bands camped peacefully near the town.

Mangas Coloradas soon delivered another blow to the halting
efforts by some of the other Chihenne to make peace with Janos. He
said such a peace would only lure people closer to Janos, where they
could be killed by treachery or by the Sonorans—as they had been
so often in the past. Mangas Coloradas conferred with Cochise at the
beginning of the raiding season, saying that a peace with Janos
would bleed away the strength of the Chihenne and so leave the
Chokonen more vulnerable. Cochise and El Cautivo, who hated the
Mexicans as much as ever, agreed to raid with him down toward

Janos. They raided the outskirts of Janos, running off a hundred horses and scattering dissension between the Mexicans and the Chihenne like nettles in bedding. The commander of Janos responded by imprisoning the band leaders who had come to the town to seek peace, insisting he would not release them until Mangas Coloradas returned the horses he had stolen. Mangas Coloradas continued on his way, glad he had broken up the peace talks with Janos. But other Chihenne and Nednhi bands continued to negotiate with the Janos people for several months, until they convinced the Janos Mexicans to release the people they had taken prisoner and provide rations to several hundred Chihenne and Nednhis who settled nearby. Just as Mangas Coloradas had predicted, the word of peace with Janos spread to the Chokonen and the Chihenne. Many of them decided to go and try that peace, especially because the Americans continued to kill people in the north, whether they were raiders or small bands just trying to live peacefully and stay out of the path of trouble.

Cochise and Mangas Coloradas remained apart, although the seeming success of the peace at Janos ate into the banks of their supporters like the rising spring waters. They combined forces to raid and spent a long time talking about the complicated choices that confronted them—like men seeking the meaning of a dream full of contradictions. Neither trusted the Mexicans, nor did they want to provoke a war with the Americans. So far, the Americans seemed the more manageable problem. They had not nearly as many people and did not want to plant corn everywhere, as did the Mexicans. They seemed mostly interested in making sure that travelers could pass safely from one end of the Chiricahua territory to the other, and with protecting the scattered ranches and mining camps. Cochise and Mangas Coloradas thought perhaps they could come to some arrangement with the Americans, although the ongoing campaign by the soldiers made it dangerous to linger long in that country. So they clung to the hope of peace with the Americans, partly because they knew from long and bitter history that any agreement with the Mexicans would end in death and treachery. They resolved to move cautiously, like a man in the dark on a cliff edge—hoping for peace with the Americans, but still placating their many followers who wanted to test this shimmering illusion of peace with Janos. They reasoned together and came to the conclusion that they must remain part of the discussion with the Mexicans if they were to maintain leadership. Even so, they thought they might play Sonora off against Chihuahua—an old game for the People.

Mangas Coloradas cautiously sent emissaries to Janos, as a man tests a hot spring with his toe. And Cochise did the same in Fronteras, to see if the Sonorans might be ready to make peace. Mangas Coloradas finally moved his band to an easily defended place near Janos so he could keep track of the other bands and the soldiers. But even though the Sonorans agreed to let the Chokonen settle near Fronteras and promised peace and rations, Cochise could not overcome his wariness and so remained aloof. But he withheld from raiding so he would not stir up the Mexicans when the Americans were campaigning actively in the north. He also hoped to stop fighting long enough to harvest the acorns to see them safely through the season of the Ghost Dance. So for all of these reasons, an uneasy peace settled in over Mexico, and the number of Chihenne and Bedonkohe camped near Janos grew gradually to total six hundred.[2] Seeing the peace take hold at Janos, many Chokonen bands also settled near Fronteras in Sonora, until nearly seven hundred people had gathered. Cochise moved his band closer to Fronteras, watching everything with a keen and wary eye.[3]

Of course, the Mexicans soon proved that even Cochise's worst suspicions were but foolish hopes. His band had not been long near Fronteras when many people grew sick and pale and pained in the belly. The shamans struggled to understand what sickness had come among them, as those stricken did not cough or have the sores of the worst diseases of the Mexicans. Instead, they simply sickened and died. The Chokonen moved away from Fronteras to live in the mountains to the north, where those who had not died soon grew stronger. Soon, they heard stories of the same sickness among the Chihenne who had been living on the rations of the Mexicans near Janos. Cochise saw that the sickness abated as soon as they stopped eating the rations the Mexicans had given them and decided the Mexicans had poisoned them. He once again regretted yielding to the temptation to believe the Mexicans and the weakness that had made him think it might be possible to end this long war, which had taken such a toll of the women and the children.[4] Mangas Coloradas also blamed himself for the suffering of his people, and many Chihenne bands returned cautiously to the agency that had been established by the Americans, hoping to live peacefully and recover now that the Americans' campaign had ended. The agent, Michael Steck, also urged them to return.

Cochise also returned quietly to the Chiricahuas in the season of the Ghost Dance,[5] determined to make peace with the White Eyes. He sent a few reliable men who spoke good Spanish to keep watch on the soldiers at Fort Buchanan near Sonoita, which protected the scattering of ranches that had started up in that grassy, well-watered valley. He found that some of the soldiers would sell them ammunition and guns in return for the money and horses and cattle and supplies brought back from raids into Sonora. He also found some traders who operated out of Tucson and other settlements who were willing to buy Mexican stock. In this way, the Chokonen lived quietly in the Chiricahuas and Dragoons all through the lean times of winter, taking care to do nothing that would rouse the American soldiers against them.

Then, in the season of Many Leaves,[6] a runner brought terrible news. Two sons of Mangas Coloradas—brothers of Dos-teh-seh—had been lured into talking peace in Sonora and then treacherously killed. Mangas Coloradas, who now had strong allies and relatives in key bands among all the Chiricahua and even among the Navajo and the Mescalero, sent the word to everyone that he would raise a great war party. Cochise called on all of the Chokonen to support Mangas Coloradas, for he had also an obligation to seek revenge for the people the Mexicans had poisoned the year before. Some five hundred warriors responded to the call of Mangas Coloradas and so mounted one of the largest war parties in the memory of anyone present. They stormed through Sonora as floodwaters that have escaped the riverbank. They killed perhaps three hundred people[7] as they rampaged through the province, killing without regard to age or sex, and set whole villages to the torch. The Sonorans seemed almost defenseless, their scattered outposts of soldiers no match for the great war party, now led by Mangas Coloradas, Cochise, Victorio, and the other war leaders of the unified Chiricahua.

Now also Cochise rode along with another rising war leader, who earned a strong name by his Power and courage in a great revenge fight with the Mexicans. His name was Geronimo, and he was the grandson of one of the greatest war leaders of the Bedonkohe, the brother people whose home territory lay between the Chokonen and the Chihenne. The Bedonkohe had suffered terrible losses from the Mexicans and could no longer raise large war parties on their own. Their warriors raided often with the Chokonen and the Chihenne, with whom they had many bonds of marriage and blood. Geronimo was stocky and powerful, his face resolute and cruel—marked by his

Geronimo. He fought alongside Cochise in his early years, but Geronimo's refusal to stop raiding helped lead to the eventual closure of the reservation Cochise fought so hard to win. *(National Archives)*

grief and anger. His band had been camped near a Mexican town with whom they were at peace when soldiers came unexpectedly and killed many women and children when the warriors were away—including Geronimo's mother, wife, and two children. Geronimo had gone from band to band—even the Chokonen—to call on warriors to help avenge the treachery of the Mexicans. In the battle that followed, he had demonstrated his great courage and great Power. His Power had promised him that bullets could not kill him and that he would die an old man, so now he flung himself at the enemy with reckless courage. He also had Coyote Power, so he could heal people who had contracted Coyote sickness by walking on the track of a coyote or eating something a coyote had mouthed or urinated on, or by speaking and thinking in a disrespectful way about Coyote or the things that were an aspect of Coyote Power. Because Coyote was so crafty, cruel, brave, selfish, foolish, and unpredictable, Coyote Power was a dangerous thing to possess—although it conferred on Geronimo great gifts in war. Now Geronimo was consumed with anger and revenge, and went constantly among the bands seeking warriors to go raiding. And even when on a raid to find horses, he would kill people who fell into his path. The People had need of warriors whose Power made them great in war, but men such as Geronimo sometimes seemed an arrow pointed at both ends. Even if his Power protected him, it did not always protect the warriors riding alongside. And because he remained so fixed on revenge, and because he often lost men on raids, he was a war shaman and not a chief. He was a useful man for leaders like Mangas Coloradas and Cochise when they had to fight, but dangerous when they had to restrain the warriors to make peace for strategic reasons with the Americans, or Janos, or the Navajo. Geronimo's anger, hatred, and Power could not be kept in a sack for future use with the drawstring pulled tight. Having Geronimo on a raid was like juggling coals, requiring courage and quick hands.

Cochise and Mangas Coloradas and Victorio and Geronimo and Juh and many others all rode together through Sonora to avenge the sons of Mangas Coloradas, who were also the brothers of Dos-teh-seh. And after they had taken more lives and horses and inflicted more destruction than any raid in memory, they turned back north before the Sonorans could gather up enough soldiers to strike back. Cochise then sent several women down to Fronteras and told them to offer to make peace with Sonora. He did not want peace with the Sonorans, but reasoned that the offer might forestall a Sonoran expedition north in the season of the Ghost Dance, so his warriors could rest through the cold months. But when the Sonorans said they would make peace and provide rations, some of the other leaders thought they should test this offer, reasoning that the great raid had finally convinced the Sonorans to yield. Cochise reminded them that no one could trust the Mexicans, any more than they could trust a flea in their bedding not to bite them. But some leaders said they could not fight forever, with the Americans coming into their land in the north. They took their bands down to Fronteras to test the peace—perhaps in part to get access to the food and whiskey of the Mexicans. Cochise noted this with grave concern, seeing that many warriors had too great a need for the powerful liquor of the Mexicans. Sure enough, the Sonorans gave the warriors plenty of whiskey and trouble soon started. The Mexicans attempted to seize

a group of warriors to lock them in the small cells that were a torture to the spirit, and fighting started. Then the Mexicans chased
them out of Fronteras and fell upon a camp of women and children,
killing twenty-six people and seizing another ten people to sell as
slaves. The Mexicans killed three band leaders in this attack. They
counted it a victory, but it would cost them dearly. They had killed
three of the last band leaders who wanted peace and remained
independent of Cochise—and so the attack strengthened his hold on
the Chokonen.

Cochise sent out runners to his father-in-law to raise a Chokonen-
Chihenne-Bedonkohe expedition to punish Fronteras once again.
Within a month, some two hundred warriors gathered near Stein's
Peak, one of the sacred mountains where the Ga'an mountain spirits danced. The warriors danced and feasted for four days, invoking
the support and guidance of the Ga'an. The leaders each consulted
their Power, and the warriors showed off their dancing and their
courage before the women, and the boys ran through the encampment, playing war and dreaming of killing Mexicans. Cochise and
Mangas Coloradas talked a long while, throwing their minds forward
into Sonora. And they agreed that they must take care not to rouse
the Americans against them, for they could not long survive a war
on two fronts. Ideally, they should make friends with the Americans
so they could sell them the horses and mules and cattle they
brought out of Mexico in return for the guns and powder and bullets they needed. But in any case, they should hold their men back
from raiding among the Americans so long as they had no peace
with Sonora or Chihuahua. So the great war party again went down
into Sonora, but this time they did not accomplish so much. They
attacked Fronteras,[8] but even though only a handful of soldiers
manned the presidio, they drove off the poorly coordinated attack
using the guns on wheels, which made such a frightening noise and
threw a sackful of bullets all at once. Cochise noted that the warriors
did not fight with good discipline, in part because they came from
so many bands. War leaders like Geronimo did not follow orders, for
he listened to the urging of his own Power. When they attacked Fronteras, groups of warriors attacked here and there instead of coordinating their attack in a way that might have overwhelmed the few
soldiers. Moreover, Mangas Coloradas seemed uncertain, so that his
great Power did not close its fist over the squabbling band leaders.
Perhaps he was still grieving for his dead sons and had lost heart.

But after the soldiers drove off the first attack, many warriors said that Power was doubtful and uncertain and so turned back for home.

Cochise remained in the area to gather up supplies and get a little revenge for the treacherous killing of the peace leaders the season before. He noted signs that the Mexicans were strengthening their defenses and sending more soldiers to the forts along the frontier.[9] In fact, the Sonorans built up their defenses so well in the next few months that they mounted an expedition of several hundred soldiers which went north and surprised a Chihenne band in its camp, killing eighteen people and capturing four more to sell as slaves.

Cochise turned his face back to the Chiricahua Mountains. But upon his return, he found that the world had changed suddenly and forever, casting a shadow in which Cochise would move for the rest of his life. The Americans had come now into the heart of Chokonen territory, building a chain of stations to keep horses for the big houses on wheels in which they traveled.[10] Several well-armed men lived at each of the rock-walled stations, each placed near a vital source of water. The stations had loopholes for firing and lots of supplies, so that the men inside could stand off an attack by many warriors—although it would be easy enough to drive the horses out of the corrals. The Americans built one stage station near Stein's Peak, another in Apache Pass, another near Dragoon Springs, and still another in the Peloncillo Mountains. These stations dominated water sources on which the People had long relied, with place-names that had stalked them and worked on them for generations. The arrogance of the Americans in building the stations so close to the water without any negotiation or presents infuriated some of the warriors and band leaders. They said the Chokonen should attack the stage stations, take the horses, guns, and supplies, and send the station keeper home with a warning to stay out of Chokonen territory. But this was the moment Cochise had long anticipated, because of his Power and his long talks with Mangas Coloradas. He did not want to start a second war so close to his sanctuary in the Chiricahuas and so resolved to make friends with the Americans if possible—despite his memory of Johnson and of Kirker.

Worse yet, soldiers had built Fort Buchanan on Sonoita Creek, halfway between Tucson and the Chokonen refuge in the Dragoons. Settlers had built scattered ranches in the Sonoita Valley, which had good water and grass as high as a horse's belly. So the soldiers now stayed all the time at the fort, to protect the cattle and the ranchers.

Moreover, miners had moved back into Tubac and started digging again.

The intrusion of so many Americans so close to their home territory alarmed Cochise. He wondered what they intended. He knew the Americans and Chokonen had clashed several times before. Some Chokonen raiders had killed two men in a wagon train passing through Apache Pass and then had eluded the soldiers sent out to find them. But Cochise had discouraged such attacks and forbidden his warriors to bother the man leading a mule loaded with the talking paper of the White Eyes, which passed regularly between Mesilla and Tucson through the territory of the Chokonen. Still, he wondered whether the Americans were still angry about the two men killed in Apache Pass, or the scattered stock raids in the Sonoita Valley.

Cochise sent warriors down to investigate the stage stations, warning them to give no offense and to make friends if possible. They reported that the station keepers were friendly and gave them presents and that soldiers also came often to the stage stations, sometimes accompanying the houses on wheels. His runners also brought him word soldiers had come to the station at Apache Pass along with Michael Steck, who was Indian agent to the Chihenne. Cochise and Mangas Coloradas had often talked about this man, who said the Great Father in Washington had given the care of the People into his hands. Mangas Coloradas said he was not a warrior, but had great influence over the soldiers, and was a fair-minded and honorable man. He had charge of the rations the Americans gave to the Chihenne and the Mescalero and often urged the soldiers not to make trouble with the warriors.

Cochise went himself to Apache Pass to talk with Steck. He met several Americans, who seemed friendly and respectful. One of them was James Tevis, a tough, cheerful man who worked at the stage station.[11] He seemed like a warrior: brave, and talkative, and a little boastful. He made a strong impression, but Cochise decided this was a man he could not altogether trust—as if you could trust any White Eye. Still, Tevis seemed a strong man with whom you could talk.

Cochise urged his warriors and band leaders to do nothing to provoke the Americans, even though they had come unbidden into the land of the Chokonen. But he walked along a narrow ridge in a high wind, for the many horses of the Americans tempted the warriors, and the arrogance of the Americans rankled many of them as well. One of the White Eyes in Apache Pass one time beat a warrior with a horsewhip, claiming the warrior had stolen some stock. Cochise then stormed down to the stage station, supported by many warriors who were the dark shadow of his words. Cochise demanded that the man who had done the whipping should be sent away. He did this partly to remove a White Eye who was likely to make more trouble in the future and partly to save face among his own warriors and partly out of his own anger. The men at the stage station seemed frightened and sobered by this display of anger, for Cochise had always been quiet and controlled in his dealings with them. When they transferred the man as Cochise had demanded, he concluded the Americans could be dealt with, and that some among them were better than others.

Cochise then called on his leading warriors to again join with Mangas Coloradas on a raid down into Sonora. They went this time more for horses and cattle and supplies than for death, for they had killed many Mexicans already in payment for the things the Mexicans had done. Besides, a settlement of traders had grown up near Cañada Alamosa, in the heart of the Chihenne territory, under the protection of the soldiers who were controlled by Steck. These traders provided a ready market now among the Americans for supplies brought up from Mexico—even sometimes providing guns and ammunition, although this was not something done openly before the soldiers or before Steck. Now they had better reason than ever to maintain peace with the Americans and mount raids into Mexico. When the Americans had first come into their country, they had said the warriors of the People should not go any more on raids into Mexico. But the Americans had done nothing further and their words seemed empty—especially now that traders would buy the things the warriors had taken from Mexico.

When Cochise returned from that raid to his camp in the Chiricahuas, he found new mules in camp with brands of the stage station. Furious, he summoned the warrior who had stolen the mules to the great dreaming stone on which he often sat, close by the great oak tree beneath which he made his camp. The warrior came, trembling, his eyes downcast but flicking to the long lance lying by the hand of Cochise. The warrior was not of Cochise's personal following, but from the band of Esquinaline—a clever, fun-loving subchief who loved to play the hoop and pole and raid and lay a long time with each of his two wives. Esquinaline had long followed Cochise, but also guarded his independence. Cochise knew he took a risk in disciplining a warrior of Esquinaline's band, but the anger was hot in him so he had to throw it, like a hot stone. Cochise scourged the warrior with his anger, saying he had left instructions for no warrior to touch anything that belonged to the stage station. The warrior said nothing, showing his submission in his shamefaced silence— hoping Cochise would not seize the long lance and drive it with the grace of contempt through his body. Instead, Cochise rose to his feet as though drawn up by his own words, then lashed out with the back of his hand and struck the warrior a blow that knocked him back off his feet. The warrior did not protest, but rose and skulked away like a whipped dog. Mastering himself, Cochise returned to the rock on which he sat and rolled tobacco in an oak leaf until his mind felt smooth and steady. Then he told Nahilzay, one of his sub- chiefs, who was standing close by, to take the mules back to the stage station and explain that it had been a mistake, that the mules had wandered.

Some while after that, the sentries Cochise had set to watch Apache Pass came back to say that Steck had returned with soldiers and wagons and a message that he hoped to meet with Cochise.[12] Cochise went cautiously to meet with him. When he arrived at the pass, he found camped nearby the White Mountain band led by Francisco, who had married another of the daughters of Mangas Coloradas. Francisco brought with him perhaps 50 warriors, 120 women, and 400 children—sad evidence of how many fighting men he had lost in the unending warfare of the past few years. The Chokonen and Francisco's band were old friends and sometimes allies—in part because of the alliance Mangas Coloradas had made with them. When the bands camped near each other, there was much talking, eating, visiting, and gambling—with many relatives who had married into Francisco's band catching up on the news from the Chokonens.

When Cochise met with Steck, he took care to meet outside of the stage station in a place where he was surrounded by his own warriors and could not be surprised or trapped, for no good had ever come of placing too much trust in the Americans. He brought with him many of his subchiefs, including Nahilzay and Esquinaline and El Cautivo, plus his sons Taza and Naiche and his wife, Dos- teh-seh. Steck proved friendly and talked well. He offered as gifts and rations to the Chokonen some cattle, much corn, 211 blankets, and 200 brass kettles—which made the women happy, although the warriors grumbled about the weight of so many pots when they moved from place to place. Steck said the Great Father had sent him to the Chokonen, to give them rations and a reservation where they could live quietly, without conflict with the settlers or the soldiers. He also urged the Chokonen to stop raiding into Mexico, reminding them that the Americans had made peace with the Mexicans and were now their friends. Cochise listened attentively to everything Steck said, but was careful to make no promises regarding the Mexicans. He did not see why the Americans should concern themselves with the Mexicans, who had so recently been their enemies. But Cochise had already learned the care with which one selected words in these talks with the Americans, as one would choose an arrow in a shooting contest. He promised he would be friendly with the Americans and protect their stock and the stage road, and let his warriors gather wood for the station keeper and grass for their horses.[13] But he made no promises concerning the Mexicans. The People hated a liar above anything else, and no leader could keep respect by breaking promises. No man who had lied could speak thereafter in council or give evidence in any dispute—and many leaders would not take a liar with them on a raid. The People had not laws as the Mexicans and Americans, but shame kept a tighter rein on them than any threatened punishment—for shame cannot be averted or outrun or faced down, and in the close intimacy of the open camps of the people, everyone knew all about everyone else. Cochise had contempt for a liar. Of course, things were not the same when dealing with people who had not earned the right to be treated as human beings, or with your enemies. Deception was a valuable tool of a warrior, and fooling and misleading one's enemy made a good story later around the fire. People like the Mexicans had proven so treacherous for so long that they had no claim on the truth. Still, Cochise took care to speak truthfully in his dealings with the Mexicans and the Americans when he was negotiating the future of the People. He knew if his enemies concluded he was a liar, they would negotiate no more. He held his silence and made no promises he did not believe he could keep.

Steck went on west, well satisfied, and met later with the Pima and the Maricopa and the Papago, river people who lived near Tucson and were starting to lose their land and their water to the settlers who were coming in growing numbers. Steck made peace with them and returned to the stage station in Apache Pass, where he met once more with Cochise. More than a hundred warriors gathered, arranged in a half circle in front of the stage station, to listen to Steck and to Tevis, who could translate a little bit. Everyone listened attentively, the warriors in the front rank and behind them the families of the headmen, and behind them the younger boys nearly ready to begin their training as warriors, and behind them the women and the children, their eyes all moving back and forth from Cochise to Steck. Cochise promised once again to keep the peace with the Americans, and to show his good faith he returned to the Americans stock that had been taken from ranches in that area and two Mexican boys who had been taken captive by raiders in Sonora.

Cochise felt much strengthened after the conference with Steck, believing he could have peace with the Americans if he could keep his warriors from raiding north of the border. He made his words as strong as possible, so they would hobble even the wildest spirits. And he conferred with Francisco and Mangas Coloradas, who were of the same mind. They again convened a great council of the Chokonen, the Chihenne, the Bedonkohe, Francisco's band, and the few Nednhi bands not already hiding deep in the Sierra Madre. They resolved to go raiding again in Sonora, to continue extracting the revenge they savored, and to get more supplies to trade with the Americans moving through their country. The war party gathered near Apache Pass, and Cochise noted that the presence of so many warriors seemed to frighten the station keepers there—which he thought might be a good thing if it reminded the Americans how many warriors the People could gather. Then they went down into Mexico, leaving only two warriors behind to keep an eye on the Americans in Apache Pass.

In the season of Many Leaves,[14] they raided down to Fronteras, where the Mexicans had so treacherously killed the sons of Mangas Coloradas and so many others. They rode toward the town. The first Mexican they encountered saw the warriors riding along behind Cochise and so ran back toward the town to give a warning. But Cochise overtook him and hurled his lance as casually as he would the pole for the hoop, and the point of the lance came out the man's front side by a length of two feet. They then rode quickly on toward Fronteras, but most of the herders and farmers escaped into the city. They captured only one man and two boys. Now the Power of Cochise rose up in him, also his anger and all of the old hatreds that ringed Fronteras like the mountains. He drove his prisoners out into the open in front of the town and showed a white flag. He waited until several Mexicans came out fearfully to talk, and then he offered to trade his prisoners for whiskey, pinole, and tobacco. But the Mexicans saw the warriors moving around to cut them off from Fronteras and ran back toward the town. Cochise rode at their heels, killing one man before shooting from the town turned him back. They rounded up the loose stock and took the boys they still had as prisoners back to Apache Pass. When Tevis saw the boys, he offered to trade ten bushels of corn for them. Seeing the value of starting a trade with the Americans for captives from Mexico, Cochise made the trade.[15] He also sent out word again to his band leaders to not molest the stage station or the mail riders or the horse herds of the soldiers or even the ranches near Tucson and in the Sonoita Valley. He wanted no trouble with the Americans.

Cochise spent the season of the Ghost Dance quietly in the Chiricahuas, telling the Coyote stories, training the boys, listening to the laughter of the children and the gossip of the women, and going joyfully to the Sunrise Ceremony for each of the young women who came of age. Each girl walked in the footsteps of White-Painted Woman, becoming an aspect of White-Painted Woman for a day and a night of feasting and ceremony. That way they could deliver messages or warnings from White-Painted Woman and from the Powers that watched over the People.

When the raiding season returned, Cochise again went into Sonora, gathering up death and horses. When he got back, he discovered warriors from one of the bands owing loose allegiance to him had raided the mining company near Patagonia and run off ninety horses and mules. Once again, a dark rage rose up in him. His Power had already warned him of the consequences of making this war on the Americans and in that future he saw the destruction of the Chokonen. He first determined which warriors had undertaken the raid against his wishes and then called upon them to return the livestock. He went boldly into their camp with several of his warriors, bringing with him Merejildo Grijalva, the Mexican captive he had raised as one of his sons and who had completed his training as a warrior. Twenty warriors had participated in the raid and they seemed reluctant to return the few animals they still had. One of the warriors, a proud and angry man whose brother had been killed by White Eyes some years ago, objected. In an insulting voice, he said they would not give the horses back and then suggested Cochise had become the dog of the White Eyes, looking for scraps they threw in the dust. Goaded to rage, Cochise drew the knife he always carried and the two warriors circled. As soon as the knives came out, Cochise felt the killing calm settle over him—for a knife fighter who had not mastered his anger had not much longer to live. Cochise killed the man, jumping in and slashing open his stomach so his insides gaped through the wound. Then Cochise turned and walked away, turning his back on the other warriors who were the kinsmen of the dead man. None challenged him, for they could see that Power stood behind Cochise and that the one whose name they would speak no longer had provoked the fight. Merejildo Grijalva stood watching all of it, seeing Cochise in a new way. Perhaps it was then he began to think about leaving the People and going to live among the Americans or the Mexicans.[16]

It seemed to Cochise that he must transform the coming of the Americans from a threat into a blessing and he tried to quiet the fears and suspicions that surrounded him, as one lies perfectly still in preparing an ambush until the birds have begun to sing again. He kept track of events in the pass and enforced his order of protection for the Americans, but traveled freely with his band and his personal following throughout the land that had been Chokonen for as long as people had been telling stories. In the season of Large Fruit, they went to the higher mountains in the north of the Chiricahuas to gather the acorns and the piñon nuts that sustained them, the gift of Usen in a hard shell. They could make the nuts into a paste, sometimes mixed with a little jerky, that a man could carry in a pouch and live off a long while when hunting or raiding. Esquinaline's band remained in the pass, partly to watch the Americans and partly to recover from a fight they'd had with a White Mountain band in which ten warriors had been killed or wounded.

When the leaves began to turn in the high places, Cochise returned to Apache Pass and met once again with Steck, who brought rations enough to feed four hundred. Cochise returned to him some more stolen stock, and repeated his pledge to try and stop any raiding by the Chokonen so the White Eyes and the People could live as brothers. But Cochise reminded the agent that he had no control of the White Mountain or the Nednhis or the Chihenne or the Bedonkohe or the Tonto or even all the bands of the Chokonen. Once again, he made no promise concerning the Mexicans. In truth, the Chokonen had long ago grown dependent on the things they took from the Mexicans and would have had to continue raiding even if they had not such a blood score to settle. The rations of the Americans were now only a token, not enough to feed a family the year round. The children would be hungry, they would have no more guns and ammunition, and no one would have the wealth necessary to host a Sunrise Ceremony if they stopped going down to Mexico and taking what they needed from their enemies. Cochise made no promise to Steck concerning the Mexicans, which was none of the business of the Americans, anyway. The Mexicans had taken the springs and mountains and camping places of the People, without any permission or payment. They had not made peace, as Steck seemed willing to do. Besides, the Americans seemed willing enough to buy the horses and cattle and things the raiders brought back from Mexico, so Cochise did not take very seriously Steck's warnings about the raiding.[17]

Then just as the season of the Ghost Dance[18] set in once again, Merejildo Grijalva ran off to join the Americans. His leaving took Cochise by surprise, for Merejildo Grijalva had grown up in his own wickiup, tended to by his own wives. Cochise had taken a second wife, who had borne him two daughters—Dash-den-zhoos and Naithlotonz.[19] Cochise had considered Merejildo Grijalva as one of his family and not as a slave, although the other boys sometimes taunted him about his blood and had not given him the respect and status of Taza and Naiche, who had their camps in the heart of Cochise. Taza was already a warrior, having distinguished himself on the raids of his apprenticeship. He was tall but stocky and fine-grained as oak, with commanding eyes and a strong face, and he had already gained a reputation for having the favor of Power. Naiche was still a boy, nearly ready to start his training. Cochise did not push him so much, nor teach him his ceremonies. He wanted Taza to lead and so taught Naiche to become his brother's strong right hand—and never his rival. But Naiche was a charming and easygoing boy, full of pranks and good nature. He eventually grew taller than his brother, but was ever the antelope to Taza's elk. He got along with everyone, his fine features so graceful and regular that people would have called him beautiful had he been born a woman.

Perhaps Merejildo Grijalva felt the preference for Taza and Naiche and perhaps this ate at him, like termites in wood lying too

NA-CHISE, -- Son of Cochise,
a celebrated warrior.
1 8 8 2

Naiche. Handsome, charming, and light-hearted, Naiche tried his best to abide by his father's injunction to live at peace with the White Eyes, but the closure of the Chiricahua Reservation finally drove him into renewed warfare alongside Geronimo.
(Tucson Historical Society)

long on the ground. Or perhaps it was simply grief. Merejildo Grijalva had come into the responsibilities and privileges of a warrior. He had set his heart on a pretty maiden, impatient to take her into his own wickiup. But then a fight started over too much bad whiskey. One warrior killed his wife, so her brother retaliated by killing that man's sister—who was the girl who had made her place already in the heart of Merejildo Grijalva.[20] He sought revenge in his own turn. Perhaps he left to avoid the retaliation likely to follow, although he was living in the camp of Cochise and so the relatives of the man he killed might not dare to strike back. But the loss of the girl seemed to kill his heart, for he lost interest in things. He began to watch the warriors coming and going with a cold stare, like a man with the Ghost Sickness already partway in the next life. Then one day he simply vanished. Later, Cochise heard he had gone to Mesilla as a translator and scout for Steck. Grijalva knew Spanish

Merejildo Grijalva.
Reportedly reared by
Cochise after he was
taken captive in Mexico,
Grijalva eventually
became a scout for the
U.S. Army and Cochise's
most dangerous adver-
sary. *(Tucson Historical
Society)*

and the language of the People and soon learned English, for he
was a clever man with a quick tongue. This made Cochise uneasy,
for he had taught Grijalva every water hole and trail and ambush in
the great sprawl of territory through which the Chokonen moved,
and in which their enemies might seek them. But Cochise quieted
his concerns, telling himself Grijalva would provide good translations and had no reason for bitterness against Cochise or the
Chokonen, who had treated him fairly and with kindness and spared
him the indignity of growing up as a Mexican.

But this was only the first in a series of difficulties, many of
them involving the Americans, who came more and more boldly into
the Chokonen territory without permission or apology. Many of the
bands were not raiding so much now and had become poor, with little stock and many hungry children. The fat horses of the Americans
were a temptation for a warrior whose daughter needed a ceremony or
whose babies fretted in hunger. Sometimes warriors went out seeking

horses and mules and cattle not closely watched. The Americans did not hesitate to kill warriors—sometimes for good reasons, other times for no reason at all. One group of warriors took some mules from the ranch of an American living thirty miles below the border in Mexico. The rancher and his men chased the warriors and killed three. A little while after that, a rancher killed a warrior who was taking a horse from his ranch. Then a station keeper at Apache Pass named John Wilson got into a fight with a Mexican captive who had grown up among the Chokonen and taken training as a warrior. The warrior went for his weapon and Wilson killed him.

Another incident involved James Tevis, the station keeper at Apache Pass. When Cochise entered the station house to trade just as the stagecoach arrived, Tevis ordered him out of the building in a tone as harsh as a man chiding a disrespectful child. Cochise's rage surged at the thought that a white man alive only at his sufferance should speak to him in this way in front of other warriors. Cochise strode out of the building, leaped onto the back of his horse, and turned back to Tevis, his lance in his hand. He said Tevis must come out and fight him—the lance of Cochise matched against the pistol of Tevis. But Tevis dropped his eyes and mumbled some apology, saying he had meant no offense, and so the watching warriors saw the White man's fear of Cochise. To make the point stronger, Cochise called Naiche over to him and roughly told Tevis to watch the boy—showing the warriors he had no fear of the White Eyes and that Tevis would do woman's work if Cochise commanded it.[21]

All these things posed a great challenge of leadership. Cochise had tried hard to keep the peace with the Americans, although the rations came only at great intervals, the People had grown hungry, and the Americans conducted themselves with increasing arrogance. Ordinarily, each of the killings would have demanded revenge and started a cycle of raids and retaliation. But each time Cochise tried to head off the reaction, so the peace with the Americans would not unravel like a poorly made blanket. But he could not hold the warriors back before such provocation for long before his authority would bleed away. Cochise had seen it happen time and again—even to his own father. Even a man of great Power would lose his influence with the younger warriors if he grew discouraged or longed too openly for peace. So after the killings of the warriors, many Chokonen from bands of the men's relatives assembled to attack the stage station. Cochise went along, angry in his own turn, but hoping he could make the raid a show of strength without a lot of killing that would destroy the peace. The warriors surrounded a wagon train going through the pass, the heavy wagons pulled by oxen. They surrounded the wagons, jeering and threatening. Several warriors rode up and lanced the oxen in their harnesses. The frightened drivers gripped their guns but did nothing, realizing their lives hung by sinew over a hot fire. When the warriors had shown their anger and courage, Cochise led them away, leaving the drivers unharmed, hoping this display would satisfy the warriors and convince the Americans to take more care. But some of the warriors were still angry, saying they had not inflicted enough punishment for the death of the warriors. If the Sonorans had done such a thing, they would have taken ten lives for each warrior—not merely killed a yoke of oxen.

Cochise sought to deflect their anger by raising a party to raid Sonora, although he knew this also might lead to trouble among the warriors left behind if he were not there to contain their anger at the Americans. In the season of the Ghost Dance,[22] Cochise led a war party of a hundred warriors into Sonora, and spent several months in an orgy of killing. They killed fifty people in one month, even women and children, for they were moving so fast they could not carry hostages and could not afford to leave witnesses who would put the soldiers chasing them on their trail. They ambushed a party of travelers seventy miles below the border. Warned by his Power after this fight, Cochise sent out scouts in all directions from the war party. The scouts reported back that fifty soldiers had found their trail and were coming along behind. Cochise set a trap, hiding most of his force on a rocky hill and putting a few men out as bait. When the soldiers caught sight of them, the warriors ran quickly up the hill where the rest of the war party was hidden. The overconfident Sonorans chased them, smelling blood and revenge. But as they came up the hill, the warriors rose up out of hiding and began to shoot, coming so close to their enemies that sometimes the fighting was hand to hand. Cochise moved among the soldiers with his lance, harvesting them the way a man with a curved blade cuts grass. They killed eleven soldiers quickly and the rest fled back down the hill, desperate to escape. Cochise considered going after them to kill them all, but once they got to better ground their guns would come into play and he would surely lose warriors. He resolved to close his hand on the victory already in his grasp.

The warriors found one Mexican wounded on the hillside, not yet dead. They amused themselves by shooting arrows into him, careful to avoid killing him too quickly, and laughing at the way he rolled back and forth in the agony of his long death.[23] The Mexicans screamed and thrashed when in pain, as though they had never learned the discipline of manhood. For a warrior, pain was a useful tool through which he could make his mind smooth and steady—for if he could ignore pain, then he had control of himself and of his mind, and might also shut out the other distractions that kept him from wisdom. A warrior often used pain as a sacrament, from a young age when the boys learned to let the sprig of sage burn down to ash and deeply into the flesh of their arms without flinching. They learned in this fashion to have command of their bodies rather than remain subject to its needs. In this way, they could run for fifty miles without paying any attention to the burning in their lungs, or remain motionless for hours at a time so they might draw to them the deer or avoid drawing to them their enemies. They practiced putting aside pain by shifting their minds somewhere else. This was one reason they sometimes tortured the Mexicans who fell into their hands. Seeing the dying men behaving like children in the face of pain helped feed the contempt the warriors nurtured for them. The Mexicans had their great numbers and their mindless persistence and their many things and their large herds—but they could not stand even a little pain before dying without losing their composure and humiliating themselves. Besides, some people said that in this way they would frighten the Chindi spirits of the Mexicans, so they would not linger and cause bad luck for the warriors who had killed them. Moreover, nearly all of the warriors had some deep reason to hate the Mexicans. Sometimes on the bodies of the soldiers they found purses made from the vaginas of the Chiricahua women the soldiers had killed. Often, the soldiers decorated their saddles and their horses with the scalps of the People. Sometimes the soldiers took babies and women and children prisoners to sell as slaves—but sometimes they would take a baby and throw him into the fire to watch him burn up. The People and the Mexicans did terrible things one to the other, each starved for revenge. It had been that way between the Mexicans and the People for as long as anyone could remember.

When Cochise returned from raiding Sonora, he found things had gone badly with the Americans. One band had stolen stock from the stage station at Dragoon Springs. Another band had raided the mining settlement at Tubac, and one of the band leaders had warned Tevis that the warriors would attack the stage station at Apache Pass. Cochise knew the warriors were angry and had many grievances against the Americans. Once again, Cochise tried to balance the anger of the warriors against the risk of war with the Americans, like a knife before throwing. The Americans had promised rations, but delivered food only once or twice a year—so the women and children had not enough to eat and the warriors could not give up raiding. In response to the demands of his warriors, Cochise led a raiding party to take the horse herd from the Santa Rita Mining Company. Of all the Americans, he liked the tribe of the miners the least, for they were ugly in their manners and drunken and likely to kill a man for no reason at all. Besides, they dug in the earth for gold, which was close to the heart of Usen because it was an aspect of the sun, and so forbidden to the People. But the White Eyes, who knew no prayers and had respect for nothing, tore apart the earth and acted like crazy men whenever they thought they could get a little gold or silver. For all of these reasons, Cochise did not mind so much raiding the miners. But Captain Richard Ewell, the *nantan* of Fort Buchanan in the Sonoita Valley, came after the raiding party with seventy-five soldiers. When he caught up with them, some of the warriors wanted to fight. But Cochise counted the many guns of the soldiers and their pack mules with lots of ammunition. He went under a white flag to the *nantan* and offered to return the stock they still had and promised payment for the rest, knowing a fight would shatter the already thin and leaky peace. Ewell had some of the men from the mining company with him who refused the horses Cochise offered, saying they were different horses of poor quality. Cochise said the Chihenne had taken some of the horses from the mines, and he had no way to get them back. Cochise returned what stock he had and said Ewell could visit the camps of the Chokonen to look for the rest. The *nantan* did this, very angry and indignant, and making many threats. But then he saw with his own eyes that the Chokonen had not many horses and few mules and almost no cattle. Cochise had spoken truthfully when he said they had not raided much and had little enough now—for the rations had not come for many months. Ewell went back to the soldier fort with only a few horses and mules. He said he would accept this partial payment now, but if the raids continued he would attack the Chokonen without any further warning.[24]

Gradually, the peace with the Americans that had such promise began to tear and fray. Cochise still tried to discourage raiding, but he could not do very much more without losing his standing. Besides, the arrogance of the Americans rankled him. They had promised rations, but had provided nothing for more than eight months. Instead, they continued to spread into the territory of the Chokonen without asking permission, so it was not safe any longer for women or children or one or two warriors in a group to go freely about their own country. Moreover, the miners and the ranchers and the settlers and the soldiers were scaring away the game and taking the best places along the riverbanks where the People had once scattered seeds of corn and squash and beans so they could later harvest the crops. The White Eyes had cut off each source of food, chopped them off like the legs of a stool.

Cochise began to cast about for some other way to protect his people, as a man will pick a camp for the night with three ways to escape. He could still rely on the strong support of his brothers Coyuntura and Juan. Coyuntura had risen to a leading position. He was fearless and cheerful in the face of hardship and loss, so that death and pain beaded up and rolled off him like water down a heron's neck. He had Power in war, so his men went safely through their enemies. He had a personal following of twenty warriors who would follow him into any danger—and who always brought back more horses than any others. Juan had not so great a following, for he had a relaxed and casual nature—not the sort to bind men tightly to him. But both Coyuntura and Juan remained fiercely loyal to their brother, and in their own alliances and relations provided a sure source of strength. Often Cochise took counsel of his brothers, relying on their insight and experience. And he felt most relaxed with them, for they could tease one another and test one another without fear or self-consciousness.

But many other band leaders resolved to go back down into Mexico to see if the Chihuahuans wanted to make peace, recalling that when the Mexicans promised rations they came every week. Cochise did not discourage these efforts, reasoning that the Chiricahua might need to play the Mexicans against the Americans—as they had long played Sonora against Chihuahua. Near the beginning of the next raiding season, some 150 warriors went in a group to the stage station in Apache Pass, and warned them to leave. However, most of the warriors had already gone down into Mexico. Cochise remained at Apache Pass, doubtful now about the Americans, but even more convinced he could not trust the Mexicans. He remained quietly among the rocks that spoke to him and the places that knew him, keeping in touch with the bands in Mexico and with the Chihenne as well. Mangas Coloradas sent word that Steck had promised a safe reservation and regular rations if Mangas Coloradas could gather many people near Santa Lucia Springs in the heart of his territory; but despite much talk and the gathering of hundreds of people, Steck never made good his promises.

The Mexicans in both Janos and Fronteras said they were interested in peace. Both provinces had suffered greatly in recent years and the people knew they could not strike back effectively at the Chiricahua, who retreated to the relative safety of the United States after they finished raiding. The Mexicans knew they would suffer less if the warriors lived near Janos and Fronteras and went raiding in the United States. Besides, a peace with the Chiricahua and the Chihenne would create a lucrative market for the horses and cattle raiders brought back from the United States, instead of the other way around. At Janos, José María Zuloaga offered peace and suggested the warriors could trade horses—so long as they did not get them in raids in Chihuahua. Many bands paid attention to his promises and moved down into Mexico, from where they launched raids into the United States. The leaders had to do this, for without raiding and no settled place where they could hunt and gather food, some bands were beginning to starve, the babies falling silent in the depths of the season of the Ghost Dance.

Steck, seeing the peace slipping through his hands because so many bands were living in Mexico and raiding north, came again to Apache Pass to meet with Cochise, one of the few remaining leaders who still seemed eager for peace with the Americans. Cochise warned Steck that he would have to go down into Mexico to seek peace with Fronteras, attending to the pleas of his headmen and the cries of the children.

Cochise sent down a few people he trusted to talk cautiously to the headman in Fronteras, including Yonis, the wife of Coyuntura. Often he sent women of good judgment and high reputation down to open negotiations with the Mexicans, for the Mexicans were less likely to simply seize them and kill them. Sometimes Dos-teh-seh went to start the talk, although Cochise was loathe to let her run such a risk. He knew Lozen often talked to the Mexicans for the Chihenne of Victorio's band, so a strong-minded woman was a great asset to a band in this way. The women he sent to Fronteras brought back word that the Sonorans seemed interested in making peace and providing rations. However, the Sonorans had made no strong promise. Cochise resolved to stay awhile longer in Apache Pass and see how the winds of opportunity shifted.

Cochise perched uncomfortably on the knife edge between peace and war with the Americans. He prayed and searched all the old stories for clues to what he must do. He remembered the story about the girl who had gone to get water and had nearly fallen and died because she had walked carelessly and not tested her footing and thought only of herself. He was grateful to that story, for through the years it had reminded him to look always where he put his foot and to walk in a selfless and prayerful way. And yet, all of the footing before him now seemed dangerous, without one flat rock sufficient to hold the weight of the People in this time of great danger. For years past, he had done everything he could to maintain the peace, for he understood the doom for his people threatened by a war on two fronts. But he stood now like a man in a rising river, trying to hold back the water with his wide-splayed fingers.

It was useless, of course.

For the Americans would soon show their true nature—just as the Mexicans had so often done in their hatred and treachery.

Cochise did not know it until too late, but a young and foolish man given great power by men with little knowledge was coming to him already, his head full of cobwebs and the name of Cochise on his lips.

Death came riding, with a baby face and a weak voice.

1861

"Cut-the-Tent"—Driven to War

It Happened at Ma'Tehilizhe (Coyote Pisses in the Water)

Long ago some people were going home after gathering acorns. They stopped on the way where the trail crossed a shallow stream. They had been walking fast and were very thirsty. They wanted to drink. It was hot. Then their leader said to them, "Don't drink until I tell you to. I want to look around here first." He went off. Their leader was wise. He saw danger in his mind.

Then, as soon as he was gone, a young woman said, "My children are very thirsty. They need to drink. This water looks safe to me. I'm going to drink it." The others agreed with her. "Yes," they said, "we must drink. This water looks good." So they started drinking.

Then, pretty soon, they began to get sick. They got dizzy and began to vomit violently. All of them got sick, including the children. They got sicker. They vomited and vomited. They were scared that they were dying. They were crying out in pain, crying out in fear. Their leader was the only one who didn't drink. He walked upstream and looked on the ground. There were fresh tracks by the stream and he saw where Coyote had pissed on a flat rock that slanted into the water. Drops of Coyote's piss were still running off into the water.

Then he went back to the people. "Stop!" he told them. "Don't drink that water! It's no good! Coyote has pissed in it! That's why all of you are sick."

Then one of those people said, "We didn't know. We were thirsty. The water looked safe. We were in a hurry and it didn't look dangerous." Those people trusted their eyes. They should have waited until their leader had finished looking around. One of those children nearly died.

It happened at Ma'Tehilizhe—Coyote Pisses in the Water.

Cochise waited quietly as a bow drawn back but not released, pondering the puzzle of the Americans. He could feel the peace sliding away, as the shifting of a slope heavy with snow. He knew this avalanche might bury the People and wondered whether he could still stop the slide. In his heart, he believed the Americans offered a better chance of a negotiated peace than the Mexicans, who had proved treacherous beyond hope of change. While other leaders went down into Mexico to seek a peace there, he held himself alert to the possibility of peace with the Americans.

He prayed often, smoothing and steadying his mind, trying to see ahead to know what he must do. He pondered his dreams, studying them as carefully as a hunter studies tracks. Power had many ways of giving a warrior warnings and sending him clues. If he sneezed, it might mean someone was talking about him. If he saw rings around the moon, he could expect a change in weather—or if he saw a snake dead and turned on its back. A shooting star will often point to where the enemy approaches and the shaking of the earth or the sudden darkening of the sun or the moon might warn of approaching epidemics in time to move the camp out of the path of the pestilence. Power often talked to people through trembling of their muscles. Dreams often offered portents. Dreaming of fire was bad, and a dream of overflowing water was a warning about death. So were dreams about losing one's teeth, or having deer or bulls or any hoofed animal running after you. Dreams often meant the opposite of what they seemed; if someone dreamed about being sick it often meant he would be well for a long time, or if he dreamed about dying he would live a long life. Dreams about summer—with its plentiful food and explosion of green—were almost always a good thing. But dreams about the dead were almost always a sign of bad news coming.[1]

When runners came with news that a detachment of soldiers had camped near the Apache Pass stage station under a white flag to meet with Cochise and exchange presents, the chief gathered up his family and his most trusted warriors to go and meet with the *nantan*. The runners said the *nantan* had come from the fort on Sonoita Creek, and seemed friendly and well disposed—although he had a large, well-armed force. Coyuntura was in camp and readily agreed to accompany him, joking that someone must go along to keep Cochise from trouble. Cochise also took Dos-teh-seh and Naiche, so they could see the White Eyes close up and so the soldiers would see that he came peacefully to the meeting. In his heart, he hoped this talk might lead to a chance to strengthen the peace with the Americans.

Cochise and his warriors went into Apache Pass in the season of the Ghost Dance[2] and camped not far from the soldier camp. They were down in Siphon Canyon, a mile from the stage station that lay close to the spring. This dependable spring was the reason this high pass between the Chiricahua Mountains and Dos Cabezas was important to anyone traveling, especially White Eyes riding horses and pulling wagons. The next reliable water one could get to with a wagon lay forty miles west at Dragoon Springs, after the long, hot crossing of the Sulphur Springs Valley between the eight-thousand-foot peaks of the Dragoons to the west and the Chiricahuas to the east. Cochise made his camp and sent out other runners. Some said they had heard the soldiers were led by a *nantan* named Lieutenant George Bascom, who was looking for a boy a White Mountain band had taken from a ranch nearby owned by a White Eye named John Ward, a hard, harsh, dangerous man. Ward had married a Mexican woman who had once been a captive among one of the bands of the People.[3] She had a warrior's baby, but took the baby, ran away, and ended up living on the ranch with John Ward as his wife. He had adopted the boy—although some people said he used the boy harshly, and beat him sometimes—until the White Mountain band took him. But the *nantan* had made no demands and seemed peacefully inclined, saying he only wanted to talk to Cochise and give his people presents.[4]

Cochise sent out runners to determine which band had taken the boy in case the *nantan* wanted that information. While he was waiting, one of the stage station men—a friendly fellow named James Wallace who had always treated the Chokonen fairly—came alone into his camp to say the *nantan* up the canyon was eager to meet with him under the flag of truce. In the meantime, lookouts posted in the canyon brought word a freight train was coming carelessly into the pass, taking no precautions. Because he had come in some measure to trust Wallace and because the soldiers did not seem worried about the wagon train helpless in the pass, Cochise decided to meet with the *nantan* in the soldier camp. He took with him Coyuntura, Dos-teh-seh, Naiche, the son of Coyuntura, a son of Juan, and another of his good friends. In all the years that remained of his life, Cochise would most regret that single afternoon when he had

Lieutenant George Bascom. Young and inexperienced, Bascom's obstinate efforts to force Cochise to turn over a captive he didn't have pushed Cochise into a war that resulted in a decade of bloodshed. *(National Archives)*

trusted the White Eyes while his Power had stood silent. Cochise went confidently into the middle of the soldier camp, although some fifty-four well-armed soldiers stood round about. He followed along behind his own eagerness for a peace to protect his People from the destruction threatening them. He brought with him his wife and child as a sign of his good faith, for he had never known the American soldiers to violate the white flag of truce. Moreover, he believed the men from the stage station would not betray the Chokonen, who had only to close their hands to take their lives. Cochise went even into the *nantan*'s tent, confident the stage station men would speak for him to the soldiers.

The *nantan* was only a boy, not far out of baby grass, his whiskers soft and his face smooth. At first, the *nantan* was polite, greeting them in a friendly manner. Ward stood beside the *nantan* to translate, which displeased Cochise. Ward was a rough and violent man, and although he had married the Mexican woman and taken in a boy in whose body ran the blood of the People, he threatened anyone who came on his land. Cochise watched Ward with a wary eye, wondering whether he was twisting the words to his own ends.

Nonetheless, the *nantan* offered them food from a table in the middle of the tent and also coffee in clever cups. But after a few polite words, the *nantan* began to speak in a rough and disrespectful tone, which Cochise could understand well enough even without Ward's sneering translation. The *nantan* said Cochise had stolen the boy from Ward's ranch and must return the boy at once. Cochise answered soothingly, saying none of his warriors had taken the boy. He thought maybe a White Mountain band had taken him. But he would send out runners to the other bands—even the White Mountain bands—and ask them to bring the boy back. He said he thought he could get the boy back within ten days.

But Bascom refused to listen, dismissing the words of Cochise in an insulting manner—as much as calling him a liar. He said he would keep Cochise and his family prisoner until his warriors returned the boy.

Cochise stood completely still, staring into the face of the *nantan* as Ward translated, although he had already heard the hardness in the *nantan*'s tone. Cochise felt his Power stir in him now, like a bear in spring. Several soldiers stood close beside the *nantan*, their hands on their guns. He could recall the many soldiers he had seen outside the tent as he entered and knew several waited on each side of the door to the tent. He could see the whole campsite in his mind, together with the details of the slope just to the east of the camp—covered with the rocks that had known him all his life. In the instant Ward finished the translation, Cochise had his knife in his hand. In a single motion, he turned and slashed open the wall of the tent with a single downward sweep of his knife before any of the soldiers could so much as shift their stances. In almost the same moment, Coyuntura and his son had their knives out as well and they followed Cochise through the cut in the tent. Cochise did not pause, but ran between two astonished soldiers. From behind, Cochise heard the blast of Ward's gun, and at the edge of his vision he saw all of the soldiers scattered around the camp turning toward him, their guns in their hands. He did not pause, but sprinted toward the hill he had seen so perfectly in his mind. But coming out behind his brother, Coyuntura caught his toe in the cloth of the tent and stumbled. In a moment, the soldiers were on him. The warrior coming out behind him ran into the guns of the soldiers, who cut him down with a volley of shots. Many fired their guns at Cochise, who ran up the hill without looking back. The bullets buzzed past his head, angry as bees. The soldiers fired more than fifty times at Cochise as he dashed without pause to the top of the hill. One bullet cut through his thigh as he ran, making blood stream down his leg, but he paid no attention to the wound. He paused at the top of the hill and turned about to see the soldiers struggling after him, far behind. None of the others had escaped. The soldiers had hold of Coyuntura, and the other warrior who had been in the tent lay broken, bleeding his life into the dust. Naiche and Dos-teh-seh and his nephews had never escaped the tent. Looking down at his hand, Cochise saw he still held the beautiful coffee cup the *nantan* had given him. He cast the cup aside and, as the bullets spattered against the rocks that had once again befriended him, turned and disappeared over the crest of the hill.

Cochise ran quickly back to his camp, where he had left the main force of his warriors. They met him, trotting toward the sound of shooting. He quickly took command of his men, stopping only a moment to bind up the wound in his leg to stop the bleeding. Perhaps later it would stiffen and the pain would hobble him, but now he ignored it. He sent out runners to bring back other bands, determined to trap the soldiers in the canyon until they had released his brother and his wife and his son and his nephews. Then he led the warriors back to the ridge overlooking the soldier camp. Cochise called down in a strong voice from the ridge, "Let me see my brother."

No voice floated back up the hill, but a moment later a volley of smoke and thunder came from where the soldiers had taken cover behind the rocks and trees, followed a moment later by the pinging and whistling of the bullets. Cochise rose up in his fury, heedless of the bullets, knowing his Power had already protected him from their hornet swarm as he ran up the hill. "I will be avenged," he called down to the soldiers in a cold fury. "The blood of the People is as good as White man's blood. We have been falsely accused, and for every harm you have done to me and mine, I will be avenged."[5] Cochise then retreated from the ridge, putting out his warriors to keep the soldiers from escaping the canyon and waiting for his reinforcements to arrive.

That night as darkness fell, Bascom broke camp and moved his men a mile up the canyon to the stage station, with stone walls that would give his men protection. The warriors followed them, keeping good count and noting the soldiers had lots of ammunition and supplies for a long siege. The warriors took up positions on the hills overlooking the stage station, setting signal fires to draw together the scattered bands of the Chokonen. They watched the soldiers through the night, waiting for the fatal dawn.

The next morning,[6] Cochise gathered his warriors six hundred yards from the stage station and put out a white flag. When they received no response from the soldiers, one warrior took the flag and approached the soldiers, walking toward their waiting guns with great courage. He called out to Bascom, saying Cochise would meet with the *nantan* halfway between the soldiers and the ravine where the warriors waited behind good cover. Bascom said he would come and talk.

A short time later, Bascom came out with two sergeants—a man named Smith and Daniel Robinson—plus John Ward. Cochise came out in his turn, along with two warriors and Francisco, his White Mountain ally who had been camped nearby and who had also married a daughter of Mangas Coloradas, whose sister was now a prisoner of the soldiers. Perhaps 150 yards from the stage station, they stopped again to parley—Cochise hoping the *nantan* would be reasonable now that his men were trapped in so dangerous a position. Cochise tried to sound calm, although in his heart he wanted to flick out with his knife and cut the man's throat clean through. Muffling his pride and anger, Cochise pleaded for the release of his family, promising to find the boy Bascom sought. But Bascom was stubborn as a mule, as sure of himself as a young warrior with the empty head and swollen pride of a rooster.

Then Cochise saw three stage station men—James Wallace, Charles Culver, and a man named Walsh—come suddenly out from behind the barricades the soldiers had put up round the stage station in the night, walking quickly toward the conference. Maybe they wanted to convince Bascom to give up his prisoners and trust the word of Cochise. But Bascom began backing away from Cochise and yelling at the three men, saying he would not trade his prisoners for them if the warriors captured them. Fearing treachery and seeing a chance to take prisoners to exchange for his wife and son and brother, Cochise drew out his gun. Shooting broke out immediately on all sides and the sergeant carrying the white flag was quickly hit. Several warriors ran out from where they had been hiding to capture the three stage station men, who now turned and ran back toward the soldiers. The warriors overtook Wallace and shot and wounded

Culver, although he made it back to the soldiers. Walsh reached the corral, climbing nimbly over the wall in a way the warriors admired. But when Walsh dropped over the wall the soldiers killed him, thinking he was a warrior. Bascom and his men made it safely back as well. The soldiers remained crouched behind their cover as the warriors gathered.[7]

All that night, the warriors kept watch on the soldiers. They lit fires and danced, working up their courage and Power for the morning. The shadow of Cochise danced crazily outward from the flames, jagged and huge and angry. His anger burned through him, searing him, changing him. He could not forgive himself now for having delivered his wife and his child and his brother into the hands of his enemy. He had been as foolish as his father and Juan José Compá and Yrigóllen, and all of the others who had been seduced by the mirage of peace. He could only blame himself now, for he had known better; he had remembered Johnson, and had remembered Kirker, and had remembered all the times his people had been betrayed. He should have remembered that Child-of-the-Water had bid them to slay their enemies, make a prayer of revenge, and fight even in the shadow of the Giant. Now Cochise swore to recover his brother and his family or never more to rest from vengeance. He danced in a frenzy, his Power reaching out to the others so they became the jagged shadows of his rage.

Cochise positioned his warriors carefully all around the stage station and throughout the pass. Near dawn, the hidden warriors watched the sergeant from the day before lead a strong group of soldiers out of the stage station toward the spring six hundred yards distant, as Cochise had known they must do. The stage station had no water, and the horses and the soldiers would have used their water in the long night, listening to the drums and the singing in the darkness. Cochise let them get the water and return safely to the stage station, still hoping that if he held his hand Bascom would come to his senses and release his prisoners. Even a boy given too much authority may see past his pride eventually.

Cochise waited until the sun was directly overhead before he made his next move. He pulled Wallace to his feet and tied his arms roughly behind him, then led his prisoner out into the open in front of the soldiers, a rope cinched up tight around his neck. Wallace pleaded with him, saying the lieutenant was an obstinate fool and promising to go and convince him to release his prisoners—but

Cochise hardened his heart and paid no attention. Then Cochise shouted out to Bascom, offering to trade Wallace and sixteen mules for his family. But Bascom refused. Cochise shouted out again, saying they were good mules—army mules. But this only made Bascom angry. He said he would only trade his prisoners for the boy he had come to find. He said Wallace had disobeyed his order and so gotten himself captured, and therefore would not trade for him. Some of the listening warriors later said one of the soldiers argued loudly with the *nantan*, insisting he make the trade and save the life of Wallace.[8] But Bascom would not relent, so Cochise dragged Wallace roughly away, anger and despair growing in him like two great trees from the same root. But he was not yet ready to give up the lives of those he loved, so he resolved to get more prisoners and to make Bascom yield up his family, no matter what that might cost.

He sent one party of warriors to guard the entrance to the pass. Then he led another group to overtake the slow-moving wagon train loaded with flour for Tucson that was by now nearly ready to leave the pass. The warriors rode up to the wagon train, whose leader had come through the pass often before. He had never been bothered by the warriors and sometimes gave them small gifts of the flour he carried. He did not know Bascom had set fire to the dry tinder of the uneasy peace that had protected him on all his other trips. The warriors rode up in a friendly way, then suddenly surrounded the wagons. They seized the nine Mexicans and three Americans. They cut the mules out of the harnesses. They had no use for the nine Mexicans, so they tied them to the wagon wheels and then set the wagons on fire, watching in grim satisfaction as the Mexicans writhed and burned. Then they took the three Americans to their camp, to trade for the family of Cochise.

Cochise told Wallace to make a talking paper for Bascom. The paper said, "Treat my people well and I will do the same by yours, of whom I have four." He left this talking paper fastened to a bush on a hill where the soldiers could not miss it.[9] Then he set himself to wait, believing that when Bascom found the note he would make the trade. Even so, Cochise knew he could not wait much longer. As soon as word of the attack on the wagon train and the trapped soldiers got out, the Americans would come from all directions. If he waited too long, the arriving soldiers would trap the Chokonen. He must remember that all of their lives were in his hands, not merely the lives of his brother and his wife and his son.

The warriors waited and danced and prayed through another night, hoping the soldiers would release their prisoners now that Cochise had so many prisoners of his own. Cochise consulted his Power and worked on the fighting spirit of his men as one stretches leather across a saddle frame—for he was determined to fight the soldiers rather than to yield the lives of his family to them. He thought of Coyuntura in the steel shackles surrounded by his enemies, feeling already a flame of sorrow even the thick smoke of his anger could not conceal.

They waited quietly all through the next day, hoping that when the soldiers found the talking paper they would send out a white flag and offer to exchange their prisoners. Moreover, Cochise had sent runners to Mangas Coloradas to bring help. However, Cochise doubted he could wait long enough for his father-in-law to come, for soldiers might already be converging on the pass from the two soldier camps within a two-day ride. He knew he was balanced here on the knife-edge of danger and the advantages in numbers and position he held now could all shift quickly against him. Still he waited, hoping the talking paper would speak for him and force the *nantan* waiting so quietly in the stage station to yield. In the meantime, he had another problem. One warrior had been seriously wounded in the shooting with the soldiers and was now dying. When the man died, his relatives would demand revenge on the White Eye prisoners he held to trade for his family. He did not know whether he could resist a demand for the death of at least one of the prisoners and still keep the warriors together, for they all had reasons of their own for fighting—not only to recover Coyuntura and Dos-teh-seh and Naiche. During the wait, the number of warriors gathered had grown. Geronimo had come with a strong party of Bedonkohe, and Mangas Coloradas had sent word as well. These strong warriors added to his strength, but reduced his absolute control—for he could only count on the unquestioning obedience of his personal following. Cochise balanced all of these things by doing nothing, but keeping his scouts well extended.

In the evening, word came that a stagecoach was heading up the long slope toward the pass. Cochise sent a war party to the west end of the pass to capture more prisoners from the passengers on the stagecoach, which would have taken two days to make the journey from Tucson. The warriors opened fire on them as they came into the pass, killing one mule and wounding the driver and another man. But another of the stage men jumped down, cut out the wounded mule, and took the reins again. The warriors did not press them too closely, for respect of their fast-shooting guns. Besides, they had already torn apart a stone bridge over a gully just ahead and knew the stage would not make the final three miles up the canyon to where the soldiers were still trapped. But the driver saw the broken bridge and lashed the wagon mules so they jumped over the broken part and pulled the wagon right on over the gully, to the surprise of the waiting warriors. They had also rolled rocks down onto the wagon road further on, but the driver skillfully maneuvered the wagon around those rocks. Soon the wagon made it safely to the stage station, so the warriors had missed their chance to gain more prisoners.

That night the wounded warrior died. His brother, who was a fierce warrior not in the personal following of Cochise, went in a fury to where the American prisoners were kept and drove his lance though the body of one of the prisoners.[10] Cochise came running when he heard the commotion and nearly drove his own lance through the body of the distraught warrior who had disobeyed his orders, but then held his hand. He would only spread disorder and anger through the ranks of his warriors and his allies if he struck now. Besides, he could well enough understand the grief for a brother—for Cochise could feel that same grief rising already in his chest.

Cochise waited again all through the following day, although he knew the ground had shifted under his feet—the tumbling of the first stones in an avalanche of death. He directed all of the women and children and old men and boys too young to fight to pack their camps and leave, scatter and make their way to a distant meeting place where their husbands and brothers and fathers could find them after the battle. Cochise held fading hope Bascom might now offer to trade and pondered what he would do should Bascom relent, for he must conceal the death of the White Eye prisoner. But his Power now told him he must fight, so Cochise kept all his warriors out of sight to convince the soldiers the warriors had left the pass. Perhaps they would grow careless and give Cochise an opening, like a slash in the tent through which Coyuntura and the others might still escape. Cochise withdrew the warriors to a distance where they danced and prayed, putting on their war paint, seeing to their weapons and their charms and consulting their Powers for the coming fight. But in pulling back, Cochise left an opening for the soldiers. In the darkness, Bascom sent out a small party of soldiers toward Tucson, the hooves of their horses wrapped with cloth to muffle the sound of their passing. They stole safely out of the pass, covering the 125 miles to Tucson in just twenty-four hours. Now the word had gone out about the trapped soldiers and Cochise had only a little time left to save his family.

The next morning,[11] the warriors returned quietly and carefully to positions overlooking the stage station and the nearby spring. Cochise now had the support of Francisco's band and Geronimo's Bedonkohe and some Chihenne bands allied with Mangas Coloradas, who joined in when they learned the daughter of the great chief had been taken by the soldiers. Bascom had answered his plea for an exchange by his silence, so Cochise knew he must make this last gamble for the life of his family. He had fashioned a plan in the days spent watching the soldiers. Each morning, they sent out their horses for watering in two groups. Perhaps if Cochise struck at the soldiers with the horses, Bascom would send men out to rescue them. At that moment, the main body of warriors could rush the stage station and overwhelm the defenders. Cochise set out the warriors and settled down to Power and luck and opportunity to summon him.

The soldiers did just as Cochise had hoped. Two soldiers came out of the stage station, moving cautiously toward the spring, looking on all sides for any footprints in the snow to warn them warriors were still nearby. But Cochise had told his warriors to leave no such footprints. The sergeants went carefully to a hill overlooking the spring, to be sure no warriors were waiting near it. Then they signaled Bascom back in the stage station to send out the horses for watering. As Cochise watched, he felt events shift in his favor. For Bascom sent all the horses out at once, instead of cautiously in two groups. Cochise held back his eager warriors, as a hunter holds the bow pulled back while the calm of aiming settles over him. He let the horses all get to water, as far from the stage station as possible, so the soldiers would relax their attention a little. But as the soldiers started back, Cochise gave the signal and a large body of warriors rushed out of Siphon Canyon to cut off the soldiers and the horse herd from the stage station, where most of the soldiers still waited with their guns and boxes of bullets. The warriors came on in all of their glory, singing war songs and riding fearlessly. The soldiers with

Geronimo. Although Geronimo was a respected war shaman, he never rose to the rank of chief and was not nearly as powerful and important an Apache leader as Cochise. *(Arizona Historical Society)*

the horses began firing as the warriors approached, abandoning any effort to control the horse herd. Many of the warriors broke away from the attack to go after the horses and mules and soon had gathered up a herd of fifty-six animals. The warriors still pressing the attack also turned aside, leaving the path open to the stage station, for they wanted soldiers to come out to rescue the ones they'd trapped near the spring. Sure enough, a strong party of soldiers set out from the stage station almost immediately.

Now Cochise appeared suddenly on the other side of the stage station with a strong party of warriors and charged across the dangerous open ground toward the stone walls of the station. But the foolish young *nantan* kept a good head under fire and quickly shifted more men with many guns to well-prepared defenses. The strong shooting killed three warriors and wounded many others, breaking up the attack before the warriors could reach the walls of the stage station. In return, they killed only one of the stagecoach men and wounded a soldier. The warriors broke and fell back. Cochise pressed the attack longest and nearly ran on into the stage

station through the bullets his Power turned aside, but finally turned
back when he saw he would only be throwing the stick of his life
into the fire of the soldier's guns. The People did not respect futile
courage or an arrogant charge against strong defenses and poor
odds. They knew how to die bravely, and when a cornered warrior
had no escape he would sing his death song and fight to the last.
But they had fought for generations against better-armed and more
numerous opponents, and had only survived because they chose
their fights and their ground carefully. It was not their way to press
this attack against many guns behind stone walls, so when the warriors saw their surprise attack had failed they turned and made their
way back to good cover. Cochise had no choice but to follow. He
knew then he had gambled and lost the life of his brother—and perhaps his wife and son as well.

The warriors withdrew and the leaders met to consider what
they should do. Runners arrived, saying more soldiers were coming,
although they were still a long way off. One shaman said a great
storm would soon find them. Cochise knew the storm would cover
the tracks of the scattering war parties. He knew he could not hold
the warriors in place any longer, even for the sake of Coyuntura,
who was loved and respected by many bands. He could not even
hold them back from killing the prisoners now, since they had three
more deaths to avenge. In truth, he had not even the heart to try—
for he felt Coyuntura was dead already. The *nantan* had seized him
by treachery and had held on like a crazy man. The *nantan* must
have come in order to start this war and kill Cochise, for all this
made no sense if all he really wanted was a half-breed boy some
other band had taken. The *nantan* had lied with his flag of truce
and had probably lied about everything since. Or perhaps he had
killed Coyuntura and Dos-teh-seh and Naiche as soon as he had
them, and so had not been able to negotiate for their release.

Now, truly, the Americans would have all the war they could
stomach.

When the families of the dead warriors demanded revenge,
Cochise gave to them the three remaining prisoners—even Wallace,
who had been friendly to the People and who had been captured
trying to convince Bascom to release his prisoners. The families of
the dead warriors circled around the prisoners. Some of the White
Eyes begged and pleaded for their lives. Some of them waited quietly, determined to die with dignity. Wallace cried out to Cochise,

but Cochise had hardened his heart. His grief rose up, burning through any compassion or human feeling for the White Eyes as fire consumes grass. He had done everything in his power to avert this day. He had kept the peace, killed those who violated it, returned stolen horses, listened to the arrogant chatter of the peace talkers among the White Eyes, and pleaded with Bascom to turn away. But all of his efforts had only brought him to this day. Now he would go forth and make war on the White Eyes, without looking back. Cochise watched grimly as the grieving relatives killed the White Eye prisoners, continuing to thrust their lances into the mangled bodies a long time after they had stopped moving and groaning. They left the bodies under a tree near the place where they had burned the Mexicans in their wagons.

Then the war party that had gathered broke up, each band leaving by a different route so they would leave no trail for the hundreds of soldiers who would soon seek them. A heavy snowstorm set in, covering up their tracks. Francisco went north, Geronimo went south, and the Chihenne went east. Cochise went south, down through the Chiricahuas toward Mexico. Now that he was at war with the White Eyes, Cochise knew he must try to make peace with Fronteras, so he would not be caught between two fires.[12]

As Cochise turned and went south with his personal following, he passed Coyote Pisses in the Water, and his heart sank in his chest as a stone in a lake. That place had warned him—and still he had gone into Bascom's tent, as foolish as the people who had drunk the water at the crossing when the chief had told them to wait. But it was worse, for he was the chief, the one who should have gone upstream to find the place where Coyote pissed. Now he understood even more clearly why his father had spent those endless hours teaching him the story of each place, stalking him with the wisdom of places, getting those stories to work on him. The places knew what he should do, if he would only listen. As he rode south, heavy with grief and loss, Cochise swore to let the places make his mind steady and smooth and to never again ignore their counsel—nor to let the White Eyes drive them from those places. For how could they be the People without the wisdom of those places, without remembering the stories that guided their behavior and thinking every time they went out from their camps as they passed by them?[13]

Bascom and his men remained in the stage station for three days longer, waiting for help to come. They crouched behind their walls

so carefully they did not realize all of the warriors had gone. They
did not venture out until another *nantan* with 110 soldiers arrived.
These soldiers in crossing the Sulphur Springs Valley had encountered three White Mountain warriors with some cattle they had just
taken from Mexico, and so took these three men as prisoners. Bascom and the new *nantan* then went looking around about the pass
for Cochise, but found only the burned-up wagon train and the bodies of the four Americans. The bodies had been so broken and torn
up by lances, the soldiers could only tell Wallace from the others by
the gold fillings in his teeth.

Now the *nantan*s argued about what to do. Lieutenant Isaiah
Moore, the new *nantan*, wanted to execute their own prisoners in
retaliation. Bascom argued against this, but the other *nantan* had
more authority.[14] Even when Bascom agreed to execute the warriors,
he argued they should not kill the woman and the young boy. The
other *nantan* said they should kill them all, because nits make lice
and Cochise should be punished for killing his prisoners. The two
*nantan*s agreed to play cards to determine the fate of Dos-teh-seh
and Naiche. Perhaps Power took a hand in this, for the game of
cards convinced the soldiers to let the family of Cochise live.[15]

Bascom went to his prisoners, who had been waiting all through
the fight to learn their fate. Coyuntura had given himself up for
dead many days earlier, and although he looked for his chance to
escape, he put his attention into making his mind smooth and
steady and calm for his death. He joked and kept a good face to
keep up the spirits of the others—especially his own son, who was
already nearly done with his apprenticeship as a warrior.[16] Dos-teh-
seh waited quietly herself, her face betraying nothing, her attention
focused on Naiche—who said little but watched the soldiers with his
intent, intelligent eyes. They all listened carefully when Bascom
came to them with a translator to explain that Cochise had killed all
of his captives and so the soldiers had decided to execute the warriors. The news did not surprise Coyuntura, who was glad Cochise
had begun already to avenge his death. He had known from the
beginning Bascom would not release him, for Bascom was proud
and stubborn and Cochise did not have the boy he sought.

Coyuntura was ready to die, for he'd spent all his life riding
alongside of death until it had become an old companion. He
answered carelessly that he was satisfied to die, having killed two
Mexicans with his own hands in the past month. He was grieved,

however, that his son must die without ever having had the chance to kill Mexicans. But he remained cheerful so his son would see how a warrior should die. Coyuntura asked for a little time to prepare himself—which Bascom granted, looking a little shamefaced. Coyuntura sat down and sprinkled the head of his son with pollen he always kept with him, and then began his death song. He was a little irritated when the other warrior who was a prisoner with him began to beg for his life. Then the three White Mountain men, seeing they had ridden into someone else's deadfall, asked for a little whiskey. But Bascom turned roughly away and closed his ears to their pleas. The other Chokonen warrior sat down beside Coyuntura and his son and began his death song as well, so he would be calm and steady for his death. The White Mountain men listened a little, then decided to do the same. Soon they were all singing and praying and appealing to their Powers to help guide them past the bears and monsters and crashing rocks and other obstacles that guard the path to the Happy Place so that only a brave man might enter there.

The soldiers took the six men to a stand of oak trees near the place where Cochise had burned the wagons and left the bodies of his hostages. The soldiers threw ropes over the branches and looped one end around each of the necks of the warriors. Then they pulled on the ends of the rope until the warriors were all hanging like venison for drying, high enough so the wolves could not jump up to pull their bodies down. Coyuntura tried not to kick and struggle as he suffocated, so he would not lose his dignity and make the soldiers laugh. He hoped the rope would not stretch out his neck so much he would look foolish in the Happy Place. He tried to close his ears to the strangled sounds of his son dying on another branch, so his mind would remain smooth. He comforted himself that Dos-teh-seh and Naiche were not hanging from these branches; and as the blackness closed over him, he thought with satisfaction of all of the White Eyes his brother would kill to avenge him.

So died Coyuntura and his son and the frail hope of peace with the White Eyes.[17]

And so began the long and bloody war of vengeance.

No longer would Cochise struggle with two minds, peace wrestling against war. Now the world seemed terribly simple—terrible and simple.[18]

8

1861

War of Extermination

Coyote Tries to Catch Turkey by Chopping Down Trees

Coyote saw Turkey in some pine trees. It was high up there in a tree. I don't know where he got the ax, but he got an ax, and he began to chop on that tree. Just about the time the tree started to fall, Turkey flew to another one.

Coyote went to that tree and tried to chop it down. He just kept doing that all day long until he was tired out. He kept chopping and Turkey kept flying to the next tree until Coyote was worn out.

Cochise sent out word to all of the allied bands that the White Eyes had killed his brother and many others, without cause or mercy.[1] He called on those loyal to him to help him seek his revenge. He had not sought this war, stepping many times out of its path although it had often rankled his pride to tolerate the intrusion of the White Eyes into the land Usen had given to the Chokonen. Now he swore to fight this war as ardently as he had tried to avoid it, until he was dead or had driven every White Eye from the territory of the Chokonen. He resolved to kill every White Eye that fell into his hands—as Bascom had killed his brother and his nephews and the others who trusted in his flag of truce.

Not even the release of his beloved Dos-teh-seh and his son Naiche soon after the fight in Apache Pass banked the flame of his anger. He had steeled his heart, like a knife heated and quenched, to losing them when he had killed his own captives. So he was moved nearly to tears when they came walking bravely into camp—Dos-teh-seh sobered and relieved to have survived and Naiche brimming with anger. Perhaps the soldiers, realizing what they had done, sought in this way to soften him. But he was past softening now. They had killed Coyuntura and challenged him in front of all of his warriors. Even if he was not consumed with rage and revenge, Cochise could not turn aside now and retain the respect of his warriors.

Cochise sent word to Mangas Coloradas to say he was going to make war on the White Eyes in Apache Pass and everywhere else in Chokonen territory, calling on his father-in-law and longtime ally for help. Mangas Coloradas sent back word that he had also resolved to make war on the White Eyes, after struggling a long time to keep the peace with them. The miners who had moved back into the diggings at Santa Rita del Cobre the Mexicans had abandoned so long ago had finally driven him to war. They had come into the heart of Chihenne territory in ever-greater numbers, scaring off the game, spreading diseases, and killing anyone who chanced into their path. They had torn at the body of the earth, in their mindless greed for the soft gleaming metals forbidden to the People by Usen. Nonetheless, Mangas Coloradas had done his best to make friends among them, knowing the Chihenne could not long sustain a war against the Americans in the north and the Mexicans in the south. Mangas Coloradas had turned the puzzle of the White Eyes over and over in his mind, seeking the solution with all the farseeing calculation of his supple mind and trusting in the guidance of his Power. Then he had gone among the miners in a friendly fashion, thinking they might leave Santa Rita del Cobre if he told them about other places they might find gold and silver. He went into their camp, telling first one man, then another, about distant places where they might find the metal that made them shake and cry out like a man in a fever. But instead of taking his advice, some miners seized the towering chief the next time he came into their settlement. He struggled, throwing them off like an elk shakes off a clinging wolf, but their numbers were too great. They took the greatest strategist and war leader the People had ever known and tied him to a framework of beams, like a deer hide to dry. Then they whipped him like a dog, until the blood ran down his back and dripped into the dust at his feet. Once he realized he was helpless, Mangas Coloradas held his words and bore the whipping without protest or complaint, scarcely seeming to notice when the whip cut into his flesh. But inside he burned, using his mounting fury to muffle the blows as he silently vowed his revenge, should they let him live. But they were foolish and arrogant men. Having offered Mangas Coloradas this terrible insult, they went away laughing—leaving him hanging all bloody and dripping rage. His son, Mangus, came quietly during the night and cut him down. Mangas Coloradas went off alone to nurse his wounds, loathe to let any of his warriors see he'd been humiliated and treated like a broken yellow dog by the miners. And as he healed, he planned his revenge. So it seemed almost the working of Power when he received the message from Cochise just as he was ready to make the miners pay for the insult they had offered him.

Cochise and Mangas Coloradas joined forces for their great war on the Americans. First they led a war party that took all the horses from the San Simon stage station. Then they split up, with Cochise going down into Sonora to camp near Fronteras. Now that he was going to make war on the Americans, he needed to quiet the fighting with Sonora. He camped near Fronteras with Esquinaline's band and also with Francisco and Delgadito, who was the second-leading Chihenne chief after Mangas Coloradas. They noted that the Sonorans had not many soldiers and later learned they were fighting a war with the Yaqui and the Mayo, two people who lived to the south and who often fought the People as well. Some Chihenne and Nednhi bands were already living peacefully near Fronteras and took alarm when the angry and agitated Chihenne and Chokonen bands arrived. The more peaceful bands feared the warlike Cochise would break the peace they had with Fronteras. Sure enough, some warriors from Francisco's band soon ran off a herd of 150 horses from a nearby ranch—but Cochise restrained most of his warriors so as not to stir up the Sonorans against them when his real target now was the Americans.

After he had traded for supplies in Fronteras to build up his guns and ammunition, Cochise returned to Chokonen territory, where the American soldiers were moving about quickly now, seeking him because of the fight at Apache Pass. But Cochise did not seek battle with the soldiers. He knew the business of the warriors was to be everywhere the soldiers were not, and to extract a heavy toll whenever the warriors did turn to fight. The bands began to watch the stage stations, running off stock and killing the men whenever they could. Cochise at first tried to lure the stage men out of the station in Apache Pass, showing a white flag. But they did not fall for his ruse, no doubt remembering Coyuntura had been seized and killed under a white flag. But Cochise only laughed at this, for he had not really expected the stage men would be such fools as to come out from behind the stone walls. Then he took a piece of black cloth and put a black flag where they could see it, showing he asked no quarter now and offered none. He sent warriors to keep a watch on the station, knowing time was his ally and he had only to wait for the opportunity to kill all of the men in those stations.

In the season of Little Eagles,[2] Cochise gathered up a raiding party. He knew the chief weakness of the White Eyes lay in their need for roads for their wagons and lots of water for their horses. The warriors knew every seep in every canyon in every mountain. They knew where a patient man could collect a skin canteen full of water by letting it drip through the afternoon. They knew where they could dig into the sand to make a space for the pool of water waiting for them beneath the surface, where Child-of-the-Water had told it to wait against their need. They could go through the mountains by a hundred paths, and find food and water all along the way. But the Whites knew only where to find the large springs low down. So Cochise knew he had only to hunt them along their wagon roads and wait for them near the water. Therefore, he led his raiding party to Stein's Peak and to Doubtful Canyon at its base, whose place-name was Tsisl-lnoi-bi-yi-tu, or Rock White in Water. This was the most reliable water between Mesilla and Apache Pass for all of the wagons and travelers crossing Chokonen territory to Tucson.

Cochise positioned his sixty warriors in the best places along that road and waited for the travelers he knew would come soon. Two men came along first and the hidden warriors killed them quickly. Two others came along a short time after that and the warriors killed them as well. Next came a wagon with five men, including some men from Mesilla whom Cochise knew and who had traded goods with the warriors in the past. The warriors opened fire on them as well, killing the two men driving in the first shooting. When the drivers fell dead, the mules began running, going about a mile before the wagon overturned. The three surviving men took up positions with good cover, using their good guns and bags of bullets. Cochise deployed his warriors and surrounded the three men, the warriors showing their rage and courage and trying to get close enough to kill them. But the Whites kept their heads and soon began to take a heavy toll on the warriors. In other times, Cochise might have not pressed the battle—for a leader who is reckless with the lives of his men will soon see his following dwindle. But he did not want these men to escape and carry the warning back to Mesilla—and he also wanted to get their guns and bullets and supplies, for the wagons were loaded with goods. Besides, he had sworn to fight to the death and had only started to satisfy his need for their blood. The warriors kept trying to work in closer all day, knowing eventually the White Eyes would run out of bullets. Once when Cochise stood up to direct the warriors—rising so they could see his signals—a bullet found him. The bullet burned deeply and the wound bled freely, but Cochise simply bound it up and paid no more attention to it. He did not want his warriors to think his Power had failed him, for they would lose confidence. Cochise had always moved fearlessly at the front ranks of the warriors, always the first into danger so any warrior who hung back would be shamed by his courage. His Power had urged him to do this and much of his influence with the warriors sprang from it, so he acted as if the wound was no more worth bothering about than the sting of a bee, although he had to set his face against the pain of it and revealed to no one how much blood he had lost. He had been surprised and moved when Dos-teh-seh and Naiche had returned, having been released by the soldiers. But when they told him how Coyuntura and the others had died, hatred for the Whites had changed his heart—as a tree buried in the sand sometimes turns to stone.

Near the end of the day, only two of the White Eyes were still alive—both men who knew Cochise. One of them signaled they wanted to talk. Seeing his opportunity, Cochise went down to talk, which gave the warriors an opportunity to come up behind and take them prisoners. They appealed to Cochise for their lives, but he was deaf to them now, and had sworn before his Power and his warriors he would have his revenge. Others had already come fearfully to him to say that his brother and nephews and the other warriors still hung from the oak tree in Apache Pass, picked at by the birds and spreading the stench of death for a long ways around. The warriors all feared the Chindi spirits in such a place and so no one went near the bodies, which were slowing turning to bone. But Cochise carried the image of them so he would not be tempted ever again to trust the White Eyes, or to show them mercy. Besides, they had lost too many warriors that day, and their relatives now demanded revenge on the prisoners. Cochise ignored the pleas of the two men with whom he might have traded supplies or even smoked in a different time. Instead, he hung them by their heels from a tree branch, carefully staking each arm to the ground. Then he built a fire under each of them, about eighteen inches beneath their heads. The warriors watched as they screamed and jerked against the ropes, until the fire burned through their heads. Then the warriors ran them through with lances so many times one could scarcely tell they had been human beings. They left them like that, so the White Eyes would understand the consequence of their own treachery.[3] Cochise did not linger to watch the men finish dying, but went through the wagon and the horses they had captured, finding thirteen good pistols and thirteen long-shooting Sharps rifles together with ammunition. Even though they had lost too many warriors, they had gained valuable supplies.

Now the war party headed west to avoid the response by the soldiers when the White Eyes discovered the nine bodies in Doubtful Canyon. They headed up one of the high ridges of the Chiricahuas, where the lookouts could see any wagons or soldiers coming across the flat valley to the west for fifty miles or more. They saw a line of freight wagons heading for the San Simon stage station with its good spring and stone building. Cochise led forty warriors down into the valley in the darkness and drove off the grazing herd of horses and mules. But some of the White Eyes chased them, with their good guns and fat pouches of ammunition, while most of the warriors were armed with bows. When the Whites overtook them, the warriors charged in among them. One warrior threw his lasso over a man, but that man tied the rope around his saddle horn and pulled the warrior off his own horse. Cochise rode up against the White Eyes, shooting at the leading man at a close distance with his pistol—but in his excitement and the movement of the horses, he missed. The warriors broke away, keeping seventeen horses but leaving three warriors dead. So already the war was taking its toll, as Cochise had known it would in the years he had held it off with his bleeding hands. And each warrior who fell was a gap in the line, while each White Eye killed was only the bending of grass in the wind.

Cochise resolved to be more careful with the lives of his men and pick his fights carefully, for the Americans were good fighters and well armed. They struck a small party of soldiers within two miles of Fort Buchanan, killing one man and taking two mules and some guns, but scattering before the soldiers could get a grip on their trail. A few weeks later, they killed one man and wounded another on a wagon leaving the mines at Patagonia. Now Cochise did not press an initial success, contenting himself with killing a man here and a man there from ambush, and all the time building up his supply of guns and ammunition.

He concentrated his attention also on the stage stations, keeping a close watch on them. Once he captured James Tevis and two other men between two stage stations. The three men surrendered, perhaps because Tevis hoped Cochise might treat him as a friend. This was foolish. Friendship had little claim in the face of the obligation of revenge and the memory of his brother and the others picked to bones by the birds and the insects. Cochise immediately killed the two men he did not know, hanging them upside down over the fire as Tevis watched. Then he gave Tevis some horse meat and let him cook it over the fire, debating what to do with him. After Tevis had eaten—watching Cochise with brave, wary eyes—Cochise told him to go stand in his boots on the coals of the fire. Tevis did not protest, but rose and stepped onto the coals, watching Cochise and scarcely shifting his weight as the coals burned through the soles of his boots. Cochise laughed, appreciating Tevis's defiance—facing death straight on like a warrior. He let Tevis leave the fire, and during the night allowed one of the warriors to cut the ropes on his hands and let him escape.[4]

When the soldiers grew too active, with too many patrols crisscrossing Chokonen territory, Cochise led the bands back down into Sonora. His men could rest a little from traveling so constantly and he could go among the Chihenne and Nednhi bands living in Mexico, seeking eager young warriors who wanted to raid among the White Eyes—who had more useful things for the warriors to take home to their families. Mostly they remained in Sonora when they swept south, partly because Chihuahua was again offering the scalp bounty, so killers were wandering all over that country.

Moving through Sonora, Cochise found the People very divided. Many bands had made their own peace with Sonora, settling near certain towns and collecting rations. Their headmen did not welcome the Chokonen, painted for war and carrying their plunder. Their arrival invariably alarmed the Mexicans and excited the young warriors who were restive under the restrictions of peace. The headmen knew the wild Chokonen—their blood boiling over with the excitement of raiding—would make trouble and would not resist the temptation of the loosely watched herds of the Mexicans. They also knew Cochise needed to recruit warriors, so the peacefully inclined leaders warned both the Mexicans and their people against the Chokonen.

When Cochise had rested and doubled the size of his war party to more than eighty warriors by attracting new followers, he returned to kill Americans. His raiders stormed through the Santa Cruz Valley, running off forty-four mules from one stage station before heading up to the Whetstone Mountains and then to the Santa Rita Mountains overlooking Tucson, which was now a city under siege—where everyone went about armed and looking often over their shoulders. Everywhere the warriors went, they spread death and claimed vengeance. They avoided the soldiers and the large settlements, but fell like lightning on isolated ranches and travelers. They destroyed ranches and killed everyone they could, stripping their bodies for anything of value and mutilating them afterward to show their contempt. Their anger had been a long time held back, tight as the reins on a thirsty horse. For all that time, they had watched the White Eyes spreading into the places that had long known and nourished and smoothed the Chokonen, their fury held by the tight-closed fist of Cochise. But now Cochise dug into them like spurs.

They struck everywhere and vanished just as quickly. They ran off the horse herd from within a mile of Fort Buchanan. Then they combined forces with the Nednhis led by Juh and Geronimo, who had come up out of their sanctuary in the Sierra Madre. Juh and Geronimo each had strong war Power. Juh was perhaps the only Chiricahua leader whose absolute authority among his men exceeded that of Cochise. Juh had a stutter that often kept him silent in council—which was one reason he came increasingly to rely on Geronimo, who was a shrewd and subtle talker. But Juh had taught his men complex hand signals, so that he could direct them in the middle of a fight—and he had great visions and foresight and a force of will that overshadowed lesser men. Power stood behind him, so that he could overawe even the outcasts from other bands who often found their way to his camp in the Sierra Madre. Only Juh could rival Cochise for the control of his men and the complexity of his strategies and his ambushes. Geronimo also had Power in war, which warned him of his enemies' designs and took the lead from their bullets so guns could not hurt him. He was not a chief, for he was entirely consumed with war and some people said he lost too many men in raiding to be trusted as a chief. But when he raided with Juh, they made a deadly combination. Now they raided with Cochise, whose raiding party had more than a hundred warriors. They laid

siege to the ranch of a tough White Eye named Pete Kitchen, who
had the largest ranch in the region. The warriors appeared suddenly,
but the cowboys scrambled back to the great ranch house—a group
of stone buildings with walls better defended than the soldier fort.
The warriors kept the men trapped in the fortified ranch house,
while other warriors ran off more than four hundred cattle—many of
which Juh and his Nednhis took back down into Mexico.

After Cochise took the horse herd from Fort Buchanan, a party
of soldiers set out after them. The soldiers chased them for twenty
miles, toward the Whetstone Mountains. Seeing the soldiers would
soon overtake them, the warriors killed most of the stock to keep
the soldiers from getting it back and then prepared to retreat into
the mountains. But Cochise saw Bascom among the soldiers and a
great fury seized him. He charged toward his enemy, calling Bascom
by name and using the curses and taunts he had learned in English.
The soldiers shot at Cochise, who charged again and again with his
boldest warriors beside him. But even though the soldiers all now
recognized him and concentrated their fire on him, his Power protected him. He lost four warriors trying to reach Bascom, for the soldiers were well armed and behind good cover. Cochise broke off the
attack and retreated into the mountains, the warriors abandoning
their horses and running up over the steep canyons and high ridges
where a rider could not follow. The soldiers, who were nearly helpless on foot, abandoned the chase.

A storm came on them quickly, helping to cover their tracks—so
Cochise wondered whether the Ga'an had sent it to help them. The
Thunder People lived in the sky, shooting their arrows of lighting.
People said the flints that warriors often picked up for arrowheads
were from the arrows shot by the Thunder People, and so connected
to Child-of-the-Water, whose father was the rain and the lightning.
Lightning flashed almost continuously in the broil of clouds over-
head, so many people fingered their charms against lightning.
Cochise made the call of the nighthawk, whose fluttering flight in
search of insects made it hard for lightning to hit. Then he said,
"Let it be well, my brother, Lightning," partly to reassure his sons,
for Naiche looked anxiously up at the sky. But despite Cochise's
prayer, one flash of lightning struck close by where Cochise and
Taza and Naiche stood, and their horses reared and bucked in fear.
Cochise remained calm, for he did not fear Lightning Power and
kept his mind smooth. So he said:

Continue in a good way;
Be kind as you go through;
Do not frighten these poor people;
My grandfather let it be well;
Don't frighten us poor people.[5]

In truth, the warm months of that year were filled with thunderstorms, more than anyone could remember. Cochise prayed often to Thunder, seeking the help of the Ga'an in driving the Whites out of the sacred mountains, where they profaned the earth. Therefore, the great number of storms heartened the warriors, and many of them gathered up pieces of chipped flint, the arrowheads of the Thunder People. Once the Thunder People had hunted for the People, so that they always had meat. But the People had gotten lazy and forgot their prayers of gratitude and respect, so the Thunder People got disgusted and went away into the sky. Now many people tied sage in their hair, to ward off the lightning strikes. But Cochise and shamans with Lightning Power prayed hard for help in the war with the White Eyes. Lightning Power had a hard time against the Whites, because they had so much metal and Power of metal. But one of the most respected shamans had Lightning Power, and his Power gave him a ceremony that would work against the White Eyes despite their metal. Cochise had hope the Thunder People would help them now, and therefore took care that all of his people should not fear Thunder, but thank It and show It their respect.[6]

Thunder heard his prayer now and so passed by them, going to seek the soldiers. Cochise watched the storm as it broke into pieces, his heart aching with the beauty of the world and a sense of reverence that they should be part of it, blessed by the rain as the poppies that turn even the meanest desert into a glory of color. Then he went to the tree splintered by the lightning strike, to take some wood, now blessed by Lightning. Such lightning-riven wood was much in demand as charms, for it had acquired an aspect of Lightning Power in the moment the arrow of the Thunder People struck it. He sang the prayers of gratitude and respect as he did so, knowing his sons would in this way learn that even deadly things that might frighten him were to be revered:

He in the sky who is holy,
He who is Black Thunder
Who put up the earth
He zigzags down with life

To impart life to her body
He in the sky who is holy,
Black Thunder, my father[7]

He went on, heartened by this reminder of the beauty of the
world and the holiness of it. Nonetheless, the mounting losses
among his warriors grieved and worried Cochise, seeing so many
women wailing in their wickiups and so many children without
fathers. But he could not relent now. He could see that the scattered
ranchers and miners and farmers had abandoned their places, heading west or taking refuge in the towns too big for the warriors to
attack. He pressed on, knowing he could not sustain such losses for
long and that the warriors would begin to slip away into Mexico if
they lost faith in the ability of his Power to protect them. Still, he
had set his course and sworn his oath. The thought of his brother
hanging from the tree in Apache Pass returned to him constantly,
like a dream of great portent. So he kept on with the killing.

And then, like a gift of Power, the White Eyes broke.

They had already abandoned all of the scattered ranches—only
Pete Kitchen remained, stubborn as a snapping turtle.

Cochise gathered up more than a hundred warriors and attacked
the mining town of Tubac.[8] They killed everyone they could catch
outside the town, then stormed through the little settlement—breaking into some houses, setting others on fire. They ran off the stock
and inflicted great damage, but the miners—well armed and determined—regrouped and fought back. They killed seven or eight warriors before the war party retreated out of the town, taking most of
the horses and mules with them. Once again, the victory had come
at great cost. But after the attack, the last miners left Tubac and the
settlement lapsed once more into the empty silence of the desert,
just as it had when the warriors had driven out the Mexicans a generation before.

Cochise now swept through the Santa Cruz and Sonoita valleys,
picking off travelers and anyone foolish enough still to be out prospecting. Then his scouts brought back the news for which Cochise
had been yearning, but for which he had nearly given up hope. The
soldiers had marched out of Fort Buchanan—all in a bunch—and set
fire to the buildings behind them.[9] Then they had marched off
to Tucson, leaving only the charred skeleton of the fort. The news
flashed through the camps of the Chokonen and was greeted every-

where with celebration and dancing. The abandonment of the forts in Arizona added greatly to the reputation and Power of Cochise, and even bands that had remained aloof from his war for fear of the White Eyes now hurried to declare their loyalty. Cochise heard the news almost disbelieving himself, for he had not expected to win his war with the Whites. The death of his brother and the rise of his Power in him had driven him to it, but he had always thought he went forth to a good death. Now he was surprised to find the White Eyes would be so easy to defeat. Perhaps they decided it was not worth dying for a land whose places they did not know and to whose voices they were deaf.

Now Cochise turned his attention to the east, where his father-in-law was fighting the Whites. Mangas Coloradas, Victorio, Lozen, and the other leaders of the Chihenne made war in their territory—sometimes joining forces with bands of the Chokonen. When the soldiers pursued them too closely, they would retreat into the Dragoon and Chiricahua mountains, to camp with the Chokonen. And when the soldiers pressed too close there, the Chihenne and the Chokonen would move back to New Mexico, just as they had sometimes moved back and forth from Sonora to Chihuahua—although the Americans were much harder to divide against one another. Cochise often raided with his father-in-law. They were the two greatest war leaders in the memory of the People—one the bow, the other the arrow. Often they waited on the outskirts of Santa Rita del Cobre to pick off prospectors who strayed too far from the protection of the many guns of the settlement or to intercept supply trains heading for the mines. Several times they mounted direct attacks on the settlement—although this posed a dangerous risk to the warriors' lives. Once they even waited for a long time watching the fort that protected Santa Rita del Cobre, learning the habits of the soldiers and then striking at just the right moment to run off the horse herd. But mostly they set ambushes along the roads leading to and from the mines, bleeding away their supplies and building the muscles of their fear. Mangas Coloradas was a patient and farseeing man. He was like a knife fighter who cuts his opponent, then hangs back to let the wound do its work. Soon they had nearly closed the road between Tucson and Mesilla, and the miners at Pinos Altos and Santa Rita del Cobre grew increasingly isolated, their numbers dwindling from fear.

Cochise and Mangas Coloradas knew the strongest weakness of the White Eyes was their great need for supplies. Set one White Eye alone in even good country and he would soon starve to death or die of thirst wandering in useless circles. They had good guns and many bullets, but were helpless as soon as they had used up their bullets. Cochise understood he must take advantage of this weakness in his long war of no quarter. He learned perfectly all of the wagon routes of the White Eyes and of all the approaches to the few places with good water the Whites needed to nourish their many horses. Apache Pass remained one of the best places to lie in wait, for it offered the only reliable source of water for horses for forty miles in each direction. Even better was the spring in Cook's Canyon at the foot of Dziltanatal—Mountain Holds Its Head up Proudly—which the Americans called Cook's Peak. In just the first two seasons of the war between Cochise and the White Eyes, the warriors killed more than a hundred Whites approaching Cook's canyon, leaving their bones scattered along the trail as a warning. For Cochise knew this was more a struggle of wills than of deaths. He knew he could not match deaths with the White Eyes—even if he killed ten of them for every warrior lost. They would come back every spring, like ladybugs that covered the trees, while the People faded like the deer from the valleys after the Whites had come. It did not matter whether he killed a soldier or ten soldiers or a hundred settlers. The deaths meant nothing—less than nothing if he lost warriors in the effort. His only chance lay in frightening the settlers away, for only greed brought them into the country of the Chokonen. He strove to enlist fear as his strong ally against greed and set those two at war in the hearts of the miners and the ranchers who came into the Chokonen territory, bringing along in their wake the soldiers to protect them. He mutilated the bodies of the Whites he killed and left them along the trail so the White Eyes would grow as crazy with fear as with greed. That is why Cochise continued to kill anyone he found and dared to attack even large and well-armed parties—despite the potential cost in the irreplaceable lives of his warriors. The Whites must know fear, even if they traveled in large groups in the heat of the day. For fear had always been the strong ally of the People. That was why Child-of-the-Water had placed on them the strong obligation of revenge before he had gone off with White-Painted Woman and the other supernaturals and left the People to fend for themselves in the midst of their enemies.

In the season of Large Leaves,[10] Mangas Coloradas and Cochise joined forces and set an ambush in Cook's Canyon with more than a hundred warriors. A small party in a mail wagon came warily into the canyon. When the warriors fired on them, the White Eyes put up a strong return fire despite their small numbers and turned the horses with great skill to go to the high ground. Cochise admired their discipline and their sense of the terrain, but mourned it as well. These men would be hard to kill. They made it to a good defensive position. Then they unloaded the wagon, taking all of the guns and ammunition, and sent the horses and wagon back down the hill without a driver, hoping the warriors would be satisfied with the horse and wagon and most of the supplies. Then the White Eyes set to building good breastworks of stones on the top of the hill to make it clear they would sell their lives dearly. The warriors closed in around the trapped Whites, sniping at them—but the seven men were in a good position and careful about showing themselves. As night descended, Cochise and Mangas Coloradas talked and consulted their Powers, trying to decide whether they should stay to kill these seven men who were dug in like badgers. Mangas Coloradas seemed doubtful, for he could not spare many warriors to kill these men, even though he would like to have their guns—most of his men were still armed with bows. Cochise said they must kill them. They had more than a hundred warriors against seven men. If these seven escaped, they would carry the word to others, and so greed would win a victory in the battle against fear on which the survival of the People depended.

The next morning, the warriors moved up as close as they could, stealing from cover to cover to get into positions from which they could shoot effectively at the White Eyes. They poured down fire on the seven men, so the rocks were speckled with smears of lead and every tree was splintered. One tree alone had 150 bullets in it by the end of that day. But the Whites kept their discipline and kept up a heavy and effective fire, so the warriors had much the worse of the exchange. Cochise hoped they would use up their ammunition in the long day of shooting back and forth, but they seemed to have an inexhaustible supply. Soon it seemed the warriors, not the Americans, would use up their bullets first. Growing desperate as the day wore on, the warriors made several charges against the entrenched positions of the Whites. The warriors paid a heavy cost in lives, but they could not get close enough to make their numbers tell. So the fight went on all day, with more than fifteen warriors dead. Cochise thought they had killed one or two of the White Eyes and maybe wounded more, but he wasn't sure. That night the mood in the camp was grim, for such losses for so little gain were a near disaster. Warriors who had lost brothers and nephews in the fighting now were wild for the blood of the Whites. But Mangas Coloradas had lost heart, saying the cost was too great and that the White Eyes seemed to have a bottomless sack of bullets. Cochise argued with him, saying they had no choice now but to stay and kill these brave, fierce-fighting men. If they all went back alive to Mesilla and to Tucson with the story of how seven men had stood off the combined forces of Cochise and Mangas Coloradas, the story would be worth three hundred soldiers in the war of fear. They discussed whether they should try to slip up to the hill in the darkness, when the long rifles and the good aim of the Americans would not give them such an advantage. But the warriors were reluctant to attack in the night, for if they were killed in such a battle they would live forevermore in the darkness in the Happy Place. Besides, owls were out at night. They would be heard off in the trees, which seemed an ill omen for an attack at night. Finally, Cochise knew he could not coordinate the attack in the darkness, and feared the warriors could come up against the guns of the White Eyes one by one.

Mangas Coloradas and Cochise talked a long time, with the subchiefs listening and supporting one or the other. Then they went aside and consulted their Powers a long time in the darkness, as their followers waited in anger and respect and fear. At length, Mangas Coloradas returned, and said he would take the Chihenne and leave the Whites. He could not afford to lose any more warriors, and every hour they remained in the canyon increased the chance soldiers would come and trap them there. Cochise listened respectfully to the decision of his father-in-law, for no man could question the courage of Mangas Coloradas or his commitment to the welfare of his people. But Cochise felt a shadow pass over him as they talked, seeing the waning of Mangas Coloradas—as the fire burns down after its rush into the new wood. Cochise spoke quietly then, saying the Whites on the hill must not leave the canyon alive, and so he would not turn away until every one of them was dead. He spoke with such certainty that his Power reached out and strengthened the hearts of his subchiefs. Then the Chokonen and the Chihenne separated. Cochise led the Chokonen warriors in dancing, acting out the courage each warrior had shown in the fight that day, then acting out the destruction of the White Eyes they anticipated in the morning.

The drums throbbed like a pulse in the night, the chants rising and falling like breath, so they all beat as one heart, breathed as one breath. They danced for hours until they were transported and transformed in a dream of war, where fear could not find their trail and death mattered not so much as the stories told about a brave man. Some of the Chihenne who were listening were drawn back to the Chokonen by the strong medicine of the dance, showing they would remain and fight alongside Cochise by dancing out into the firelight, where the drums throbbed and the breath of the song filled them. But in the morning, most of the Chihenne slipped away with Mangas Coloradas, only a few remaining with the Chokonen in obedience to the will of Cochise.[11]

Now Cochise turned back to the Americans, considering what he should do. The Apache had tried to gain high ground where they could pick off the Whites without risk all through the day before, with little success. The White Eyes had picked good ground and they were better shots than the warriors. Now Cochise resolved to trust to his Power. He spoke to the warriors, building up a fire in their blood with the kindling of his words and the logs of his Power. They could see Power rising up in him until they could almost touch it—like a great stallion on a tight reign trembling to run. Now Cochise turned to the White Eyes, knowing they had listened to the dancing and the singing through the night, knowing Power and fear had worked on them and hoping they had fewer bullets left than it had seemed the day before. Cochise led the attack himself, running in the front rank with Taza beside him, relying on his Power and on shame to draw the other warriors along after him. The Whites saw them quickly and started a strong fire, but Cochise ran through the bullets. He had covered half the distance to them and was starting up the hill when a bullet grazed him, drawing a gush of blood but causing him to pause only a moment. Taza came up beside him, fearless and excited. Then a bullet hit Taza, knocking him back down onto the ground. He struggled to rise, then fell back again. Cochise felt anger and rage and Power rise up in him with the image of his son bleeding on the ground and his brother hanging like a gutted deer from the oak tree in Apache Pass. He turned back to the White Eyes, with his brother Juan now appearing from nowhere at his side as they ran together up the hill. The Power of Cochise turned the bullets aside and stiffened the courage of his men coming on behind, so the charge carried them up over the breastworks of the Americans. As he came over the line of stones, Cochise thrust his lance through the body of one of the men—a bearded man with a fierce and resolute face, willing as a warrior to face death and make his enemies pay the price for it. He seemed surprised when the lance entered him, the tip coming out his back. But he only grunted and struggled to raise his gun to shoot again. Cochise pushed him back to the ground, then wrenched out his lance and thrust it through his heart this time, so the white man shuddered and died in a moment, gripping the shaft of the lance that pinned him to the ground. The other warriors were among the White Eyes in a moment, hacking them to pieces. Three of the Whites fell back and warriors pursued them, bringing two of them to bay fifty yards down the slope and killing them there. The last man ran another hundred yards before the warriors closed in. He turned and kept shooting as they overwhelmed him, killing one warrior and wounding another as he died. The warriors fell upon the bodies of the White Eyes, stripping them of anything valuable—especially their deadly guns. Sometimes Cochise did not mutilate the bodies of men who had died bravely, but the warriors were in a fury. They broke every bone in every body and shot each man in the head and cut and mutilated them.

Cochise went back down the hill to tend to Taza, who made no complaint, sitting against the rock with a fierce, happy look on his face. Cochise let the warriors vent their fury on the bodies of the Whites for a while, then called to his subchiefs to get the warriors moving south. He totaled the losses, dismayed to discover that killing these seven White Eyes had cost the lives of twenty-five warriors—both Chihenne and Chokonen. He knew he could not go on fighting long if he won many such victories. But at least this fight would make the Whites afraid, knowing even a well-armed and determined party could not pass safely through Crook's Canyon. But in his heart, he wondered that his Power had led him to such a fight and felt a sick fear growing for Taza. After he had watched the warriors breaking the bones of the White Eyes for a time, Cochise sent several warriors to the hiding place where they had left the women and children when they went to set the ambush, telling them to head south for Janos. Then he gathered up the warriors and directed them to scatter so they would not leave a trail the soldiers could follow. The Chokonen made their way back down to Janos, with gold and watches and goods to trade to the Mexicans for bullets and powder and food.

Many warriors had wounds, so the people who had healing ceremonies were much in demand. Some shamans specialized in finding out what had caused a sickness; they would do ceremonies and then reveal that the sick person had Coyote Sickness because he had stepped on a coyote track, or Bear Sickness because she had spoken disrespectfully about bears. Then the family would have to find someone with a ceremony for Coyote Sickness or Bear Sickness. The power to heal was a valuable but sometimes dangerous gift. Sometimes people would themselves kill a shaman whose Power had started killing people he treated. But everyone was also a little bit afraid of these shamans, because sometimes Power would tempt these men and women to trade the lives of others for a longer life for themselves—especially relatives. The shamans with the best reputations were in much demand. Some of the warriors sent family members to shamans who had strong Power in healing and against bullets and asked them to come, using their real names so they would be shamed to reject an appeal. Of course, Cochise and Taza had no need to ask in such a way. But Dos-teh-seh went with two fine horses and two good guns to one man who had Gun Power, offering these gifts to him with wordless respect. In accepting them, he agreed to use his Power to help Cochise and Taza, who were side by side.

The shaman came to prepare the four-day ceremony, bringing turquoise, abalone shell, red coral stone, eagle feathers, pollen, black flint blades, white shell, and obsidian, representing all the sacred stones and all the sacred colors. He brought with him also a basket with white clay, red ocher, coral, rock crystal, opal, jasper, gypsum, snakeweed, grama grass, and cigarettes—wild tobacco rolled in oak leaves. The family gathered around to participate in the Power of the healing ceremony and to add their prayers and right thoughts. The shaman brought with him two assistants, one of whom beat the drum throughout the long ceremony, to help smooth and steady the minds of the listeners so they could feel the Power gathered around the shaman and release any fears that might offend that Power. The shaman first marked Taza and Cochise with pollen, forehead, foot, and chest. Then he lit the first of his cigarettes and reverently blew smoke in each of the four directions, saying:

May it be well
There are good and evil on this earth.
We live in the midst of it.
Let all believe in peace.

I want nothing to harm us.
We only want food and other good things.
This man is wounded.
I want him to live.
He has been searching for something good.
This evening I hope what is wrong will disappear and he will live
    a good life.
Now I am going to tell you something.
Now you must do right as you promised me to do.
Your Power must go into the life of this poor man.[12]

With motions so careful and graceful his hands were another prayer, the shaman used the minerals from the basket to mark first himself and then Cochise and then Taza with pollen, then with red ocher, then with specular iron ore, then with white clay. Next he took the pollen and marked everyone present. He offered the pollen to the sky, to Thunder, to the Powers watching, turning in a sunwise direction a full sacred circle, singing songs his Power had taught him. As one assistant beat slowly on the drum, which was the pulse of everyone present sounding in their ears, the other shook rattles made of eagle claws. In this way, the ceremony went on—the formal songs with words passed down carefully from Child-of-the-Water and White-Painted Woman, and the improvised prayers in which the shaman drew on his knowledge of his patient and his family. In this way, the shaman could help even Cochise correct bad thinking and bad behavior and find with his feet the path of Child-of-the-Water, for all ceremonies were a way to restore social harmony and smooth anger and jealousy and fear. The shaman sang sets of songs for each of the four directions, the four stones, the four colors:

Black is for the east
Blue is for the south
Yellow for the west
White for the north.[13]

At the end of the fourth set of songs, the shaman held himself still, tilting his head up, listening with complete attention to his Power. The silence fell absolute on the wickiup and they could hear something moving over the roof, up above them. Then after a long time they heard the shaman talking to his Power, a murmur like a mother to a child in a language of their own. Now he turned back to a carefully prepared piece of buckskin that had been unblemished and stretched empty in the middle of the space between the shaman and Cochise. But when people looked back down at the buckskin, they saw a certain plant there, which had not been there before the shaman had talked to his Power.[14] The shaman knelt in front of the plant, talking to it in a friendly and respectful way, then singing the songs his Power had given him. He took the plant and broke some of it into a cup of water, which he gave to Cochise and to Taza. Then he set some of it on fire and fanned the smoke over them with an eagle feather. [15]

Cochise and Taza rapidly recovered their strength, for their bodies were strong and their minds smooth and the shaman who tended them had a good relationship with his Power. A month later, Cochise led his warriors back up to Cook's Canyon, knowing the fear from the last fight would have settled a little and the soldiers would have gone back to the fort after seeking the Chokonen everywhere. As they waited there, Mangas Coloradas returned with many warriors. He was full of compliments for the way the Chokonen had finished the fight with the seven men, for Mangas Coloradas loved Cochise and knew how much they needed each other in this war. Still, knowing that Mangas Coloradas had left before the end of the last fight in the canyon lay like a shadow between them. Cochise was careful not to deepen that shadow and his warriors knew he would not tolerate any criticism of his father-in-law, so the Chihenne and the Chokonen joined forces again with no hard feelings between them. Each warrior knew every leader must listen to his Power and select among hard choices, just as each warrior must decide whom to follow.

They had not long to wait in the canyon. A pack train with nine Mexican mule drivers came carelessly into it, perhaps because they had heard that soldiers had scoured the area and found no warriors. The hidden warriors held their fire until all of the men were in the canyon and killed them quickly, suffering no losses. This reassured the warriors whose faith in the Power of Cochise and Mangas Coloradas had been shaken by the last, costly fight in the canyon. They left the canyon for a while out of caution, but circled back around when they were sure no soldiers were coming out to hunt them.

Some days later, 6 large wagons, 2 buggies, and a smaller wagon came slowly along into the pass, with 24 men, 16 women, and 7 children herding several hundred cattle, sheep, goats, and horses.[16] Cochise recognized some of the men and the horses, for they had

been settlers living in Tubac and Sonoita Creek in Chokonen territory. They had gathered together when the soldiers had left, as they
no longer had protection against the warriors. They came on carelessly into the canyon, relying on their numbers for protection. And
perhaps in normal times, their many men and many guns would have
deterred an attack. But Mangas Coloradas and Cochise now had
gathered 200 warriors together and were determined to drive the
White Eyes out of Chihenne territory, as they had already cleared
Chokonen territory. Besides, Mangas Coloradas wanted to regain the
face he had lost in leaving the fight with the seven, so he was as
eager for a fight as Cochise. They waited until the last wagon entered
the canyon, noting with satisfaction the Whites had not sent an advanced guard and did not have skirmishers moving on each side of
the slow-moving column of wagons and livestock.

The warriors swarmed out of the rocks, first making for the herd
of cattle and horses. They stampeded the herd, spurring them to a
run through the canyon. Several of the Whites on horseback who
had been tending the cattle bravely charged at the warriors to give
the others in the wagons time to respond. They stopped the charge
of the warriors, who were mostly interested in rounding up the
horses and cattle. The warriors shot one man dead out of his saddle
and fatally wounded a second. Two other White Eyes were badly
wounded in that charge, but the Whites by their courage had prevented the warriors from sweeping in immediately among the wagons. Meanwhile, the Whites abandoned the lead wagon, which was
too far ahead of the rest, its occupants running back to the next
cluster of wagons in line. At the same time, the wagon in the rear of
the straggling column turned and fled, taking with it most of the
women and children.[17] Cochise let them go, concentrating his attention on the herd and on the other wagons now trapped in the
canyon. While some of the warriors plundered the leading wagon,
the rest kept up a strong fire on those remaining. They killed one
more man, but the half brother of the scout Kit Carson was guiding
the party and led a strong defense.

Cochise noted one of the women stood behind the White Eyes,
fearlessly loading their guns through the battle and earning his
admiration. Usually, White women did not fight—perhaps because
they were afraid, and perhaps because their men would not let
them. The White women usually stayed in towns or on ranches, not
moving constantly and sharing the hardships of the men as did the

women of the People. Cochise was impressed to see the way this woman fought, brave as a warrior. The warriors did not press the attack closely, as they already had all the livestock and as much plunder as they could easily carry. The lives of these strong fighting men still in the wagon had no value. So when a lucky shot from one of them killed a warrior as the day dwindled, Cochise and Mangas Coloradas decided to break off the attack and leave before the soldiers came. They left with 400 cattle and 900 sheep, moving slowly toward the safety of the Florida Mountains, where they would kill many of the sheep and smoke the meat. The large war party split into three groups, to make it harder to follow. But as the Chokonen approached the foothills of the Florida Mountains, a well-armed force of perhaps 35 soldiers attacked them from ambush.[18] Cochise then had only 80 warriors and was burdened with the livestock, so he could not stand and fight. In a long, running fight, the soldiers killed eight warriors and recovered some of the livestock, spoiling the victory. The deaths cast a pall over the group, so they did not celebrate that night. Still, Cochise knew he had delivered another blow to the White Eyes, demonstrating that no party was safe in passing through the territory of the Chihenne and the Chokonen.

He knew his men needed a rest, so once they had slaughtered the remaining sheep and cattle and prepared the meat, they traveled quickly on down to Fronteras. There they discovered that Mangas Coloradas had led his men down to Janos, where things were dangerous and uncertain. The Chihuahuans had struck back against bands raiding in Mexico, killing eleven warriors and women living down there while Cochise and Mangas Coloradas were killing the Whites in Cook's Canyon. Shortly after Mangas Coloradas arrived in Janos, the spotted sickness broke out in their camps, so they quickly moved away. The sickness appeared also in the camps of the Chokonen near Fronteras, so they moved away as well—having already traded with the Mexicans for the things they had taken in Cook's Canyon. The Chokonen retreated into the Animas Mountains in the season when the Earth Is Reddish Brown,[19] building up their strength. Cochise kept in touch with Mangas Coloradas and debated whether to send out raiding parties to gather more food and supplies down in Mexico or north to the miners remaining at Pinos Altos. At length his fresh hatred for the White Eyes overcame his old hatred for the Mexicans, and he led raiding parties back to the mines near Pinos Altos, joining up again with the Chihenne. Besides, he had decided to try to avoid fighting the Sonorans so he would have somewhere to go to trade the plunder taken from the Americans.

The war parties first probed the defenses of the miners at Pinos Altos, finding them weaker as the mining camps continued to bleed men, but still too strong to press a direct assault. They circled back to their favorite places along the approaches to Cook's Canyon, knowing supplies going to Pinos Altos must pass through this snare. They lay in wait for a wagon train the scouts had spotted, but lookouts reported that a strong force of well-armed soldiers had joined the party, led by a skillful *nantan* named Thomas Mastin. So Cochise resolved to attack Pinos Altos instead, while the soldiers were busy protecting the wagons. But perhaps Mastin had Power himself, for he seemed to sense Cochise's intentions. He left the wagon train and marched his soldiers quickly to Pinos Altos. He was camped there when the Chokonen and the Chihenne came swarming out of the hills, perhaps two hundred strong. They swept through the town, killing anyone they caught in the open. But the miners were wary and ready for attack and retreated into their well-fortified buildings. The warriors cornered some miners in their diggings, killing them quickly. But once the miners had gotten into their houses with their good guns and plentiful ammunition, they were hard to kill. The warriors tried to get close enough to set fire to the houses, without much success. Then Mastin's soldiers appeared suddenly. The warriors turned on them, killing some but suffering their own deaths in return. The soldiers soon found themselves on the defensive, so they retreated to a strong cluster of buildings in the center of town. The warriors, flushed with the Power of Cochise and eager for the blood of the soldiers, pressed the attack. They fatally wounded Mastin and killed two other soldiers in the hard fighting at the store in the center of town. But then the soldiers started firing cannons loaded with nails and bullets, driving the warriors back. Seeing the warriors falling back with heavy losses, the miners rallied and chased them. Cochise broke off the attack several hours after it had started, reluctantly abandoning the bodies of ten dead warriors and carrying others both dead and wounded. The warriors had killed only five Whites and wounded seven others–but they had demonstrated that the Whites were not safe even in their strongest settlement with soldiers to help them. The White Eyes understood this lesson, and within a week the last of the miners fled to Mesilla or Tucson. The Chihenne and Chokonen had nearly cleared their territory of Whites for the first time in more than a generation.

The Whites had been thrown onto the defensive everywhere in the territory of the Chiricahua and were now concentrated almost entirely in Santa Fe, Mesilla, and Tucson. Only a few scattered mining camps were left, with the men working always with their guns at their sides. Their soldiers had run away in fear, leaving only a few groups of poorly disciplined irregulars to come out carefully and fearfully.

But the victories had come at great cost, so every family had its losses to mourn and spoke no longer the names of warriors they had loved and remembered as boys, playing in the camps of the People. Even so, Cochise closed his mind to the cost. He knew they must drive the Whites out now, for they and the Chokonen could not live in the same places, drink the same water, cast their spirits out to the same horizon. He must gamble everything on this war to the death, as a man bets everything he owns—even his life—on a single cast of the pole as the hoop rolls on.

And had he not already nearly won this war?

Had his Power not stood beside him, its shadow as long as a dancer at sunrise?

And if his Power stood beside him and if all the Chiricahua were in the shadow it cast, then what could the White Eyes do against them? Their enemies must falter and die and fall back—for they knew not the proper prayers and did not belong to these rocks, these mountains, these springs. The Chokonen were of these places—shaped by them, remembered by them, smoothed and steadied by them. They knew the stories for each ridge and spring and undercut stream bank, which they practiced in their minds as they passed from place to place, until they had learned the lessons of those places, until wisdom sits in those places.

So it was right and proper that his Power had shown him how to kill the Whites and set their fear against their greed until they left the places Child-of-the-Water had prepared for the People. So Cochise felt his spirit rising up, even under the weight of the deaths of so many good men.

For if the People fought with courage and reverence, remembering their obligation to the stones, learning the wisdom of places, and practicing the discipline of a warrior, how could these soulless creatures who knew not a single prayer overcome them?

9

Cochise Triumphant

It Happened at Tliish Bi Tu'e (Snake's Water)

The people came to get water at the spring at Tliish Bi Tu'e and saw there was none. They were shocked! The women began to wail. The men stood silent and still. "Why has Snake's Water dried up? Why has this happened? What have we done to cause this to happen? Water must surely be angry with us." This was what they were thinking.

Now they were walking away, thirsty and shaking with fear. The women were wailing, louder and louder. Their children were crying, too. They were wailing as if a relative had died. "What if this happens elsewhere?! What if this happens everywhere?!" They were deeply frightened because of what they had done.

"Our holy people must work on this for us." This was what they were saying as they walked away from Snake's Water. "Our holy people must help us by making amends to Water. They must help us so we may live! They must ask Water to take pity on us! What if this happened everywhere!" This was what they were thinking. This was what they were praying. They did not understand. They were terribly afraid. The women were wailing louder, as if a relative had died. Already they had started to pray.

Now the People went freely about in their own country, for most of the White Eyes had fled. Only a few settlements remained and the people there hid in their towns, venturing out only in well-armed groups, looking about on every side for an ambush. Sometimes large parties of men set out from Tucson or Mesilla or Santa Fe, hunting for raiders. But it was not difficult to stay out of the way of such men, or to set an ambush to send them running back to the relative safety of the few towns too big to attack. So the People lived as in the old days, when they could camp again in the best places and go hunting—for the game returned as the Whites left.

160

Now they could once again hold the ceremonies that connected scattered bands and formed the beating heart of the People. They all loved best the ceremonies that involved the masked dancers, whose prayers and preparations and costumes made them for the four days of the dance an aspect of the Ga'an Mountain Spirits, who lived in the heart of the sacred mountains and whose drumming a quiet and steady man could hear through the rocks—like Tipping Beetle with his head against the ground. Cochise had learned the songs and the dances and the demanding prayers to prepare the masked dancers, for he had dedicated his life to protecting his people and knew they could not long survive without the goodwill of the Ga'an.[1] His reputation for Power was great, so when he indicated his willingness to prepare dancers for the ceremony, the best dancers volunteered eagerly. They happily bore the restrictions necessary to the dancers, knowing that assuming an aspect of the Ga'an was a risky and delicate matter. If a dancer made any mistake—even a small one—he might fall ill and perhaps die.[2] One dancer must not touch another dancer—especially one prepared by a different shaman—or he might suffer spasms or trouble in the ear or eye or a swollen face. In such an event, all the masked dancers must blow the sickness away. Each item of the costume must be put on in the proper order with the proper prayers, for dancers who were arrogant and put the mask over their heads without the proper words and gestures could go mad from that disrespect. Then only the intervention of the Masked Dancer shaman could cure him. So all of the dancers relied on the ceremony given to the shaman by his Power.

But the dancers also brought their skill and prayer to the ceremony, for the best dancers had a great following—although they must remember they were only an aspect of the Ga'an and so not offend Power through their vanity. No one could even call the dancers by their names in the many days of the ceremony, or they would anger the Ga'an and bring bad luck. Still, each dancer first learned the steps, but remained free to embellish the dance—just as storytellers made each story their own. For the People loved the differences that made each person and tree and stone an individual; they did not make everything the same so one object was indistinguishable from another, as did the White people. You could not steal a bow or a shield or a basket—because the handiwork of the person who had made it was obvious, and you would be immediately shamed if you took it and pretended you had made it. In the same way, no man could steal another man's ceremony or his dance or his song—for everyone knew the style of each dancer and singer. Each ceremony and dance and song was a prayer—and who would be so foolish as to steal a prayer?

Cochise took great care in the songs and designs and prayers with which he prepared the dancers, knowing Power was a knife held carefully by the blade. And when Taza said he would learn the part of a dancer, Cochise took him aside and spoke carefully to him.[3] He said, "My son, I want to tell you some things before you start, for this is your first time. Putting this mask on and getting everything tight is going to feel awkward. When you are led out to the fire by the leader, there is going to be a big crowd of people, but they don't know who you are. Don't be bashful. This is your first time and the way you dance now is going to influence all the dancing you ever do. If you act bashful when you start to dance, that habit is going to stay with you. If the other dancers are lively and are trotting around there like wild steers and you drag and aren't lively, you'll always dance like that. The leader is the one who is the best dancer. Watch your leader. Watch how he holds his hand up and do as he does. Don't watch the last man. Take short steps. Don't spread your legs. Don't have your head down. Look at your sticks. Keep the horns of your headdress in line. When you get over there and start to dance, you must be singing for yourself, humming a little."

Each Masked Dancer shaman would prepare four masked dancers. Each had an elaborate headdress with horns and sacred symbols, a deerskin skirt hung with charms and fringes, beautiful moccasins with the toes turned up, and a stick with symbols for Lightning and Moon and Sun. Cochise prepared also the Gray One, the clown who wore a mask of scraped rawhide with a big nose and big ears, with only moccasins and a G-string, and the rest of his body covered with white paint. The clown danced around the masked dancers, making people laugh—like Coyote showing that life is ridiculous and full of surprises. The Gray One made rude gestures and rolled on the ground, kicking in the air like a horse in a wallow, and danced all about in no particular order, making fun of everything. He was the servant and the messenger of the masked dancers, giving people instructions—telling the singers what songs the dancers wanted, telling people when to smoke tobacco, and carrying messages from a boy to the girl who had captured his heart.

But in some ways, the clown was the most powerful dancer of all, and was essential in any ceremony to cure sickness.

Cochise spent hours preparing the dancers, neglecting nothing. First they stood facing east while he smoked a first cigarette and prayed: "Under the heavens to the east, inside Big Star Mountain, can be seen the great Black Mountain Spirit. His body has been designed and the uprights of his headdress have been made with the big star. I use the sound of the Mountain Spirit rattling his headdress as he dances to the fire. By means of it, I walk the earth. It drives all evil away. With it, I perform this ceremony. With this, I walk. That is all."

Then he painted the lead dancer with the help of some others who used softened sticks, sometimes a finger, to apply the paint. Sometimes the dancers also painted one another. But Cochise directed every design, singing and praying and beating the drum as they worked, sometimes stepping forward himself to create a particularly important or intricate design on their bodies. He put his attention into the songs, for he could harm the dancers if he made even a small mistake out of lack of respect. His songs called on the Mountain Spirits to give the dancers strength, so they could dance for hours in the center of the circle of the People. He sang in this manner:

Inside the holy home
At the place called "Home in the turning Rock,"
The Mountain Spirits, truly holy,
Rejoice over me to the four directions.
And make sounds over me.

In the middle of the Holy Mountain,
In the middle of its body, stands a hut,
Brush-built for the Black Mountain Spirit.
White Lightning flashes in these moccasins;
White lightning streaks in angular path;
I am the lightning flashing and streaking!

This headdress lives; the noise of its pendants
Sounds and is heard!
My song shall encircle these dancers!

Cochise worked carefully so he would finish the painting just before sunset and the dancers would have time to eat a good meal provided by the feast makers. Below, in the camp, people had started a great fire for the ceremony and the social dancing to follow. When the people had begun to gather in eager anticipation of the entrance of the dancers, Cochise lined them up in a row facing east, each holding his headdress, as he blessed them. He sang very slowly:

Thus speaks the earth's thunder;
Because of it there is good about you,
Because of it your body is well
Thus speaks Earth's thunder.[4]

As he sang the dancers turned clockwise, calling out at each mention of the Mountain Spirits and motioning with their headdresses in the four directions in respect. When the songs had ended, they each spit into their buckskin masks four times, made three ritual passes over their faces with the masks, and then drew the masks over their heads on the fourth pass. Now they went down the hill toward the fire, led by the chief dancer. They came with their yellow buckskin skirts held in place by a broad belt with many pendants and sacred charms and their naked upper bodies and arms entirely painted, black, white, and yellow in narrow bands of color. Cochise also painted on them a branching design for the saguaro, a jagged row of peaks, a zigzag line, a triangle, crosses, a stepped line, and a four-pointed star—with different designs on different nights. Each dancer carried a pointed wooden stick in each hand. Tied at their elbows they wore long, buckskin streamers trailing eagle feathers. The mask was a buckskin hood drawn tight around the neck; it had small holes for the eyes and was painted black, or sometimes yellow and blue. Above the nose hung a piece of turquoise or abalone shell, so the dancers could enjoy the strength of the abalone. Prongs of soaked and shaped oak on top of the mask held a frame of yucca to make a branched structure of wooden slats on top of the head, from which dangled earrings that jangled musically as they moved. The headdresses were decorated also with turkey and eagle feathers, and the slats were colored black, yellow, green, and blue—but never red, for that would be a witch color.

Coming close to where the fire burned and the people waited, the masked dancers paused as people came to them for curing. The dancers would dance around each person for fifteen or twenty minutes as Cochise sang and drummed, blowing the sickness away. Then, when they had danced cures for everyone who sought their medicine, the dancers turned and all together burst into the open space around the fire. The people greeted them with a great cry of triumph and reverence—the trilling cry of the women recalling how the heart of White-Painted Woman had leapt up when her sons came home to her. They danced to each home, bringing the blessings of the Ga'an of whom they were an aspect. They went throughout the entire encampment, taking special care to dance in front of any home suffering from sickness or discord. Then they went around the fire four times, dancing high and proud, gesturing and singing in a way to scare sickness and bad luck away from the camp. After the dancers had arrived, no one could call any dancer by his name nor point with hands or lips to a dancer nor touch any dancer, lest the Mountain Spirits whose attention the dancers sought to attract should be angered by this show of disrespect.

The dancers now danced the way a warrior runs to battle, without fear or hesitation or fatigue. If they grew tired, they had only to pass the sacred sticks over their muscles and they would be restored. When the leader threw his arms out wide, the singers with drums and long memories and strong voices would begin—often taking their lead from Cochise, who watched his dancers and coordinated their steps with his strong, clear voice. He would speak the beginning of the song alone in his great voice and then everyone would join in the refrain, which they had learned through countless repetitions on countless nights such as this. In this way, the song rose and fell—first a single voice that pierced your heart like an eagle call, then a burst of melody like waters rushing over rocks which rose and peaked and died away again, yielding to the single voice. Each singer made his own songs, so the best singers were always in demand. The dancers responded to the songs as the leaves tremble before the wind, each song demanding a different step. The lead dancer must know the steps and the songs. First they would dance the free step, where each dancer improvised. Then they would dance the short step, with a rigid posture and staccato steps that gave them a rest so they could dance straight through to dawn. Finally they would dance the high step, forming a circle around the fire facing out as they strutted and pranced and flung themselves about to the delight of the onlookers. Often the onlookers called out for the high-step songs, but a skillful singer would not always yield

to the crowd lest he too quickly wear out his dancers. Cochise sang
the free-step song in this manner:

> At the place called "home in the Center of the Sky,"
> Inside is the home's holiness.
> The door to the home is of white clouds.
> There all the Gray Mountain Spirits
> Rejoining over me
> Kneel in the four directions with me.
>
> When first my Power was created,
> Pollen's body, speaking my words,
> Brought my Power into being,
> So I have come here.[5]

Sometimes in the headlong high-step songs, one whirling, leap-
ing dancer would collide with another or drop his stick. Then the
dancer would stagger about as though dazed, so the other dancers
would see the danger. Then they would line up single file and pray
to the wand he had dropped until it was safe for the leader to pick
up the stick and return it to the dancer.

In this way the masked dancers brought the blessings of the
Mountain Spirits on the camp. They showed their reverence and joy
in everything they wore, in every design on their bodies, in every
gesture, every step, every voice, every song—not becoming the Ga'an,
but securing their blessings for everyone present.

Eventually, the masked dancers would leave. Then the singers
would take up the social dance songs, for these ceremonies brought
together friends and relatives and allies eager for the feasting and
the blessing and the chance to socialize. The People were modest
and chaste, and no one respected those who were loose in their
ways. That was why boys who could watch sticks burn down on their
arms, run to the top of the mountain without swallowing a mouthful
of water, or dodge arrows as a game were nonetheless too ashamed to
say a word to a girl they desired. The social dances went on for hours
after every ceremony, giving the young people a chance to look at
one another, touch one another, and give gifts to one another as
tokens of their interest. They danced in circles, with girls on the
inside moving around the fire with an easy, sidewise step, and boys
around the outside moving with a longer step, shy and proud and
eager and abashed. One singer or another would offer a social song,
sometimes with clever verses to make the young people blush, and

sometimes with a single phrase like "What belongs to us?" which reminded everyone they were defined by their traditions and prayers and families, and not their possessions.

Many of the social dance songs made people laugh and wink, the young people flushed and the old people fondly remembering when such songs made them tongued-tied and embarrassed. So went one song:

> She married an old man
> With big buttocks!

Or

> I see that girl again,
> Then I become like this;
> I see my own sweetheart again,
> Then I become like this.
>
> Maiden, you talk kindly to me,
> You, I shall surely remember it,
> I shall surely remember you alone,
> Your words are so kind,
> You, I shall surely remember it.
>
> My sweetheart, we surely could have gone home,
> But you were afraid!
> When it was night we surely could have gone home,
> But you were afraid!

And when the singer interjected such a verse, Cochise would catch the eye of Dos-teh-seh and they would smile. They remembered when they had first found each other in the camp of Mangas Coloradas—Cochise a young warrior so serious and intent on earning a great name. They remembered how they had caught each other's eye and looked away blushing, and how Cochise had followed her sometimes when she went for water, longing after her but afraid to speak to her—though he would ride without pause through the bullets of a dozen Mexicans. Now Cochise watched his own sons dancing around the fire. Now he understood why he must risk everything in the war against the Mexicans, against the Whites: so the People might endure. He fought so the cycle of life and ceremonies might go on, comforting and shaping and teaching his children as it had taught him and his father and every one of the People since before

the first memory. Now they had cleared their enemies from their
land, so they could build a great fire with smoke visible for miles
and stay through four days of the ceremony, safe from their enemies because of the courage of their warriors and the reverence of
their prayers. Then the teasing, laughing voice of the singer pulled
Cochise again from his thoughts, and he laughed out loud as the
singer sang:

> Man from a distant land,
> Why do you talk to me?
> Why do you talk to me?
> Why do you talk to me?
> What have you done for me
> But just talk to me?[6]

The ceremonies restored Cochise's spirit, which had been
wounded by the death of each warrior who rode with him against
the White Eyes. Sometimes, when he thought the war was only to
avenge his brother and his father and others whom he loved, he
grew weary with the cost of it. But when the People gathered in
these dances, joyful and prayerful, he remembered why he fought
and what was at risk. Always, the counsels of the People were divided
between the war chiefs and the peace chiefs, having the same argument in its hundred forms. Some argued only peace could save the
People, for the old days had passed away forever and they must live
quietly in what space was left to them, depending on rations and
wood rats. Others argued this was only a slower death, which would
turn all the ceremonies into Ghost Dances and the glad call of
Mockingbird into the hooting of Owl. Cochise saw this was true as
he watched the girls blush and the boys strut as they had always
done. And beyond them the firelight reflected off the silently watching rocks, which had ever been the steady friends of the People.

When the four days of feasting and dancing had concluded,
Cochise resolved to consolidate the gains the warriors had made
against the Whites, so the Americans would not be tempted to reoc-
cupy the places they had abandoned. He knew this required a peace
with Sonora so they could continue to trade for guns and powder to
use against the Americans and have a place to camp where they
could store food. He took his band back down into Mexico, hoping
to make peace with Fronteras—for Chihuahua to the east was at war
with the Chihenne. Led by a strong fighter named Joaquin Terraza,

the Chihuahuans had hit the Chihenne hard—even killing the brother of Mangas Coloradas, who thereafter took the obligation of revenge all the more seriously. Chihuahua was now a killing field, patrolled by both soldiers and scalp hunters. Realizing he could not make peace with Janos while Mangas Coloradas fought them, Cochise sent an offer of peace to Fronteras through Yonis, whom he had taken into his wickiup as a wife after the death of his brother, her husband. The Sonorans agreed, promising safety and rations if the Chiricahua settled near Fronteras. The Sonorans had seen the death and destruction in neighboring Janos and among the Americans, and realized Cochise had become the leading man among the Chiricahua. Besides, they knew they could benefit from lucrative trade if the Chiricahua warriors brought the livestock and goods they plundered from the United States and Chihuahua. Cochise noted their answer and restrained his warriors from raiding in Sonora, but he did not move to Fronteras and accept rations—for he had not forgotten the poisoned rations that had made so many widows and orphans among the People already. Instead, he joined with Mangas Coloradas to raid in Chihuahua to replenish his supplies for when he would return to the Dragoons. But other subchiefs did take their bands to live near Fronteras, and through them disease soon spread to the camps of the People, claiming more lives than the guns of the soldiers. Cochise believed that the Mexicans spread these diseases among the People on purpose, by giving them blankets of people who had died in the plagues. The pox spread quickly, and in the season of the Ghost Dance, thirty-two Chiricahua living near Fronteras died—including seventeen irreplaceable warriors.

When his raiders had replenished their ammunition and taken enough beef from the Mexicans to feed their families, they left their women and children camped in a safe place and went north to continue the war. Cochise now turned his attention to one of the last settlements outside of Tucson, the Patagonia mines. He had been questioning captives and sending scouts to watch the mines ever since the soldiers had left Fort Buchanan, waiting for the right moment to drive off those miners as he had cleared Tubac. But the miners were well armed and the settlement was well fortified, with stone walls and loopholes for firing—so he waited. In the season of the Ghost Dance,[7] Cochise returned to the Dragoons and Chiricahuas, setting scouts out to constantly watch the mines. They also watched Tucson and San Xavier, the mission near Tucson where many tame

Papago and Pima lived. The warriors ran off 181 cattle from just outside Tucson, but lost several warriors when some Americans and a hundred angry Papago gave chase.

Cochise went out alone often, without fear, protected by his Power. One time he was riding along near Tucson when he saw a white man approaching on a fine horse. Cochise had known the man before the war. He was a rancher who had maintained friendly relations with the Chiricahua and had traded sometimes with them. Cochise rode carelessly up to him, his rifle across his saddle, eyeing the man's fine horse. He could see the man was wary, fingering his gun, but he stopped his horse and greeted Cochise in a friendly fashion—although his fear showed through plainly enough. Cochise made a sign of peace as he rode up to the man, keeping his eyes on the White's gun hand. Then, using only his knees, Cochise maneuvered his horse until the barrel of the rifle across his saddle was pointed at the man. With the smallest of motions, Cochise dropped his hand to the gun and pulled the trigger, shooting the man from his horse. The man fell with a groan and lay in the dirt. Cochise looked down at his enemy and wondered whether his need for revenge would burn out before it consumed him entirely—as it had Geronimo—leaving nothing but ash and melted metal. He considered finishing the man with a lance thrust, but decided to let him lie there, remembering he had not been a bad man—for a White. Cochise took the horse and rode away, his eyes moving along the ridges of the mountains he knew as well as the creases in his palm.[8]

Cochise sent out runners, hoping to assemble a large force to attack the mines, but the Nednhis were debilitated by outbreaks of disease and Mangas Coloradas was busy killing Mexicans, so he could not gather enough warriors. Instead, Cochise took his personal following and haunted the road to Tucson. They ambushed two men in a canyon near the mines—one of them a Delaware Indian and the other a White Eye. They killed the Indian in the first volley, but the White Eye ran quickly down to the end of the canyon, fighting with great courage as he retreated, shooting with a shotgun and a revolver. He had nearly reached safety when Cochise brought him down with a bullet through the thigh. He still tried to fight, but another warrior finished him with a bullet through the brain. Cochise was impressed by the way the White man fought—even with so little chance—so he ordered his warriors to leave the body alone so the brave man would have all his parts about him in the Happy

Place—if the Whites went to such a place. Maybe they just went to a deep hole where they dug for silver and gold, never seeing the sun. Cochise left the body where it lay and took the man's gun, which had a beautiful handle with an inlaid grip.

His scouts soon brought him word that a small contingent of soldiers had returned to Tucson, with different uniforms than the soldiers had worn before.[9] Some people said the White Eyes were busy fighting each other a long way off, but Cochise did not know whether to believe such a story. Even if they were, it did not seem to have made them any less reluctant to kill any warrior or woman or child of the People they encountered. He continued to move silently through the mountains near Tucson, hoping his ally, fear, would wear down the will of the Whites. He ambushed a small party leaving the mines, killing all seven people. The warriors butchered the oxen for the meat and took also a rifle, two pistols, and some gold they could use to trade with the Mexicans. Cochise also claimed a beautiful, big-chested, surefooted chestnut mare he rode for some while.

After several months, the gray soldiers who had moved into Tucson left again, perhaps discouraged they could do nothing against Cochise, who learned quickly of their departure and hurried to intercept them. The Chokonen had been camped near a White Mountain raiding party led by Francisco, who was a kinsman of Cochise because he had also married a daughter of Mangas Coloradas. They went together to Dragoon Springs, knowing the soldiers would struggle across the desert and camp near the springs at the abandoned ruin of the stage station, which the warriors had burned and scattered. They lay in wait and attacked the thirsty, weary soldiers, taking them by surprise. They killed four men and ran off thirty mules and twenty-five horses without suffering any loss. They celebrated this great victory that night, and Cochise took satisfaction in knowing the soldiers would remember they had been beaten and would not come back.

Soon Chihenne runners came to the camps of the Chokonen with a request for help from Mangas Coloradas, who was having a hard time with the soldiers who had returned to his territory. Many soldiers had come into New Mexico from the east, occupying Santa Fe and opening up forts that had been abandoned. Some said these were soldiers having a war with other Whites, but mostly they seemed interested in killing the People. The warriors had shadowed them and run off their horses. The gray soldiers had retaliated by hunting down anyone they could find—even crossing the border into Mexico to chase raiding parties. They took no prisoners. When they did surprise a band and took prisoners, they executed everyone—warriors, women, and children.[10] Cochise took his warriors east to support Mangas Coloradas, for they had long been as the fingers of one fist. They struck the gray soldiers hard. After a time, these soldiers mostly left the towns and forts and marched off north, so it seemed the Chiricahua had again won their war with the Whites.[11] The Chokonen raided awhile in New Mexico before retreating again to the Chiricahuas, where no White Eyes dared to venture.

Cochise returned to disturbing news. The shaman with Lightning Power who had the ceremonies to negate the protection of the iron used by the Whites had died some months previously, taking with him his ceremonies and wisdom. Now many soldiers had entered Tucson from the west, wearing the old uniforms with hundreds of wagons.[12] In the season of Many Leaves,[13] his scouts warned him that a small party of soldiers was approaching Apache Pass from the west. Warriors hurried to intercept them in the pass. They waited until the three soldiers had dismounted to water their horses before shooting from their hidden positions, killing one man and wounding another. The man not hit in the first volley jumped on his horse and, ignoring the pleas of the wounded man, spurred his horse out of the pass. Several warriors gave chase, crying out happily, "Let's have a race. *Mucha buena mula, mucho bravo Americano.*"[14] But he had a good horse and many bullets and wounded several warriors who came up too close behind him in the six hours they chased him.

Now Cochise turned west to face this new threat, scarcely believing the rumors that filtered through to him about the great numbers of soldiers who had returned to Tucson. He sent word to Mangas Coloradas, saying that the soldiers had returned in greater numbers than ever, in hopes his old ally and kinsman would rally once more to his side, for they had always burned as two fires in one ring of stones.

Cochise set scouts out to watch the approaches to Apache Pass, knowing the soldiers must come through there. He was determined to make them pay so dearly for the passage that they would reconsider whether they wanted to take back Chokonen land they had abandoned at the cost of so much blood.

He did not know then that Power and luck and pity had turned against him. He did not know then that the year during which the Chokonen had been masters of their own land was but a lull in a storm stretching beyond the furthest horizon. He did not know then that his Power and his strength and his courage had only been tempered in all of the loss and pain of his life for the time just ahead. Now he must face a foe greater than the Giant, although he had not the breath of Power that could shatter a tree. He wondered whether the People had done something to bring this on themselves, like the people who had gone to Snake's Water and found the spring flowed no longer. Sometimes he would go and sit at Snake's Water and think on this, trying to understand the nature of the offense he had committed that the Whites had come back. He could not think what he had done, but nonetheless resolved to keep his courage and do all things in a right and prayerful manner. That was surely the lesson of Snake's Water, which whispered to him as the Ga'an whispered to Tipping Beetle. For when he also listened to the Ga'an through the stones through the sky, he knew that he had set out on the path of Child-of-the-Water and could not turn aside now, though the Giant should blot out the sun and the springs go dry. For he was now the shield of his people, gripped in their hands. He had come to the deep box canyon of his life, with his enemies gathered at the only entrance and no place left to go but back through them—singing his death song.

10

Battle of Apache Pass: Return of the Americans

Coyote Helps Lizard Hold up the Sky

Coyote went along and came to an old tree, a tall one, with all the limbs off, standing there like a post. He saw a lizard up there, a fat brown lizard.

He stopped under there and looked at him. He said, "I'm a person who eats nothing but fat. Come down here and let me eat you."

Lizard answered, "Old man, don't talk that way. The whole sky is going to fall on us. I'm here because this tree is holding up the sky and I'm holding up the tree." Then Lizard said, "Catch on! Hold it! I'm tired."

Coyote grabbed hold of the tree. The clouds were moving, and every once in a while as he watched the sky it looked as if that post was falling.

Lizard said, "You hold it while I go and get some fellows to help us."

So he went off. Coyote was there alone. He was holding that tree with all his might and main. Every once in a while he got scared and looked up. He thought the sky was falling. He stood there all day and was pretty nearly all in. He began looking for some hollow place to go into before the sky could fall. He was nearly ready to run for it.

Finally he just jumped and ran to a hollow place. He lay there frightened, looking up, and then ran as fast as he could to another hollow place. He did this, going from hollow to hollow, until he got to a bank, and he saw that the sky wasn't going to fall after all. Then he went on his journey again.

Cochise sent out runners to all of the allied bands and set out scouts to watch all of the approaches to Apache Pass. He knew any force of soldiers entering Chokonen territory would go first to Dra-

goon Springs and then forty miles across a hard and waterless stretch
to Apache Pass. Cochise set a watch on both places, waiting for his
allies to gather. Then scouts brought word that a strong force of soldiers—perhaps 140—was already approaching Apache Pass.[1] Cochise
gathered up his following and hurried there, praying to his Power
and stripping his mind down to the fight ahead, for a warrior casts
aside everything but his weapons before a battle.

The warriors took up positions where they could watch the soldiers, who were careless as they reached the springs. They let their
horses loose without many guards and went about in small parties,
pitching their tents here and there and neglecting the thorough
scouting and posting of sentries any experienced war party would
have used. They did not seem prepared for a fight, but Cochise did
not seriously consider making peace with them. The death of his
brother had set his course long ago, as a man picks out the distant
mountain to guide him across the desert. Some warriors set to watch
the soldiers took an opportunity to kill four of them who wandered
too far from the main body, which was camped near the abandoned
stage station. The shooting alarmed the soldiers, but the *nantan*
nonetheless put out a white flag to show he wanted to talk.

An hour later, Cochise came, mounted on a white stallion with
his fine rifle with silver inlaid stock, two pistols, and seventy-five
warriors—their guns and lances flashing in the sunlight. He rode up
close enough to shout to the *nantan*, careful not to put himself in
the power of the Americans ever again in his life. When the *nantan*
came out, exposing himself to their fire, Cochise rode forward to
parley backed by a dozen trusted warriors.

The *nantan* greeted him in a friendly manner, just as Bascom
had done when he had no cause for war. The *nantan* said, "We wish
to be friends of the Apache. At the present, my men and I are the
only ones traveling through your country and we desire that you not
interfere with my men or animals. There is a great captain in Tucson with a large number of soldiers who wishes to have a talk with
all the Apache chiefs and make peace with them and give them
presents."[2]

Cochise listened to this speech with amused contempt, wondering whether the White Eyes really believed he was such a child he
would step again into the snare of their lies. But he kept the anger
and the hatred away from his face, as one would ignore a wound.

"We wish to live in peace as well," he said, his eyes glittering. "I will return later and we can talk further," he added, wishing he might see this man's smooth, ugly face when he found the bodies of the soldiers, already stripped, shot through the chest, and lanced through the neck. He often had trouble telling one White from another, in part because so many grew hair all over their faces like beasts. They stank and rarely washed and covered themselves with filthy clothing. The People never failed to bathe when there was water anywhere close, giving themselves sand baths by rubbing vigorously all over their bodies with fine, clean sand when they could find no water. When they were in camp, they would walk several miles away to defecate, while the stinking water from foul toilets of the Whites and the Mexicans often ran down the streets in their towns. But it only made it more galling that such an ugly people so without personal pride should think they might take the land of the Chokonen. Nonetheless, Cochise gravely accepted the presents of tobacco and food, appreciating the irony but also wondering that these fools thought so little of the People that they sought to pay their deep debt of blood with a little tobacco. So he rode away to join the many hidden warriors keeping watch on the soldier camp. Soon the soldiers found the bodies of the missing men, and hastily struck camp to move to a place easier to defend. The warriors followed them, and that night shot into their camp, wounding one man and killing a horse. The soldiers left quickly, going through the pass to the east.

Cochise began his preparations in earnest, taking heed of the warning the *nantan* had given that more soldiers were coming soon from the west. Mangas Coloradas, with Victorio and Lozen and his many warriors, arrived soon. Along with him came Juh and Geronimo and many Nednhi warriors. Cochise could sense the convergence of their Power and began to hope they might stand together and drive the soldiers back before they could set down their stubborn roots, tenacious as a cottonwood in a rocky streambed. The war leaders of the gathered bands met in council to plan their strategy for the approach of the soldiers. They decided to build rock fortifications on the hills overlooking the spring in Apache Pass and wait there for the soldiers. They knew the soldiers must cross forty waterless miles in the hottest season of the year and so would come carelessly to the spring. And even when they found the spring defended, they must press up to it or perish—for they could not cross the desert again without water. They would throw themselves against the bullets and arrows of the warriors well concealed and behind good cover on the slopes above. Several hundred warriors had gathered now from all of the allied bands of the Chiricahua—all in the grip of the war Power of their greatest warriors—so they believed no one could break them here in the heart of their own country.

Now the soldiers came into the trap Cochise had so carefully prepared, just as his Power had told him, watched by the warriors set out to shadow them. A large force with many wagons stopped at Dragoon Springs,[3] but the warriors did not molest them so they would not be on their guard when they reached Apache Pass. Then the larger part of the soldiers set out in the darkness for Apache Pass, sixty-eight men with some of the livestock and two heavy black tubes on wagon wheels. They crossed Sulphur Springs Valley in a grueling nineteen-hour march and came straggling into Apache Pass with the sun directly overhead, thirsty and tired and eager for the water.

But things quickly began to go wrong. First some warriors spoiled the trap by attacking the rear of the column, trying to drive off the livestock. The soldiers kept their discipline and turned back around quickly. The warriors killed one man and wounded a wagon driver, but the soldiers rallied and drove off the warriors, killing four.[4] Now alert, the soldiers escorted the wagon train and livestock to the ruins of the stage station just down the canyon from the spring. Still, Cochise felt hopeful. The horses and cattle could not last long without water, so the soldiers must still come to the springs—and the waiting warriors would extract a heavy toll of them there.

The *nantan* knew his business, now that he knew he camped between the high ridges of danger. He deployed his men carefully—spread out across the narrow canyon—and moved cautiously toward the spring. As the soldiers approached, the warriors opened fire from their well-hidden position, killing one man and wounding another. The soldiers did not press the attack, but fell back out of easy rifle range. Now the *nantan* sent strong parties up the hillside along the ridge, hoping to flank the positions of the warriors overlooking the spring. But they ran into strong fire from the warriors Cochise had placed there to prevent his enemy from going around the flanks. The soldiers even brought a brave dog with them, which ran all over the slope, his barking showing the soldiers where the warriors were hidden—until one of the warriors shot off that dog's toe, sending him yelping back to the soldiers. Cochise had prepared his defenses carefully and the soldiers could not get around behind the warriors. But now the soldiers rolled out a surprise, which turned the battle against Cochise.

They brought up the great guns on wheels and began to shoot giant bullets that exploded after they struck. The bullets arched up into the air and came down on top of the breastworks overlooking the spring behind which the warriors waited. The shells exploded with a terrible noise, scattering fragments everywhere—even shattering the rocks themselves. The warriors shrank down behind their rock barricades, steeling their nerves against these deadly explosions. They waited for the shooting to stop, thinking the soldiers could not have carried an endless supply of such large bullets. But the shooting went on and on for more than two hours, the injuries among the warriors mounting. Finally Cochise passed the word to the warriors to pull back from the face of the slope to positions where they would have more protection from the guns on wheels.[5] After about four hours of fighting, the warriors withdrew out of range and the soldiers moved cautiously forward to the springs, watering their stock and filling canteens and barrels with water. Cochise watched them with dismay, for despite the advantage of numbers and terrain the warriors had killed only two soldiers, wounded four, and kept them from water for a few hours.

Watching from the high ground, Mangas Coloradas saw several soldiers from the rear of the column go galloping back to the west, to get the many soldiers coming along behind. Frustrated at the course of the battle, feeling the doubts of his warriors, Mangas Coloradas seized the opportunity for action and summoned several warriors to go with him after the three men. They rode along a back path to the entrance of the pass, hoping to cut off the soldiers before they could escape. They nearly came too late, and the soldiers had a lead on them. The warriors pressed their horses, coming up close enough so one of the bullets of Mangas Coloradas brought down the horse on which the hindmost soldier rode. The other Whites cast frightened looks over their shoulders, but fled on out of the pass. Seeing they could not overtake these others, Mangas Coloradas turned to console himself with killing the one man who had fallen into their hands. The warriors surrounded the man, who took cover behind the body of his horse and began shooting. The warriors worked their way in closer, waiting until he ran out of ammunition or had to reload so they could rush him. But he had a good gun, which seemed never to need reloading. Then he made a lucky shot, hitting Mangas Coloradas and inflicting a dangerous wound. The other warriors hurried to the great chief and carried him to safety, desperate to take him to a shaman, their confidence shaken because Mangas Coloradas's Power had not protected him against a single soldier with a good gun.

The Chihenne were dismayed when they learned Mangas Coloradas was badly wounded. Most of the Chihenne left that night, seeing they had no longer the Power of Mangas Coloradas to protect them. A large party of Chihenne warriors took him down to Janos, where there was a Mexican doctor of great skill who had been friendly to the People. The warriors went to that man's house with their grievously wounded chief, warning the doctor they would kill everyone in the city if he failed to save the chief or performed witchcraft on him in his weakened condition.

Cochise felt his own courage sag when he saw his father-in-law's wound and watched the Chihenne depart. But he held his Chokonen in the grip of his Power and would not yet leave the pass to the Americans. In the night the warriors returned to their position on the hills overlooking the spring. But in the morning, the soldiers brought out their guns on wheels once again and Cochise realized the battle was lost, that he could not keep the soldiers from the water. He pulled his men back out of danger. The rear guard of the soldiers had come into the pass during the night, so now they had cavalry as well.

Cochise moved his men away from the pass, wary lest more soldiers coming from other directions should trap him in a bad place. He set out scouts in all directions to look for danger and to keep track of the soldiers, moving now unmolested through the land Child-of-the-Water had given the Chokonen. The soldiers left the pass quickly, but within several weeks a strong party returned and built a fort in Apache Pass, overlooking the spring. They left a hundred men, well mounted and well armed, to guard the approach to the spring and hunt down any raiders who attacked the growing number of wagons now on the old stage road. Warriors set to watch the soldiers killed one man who wandered too far from the walled fort as they built it, but most of the soldiers stayed safely in large groups behind their fortifications.[6]

The warriors watched the road, attacking the unwary. Cochise's sentries warned him of one party of nine men coming into the pass from the east, their progress clear from the dust raised by the hooves of their horses when they were still nearly a day's ride away. A party of warriors concealed themselves in a gully in the flat terrain just before the pass, where the riders would not yet expect an ambush. The gully was seven feet deep, four yards wide, and a quarter mile long, but you could not see it until you had ridden right up to the edge. When the men approached, the warriors sprang up and killed eight of them in the first round of shooting—most of them before they could raise their guns from their laps. They captured one man alive and tied him to a post, burning him as though he were a witch. Cochise knew he must once again call on his old ally—fear—to make the White Eyes understand the price they would pay if they wanted to take land that was not theirs, whose places they did not know.

Now the main body of soldiers came through the Chokonen country and on into Chihenne country, so many soldiers Cochise did not even consider attacking them. The soldiers returned to all of the old forts—and built new ones. They began to move ceaselessly about the country, killing any band they encountered, not caring whether that band had been raiding or not. Some bands approached them with white flags, hoping to make peace now that the soldiers had returned in such numbers. Even these the soldiers shot down without stopping to talk.[7]

Everywhere, the war had turned against the People. The soldiers came like the spring flood that escapes its banks and spreads out, changing everything. Cochise struck at them until his arms grew weary, but the water only closed over the cut he had made with his strongest blow. Now he was on the defensive once again. The battle at Apache Pass had convinced him that he could not stand upright against even a relatively small band of soldiers—not even when he had an advantage in numbers of three or four to one. For the Americans were good fighters, well led and disciplined. More important, they had good guns and lots of bullets. They could be careless in their use of bullets, as one would cast handfuls of pebbles just to see them spatter in the water.

Cochise struggled a long while, trying to decide what he should do. Going out alone to pray and seek the guidance of his Power, his horse brought him to a place where the burned snag of a cotton-wood tree loomed against the sky. That tree reminded him of the time Lizard had saved himself by tricking Coyote into pushing on the tree to hold up the sky. Now Cochise understood this story, which had worked on him all these years, waiting for this moment. When his warriors had driven the soldiers from their fort, he thought the People were as the Giant. But they had always been Child-of-the-Water—small and dependent on Power and courage to survive. Now they were Lizard, trapped out in the open by their hungry enemy. They could not overpower such a one as Coyote, with his long white teeth set against the tiny teeth of a lizard. They must rely on strategy, like Lizard. Cochise went back to his camp after thanking the tree and the story, better understanding every day the wisdom of the People who remembered such stories. He resolved not to again make the mistake of fighting the Whites head on. Besides, he knew now what lay ahead. They would keep coming, no matter how many he killed. Now each warrior was even more precious. He could not afford anymore to trade the lives of his men for the fear of the Whites—for the Americans would not simply go home. He must ration his warriors, like a man two days from water with only a swallow in the water skin. He must go where the soldiers were not, strike when they did not expect it, and leave no sign of his passing. No more would the People gather in their hundreds for ceremonies and feasts, sending up a column of smoke from the ceremonial fire for four days running. Now they must camp again in their secret places, moving often and never neglecting their sentries. They must kill quickly and silently and rely on Power to keep them out of the path of their enemy.

Cochise turned to this new war with a heavy heart, but without hesitation. What other course lay open to him? Had he not promised with his first steps to walk in the path of Child-of-the-Water? Had not that child gone out to face Buffalo and Antelope and Eagle and the Giant—just a boy with a bow and the favor of Power? Could he do less now, with the eyes of the People and the gaze of his own sons turned toward him?

11

Death of Mangas Coloradas: The Shadow of the Giant

Coyote and Dog Argue

Some dogs were out in the woods. Some coyotes came to the dogs.

One of the coyotes said, "Why don't you dogs come and join us out in this wilderness? We live out here, happy, free. We eat all kinds of wild fruits. No one abuses us. We live among the little bushes and live very happily, free from getting whipped or scolded!"

One dog said, "Ho, we live with some people and they take good care of us. We live on meat and fat that they bring us. We sleep in a camp with these Indians. They tell us, 'My dogs, I love you.' They take very good care of us."

Then the coyote told him, "We've heard you dogs from the hills; they have been whipping you dogs, and we have heard you crying over there."

Then the dog said to the coyote, "We all have to learn to obey our masters. Sometimes we don't obey; that's the only time we get a whipping."

Coyote said, "They whip you just the same."

Dog told them, "You live out in the woods and have many enemies."

Coyote said, "We eat nothing but fat out in the woods, all kinds of meats are what we eat. We eat prickly pears, yucca fruit, and all kinds of wild fruits." Then Coyote told him, "We hear you get whippings all the time anyhow. We hear you crying all the time they are whipping you."

But Dog said, "We get plenty of meat and a good place to sleep. We do not have to dodge anyone the way you do. We cannot agree with you that we should go back to the woods with you."

Mangas Coloradas—the greatest war leader in memory, whose Power and shrewd strategy had formed alliances with so many squabbling bands—seemed changed by his wound. He recovered slowly, so the Chihenne did not harm anyone in Janos. It seemed he had made a journey to a far place and returned reluctantly with grim tidings. The Chihenne and Chokonen continued to raid, sometimes together, but mostly in smaller bands, harder for the soldiers to follow and trap. Sometimes Cochise would stay a while in the camp of his father-in-law, for Dos-teh-seh worried about him now—seeing his hair so gray, his eyes so distant, his giant frame hollowed out like a sotol stalk rattling with bees. He talked about the battles he had fought, making oblique reference to the great warriors and chiefs whose names he could no longer openly speak. He and Cochise talked long—as they had always done—about how to protect their people.

Cochise was dismayed to find that Mangas Coloradas had grown weary of fighting, having lost faith in the outcome. He said the Mexicans could never be trusted, for the hatred between them was too deep and too long, like two great trees grown so into each other that they must be cut down together. A peace with the Mexicans was only the musk smeared on the jaws of the trap to lure the People in close enough to kill. Moreover, the People could not survive a long war with both the Mexicans and the Americans, trapped like a low sandbar between two rivers. Even if they could somehow sustain the steady loss of warriors, they could not survive through many cycles of the seasons with the White Eyes and the Mexicans both chasing them, destroying the caches of food on which they must survive through the season of the Ghost Dance. The People must find a way to make peace with the Whites, who might be trusted to honor their agreements if the leaders could restrain the warriors from any raiding north of the border. Cochise argued a long time with Mangas Coloradas, reminding him of Kirker and Johnson and Bascom and the miners at Pinos Altos and of the way the soldiers now killed people even under a flag of truce. Better to continue to trick and manipulate the Mexicans, who were confused and greedy and divided enough to give the People an opening. Even if the Whites gave the People a little bit of land on which they could live, they would all be like the dogs who traded a warm bed for whippings over which they had no control. But after a time Cochise could see that his words were wasted, a distant sound Mangas Coloradas could no longer hear clearly. Cochise stopped arguing with his father-in-law, respecting the decision that the Power of Mangas Coloradas seemed intent on forcing upon him.

Sometimes Cochise would stalk him with places, shooting the arrows of those stories at Mangas Coloradas.[1] He would find ways to mention places with stories about people who had placed trust too easily or neglected their obligations or grown tired and careless. Once he found the opportunity to recount the story of the argument between Coyote and Dog, hoping that the story would work on Mangas Coloradas so he would not play the part of the dog. But Mangas Coloradas would counter by mentioning places whose stories taught about protecting the helpless or not remaining flexible and clever. This stalking of each other revived Mangas Coloradas a bit, for he was a master of talking in places and the complex stringing together of lessons and places, beautiful and intricate as beadwork on a dress of white buckskin. Only Cochise could have matched wits with Mangas Coloradas in this way, each trying to find the places that would win their point—all in the respectful indirection of talking in places, which avoided confrontation or direct criticism. Still, it grieved Cochise to see so great a warrior thinking in this fashion, and he remembered with a sharp pang how dismayed he had been as a young warrior when his own father had begun to talk in a wistful way about peace with the Mexicans. He remembered too well what tragedy that thinking had caused for his father and his band, like a man who loses heart to pray and goes about with the carelessness of despair—not looking where he puts his feet, like the girl in the story who went to gather wood.

Mangas Coloradas went back to Chihenne country with his family and his personal following, chasing a rumor some White Eyes had camped near Santa Rita del Cobre, saying they wanted to talk to the Chihenne. Mangas Coloradas talked it over with his subchiefs. Victorio and Lozen pleaded with him not to go into the camp of the Whites. So did Geronimo, who was camped with Mangas Coloradas with the dwindling remnants of the Bedonkohe, who had been nearly all killed in Mexico. But Mangas Coloradas was adamant, as though Power talked so loudly in his ear he could not hear the others. He went to the Whites, trusting in the white flag they offered—as Cochise had trusted in Bascom. But they seized him, saying they were only passing through Chihenne territory and would keep him close to them until they were safely through it.

Perhaps that was what they intended at the first. But soldiers came along soon after and took charge of Mangas Coloradas, who saw his death coming on quickly. He withdrew his mind from the soldiers, so his thinking would be smooth and steady no matter what they did. The *nantan* was a small, fierce, strong-fighting man who hated the People. He gave Mangas Coloradas over to the guards, saying that he must not escape—and adding that he must not live. During the night, the two guards amused themselves by heating their bayonets in the fire and holding the glowing metal against the feet of Mangas Coloradas. He ignored them for as long as he could, remembering the places that knew him and recalling the Mexicans and the White Eyes he had killed. But finally he rose up on his elbow and said to the two guards in his strong voice, "I am not a child that you should play with me." Shamed by him, they shot him. The *nantan* was well satisfied and they buried Mangas Coloradas nearby. But then they thought perhaps they had not done enough to him, so they dug him up again and cut off his head and boiled it in a pot, so they could keep his great skull. After that, soldiers went to find his followers, who were camped not far off waiting to see whether they might have peace. The soldiers fell upon them without warning, killing nine people, including Mangas Coloradas's son, and wounding his wife, the mother of Dos-teh-seh.[2] The soldiers happily scalped the people they had killed, even the women and children, and hung the hair from their bridles.

The news fled quickly to Cochise when Geronimo and the bits of the Bedonkohe came to join the Chokonen, for the Chihenne were nearly broken and scattered and hard-pressed in their own territory. Dos-teh-seh cut her hair off ragged with grief, keening and moaning a long while in missing her father and her brother—mourning the lost hopes of a free people. Cochise hardly knew what to do, for he was so full of anger and vengeance and grief already that he did not see how he could hold any more. But then he heard that the soldiers had cut off the head of the one whose name he could no longer speak and boiled it in a pot—so the father of his wife must go headless in the Happy Place. Cochise resolved to kill any White that fell into his hands, and do to each of them as they had done to Mangas Coloradas. After that, he tortured his prisoners more often and mutilated their bodies, cutting off their heads and hearts and testicles. Cochise renewed the oath of vengeance he had taken for his father and his brothers—helpless otherwise to ease the grief of his wife for her family.

Soon after he heard of the death of his father-in-law, Cochise went to Fort Bowie, sending emissaries to pretend they were seeking peace so they could gather information about the number and strength of the soldiers. The garrison there now numbered eighty— too strong to attack between their thick adobe walls on the high ground overlooking the spring. He faded away into the stone dream of the Chiricahuas. Power was with him in this, for the soldiers soon received orders to seize any of the People appearing under a flag of truce and make even women and children prisoners.[3] Now,[4] Cochise took his people back down into Mexico—perhaps three hundred strong. He sent out scouts to find out how things stood with Fronteras, which was guarded by only thirty soldiers, for the Sonorans had not much protection and not many soldiers. Other Chokonen bands were camped near Fronteras, having fled Janos after they were attacked by soldiers there. These Chokonen headmen had nearly three hundred people in their bands and said the Sonorans were frightened and ready for peace, but Cochise did not trust them and so made no treaty. Nonetheless, he held his warriors back from raiding in Sonora so they would not stir up the soldiers or make trouble for the friendly bands already living there. He took his people to stay in the Sierra Madre, camping alongside Juh's Nednhis. Geronimo and Juh were strong allies and Cochise respected Juh's Power and his fighting spirit.

Cochise sought to stay quietly in the Sierra Madre, remembering his principal aim now was to kill Americans to punish them for what they had done to Mangas Coloradas and to his brother. But the weakness of the Sonorans was a great temptation to some of the war leaders, who said the Mexicans were fighting other Whites far to the south.[5] Some bands raided in Sonora, prompting the Sonorans to offer a new scalp bounty and to cut off trade with many of the Chiricahua and Chihenne bands. Cochise then did a little raiding in Sonora, but mostly he went quietly on raids among the Americans— for the big American horses could be traded for food and bullets in Sonora. Many warriors also eagerly traded horses for whiskey, which made them violent and quarrelsome when they returned to their camps. But despite the uncertainty and risk of remaining in Sonora,

Fort Bowie ruins. After the disastrous confrontation between Cochise and Bascom, the army built a fort near the critical spring in the heart of the strategic Apache Pass. The fort served as a major staging ground for the army in the war with Cochise, but was abandoned in the early 1900s. The haunting ruins now lie silent and rarely visited at the end of a five-mile hike.
(Peter Aleshire)

news of the campaign of the Americans filtered down to him, keeping Cochise's band in place. Soldiers hit one mixed band of Chokonen and Bedonkohe camped on the Rio Bonita in New Mexico, killing twenty-five people before anyone had a chance to parley or surrender. Cochise kept the women and children in Sonora, restrained raiding there, and raided cautiously across the border. Once Cochise went all the way to Fort Bowie and ran off the horse herd, staying ahead of the soldiers who chased the war party all the way back down into Mexico.

Cochise kept his band moving in Mexico, spending most of their time in the Sierra Madre—but sometimes going down to Fronteras to trade. The Sonorans seemed frightened and unpredictable and many of the Chokonen, Bedonkohe, and Chihenne bands camped near the Mexican towns were wary and hostile when Cochise brought his own following close. Some of the Chihenne—and even some of the Chokonen—offered to guide the Sonoran soldiers against Cochise. But although these treacherous people led the soldiers here and there seeking Cochise's Chokonen, they had little success. Perhaps they did not truly wish to find Cochise. Nonetheless, after returning from a raid on the Americans with goods to trade, some of his sub-chiefs camped near Fronteras. But instead of trading, soldiers from Fronteras attacked them, killing several warriors and several women. Cochise led a raid on Fronteras, killing anyone he could. After that, the tenuous peace that some of the bands had fashioned with Fronteras came to pieces like an old shirt, and the war resumed. At the same time, Chihuahua offered its scalp bounty, so the People were hunted everywhere on both sides of the border. The full resumption of the war with the Mexicans fell heaviest on the Nednhis, who lived mostly in Mexico and so could not escape easily across the border. The bands that lived near Carrizelenos and Janos were devastated, and only the Nednhi bands that remained mostly in the Sierra Madre—like Juh's—survived the new offensive.

Cochise now resolved to live along the border, so he could move back and forth depending on which army pursued him most closely. Sometimes the Americans and the Sonorans would cross the border on a fresh trail, but they usually broke off the chase if Cochise went far enough beyond the border. So he remained hidden in the north-south running mountains on both sides of the border, remaining invisible in the vicinity of the camps where he had hidden the women and children. They would ride hundreds of miles to raid, then scatter so they could not be tracked back to the camps of the children.

Galled by the constant raids, the Americans mounted a great campaign against the Chokonen and the Chihenne, who had regrouped under Victorio and Lozen and a grizzled war chief named Loco. Some said Loco got his name because he was crazy for killing Mexicans. One side of his face drooped, for when he was a young warrior he had surprised a grizzly that mauled him before he killed it with his knife. This was a Powerful thing, for the People feared and deeply respected bears, which some people said were sometimes an aspect of the spirit of a dead warrior. Victorio and Loco had become the leading men among the Chihenne, trying to fill the great gap in the ranks of that band created by the loss of Mangas Coloradas. Cochise and his Chokonen raided with them, combining forces for a big strike and then scattering to throw off the inevitable pursuit. Often they would go to Cook's Canyon to wait for opportunities, as Cochise and Mangas Coloradas had once done.

In the season of Large Fruit,[6] they attacked a supply train with an eight-man escort. The soldiers abandoned three wagons and nineteen mules, but killed four warriors while suffering only four wounded themselves. Two weeks later, a force of more than two hundred Chokonen and Chihenne ambushed a detachment of soldiers in Cook's Canyon, killing one man and wounding several others. But the soldiers circled their wagons and held off the warriors in five hours of skirmishing. Cochise directed his warriors to fire the grass, hoping to stampede the horses, but the grass was too wet to burn. The warriors split up to attack from three directions, Cochise directing the attack from high ground where the subchiefs could see his signals. Few other leaders could have coordinated such an attack—only Juh and Victorio among the Chiricahua still living. Hard pressed, the soldiers gave way and retreated out of the canyon, abandoning their wagons and horses. Satisfied with this windfall of supplies and stock, Cochise let them go—he would not trade the lives of his warriors for the lives of soldiers.

After this, the Americans built a fort in Cook's Canyon, placing in it a strong force of soldiers.[7] Cochise left Chihenne territory and returned to the Chiricahuas. There he could remain hidden in the deep, forested canyons whose places he knew, so he could journey through that whole country in his mind, opening himself to the wisdom of those places as he went from one to the other. He did this sometimes when he needed guidance and his Power was off somewhere attending to the business of Power. Now he camped in the Chiricahuas near Fort Bowie—careful the soldiers should not know he was there—and went to watch the fort from a hidden high place for several days running, until he had learned their pattern. Then he led seventy-five warriors out of the rocks at just the right time to steal the whole horse herd from the fort before vanishing back into the mountains, easily eluding the attempts of the dismounted soldiers to find him. He remained awhile longer in the Chiricahuas, until the accumulated effect of his raids had so aroused the soldiers that they sent more men from a long ways off, then he slipped back down into Mexico.

Cochise would have liked to find a remote campsite and simply remain hidden, until the efforts to kill him faded some. But the war on two fronts had taken a toll on the People—especially in their effort to accumulate enough food to get through the winter. They could no longer go openly among the oaks to gather the acorn harvest or on the slopes dotted with agave to cut out the great, sweet hearts of that plant to bake mescal. Nor could they safely remain in one place long enough to dig the dip-roasting pits and prepare the mescal. The soldiers and the settlers who had returned in their wake had once again driven off the game. Only the cattle and sheep and grain brought back from the raids held starvation at bay—even in the good months when they should have been piling up surpluses to carry them through the season of the Ghost Dance.[8] The raiding had become essential to survival, for they had not enough bullets to use all of their guns. Usually the warriors fought with bows and lances against the good guns of their enemies. Even so, many of the warriors said only the strong Power of Cochise saved them from extermination. Every time they came across other bands, they heard new stories about Nednhi and Chokonen and Chihenne bands camping in some out-of-the-way place when the Americans or Mexicans wiped them out. Sometimes bands tried to move further north to get out of the way of the Americans—but then they were attacked by the Navajo, who were also hard pressed in their own land by the soldiers. The Bedonkohe had nearly ceased to exist, their few warriors raiding now with the other bands. Word filtered in that the Sonorans from Bavispe had wiped out a Nednhi camp near Janos, killing 21 and capturing 7—mostly women and children. Then the Americans found a Chokonen camp in Turkey Canyon in the Chiricahuas and killed 30 people, just as the band had set out for Sonora to make peace and take their chances there.

The Bedonkohe leader, Luis, led a war party to the mines at Pinos Altos, but found the soldiers ready for them. In that battle the soldiers killed 13 of the 18 warriors, including Luis and 9 Chokonen warriors. Some Mexicans in the fight scalped all the dead warriors and took their hair down to Chihuahua to sell it. The war party had been driven to the risk of the raid on a strong settlement with soldiers nearby because their families were starving, their clothing in rags, their stock all run off or eaten up, and their ammunition exhausted.[9] Some relatives of the dead men raised a raiding party and ran off the horse herd from the camp of the soldiers who had killed Luis, but those soldiers followed them back to Mount Graham, where the Mountain Spirits live. The raiders had rejoined the camp of Cochise, some 250 strong. But camping in that holy place brought them no luck, for the soldiers found their camp and attacked them at dawn, killing 21 people. Cochise rallied the warriors and skirmished with the soldiers to give the women and children time to escape up the steep canyons. But his whole force of warriors had only a few guns with bullets among them, and they could do no more than make the soldiers come on slowly from caution.

Seeing how the wind now howled around the ears of the People, Cochise sent runners to the scattered bands to mount a strong war party to avenge the many deaths of that season. He led nearly two hundred warriors quietly to Doubtful Canyon near Stein's Peak, where he set an ambush. Some sixty soldiers came along into that ambush, which Cochise sprang on them just after they passed the abandoned stage station in the canyon. They took the soldiers entirely by surprise, but only wounded four in the first volley because they had so few guns. The soldiers rallied, pouring bullets on the warriors, who fought back for forty-five minutes before Cochise gave the signal for them to retreat to higher ground. They killed two soldiers and wounded four others, with more than ten casualties among the warriors. Even so, the warriors took heart from having returned to the attack after having run so long before the wind of the soldiers.

But now the soldiers redoubled their efforts against the People. Some said the soldiers had finished their war against the Navajo. The soldiers were led by Kit Carson, who some of the subchiefs had once considered a friend of the People. They said the soldiers had gone into the heart of Navajo country, where no raiding parties of the People would have dared to venture. The soldiers had burned all of their crops and taken all of their sheep and even burned all of the peach trees growing in the heart of the canyon that constituted their best fortress. The chief *nantan* would accept no surrender, nor would he let them stay in their own land. Instead he rounded the Navajo up and made them all move to a terrible place—hot and barren and diseased—on the banks of the Rio Grande called Bosque Redondo. Then the soldiers turned their attention to the Mescalero, harrying them everywhere and killing them without pause. Finally the survivors surrendered and were sent to Bosque Redondo to live among the Navajo, their longtime enemies.

Now the soldiers turned their full attention to the White Mountain Apache, the Chokonen, and the Chihenne, aided by large parties of heavily armed people from the towns who roamed around the countryside killing anyone they found. The soldiers concentrated first on the forested country of the White Mountain bands, and so Cochise came to the aid of his old ally and kinsman, Francisco. They shadowed the soldiers, striking them sometimes, then fading into the forest and canyons. They hoped to keep the soldiers busy and away from the hidden camps of the women and children. But the soldiers proved dangerous and good at hanging onto their trail. Cochise wondered if they had finally begun to read signs better, for it seemed the soldiers clung to their trail now like snapping turtles. Once, as they moved ahead of the stubborn pursuit of a large body of soldiers, Cochise went alone and circled back to watch them tracking. There at the head of the soldiers he saw Merejildo Grijalva, who had learned from Cochise himself how to read a trail. Cochise then scattered his band, to confuse the trail. The soldiers continued into Broad Water Going, where a brave and funny warrior named Plume was camped with his family and a few other men. The soldiers came upon them suddenly and Plume warned the others to run quickly up the canyon, but he himself ran back toward the soldiers, dodging and jeering at them. He shot all of his arrows and then jumped out into the open in front of the soldiers, dancing about like Coyote, picking up rocks and throwing them. At first the soldiers laughed at his antics and stopped shooting, for they didn't know warriors practiced throwing rocks from the time they were old enough to walk. Plume hit one of the soldiers, nearly cracking his head open. All the soldiers shot, killing him quickly. But he died a happy man and a brave warrior, for he knew he had given his family and his relatives time to escape. When Cochise heard how Plume had died, he almost envied him. Plume, at least, had died as a true warrior—protecting his family—so he could walk proudly past the bears and the monsters guarding the path to the Happy Place.

Seeing how strong the soldiers now were in the Chiricahuas and knowing Merejildo knew all of the best camping places, Cochise led his band back down into Sonora. He also went because the Whites had built another strong fort in the heart of White Mountain territory. At first they called it Fort Goodwin, and later Fort Apache. After that, most of the White Mountain bands gave up fighting and begged the Whites to let them remain in their own country, promising to stop fighting and to help the soldiers track down the Chokonen. All this convinced Cochise to go to the Sierra Madre and Fronteras.

They stole some stock from near Fronteras, for their families by then were starving. The Sonorans chased them, to little effect. But later, Sonorans went quietly into the Animas Mountains and surprised a camp of people huddled in the snow, killing thirty-nine people immediately—only nine of them warriors. They captured twenty-eight others, taking them back tied together to sell as slaves.

The cold was so bitter that three babies froze to death on the march into slavery, which seemed almost a mercy to Cochise when he heard of it.

But Cochise kept his personal following out of harm's way—moving constantly, lighting no fires that could be seen in the day, and raiding carefully. They made sure to leave no witnesses and no tracks to bring the soldiers to where the women and children remained hidden. Cochise leaned heavily on his Power, which directed his movements and warned him of the approach of his enemies. While other bands fell into the pit, Cochise ran along the ridge—with a drop to death on either side. Still, his courage faltered when he heard news that even Victorio and Lozen had sought peace with the Americans after they had learned that a good man who had been agent at Pinos Altos before had come back. His name was Michael Steck and he treated the People with justice and courtesy, so Victorio thought he might honor his word—something Cochise had long decided no White man would do. Loco led the way toward peace, for he had grown old in the service of his people and spoke more and more about the benefits of peace—even at the great risk of trusting the White Eyes. Victorio held back, heeding the counsel of Nana, one of the most respected holy men and war leaders of the People. Nana had a great name before Mangas Coloradas rose to the leading position among all of the Chihenne. He was now an old man, but seemed the unquenchable spirit of the People. He appeared frail and bent, and was limping from an old injury. But he had Goose Power, so he could ride a day and a night and a day and a night, seeming fresh when warriors thirty years younger faltered and slipped from their saddles. He had great Power and knew things no one else remembered and seemed undeterred by any disaster or loss. But even Nana now conceded the need to talk peace with the Whites in hopes the Chihenne might live quietly in some small piece of their home. They most yearned to settle at Ojo Caliente, the place where the world began and whose sacred waters had soothed and restored the Chihenne since before the first memory. Victorio and Nana and Loco cautiously sent emissaries to Steck to see if he would give them rations and let them settle at Ojo Caliente. But Steck said they must live at Bosque Redondo with the Mescalero and the Navajo, and also convince Cochise and his Chokonen to do the same. But Victorio answered he would not live at Bosque Redondo. Furthermore, he said Cochise would never surrender. "He does not wish it and will never be friendly more," said Victorio to Steck.[10]

Soon it seemed all of the other leaders would falter and begin to look like Wood Rat for a hole in which they could hide, or follow the advice of Dog and trade scraps for whippings and cringing. Cochise rose up in his Power and strength, drawing the warriors who still had the heart to fight to him. Now he understood the stories about Child-of-the-Water he had heard since he was in baby grass and why Child-of-the-Water fought even hopeless odds. Now he knew why Coyote could never live on scraps and accept whippings like Dog. Now he knew that fighting was a prayer. In the same manner that he prayed to the dawn and the wind and the thunder, he held his thoughts smooth and his heart steady by fighting past even the hope of victory, knowing it was enough merely to continue. He resolved to hoard the lives of his warriors and squander the lives of his enemies. Perhaps the White Eyes would overwhelm him. Perhaps they would lose heart. It did not matter. He would go on, walking the path on which his feet had been set.

Cochise haunted the Dragoons and the Chiricahuas, where he could count on the long, deep friendship of the rocks. He moved his camps constantly and set out a network of sentries so they could see his enemies coming for miles off. They could also see horses and soldiers and wagons approaching from half a day's journey, so he could move his warriors quickly into position for an ambush. With thirty warriors he attacked the mail wagon between Fort Bowie and Tubac, letting the drivers escape but gathering up the horses and the mail—which sometimes had things he could trade down in Sonora. Two days later he ambushed a wagon near Tubac, killing one man and wounding another. A month later he took twenty warriors and attacked a ranch at Santa Rita. Then he swung north and attacked an army supply station, killing several soldiers. The soldiers fled the station and the warriors gained 6 horses, 250 cartridges, 2 good rifles, and rations. Two days later they struck the outskirts of Tubac before finally turning south out of the path of the soldiers forming up to chase him.

Cochise could feel his Power rising up in him, unfurling itself like a waking bat hanging from the ceiling. He remembered how he and Mangas Coloradas had stalked each other with stories, debating the issue of peace and war. He had told the story about the argument between Dog and Coyote, hoping it would work on his father-in-law. But stories had a will of their own, so instead the story had worked on Cochise. Now he felt he understood it for the first time. He understood all of the other stories about Coyote in a different light as well, and was grateful that although Child-of-the-Water and White-Painted Woman had gone from the People, they had left behind these stories to teach them and protect them. Cochise turned to fight, shedding the doubts and fears and second thoughts as the lizard slips out of its skin and leaves behind its tail to fool his enemies—as clever as when Lizard made Coyote hold up the sky. And as his mind grew smooth and steady, he felt his Power strengthen, so he could hear the voice of Power every day. The warriors could feel it as well, and his following grew as the word spread that a raiding party with Cochise could not be surprised and slipped through dangers with few losses. He did not make arrogant demands of Power, of course. Caution became his habit and he selected his camps with terrible care—never in the obvious places and always with three ways to escape in the middle of the night. He never neglected his sentries. He planned his attacks with exquisite care and developed great authority over his subchiefs so he could mount sophisticated, layered ambushes or coordinate a complicated attack or retreat. His closest allies—El Cautivo and Nahilzay—had been with him for many years, so in war they thought as with one mind. Moreover, he had strong alliances with all of the fighting bands, especially Geronimo and Juh and Victorio and Lozen and Francisco. And even though the number of the People had dwindled and the children had not enough to eat, Cochise felt a certain relief now that everything had come down to fighting and killing and surviving.

He was vengeance, well mounted. His enemies would have cause to fear him now—and regret that they had made him so.

12

Late 1864

Cochise the Avenger

It Happened at Gizhyaa'itine
(Trail Goes Down between Two Hills)

Long ago, right there at that place, there were two beautiful girls.
They were sisters. They were talking together.

Then they saw Old Man Owl walking toward them. They knew
what he was like. He thought all the time about doing things with
women. Then they said, "Let's do something to him."

Then one of those girls went to the top of one of the hills. Her
sister went to the top of the other one. As Old Man Owl was walking
between them, the first girl called out to him. "Old Man Owl, come
here! I want you to rub me between my legs!" He stopped. He got
excited! So he started to climb the hill where the girl was sitting.

Then, after Old Man Owl got halfway to the top, the second girl
called out to him. "Old Man Owl, I want you to rub me gently
between my legs!" He stopped! He got even more excited. So he
turned around, walked down the hill, and began to climb the
other one.

Then halfway to the top, the first girl called out to him again in
the same way. He stopped! Now he was very excited! So Old Man Owl
did the same thing again. He forgot about the second girl, walked
down the hill, and began climbing the other one.

It happened that way four times. Old Man Owl went back and
forth, back and forth, climbing up and down those hills.

Then those girls just laughed at him!

It happened at Trail Goes Down between Two Hills.

Cochise moved through the mountains along the border, his Power
drawing allies to him. He yearned sometimes for the rocks of the
Dragoons, which stood around him in his dreams, making him feel
safe and secure as when he had slept curled up between his mother

and his father in the days before the world had collapsed into unending war. He knew all of the canyons and springs and hidden places of every range of mountains in a vast sprawl of territory—even if he did not know all of their place-names. Fortunately, whenever he gathered up a large raiding party some of the warriors from allied bands knew some of those stories, and would repeat them to Cochise as they traveled. When the season had come when he could seek revenge for his father-in-law, Cochise sent out runners to the scattered allied bands, seeking to gather up a large raiding party for a sweep through Mexico. Juh brought his large force of Nednhis from the Sierra Madre, and so they amassed nearly 200 warriors for the raid, spearheaded by relatives of the people the Sonorans had killed not long ago in the Animas Mountains.

They set up an ambush on the road between Bavispe and Janos where it passes through the many canyons of the front edge of the Sierra Madre. They ambushed one party, killing ten and capturing one man, whom Cochise turned over to the relatives of dead warriors. Then they ambushed a wagon train out of Janos, killing eleven men and taking four women and children prisoner together with sixty head of stock. When a party of seventeen soldiers came looking for the wagon train, the warriors attacked them as well—with only three escaping. The warriors turned back to where their families were hidden along the border, well pleased because they had gained guns and ammunition and food. They held a feast and dance of celebration, although Cochise insisted that the warriors should smoke and dry out most of the meat to make jerky against future hunger.

Francisco's band soon joined them with news that the *nantans* had changed among the Whites[1] and that a patrol had hit them while they were camped on Mount Graham. Francisco had moved south to get out of their way. Now he joined Cochise for another raid along the border in the season of Many Leaves,[2] the two great fighters leading a force of more than 150 warriors. They attacked one wealthy ranch, taking two boys as captives to train as warriors and killing everyone else. They also took with them sacks of gold to trade in Sonora. They killed a man, a woman, and their children and some Mexican ranch hands near Tucson, then swung east and attacked a supply wagon, killing one of the soldier guards and wounding all of the others. They let those men flee out into the desert, content with the supplies in the wagons. Knowing the soldiers would soon follow to take up their trail, Cochise and Francisco then turned south into Sonora.

Cochise kept scouts out all around the main party of warriors, and those scouts soon warned him that soldiers following his trail had crossed into Sonora. Cochise sent warriors back to watch the soldiers. When two of them went off to hunt, the warriors killed them quietly. Two more came to find the first two, but they escaped—so the soldiers knew the warriors had them under watch. The soldiers rode out after them, but came up against the warriors in a strong position on a hillside with Cochise on the ridge directing their movements with hand signals. The soldiers soon found themselves surrounded, the snare drawing tighter with each gesture Cochise made up on the ridge. Cochise did not want to risk too many losses, so he patiently worked the warriors into position. But perhaps these White Eyes were protected by Power, because a rainstorm came up suddenly in the late afternoon, wetting the bowstrings of the warriors and making their firing ineffective. Cochise pulled back the warriors and let the soldiers go—but the fight had revived the pride of the warriors, as the rain revives the poppies. They held a dance of victory, the warriors pantomiming how they had killed the two soldiers and everyone feeling strong and hopeful. Watching the warriors dancing in the firelight, Cochise noted men from many bands— White Mountain, Chihenne, Chiricahua, Bedonkohe, and Nednhi. This demonstrated that talk of his Power had spread, drawing the most ambitious and warlike spirits from many bands. This offered strength, but also danger. He must keep control of the warriors, for only coordination and careful planning would enable the Chokonen to survive among so many enemies. However, he also noted that many of these warriors had come on their own, without their band leaders. He knew Victorio and Loco and other Chihenne leaders still hoped for peace with the Whites. And he had a long talk with Francisco, who said most of the other White Mountain bands were seeking peace with the White Eyes as well. Some were even agreeing to help hunt down the Chokonen. While Cochise felt grateful to his Power for making his Chokonen so strong, he also knew his following was as a loose and shifting sandbar in a rising river—dependent on his success in each raid.

Cochise went down into Sonora in the season of Large Fruit, to trade and see if he could talk the Sonorans into leaving his band unmolested through the season of the Ghost Dance. He discovered that the northern forts had been stripped of soldiers, for the Mexicans were still fighting their war in the south with other White Eyes.[3] Cochise opened negotiations at Fronteras warily. But the Sonorans had not much to offer as rations, and Cochise thought they sought only to hold him in place for some trick. When his far-flung scouts warned that a large party of heavily armed White men was coming from the north toward Fronteras, he moved his band away from Sonora.[4] He spent the summer months moving through Sonora and Chihuahua, living quietly to avoid the soldiers.

As the season of the Ghost Dance approached, Cochise turned back to the Chiricahua Mountains, whose deep canyons and varied plants might help get the women and children through the cold months. Hunger stalked them, holding to their trail. He gathered rumors and reports, and was discouraged to learn that Francisco had moved back into the White Mountains and offered to settle on a reservation near the fort. Moreover, Loco and Victorio were talking to the Whites at Pinos Altos. Cochise cautiously sent emissaries to Fort Bowie, thinking perhaps the Whites also had grown weary of this long war and might offer something useful. If nothing else, the talking might give his warriors and their families a little rest and a chance to build up their food supply.

Cochise went to a ridge overlooking Fort Bowie with a white flag and signaled his willingness to talk. The *nantan*[5] came out and said he had no authority to make a treaty, but urged them to come back in twelve days. Several women agreed to go down into the fort to count the soldiers and see if they seemed friendly. Dos-teh-seh insisted on going, although she knew Cochise was loath to let her run such a risk.[6] The soldiers gave her food and clothing and seemed well disposed—but who could know anything with the White Eyes? They covered their faces with fur and changed their words the way some lizards changed their color. You could only count on them when they were trying to kill you; everything else was a trick.

Sure enough, while the Chokonen were camped in the mountains some thirty-five miles from the fort, a strong party of soldiers guided by Grijalva tried to take the camp by surprise. Fortunately, the lookout, whom Cochise with his customary care had posted overlooking the approaches to the camp, spotted them and gave the alarm. Nonetheless, seven people were killed in the confusion as the band scattered and the soldiers seized and destroyed the supplies of

dried meat and heart of agave that would have helped carry them
through the season of the Ghost Dance. Cochise learned again the
cost of trusting in the Whites—even if it were while waiting to talk.

Nonetheless, Cochise decided to remain in the Chiricahuas.
Here, at least, they knew where they could find oaks with acorns
and certain roots, and patches of corn they had scattered in the
warm months, and a hundred other plants that would carry them
through the hungry months. They moved carefully from the Chiricahuas to the Huachucas and the Dragoons and back again. They
never remained long enough in one camp for the soldiers to find
them—although the soldiers rarely sought them in the snows of winter, which sometimes lay heavy in the high places. But now the soldiers set out in force. They struck one party near Sulphur Springs,
killing one man and wounding two others. The soldiers scoured the
Dragoons, guided by Merejildo Grijalva—but Cochise saw them coming from the high places and took all his people and fled south,
crossing the dangerous open ground of the Sulphur Springs Valley
under the protection of night, praying to the darkness in gratitude as
they went.

Cochise worked to make his mind smooth and resilient and
steady, practicing gratitude for the gifts the Chiricahua had been
given with open hands, remembering the stories to instill reverence
and feeling the Life Force in all things—even the wind and the lightning. He would often gather the children and the young boys
around him at night to tell them the stories he had learned to
steady his mind, so that they would see these reminders everywhere—as he did. He loved to tell the story about the argument
between Wind and Lightning, for it taught them the importance of
working together in a land surrounded by enemies. He told the story
in this manner:

Lighting and Wind got into an argument as to who did the most
good and was the most powerful. Lighting told Wind that he was
most powerful: "You can't do the things I can." Wind got angry and
hid from the earth. They looked for him. They hired all the hawks
and other birds to look for him. They were having too little rain.
They hired the black and yellow bee too, for he can go into small
crevices.

At last they found Wind in a far region. Bee found him there. A
continuous odor of grass came from the place where he sat and the
vicinity. Bee could not approach because of it. So Bee went on the

four directions. He kept in the air. All at once the wind saw Bee before him.

Wind spoke to him. He said, "You must have got help from some supernatural being, for no one can approach me in this manner."

Bee called the name of the wind, for it was an emergency, and he called his name to his face. "Wind," he called, "you are wanted back. The People are suffering. It is your duty to come back and do your work."

"But Lighting said he could do without me. That is why I left. How is it that you people want me back now? I have many things to say to Lightning, but I guess I'll just send him about four messages. I'll be at a certain mountaintop and Lightning can wait for me on a rainbow and I will speak to him. Four days after you go I will be there."

On the fourth day Sun was there and Lightning and Earth were there too. Sun came from the east in the form of a little cyclone. Wind and Thunder embraced.

Lightning said, "We've been wondering where you've been."

Wind replied, "You said you were more powerful; that is why I went away. Why is it that the earth is so hot that it is about to burn up?"

The breathing of the thunder created four persons and these were sent out in the four directions, and they were told that whenever the earth trembles they should come to the center. Lightning and Wind used that Power to make the earth as it was before, with green grass and the proper amount of water. Sun had a pipe for them. They smoked and agreed to have no more trouble after that. At this conference the seasons were made.[7]

Cochise told that story many times to the young people, knowing that thereafter the wind and the clouds and the sun and the bees and the changing of the seasons would all remind them of their dependence on one another and the foolishness of pride. He told it in the night even as they fled their enemies to help keep up the courage of his people.

The Chokonen went on down to Fronteras, but found that town so impoverished it was hardly worth raiding. Cochise left the women and children in a safe place and drifted back up along the border, gathering supplies and rumors. Hard news came to him there. The White Eyes had killed Francisco, who had fallen into their hands when he offered to make peace—as most of the other White Mountain

bands had already done. But once he had surrendered, the White
Eyes imprisoned him for things he had done while at war. After a
while, they killed him just as they had Mangas Coloradas. In the
meantime, White Eyes had also killed some leading Chihenne who
had gone into Pinos Altos on the promise of peace. Victorio was
with them, drinking coffee in a house when the White Eyes attacked
them treacherously. Victorio escaped, but the Americans killed three
of his headmen. Victorio gathered up his warriors and took his
revenge by killing four soldiers just outside of Fort Cummings.

Cochise now moved the Chokonen back down to Janos to trade
things taken in his raids on the Americans. He attempted to live
quietly there, resting his warriors and staying mostly in remote camps
out of harm's way. But the Americans sent soldiers down into Chihuahua to find them. Cochise heard the rumor of their coming and
evaded them easily enough, but the cooperation between the Mexicans and the Americans was a worrisome sign. He could feel the
tightening of the snare around his leg, the hunger of the children
biting into his flesh. Then some warriors who had been raiding
north of the border brought back even worse news, saying both the
army and the people in Tubac continued to hunt the People, now
guided increasingly by White Mountain warriors. This was grim
news indeed. Cochise could elude the soldiers indefinitely, but not
warriors who could call on Power and smell out a trail the way a
vulture smells carrion.

Nonetheless, Cochise organized a raid as the season of Little
Eagles[8] approached. He had little choice, as his people were eating
mostly roots after the long, cold months. He raided not so much for
revenge as for survival. They swept through the Santa Cruz and
Sonoita valleys, hitting isolated ranches and moving on before the
soldiers could respond. They raided the ranch of one brave man
named Rafael Saavedra, who retreated to the well-fortified ranch
house with his servants and his cowboys at the first attack. But the
warriors captured one woman, who screamed for help. Saavedra
came running out of his safe place, shooting and shouting, finally
driving off the warriors and rescuing the woman. But he was mor-
tally wounded trying to get back to the ranch house. Cochise admired
his courage but was glad of his death, for that man was a strong
enemy. The Chokonen moved quickly on, hitting one ranch after
another and running off hundreds of head of horses and cattle.

As Cochise had feared, the ranchers sent for tame warriors—mostly White Mountain men—who could follow a trail. Using the skills of the warriors, the White Eyes found the camp where Cochise had stopped to smoke and dry meat. They attacked by surprise, so the sentries gave only a little warning. The women and children scattered, as did most of the warriors. One man rallied three other warriors and they stood their ground, giving the others time to escape. Finally the White Eyes killed all four, cutting off their ears and taking their scalps. Cochise understood then that he must also fight his own people and that the White Mountain band, which had once been his allies, were now his most dangerous enemies.

Still, he gathered up his warriors again and three weeks later led a hundred men against a military outpost north of the Huachucas, running off 57 horses, 10 mules, and 72 head of cattle.[9] Five soldiers took the only 5 horses left to the post and gave chase, getting close enough to see Cochise and his many warriors before returning to the army camp. A strong force from a nearby fort with 56 soldiers and 16 White Mountain scouts arrived the next day to pick up the trail, but Cochise scattered his warriors, so their trail dispersed like smoke.

Cochise turned back to Janos, nearly out of bullets. Fortunately he had plunder from his raids and the traders at Janos soon resupplied him with ammunition and food for the families of the warriors still hidden in the mountains. He remained in the mountains in well-guarded camps, sending warriors into Janos every Saturday to trade. He warned them not to get drunk in the town, reminding them of all of the treachery of the Mexicans. Cochise also mostly restrained his men from raiding around Janos, so they would not stir up the Chihuahuans against them. Instead, he sent raiding parties into neighboring Sonora, which remained mostly at war with the Chokonen.[10] He sent word to Juh in the Sierra Madre and to Victorio and Loco, so they sometimes joined forces with the Chokonen raiders in Sonora.

Cochise himself led a raid on Fronteras in the season of Large Fruit,[11] riding straight through the town. They killed several people and ran off most of the stock. One man shooting from his house wounded Cochise in the neck as he rode through the streets on his great black stallion. The blood ran down across his chest, spreading dismay among his warriors. But Cochise kept his saddle and ignored the wound, convinced his Power would not let any bullet kill him.

They paused only a little while as Cochise called on the medicine man who had healed other wounds. Then they continued raiding, gathering up horses and deaths until their arms were full and their anger sated. Mostly they struck in isolated places, leaving no witnesses. Sometimes they raided just outside of the largest towns, so no one felt safe in all the northern reaches of Sonora. Usually they retired into the Sierra Madre when they needed to rest and jerk and smoke the meat they had taken. Once a party of Mexicans surprised their camp and killed five warriors and one woman, and captured four other women and children. They scattered in that attack and reassembled at the distant meeting place on which they had all agreed. Every day they all agreed on a meeting place, so they could scatter in an instant and reassemble in the next several days. Then they retired to the Sierra Madre to rest.

A hard and shifty man from Janos who had married a woman of the People found their camp in the Sierra Madre. The warriors let him approach, because he had sold them valuable guns and ammunition in the past. He offered to help them in their raids on Sonora by finding traders who could quickly get them bullets and guns in return for things the warriors brought back on raids. He showed them the value of the bits of talking paper the Mexicans and the Americans always seemed to carry and urged them to always look for gold and silver, which were portable and of great value. He urged them to concentrate their attacks on the mail riders, who often carried paper money and other valuable things. Cochise sent that man along with some of the raiding parties moving along the border, so he could show them which things were most valuable. In this way, they increased the return on their raids and began to rebuild their supply of ammunition—which was always their most worrisome weakness in this never-ending war on both sides of the border.[12]

When he had rebuilt his supplies, Cochise turned his attention once again to the Americans. Only one in four of his warriors had firearms, and even they had only a few bullets. Late in the season of the Ghost Dance,[13] his raiders announced their return by killing a mail rider near Fort Bowie. Then he led sixty warriors in an attack on the Mowry Mines. They trapped five miners in their house, wounding one as he ran in the door. Cochise tried to get close enough to set the roof of the building on fire. Although he killed one man by shooting through the window, the firepower of the men at the loopholes in the walls of the stone building was too strong and the warriors fell back. During the battle, a mail rider rode up, surprising the warriors who were concentrating on the miners. Although they shot the man's horse and wounded him in the leg, he made it into the building. Two other men came upon the fight and turned and fled before the warriors could catch them, so Cochise knew he could not remain much longer at the mine. He hated the miners more than almost any other tribe of White Eyes, for they profaned the earth and violated the will of Usen. Their very presence was an affront to Power and seemed a failure in his duty to Usen and to the People. Cochise retreated then from the mines, leaving those men for another time. Instead, he concentrated on vulnerable travelers and isolated ranches, trying to accumulate enough easily carried goods and easily driven horses to trade in Janos.

Soon Cochise noted another worrisome trend. For all the years of his war with the Americans, he had used the border to his great advantage. That was something the place called Trail Goes Down between Two Hills had taught him. He had not known what that place was trying to teach him when his father first told him the story. He had simply laughed at foolish Old Man Owl and felt hot for the two pretty sisters who had made a fool of him. Now he understood that that place had been telling him something about war, and how he could keep the Mexicans and Americans going back and forth between the two hills by crossing and recrossing the border. That was how those places worked—they taught a warrior valuable lessons long before he understood their meaning. But now both the Mexicans and Americans often ignored the border and continued on his trail far across it in both directions. One band of Sonorans even went all the way to the Chiricahuas and surprised a Nednhi group headed by a subchief named Tuscas, killing eight warriors and four women, and capturing twenty-six women and children to sell as slaves.[14] Cochise later learned from traders at Janos that the Sonorans and the Americans had agreed to cooperate in their war with the People, coordinating their patrols and giving each other permission to cross the border freely.

When he learned of the attack on Tuscas's band, Cochise gathered up a party of seventy warriors and went raiding in retaliation. They looted a wagon train and raided several ranches. But this time the soldiers came after them quickly, guided by Grijalva. They overtook the warriors, driving them from their camp and killing three in a running fight. The soldiers destroyed a five-month supply of food and hundreds of carefully tanned skins for clothing and moccasins Cochise had gathered in his camp. Once again, Cochise had reason to bitterly regret the good training Grijalva had obtained at his hands. He resolved to kill Grijalva when he had the chance—more in sorrow than in anger. He understood the choices Grijalva had made, just as he understood why even Mangas Coloradas had yielded to the yearning for peace and the hope their children might grow up and die in the fullness of their years. He would not question each warrior's right to make his own choices—nor could he hold back from killing him when his choices made him his enemy.

When Cochise returned to Mexico to evade the gathering American troops, he found the Sonorans had gotten stronger, with many well-armed patrols moving constantly along the border. He surprised one small patrol and killed 2 men, but then a force of 137 soldiers scoured the mountains, destroying two camps of allied bands. Cochise and the other Nednhi and Chokonen war leaders struck back in their accustomed way, killing 5 people on the road near Arizpe, then several farmers, then a cowboy near Bacoachi. The efforts of the Sonorans had only stirred up the Nednhi and Chokonen, giving them reasons to seek revenge—so they killed more people in Sonora in that season of raiding than they had for several years. However, Cochise restrained them from raiding in Chihuahua, for the trade with Janos was a toehold on the cliff face.

Eventually the Mexicans understood this and chipped away that foothold. The Sonorans complained bitterly that the people at Janos were helping the warriors—even warning them when Sonora sent soldiers into Chihuahua. Other officials investigated these claims and decided Janos should not trade any longer with the warriors, who were now raiding mostly in Sonora. They sent new soldiers to Janos with orders to attack any bands that had been raiding instead of buying their supplies. The change in Janos was a deadly blow to the hopes of the Chokonen, but it did not much surprise Cochise. He knew the Mexicans—both Sonorans and Chihuahuans—would always be his enemies. The People and the Mexicans were as the wolf and the deer—enemies by their natures—although many Mexican women and children had been raised up in the band and had become as the People themselves. Once Janos was closed to him, Cochise had to turn north in the hope the Americans had relaxed their guard during the months he lived in Mexico.

In the season of the Ghost Dance,[15] Cochise camped at Black Mountain in the Peloncillo Mountains northwest of Fort Bowie so he could raid along the wagon road leading to Apache Pass. His warriors killed a *nantan* and a mail rider only a few miles from the fort and then tried to run off the fort's horse herd, but alert sentries drove them back. Cochise withdrew again into the remote security of the Peloncillos, where the Americans rarely patrolled and which was too far north for the Sonorans to reach, although they now had the permission of the Americans to go a hundred miles or more across the border when pursuing raiding parties. But to Cochise's surprise, a Sonoran army followed some raiders all the way to the Peloncillos and struck his camp, capturing a boy and some horses. Cochise harried the Sonorans back out of the mountains and down toward Sonora, but the attack demonstrated that no place could be considered safe anymore, now that the Americans and the Mexicans and even the White Mountain bands had made common cause against the Chokonen.

In the season of Many Leaves,[16] Cochise took a hundred warriors and tried to drive off the Fort Bowie horse herd—in part to dismount the soldiers who might otherwise chase him. But the soldiers had new quick-firing guns, so each man had the firepower of three or four men. The raiders shifted south, then circled back and attacked a mail coach ten miles from the pass. The warriors wounded several men in the first attack, but the driver whipped the team and the warriors chased it for six miles before they stopped it. They expected a hard fight, because the two soldiers and two others were well armed with plenty of ammunition. But the White Eyes were foolish and frightened so they surrendered, pleading for mercy. Perhaps they did not know that the bones in the pass belonged to the brother of Cochise. Many of the warriors with Cochise had a debt of vengeance to fulfill. They seized one wounded man, ripped off his clothes, scalped him, then tied a rope to his feet and dragged him through the rocks and cactus until he died. They took the other prisoners some distance from the road and killed them as well, mutilating their bodies as the soldiers had mutilated Mangas Coloradas. One man they cut open and removed his heart, setting it neatly on his splayed-open chest. They cut off the testicles of another man and stuffed them into his mouth. The warriors got some satisfaction from this, for they had all nursed their hatred for the Whites a long while. But Cochise was most glad of the guns and ammunition he got from the foolish Whites—so stupid they did not recognize the time for their own death song.

Cochise retired once more into Sonora, knowing the soldiers would be stirred from their hornet's nests. But Sonora proved not much safer, with soldiers everywhere. Cochise sent six people to see if perhaps Janos had changed its mind again about trading with the warriors. While they were talking with the Janos headman, a Nednhi band ran off a horse herd, so the Janos headman seized the six Chokonen and put them in a jail. Things went from bad to worse, and the Sonorans mounted a major campaign against the People. They had reportedly won their war with the other White Eyes in the south and had also broken the Yaqui, so now they turned their full attention to the People, who had killed more than a hundred Sonorans in the past year. The Sonorans even ventured into the Sierra Madre, where Juh's band had been safe for years, hitting one of his camps and killing several warriors. They surprised another camp some weeks later, killing twelve people and taking nine prisoners for sale as slaves. Fear and uncertainty spread through even the Chokonen, testing the loyalty of all save the personal following of Cochise. Some of the subchiefs went back to Janos, hoping to negotiate a peace with Chihuahua. But soldiers attacked the bands seeking peace, killing two leading men who had been friends and allies of Cochise for most of his life—along with eight women and two children. Then the people of Janos, seeing that any chance for peace had passed over them once again, sent out soldiers to kill as many warriors as possible. They hit another camp, killing the brother of Mangas Coloradas and marching back into Chihuahua City with twelve scalps and ten prisoners.

Cochise moved north to the Mogollon Mountains to stay out of the way of the Sonorans' war. He had lost more than a hundred people in the past year, most of them to sickness that plagued them whenever they had dealings with the Mexicans. His strength had dwindled alarmingly, for he knew he could not supply the needs of the women and children if he could not recruit enough warriors to mount an extensive raid. After his warriors had rested, Cochise led a war party over to the White Mountains, to see what kind of peace the White Mountain bands had made with the Americans. He was going to find an old friend of his—a White Mountain headman named Pedro—when he encountered a White Eye trader and his party. The Chokonen seized them and all of their supplies, then stripped them so they stood fearful and trembling, wearing only their shoes. He might have killed them to satisfy his warriors and his own old ache for blood, but Pedro pleaded for their lives, saying the traders came often among the White Mountain bands bringing things they needed. Cochise let them go.[17]

Finding that the White Mountain bands seemed satisfied with the peace and the treatment of the soldiers, Cochise cautiously sent an emissary to the soldiers, testing the thin ice of peace. He had lived now some sixty years and had watched as his people melted away like snow out of season. He had come by painful degrees to see the wisdom of Mangas Coloradas and of his own father, who had seen ahead to this time as though they stood on a high place. He understood he could not win this war with the Whites by driving them out of his country. Now with the Mexicans and the Whites both against him, he could not even keep on fighting indefinitely. He had lost so many warriors and so many children in the past seven years of constant war he doubted his own children would finish their lives as free men. The People must either have peace or die. He was not frightened for himself, for a warrior can only hope for a good death. But it grieved him to think of the women and the children all dying out of their time. If he could not win this war by driving out the White Eyes and could no longer play the game of the pretty girls mocking Old Man Owl, he must convince them to make the same arrangement with the Chokonen they had made with the White Mountain bands.

Cochise sent word to the *nantan* at the fort and waited hopefully for the reply. But the *nantan* said he would only talk if Cochise turned over his family as hostages. This stirred the dark memories of the last time Cochise had put those he loved in the power of the White Eyes and of all the blood that had spilled out of that old wound. Besides, malaria had broken out in that country. Cochise therefore took his band to the Dragoons. Still, he sent word to one of the *nantan*s who some people claimed was a good man, saying he would end the war he had waged for seven cycles of seasons if the Americans would let him remain in the Chiricahua Mountains. Cochise even offered to protect the road through Chokonen territory if the Whites would let him live in peace. He met for a little while with the *nantan*, who said he could make no promises. Cochise consulted his Power and reluctantly concluded the Whites were not ready for peace—and were perhaps once again trying to hold him in place to trap him. He faded from that country, going quietly and leaving no sign of his passing.[18]

Weeks later,[19] a brave *nantan* named Captain Frank Perry came with sixty-three soldiers led by a White Mountain warrior who knew Cochise and had offered to lead the soldiers to his camp. The soldiers captured two Chokonen as they approached the Dragoons, but instead of killing them, the *nantan* released them to carry a message to Cochise saying he wanted a peace talk. Seeing the glimmer of a hope for peace, Cochise agreed to meet the *nantan*, backed by his warriors on open ground where the White Eyes could not indulge their usual treachery.

Cochise, still straight as a reed and standing six-feet-two-inches tall,[20] had broad shoulders, a slender waist, and long legs all of muscle and sinew. Gray threads streaked in his long, black, braided hair and his face was striped with vermilion. He regarded the *nantan* steadily with his keen eyes, which now had a glimmer of melancholy about them—for he had seen hard things and many deaths.

"What are you doing out here, Capitan,"[21] said Cochise in a friendly way, his eyes moving from the *nantan* back toward where the soldiers waited, alert for any trap.

"Come to see you and prospect the country generally," said Perry.

"You mean to come to kill me or any of my tribe—that is all your visits mean to me," replied Cochise. "I tried the Americans once," he added, not sure whether this man knew the long and bitter history of the Whites' betrayal of the Chokonen, "and they broke the treaty first—the officers I mean—this was at the Pass. If I stop in, I must be treated right—but don't expect they will do all they say for us. I won't stay at Goodwin, it is no place for Indians. They die after being there for a short time. I will go to [Fort] Goodwin to talk to you, after I hear how you treat Indians there. I will send in two of my Indians who will let me know. I lost nearly one hundred of my people last year—principally from sickness. The Americans killed a good many. I have not one hundred Indians now. Ten years ago I had one thousand," he said, speaking honestly as he would to a warrior without any attempt to disguise the weakness of the Chokonen. "The Americans are everywhere and we must live in bad places to shun them. I can't give you any mescal, as there is another scout on the other side and we can't make any fires to roast it. The White Mountain bands are stronger than we are and steal stock from us; some of them say you came to kill us, but some Indians lie. My Indi-

ans will do no harm until I come in, which I may do inside of two
months," he concluded, although he did not trust any promise of
the Americans and was not certain he would surrender in any case.
But even if he did not, perhaps the soldiers would stop chasing him
for a little while if they thought he would come in.

"I heard you were wounded, but you walk all right," said Perry.

"I was wounded twice. First near Santa Cruz, in the leg twelve
years ago. I had a bad leg for some time afterward. Next near Fronteras, two years ago, in the neck. I would like some bread and tobacco
and a blanket," he added, to gauge the man's reaction.

Perry gave him presents—including so much of the rations for
the soldiers that his men went hungry for three days. But Perry had
fought long enough already to know how many lives and how much
money it would cost to finally hunt down and kill this warrior—even
if he had only a hundred men left as he claimed. If he could convince Cochise to come in, it would be worth the lives of his entire
detachment—much less their rations.[22] Perry promised Cochise he
would carry his words back to his superiors and speak strongly himself for peace, urging Cochise to come to Fort Goodwin to receive
more presents and talk more about peace as soon as possible. But
Cochise remained unconvinced. Perry seemed like a good man—
brave and honorable. But he was only a little *nantan* and Cochise
did not believe that the great *nantan*s would stand behind Perry's
words.

But Cochise held off raiding in Arizona for a while, until he
received word that a strong force of soldiers had set out from Fort
Bowie and other posts, once again hunting the scattered and carefully hidden bands. He also resumed raiding, stalking ranchers and
wagons and settlers in the still fearful and lightly settled Santa Cruz
and Sonoita valleys. He realized he could not depend on the mercy
or honor of the White Eyes. They would only give him what he
sought if he forced them into it, by making the war so terrible they
would yield his own land back to him as the price of peace. He saw
clearly now why Child-of-the-Water had imposed the sacred obligation of revenge—blood for blood. Fear remained the strongest ally of
the People in a land filled with their enemies. Cochise sent runners
to other bands, including the Chihenne to the east and the Nednhis
to the south, promising the protection of his Power and the rich
plunder of the Americans to warriors who would join him, even if
they were outcasts from other bands.

When Cochise had assembled a large enough war party, he staged
a surprise attack on an army supply train approaching Camp Crittenden, killing two soldiers and capturing 12 mules. Then he attacked
a ranch near Tubac and took 130 horses, nearly trapping the fifteen
cowboys who chased them for a time. He attacked nearly every
ranch in those valleys, usually killing one or two unwary men before
they knew he was stalking them, and vanishing with the livestock
before the soldiers came to find him. His warriors killed the mail
riders between Tucson and Mesilla so often the White Eyes finally
stopped sending them altogether, relying instead on strong parties of
soldiers or settlers to carry mail at long intervals. Throughout the
warm months, he camped in the Dragoons. He never neglected his
lookouts on the high places from which they could spot soldiers or
a wagon moving fifty miles away. Whenever the soldiers did find
their trail with the help of their White Mountain warrior dogs,
Cochise had half a day or more to run through the canyons to the
other side of the mountain, or cross the low desert into the Chiricahua Mountains.

Cochise had by now nearly perfected this mode of warfare,
which spread fear among his enemies but hoarded warriors' lives.
He kept his scouts spread out far and guarded against surprise as
diligently as the bee gathers pollen. But he never missed an opportunity to strike a rich target with little risk—or to take advantage of
surprise. When his sentinels saw the mail coach crossing the flat,
dusty Sulphur Springs Valley, Cochise and a party of warriors hurried to Dragoon Springs, where he placed his men in a small gully
by the road, covered with grass. As the mail coach approached, the
warriors rose as if by the will of Power out of the earth and show-
ered the stage with arrows and bullets, killing the driver and three
soldiers immediately. The stage fled south—as Cochise had known
it would—where it encountered the rest of the warriors, who were
mounted and waiting. They quickly killed the two remaining Whites.
All told, the Whites had time to fire only six shots, and the warriors
suffered no casualties—which was precisely the sort of clever and
bloodless victory the warriors most happily celebrated.

That night several warriors brought into the camp three White
Eyes—rough, wild men who for the past several years had carried on
a secret trade with the Chokonen. They always had whiskey and ammunition to trade, moving along the border and appearing at the
camps of the people. Sometimes they moved down into Sonora to

trade there. Cochise did not trust such men, who had effectively turned on their own kind. But he had need of them, for he could not count on obtaining all of the bullets and powder he needed in his raiding. He put out a strong word to the warriors not to kill these men, who were otherwise tempting targets—riding alone with pack mules loaded with goods. But neither did he trust them. They were like Kirker and Johnson—renegades from their own people whose Power was greed and who would turn on anyone for money. Nonetheless, he kept them close and made a good trade with them, offering the gold and valuables from the mail train for more ammunition.

The three men were still with the warriors when they struck a herd of 250 cattle run by five cowboys twelve miles west of Sulphur Springs.[23] Traveling with the herd was a wagon train with seventeen men, one woman, and two children on their way to California. No doubt the cowboys thought the seventeen men with the wagon train would help protect them. But a cattle herd strung out over a long distance was too tempting a target, so Cochise led his warriors in a dash toward the herd. They fought a running battle for three hours, as the warriors harried the strong party of well-armed men, hoping to force the White Eyes to take up a defensive position so the warriors could run off the cattle. Cochise led the charge repeatedly, for the Whites soon noticed him on his black stallion and concentrated their fire on him. But he was protected by Power, so he tried to draw the fire away from his warriors. He slipped down on the side of his horse, looking under the horse's neck and directing his mount with his body and the rope tied around the jaw and his Horse Power. He rode up against one of the cowboys, who could not touch him with his gun. Straightening up as he neared the man, Cochise drove his lance clean through his body, so the man was dead before he left his saddle. Seeing this evidence of Power, the warriors pressed their attack until the cowboys fell back and abandoned their herd. The warriors let them go, for cattle to feed their families had far more value to them than dead Whites.

The next day, they returned to the wagon road where soldiers had found the coach they'd looted several days before. The warriors made several charges against the soldiers, but did not press the attack against the discipline and firepower of the White Eyes. Then they hurried the slow-moving herd to the Dragoons and at night crossed the Sulphur Springs Valley to the Chiricahuas, trying to reach a safe place where they could kill the cattle and jerk the meat.

But soldiers converged from several directions—one band of them
guided by Merejildo, who quickly found the trail of the cattle and
the war party crossing the valley into the Chiricahuas. The soldiers
marched for twenty-two hours without stopping and without sleep,
until they finally came up against the rear guard of the war party.
The soldiers charged the five warriors in the rear guard, killing three
in the first rush. Alerted by the shooting, Cochise turned with the
main body of warriors, hoping to draw the soldiers off so those
remaining could still escape with the herd. Cochise boldly led his
men back toward the soldiers, charging them and then drawing off.
He and Merejildo quickly recognized each other. Cochise tried to get
close enough to kill him, but Merejildo dropped back among the
soldiers—who soon concentrated their fire on Cochise. But Cochise
was sheltered under the wing of his Power, so none of the bullets
could find him. Whenever Merejildo or one of the soldiers took aim
at him, Cochise slipped down on the side of his horse and shot
under his steed's neck. But despite his Power and courage, the war
party was in a dangerous position, caught out in the open with their
bows matched against the good guns of the soldiers. After fighting
for ninety minutes, Cochise had lost twelve warriors with little damage inflicted in return. He gave the command to abandon the cattle
herd and retreat into the foothills of the mountains that waited for
him nearby—old friends with their arms extended.[24]

He went to those mountains and those rocks whose place-names
had schooled him, knowing his enemies would seek him there. The
warriors riding with him were shaken and grief-stricken, for they
had lost twelve of their brothers and nephews and uncles and lifelong friends. He could feel their doubts cutting away the sand of
their courage, like floodwaters in the cottonwood roots. He knew he
should scatter his war party before the soldiers concentrated against
them, knowing the word would have gone out to all of the surrounding forts. But he could sense the dismay among the warriors,
the wedge of fear amidst the anger and the grief. Moreover, he felt
his Power standing behind him. Instead of scattering the band so
the warriors would make their way by twos or threes down into
Sonora, he led them into the heart of the Chiricahuas.

There, Merejildo found them in Tex Canyon, at the place Power
told Cochise he should turn and wait for the soldiers. There he
missed his chance to kill Merejildo—who it seemed had the protection of his own Power. And there Cochise and his warriors stood off

the best efforts of the soldiers, coming from everywhere against them.

This great victory was like a high ridge in the storm, one from which the waters must run down one side or the other. After the soldiers had gone limping back to the forts for more bullets and more men, Cochise led his men north to the Burro Mountains, partway between the territory of the White Mountain bands and the territory of the Chihenne. On the way he passed by Trail Goes Down between Two Hills, which reminded him of foolish Old Man Owl. The place congratulated him on his cleverness in leading the soldiers from one hill to another, back and forth until they looked foolish in the eyes of his warriors. But that place also reminded Cochise that not even the soldiers would go back and forth indefinitely between the same two hills. Cochise understood that he must find some way out of the war, which he could not win. He had done great damage for more than eight years. He had long ago lost count of the White Eyes he had killed, but knew they totaled in the thousands.[25] Now the White Eyes had seen he could still strike in the middle of the territory they thought they controlled and stand against many soldiers.

Perhaps now—finally—they had grown weary of passing between two hills.

Perhaps now—finally—they might give the Chokonen the only thing they had ever wanted—the land that was their own.

Cochise turned his back on Fort Bowie, whose *nantan* he did not trust, and put himself between two hills. On the one hand, most of the White Mountain bands had made peace, so some of his kinsmen among those bands might serve as intermediaries. He sent Dos-teh-seh and some other people into the White Mountain country, for she was the daughter of Mangas Coloradas and was kin to Francisco. Although Francisco had been killed treacherously by the White Eyes, Dos-teh-seh still had relatives with his band who would help her. On the other hand, Cochise also sent word to Loco, who was leading the Chihenne faction talking to the White Eyes about establishment of a reservation near Ojo Caliente or Cañada Alamosa. A new agent had come to the Chihenne—a *nantan* named Charles Drew, who seemed brave and honorable. He treated the Chihenne leaders with respect and seemed intent on restraining the soldiers and providing an opportunity for peace.[26] Cochise sent out feelers both east and west. As he rode on down the steep ridge of his decision, he thanked Trail Goes Down between Two Hills for its wisdom and remembered his father with love and longing.

As he waited for word about peace, Cochise moved his band frequently and tried to restrain the raiding of the warriors, even though their families were hungry. Deep in the season of the Ghost Dance[27] they crossed the dangerous Sulphur Springs Valley at night and took refuge in the Dragoons. But soldiers followed them there. Cochise kept his band moving from peak to peak so the soldiers could not find them, but Merejildo came upon a track that led him to the camp of one of his subchiefs. There the soldiers killed thirteen and captured two before the survivors escaped. The people who escaped made their way to Cochise's camp, having lost all of their food and possessions, so that Cochise must stretch his small supply of food even further. Of course, he did not consider turning them away, although everyone already had their belts cinched tight. The need to freely share food and shelter was one of the most powerful values of the People, and it would be far better to starve than to have people say he had been selfish.

Cochise kept his band moving from mountain range to mountain range, taking care that no fire should leave a tattletale of smoke and praying constantly to his Power. He gathered rumors that large, armed parties were moving in all directions from Tucson and other settlements. He also learned Sonora was again offering a scalp bounty and Chihuahua had mounted a major campaign, keeping hundreds of soldiers constantly in the field. Nonetheless, Cochise left the women and children in a safe place and raided down into Mexico to bring back cattle. They captured a herd of two hundred, but were so slowed by the cattle that Mexican soldiers overtook them, killing five people in the camp. The rest of the Chokonen moved north with what cattle they had left. The Mexicans followed them all the way to the Dragoons and hit another Chokonen rancheria. Hearing the shooting, Cochise rallied his warriors and went to rescue the other band. He found the Mexicans in strong positions, shooting down at the warriors who had stayed behind to give the women and children time to escape. Cochise selected his four best marksmen and gave them the best guns and most of the ammunition. He sent these four men to a position where they overlooked the Mexicans, then launched a carefully coordinated attack from three sides, so that suddenly the Mexicans were the ones in the trap. The Mexicans stood their ground for a time, but retreated after the marksmen killed two of them.[28]

Now Cochise tended to his wounded and distributed the cattle and horses they had brought back, pushing hunger away to the edge of the camp. Then he mounted another expedition, this time raiding ranches in the area. They burned several ranches, then boldly attacked Tubac, which had galled Cochise in the many years it had existed. The thirty residents took shelter in the few strong buildings while the warriors looted the rest of the town.[29] Then they turned south, circled around, and attacked a wagon train near Camp Crittenden, killing three men. Soldiers set out after them, but Cochise attacked the twenty White Eyes with nearly two hundred warriors, putting them to flight. Cochise did not bother to pursue and destroy them, for he loved his warriors more than he hated the Americans.

Cochise now sent Dos-teh-seh once again to the White Mountain bands. She returned saying the *nantan* at Camp Mogollon—a man named Major John Green—seemed willing to talk.

Cochise resolved to go and talk to the *nantan*, after ten seasons of seeking his revenge. He had drunk death until it ran down his face, pooled around his legs, and threatened to drown his people. He would talk. He wouldn't forget his father or his brother or start licking the hands of those who whipped them, like Dog in the story. But he would see what the White Eyes offered, and not turn away if they offered any honorable escape from the slow dwindle toward death that otherwise awaited the People.

Perhaps it was his Power that turned him to it now, after urging him to fight for so long. For perhaps his Power knew that a slender chance would present itself now in the most unexpected of forms—a White man a warrior might trust.

13

Early 1871

Turn toward Peace: Thomas Jeffords

The Boy Who Trained an Eagle and Taught It to Hunt

A young boy climbed up a cliff and reached an eagle's nest.
He brought down one of the eaglets. He took it home with him.
   People said to him, "Throw it away! It will make you sick!"
But he didn't.
   He kept it and fed it and raised it. It became his friend.
Wherever he went, the eagle went with him. It flew along by his
side. When he saw a deer he told the eagle to get it, and the eagle
would catch it for him. The eagle would bring him a rabbit or
anything he wanted.

In the season of Large Leaves,[1] Cochise went to meet with the *nantan* at Camp Mogollon. He went that long distance because he knew
the soldiers at Fort Bowie were treacherous. Nor did he trust the soldiers at Fort Goodwin, which was in Chihenne territory. Cochise still
hoped he might find that rare treasure—an honest White man who
would keep a good hold on his promises. Dos-teh-seh's report about
Green made him hope that perhaps this *nantan* was such a one, for
he did not address her with either a sneer or a dangerous smile.
More than a thousand White Mountain people were already camped
near the fort, living on the rations of the soldiers. They went no
more out to raid, but many of them now worked with the soldiers,
helping hunt the bands still fighting. He went cautiously into that
country, for bad blood had grown between the Chokonen and the
White Mountain people, who now helped the soldiers hunt them.
Their bands had many ties of kinship and friendship, for Francisco
had for a long time been one of the chief allies of Cochise. They still

Thomas Jeffords at his ranch. A trader and sometime scout, Thomas Jeffords was the only White Eye that Cochise trusted and played a key role in bringing about peace between Cochise and the Americans. *(Arizona Historical Society)*

had friends among the White Mountain people, who were anxious to feed the possibility of peace between the Chokonen and the White Eyes. But now they had enemies as well, so Cochise moved cautiously through the White Mountain country and selected the place where he would meet Green with great care.

He was impressed with the *nantan*, who seemed a strong and quiet man—not given to boasts or bluster. Green listened quietly and was careful in his promises.[2] Green showed respect and courtesy unusual in a White man, as most of them spoke brusquely and without preamble, treating even great leaders like errant children in need of scolding.

Cochise returned the courtesy, saying he had heard Green was a good man who kept his word like a true warrior. He said he had looked around and talked to the White Mountain people, who said Green treated them well and had allowed them to settle in their own country. Cochise asked for no more than that, and in return said he would stop all raiding among the Americans. He said, "I was treated very badly at Camp Bowie some time ago. I have been fighting for thirteen years and now am tired and want to sleep. The troops have worried me and killed almost all my band. But now I think that I have killed about as many as I have lost and we are about even.

Now I would like to come on the reservation in our own country—
and then I will protect the road from Camp Bowie to the San Pedro.
If I come in, many other bands might come in as well. For whenever
I need a large war party, I send to the other tribes for volunteers
and they come. But remember, I did not start this war—but fought
only for revenge and in self-defense."[3]

They talked awhile, until Cochise was sure Green understood
the reasons for the war and his desire for peace. But Green was
careful to make no promises. Cochise respected this in him, for he
knew the Whites made decisions in a complicated and confusing
way. They were not like the People, who each made decisions for
themselves and therefore could be relied upon to hold onto those
decisions—for they would be disgraced if they lied. Among the
Whites, the band leaders could not decide anything for themselves—
even strong and honorable ones. They must always send up to a
higher chief to see what they could think and do and promise. Usually that chief must send up to a higher chief—maybe all the way to
this mysterious Great Father. If Green had promised them a reservation and told them to camp in a certain place, Cochise would have
immediately suspected a trap. Instead, Green said he would give the
words of Cochise to his commander and urged Cochise to come
back in several weeks for an answer. Cochise went on his way again,
as a man who ponders a dream whose meaning remains unclear. He
turned south to the Chiricahuas, feeling uneasy and threatened in
the White Mountain territory now that their warriors were the hunting dogs of the soldiers.[4]

Cochise talked a long while with his subchiefs in the Chiricahuas, seeking the consensus by which the Chokonen made all their
important decisions. Cochise could not command his warriors or
even the subchiefs. He could only sway them with his eloquence
and his Power and the deep loyalty forged in years of fighting
together. They smoked and prayed and talked a long time, trying to
decide whether they should return to the White Mountains and trust
in Green—even though they now had enemies among the White
Mountain bands. Gradually they decided they should instead turn
their faces to the east. They had word already from the Chihenne
that the Whites had sent Lieutenant Drew as the new agent. The
Chihenne had been fighting the soldiers for as long as Cochise but
had suffered even more in their war, for they had not so many good
places to hide. The soldiers had early on broken the Mescalero, who

Victorio. Victorio's Chihenne Apache often fought alongside Cochise's Chokonen. After the death of Cochise and the breakdown of the peace he had won, Victorio led his people in a doomed but brilliant flight across the Southwest and Mexico. Descriptions of Cochise suggest that he may have in many ways resembled Victorio physically. *(National Archives)*

had been the allies of the Chihenne. The Whites had at first imprisoned the Mescalero in the midst of their enemies—the Navajo at Bosque Redondo. But seeing that remaining there would mean death from disease and starvation, the Mescalero had gone back to their own country, living quietly and hurting no one. The soldiers had finally decided to let them stay there. This had given the Chihenne hope, seeing that the soldiers had relented and let the Mescalero stay in their own country. Loco, Victorio, and Savadora, a son of Mangas Coloradas, had sent word that they wanted peace. They met with Agent Drew in the season of Large Fruit,[5] and said he seemed an honest and respectful man who favored peace and promised to try to establish a reservation for the Chihenne near Cañada Alamosa, close by the sacred waters of Ojo Caliente. This seemed hopeful, as Cañada Alamosa was a good place, with grass, water, game, and a small settlement of Mexicans with whom the Chihenne and Chokonen had long maintained friendly relations, for they traded there the goods they brought back from Mexico.

Hearing these hopeful tidings from Victorio and Loco, Cochise sent word he would also talk to Agent Drew. But he did not move his band to Cañada Alamosa, for things still seemed uncertain and unsettled. He came and camped nearby for short periods sometimes, so he could see how things stood. But he was wary and careful, for scalp hunters coming up from Sonora often prowled about that area, killing anyone they found alone or in small groups and taking their hair back down into Mexico. Moreover, although Agent Drew seemed like a good man, he never settled on a promise—like a fly you cannot quite catch. He would say something hopeful, but then wait a long while for word from some other *nantan*.

In addition, Agent Drew seemed to have trouble with the other Whites and the Mexicans. He tried to prevent the Mexicans at Cañada Alamosa from trading with the warriors. The headmen in Cañada Alamosa objected. Chihenne who came to the Chokonen camps brought some puzzling and confusing stories about the fighting among the Whites. Agent Drew sent soldiers to arrest the Mexicans who were trading with the Chihenne, who called up their own soldiers to protect them. Then the Cañada Alamosa Mexicans sent men to take Agent Drew prisoner. It went back and forth like this, until the Chihenne were completely confused, not knowing whom to trust.[6] Agent Drew said they must remain quietly nearby until he got permission to set up a reservation for them. But the traders at Cañada Alamosa warned the Chihenne that Agent Drew was lulling them with his promises so they would remain long enough for him to send the soldiers to kill them—as the Whites had killed the Arivaipa.

The situation grew even more confusing when Agent Drew got in a bitter argument with two post traders the Chihenne trusted. One of these men was named Elias Brevoort, a loud, smooth-talking man who had been selling the People food and knives and pots and pans at the post fort. He also came more quietly to their camps to sell them guns and ammunition—all in return for loot brought back from Mexico.

His partner was a tall, quiet, red-haired man named Thomas Jeffords who treated the People with respect and compassion. The People called him Red Beard, and Cochise would soon find his fate twined about the trunk of this most unusual of White men. Cochise had heard people talking about Jeffords for some time, for Jeffords sold goods to the People.[7] He was very tall, with bristling red whiskers that seemed so strange they might be a sign of Power. He did not brag and talk in a rough, loud voice like most White Eyes, but watched everything with his bright blue eyes—which sparkled with humor and intelligence. He also had a strong laugh and loved to make jokes and fool around. He did not make a big noise to draw attention and credit to himself and paid little attention to what other people said. He just went on his own way—doing as he thought best without fear. In this he was like a warrior of the People, who did not complain or chatter foolishly nor break their word—but who also loved to laugh and play jokes on one another and roll in the dirt for the joy of living, like Coyote.

Jeffords had been born in the east.[8] Some said he had been the captain of a ship big enough to hold a whole village, on a lake so big you could not see the far shore, so now people called him Captain. He moved west then. First he worked on making a great road. Then he practiced law in Denver. But he was a restless man, so he went to Taos, where he was seized by the gold sickness of the Whites and so took up prospecting. When the Whites began to fight each other, Jeffords served as a scout for the blue soldiers—even the ones who had come from the west and fought Cochise at Apache Pass. After that, Jeffords worked for a while in charge of the mail riders who carried messages from Santa Fe to Tucson. But he got discouraged because the Chokonen killed so many riders.[9] He quit and did some more prospecting, this time even passing through the territory of the Chokonen. He made friends with some of the Chihenne bands, for he was a strong, friendly, and respectful man who treated the People like human beings instead of animals to be hunted. He even learned their language—something White Eyes almost never did. People who knew him said he was a rare man—not like a White man at all. That is why the Whites sometimes turned to him to talk to the Chihenne and sometimes Loco sent messages to the soldiers through Jeffords.

Loco and Victorio were glad when Jeffords got the license to serve as a trader at Cañada Alamosa, for he seemed a white man they could trust—at least a little. They were puzzled and unsettled when Jeffords and Brevoort got in a great argument with Agent Drew, who also seemed like a good man. It all started with trouble about Loco, who was trying to stay on good terms with all three men. One night Loco got drunk on whiskey. Agent Drew and Brevoort got into a fight about whom to blame for giving the warriors whiskey—each blaming the other. Agent Drew won that argument, so the faraway men who had charge over all the traders took away the license of Jeffords and Brevoort.

After that, Jeffords sought out the camp of Cochise, who was then staying not far from Cañada Alamosa. Jeffords rode openly and fearlessly, displaying the casual courage of a warrior. Perhaps he felt protected by his relationship with Loco, or with the friendly contacts he had made with some Chokonen bands when he was prospecting in their territory several years earlier. Still, it was a brave thing—for Cochise had remained aloof from Loco's peace talk, waiting to see whether the wind would shift and blow toward peace. The lookouts saw Red Beard coming and sent word back to Cochise to see if they should kill him. Cochise sent word back that they should not harm him, but that they should meet him and bring him into camp to see what Jeffords had to say. Perhaps Jeffords wanted to begin trading with the Chokonen, now that he had been sent away from Cañada Alamosa.[10] Cochise greeted Jeffords with grave courtesy, impressed at the fearless way he came alone among the Chokonen—not boastful and swaggering like a man trying to work up his courage, but quiet and confident like a warrior. Every other white man Cochise had known seemed to think of the People as not quite human. Even the other traders who came among them either swaggered or smiled so much you could not trust them. Most of the traders were worthless people, interested only in money, or men without a conscience who would kill even their own kind for a small advantage, like Johnson or Kirker. Red Beard seemed different. He seemed a true man, sure of himself and willing to judge other men on the same terms—whether they were of the People or of his own race. Cochise felt the whispering of his Power, saying Red Beard might prove useful to the Chokonen, for he was independent, fearless, and honest, and he spoke their language. The Chokonen always had need of such a man in their negotiations with the soldiers, who could twist words tighter than a horsehair riding crop. Cochise sat with Red Beard for several hours, smoking and talking—taking his measure. He had aways done this, relying far more on the character of a man than on words or promises. For the People, everything depended on their relationships and on their sense of shame and honor. He had never had such a feeling about a Mexican or an American—save the beginnings of it now with this quiet, funny, dignified man with his flaming red hair and great bushy beard.

Now came strange news from the Chihenne. Agent Drew, whom many of them trusted, had gone out with some soldiers after warriors who had stolen some horses. But he got lost trying to get back to the fort and wandered for days without food and water. By the time some other soldiers found him, he was too far gone and died. Cochise shook his head upon hearing this news, baffled the People should be running in fear from a people so foolish and weak even a *nantan* would starve or die of thirst in a place where an apprentice warrior would thrive. Wary of the new agent, many of the Chihenne warriors remained at a distance from the fort and the agency, although many of their families camped nearby and collected rations. They had come to depend on those rations, for the warriors were no longer raiding much among the Americans, nor did they go so often down into Sonora and Chihuahua.

Loco and Victorio sent word to Cochise in the season of Large Fruit[11] that they would meet with the new agent, Lieutenant Argalus Garey Hennisee, to talk further about peace. Cochise brought ninety-four Chokonen to camp near Cañada Alamosa, including thirty-four warriors, which constituted his personal following. Jeffords also attended the conference, which reassured Cochise, who had already begun to think Red Beard was different from all other White Eyes. Another agent was there as well, who had authority over Hennisee. This man—William Arny—had already visited the Navajo and Zuni and Hopi, saying the Great Father had sent him to make peace with all his children. Cochise met warily with him, standing with the Chihenne leaders—his well-armed warriors alert to any treachery.

Arny addressed Cochise in a friendly manner, although condescending in the way most Whites tried to be friendly—as though the People were children in ignorance. "The Great Father wants to know what the Indians want so as to keep the peace," said Arny, as though the warriors had started the war.

"I have been to the White Mountains to learn how they talked and am now here to hear what you have to say so that I can take my word back to my people in the Chiricahua Mountains," said Cochise quietly. He had brought his following here to test the possibilities of peace, but the greatest part of the Chokonen remained waiting at home.

"This paper was written by the Great Father," said Arny, displaying a large paper as though it were a talisman blessed by the strike of lightning, "and I will read what he says to his children."

"I want to talk first, I have come to hear you talk," said Cochise, still trying to decide whether Arny was a man who could be trusted or whether he split his words between truth and trap like the tongue of a snake. Besides, he did not trust the talking paper of the Whites, which had not the face or honor of a man, which was why the Whites so easily tossed them aside when it suited them. Some people said the talking paper was a form of witchcraft—like the pictures the Whites made of people—and did not trust anyone who was scribbling all the time in that incomprehensible way. "If the government talks straight, I want a good peace. My people hide in the mountains and arroyos to keep out of the way. I want the truth told. A man has only one mouth and if he won't tell the truth he is put out of the way," he said earnestly, hoping Arny would understand the importance of this. Among the people, a liar was despised, and could not speak in council or give witness in any dispute or carry messages. Many leaders would not have a liar in their war party. But all the White Eyes had ever done was lie to him, so he wondered whether they put any value on the truth at all.

"The Great Father wants a good peace," said Arny smoothly, "and the warriors must stop the killing and stealing and go upon a reservation or he will send soldiers after them again and continue to do so until they are willing to make peace."

"The People want to run around like a Coyote," said Cochise. "They don't want to be put in a corral."

"The Great Father does not want to put them in a corral," replied Arny. "He wants them to eat and dress like a white man, have plenty of everything and be contented—wants them to know where they want to receive their rations. Talk it over among yourselves and tell me early tomorrow what you want, where you want the rations issued," he added shrewdly, talking past Cochise to the hungry women with their babies so thin you could count their ribs like counters in the stave game. Cochise understood the snare in this statement, for the story of the argument between Dog and Coyote had been working on him. He understood that a little bread and bad beef might bait the deadfall, so that even if they lived, the White Eyes would crush their spirits.

"We want it so that the Whites and everybody can travel where they please, build their fires at night, lay down and rest in peace," he replied, so Arny would understand they would not trade their freedom for a little beef. "I will talk to the tribe and learn what they want so that I can talk straight. I am going out to talk to the other Indians and have them leave the roads clear," he said.[12]

Arny talked soothingly and promised he would talk with the Great Father to get a reservation for the Chihenne and the Chokonen. Hearing him talk like sun on grass, Cochise and Victorio and Loco felt hopeful. They did not learn until later that Arny made a list of six places for a reservation, most of them places the People would not want to live. The place he recommended to the Great Father was Tularosa, nearly a hundred miles from Cañada Alamosa—far from any White Eyes. But it was a high, cold country without enough game, where crops would freeze quickly. Besides, some people said it was cursed—a witch place. Moreover, it was far from the traders at Cañada Alamosa, who supplied many things the People needed—as well as a place to quietly dispose of plunder brought back from Mexico. In the end, Arny talked well but acted badly—although Cochise only realized this much later.

The Chokonen remained camped quietly near Cañada Alamosa, drawing rations and waiting to learn what the Great Father would decide. Cochise resolved to keep the peace while they waited—and to build up his strength should the White Eyes once again prove treacherous. Red Beard came often to his camp, bringing things to trade. Sometimes he had whiskey, other times trade goods. Sometimes he brought bullets, which he traded quietly.[13] Gradually the trust grew between Red Beard and Cochise, so Cochise leaned more and more heavily on his advice to find his way through the thickets of words the Whites always planted. Jeffords urged him to wait quietly to see what happened next, noting that the *nantan* at Fort Bowie was worried Cochise was only feigning peace so he could accumulate supplies and get more guns from the traders. Cochise smiled grimly at this, for he *was* storing up his supplies—not because he intended a trick, but because he had learned always to prepare for the next trick of the Whites. Cochise waited quietly in his camp for several weeks, his uneasiness growing with each day. Finally, heeding the cautions of his Power, he slipped away from Cañada Alamosa and returned to the Chiricahuas, relying for news on the people who passed back and forth between the Chokonen and the Chihenne.

Several months later, he returned just as quietly to Cañada Alamosa. There he discovered to his alarm that Agent Hennisee had been replaced by Agent Orlando Piper, a wizened little man with a bird voice and an ugly scrabble of whiskers on his chin, who seemed more like an old woman than a man who could command the respect

of warriors. Moreover, Piper now said the Chihenne could not stay
at Cañada Alamosa, close to the hot springs they loved, but must go
to the Mescalero Reservation near Fort Stanton and the Rio Grande,
with its cold winters and places whose names they knew not. Hearing this, Cochise returned just as quietly to the Chiricahuas. Even
Loco refused to move as Agent Piper demanded and the Chihenne
remained camped near Cañada Alamosa, alert to treachery. They
hoped that if they continued to cling to their own land the Whites
would weary of trying to force them to move—so long as the leaders
could keep the warriors from raiding among the Americans. Agent
Piper nagged them like a mother-in-law, but they stayed in place,
like a turtle in the mud. Agent Piper would often ask them about
Cochise, and they would say he had gone back to his own country
and would never consent to live near Fort Stanton.

So everything remained suspended—like the time after a warrior
has been wounded but does not yet feel the pain. Cochise and Victorio and Loco all tried to restrain their warriors, sometimes sending
them down into Mexico to raid when the children grew hungry or
the warriors too restive. But gradually, problems grew up again with
the Americans. Deep in the season of the Ghost Dance,[14] a party of
sixteen miners headed for Apache Pass because a woman told them
they might find gold there. About thirty miles from the pass, they
were ambushed by some young warriors eager for the miners' horses
and guns and angry at the idea of these ugly bearded men digging
in the sacred Chiricahuas. They wounded two of the miners, but the
men all took a strong position so the warriors could not get at them
without losing too many lives. After that, soldiers came out quickly
from Fort Bowie, but they did not have Merejildo with them and so
could not find the raiders.

Warriors slipped out of the camps of Cochise and his subchiefs
one by one and by twos or threes as the cold season hardened
and their families were forced to live on roots and dried acorns—
sometimes chewing on old leather to remember the taste of meat.
Loath to see their children hungry when they still had their weapons,
the warriors went out to find horses and cattle—although Cochise
and the other leaders warned them against raiding. A few warriors
stole fourteen horses from near Silver City, but a party of thirty settlers and soldiers followed them from mountain to mountain back to
the Chiricahuas and surprised a Chokonen camp that had neglected

its sentries in a blinding snowstorm. They killed fourteen people, wounded twenty, and captured one more. They also burned the seventeen wickiups with the 2,500 pounds of beef and blankets and supplies. The survivors, who were Chokonen and Nednhis, scattered. Many sought shelter with Cochise and other band leaders, adding to the mouths they must feed through the season of the Ghost Dance.

Facing starvation in earnest, Cochise now sent out a raiding party that took sixteen horses from Fort Bayard. They hurried back to Cochise's camp, but the settlers and soldiers followed them. Fortunately, Cochise never neglected his sentries. The warrior who had been set to watch the approach to the camp saw the soldiers creeping up on them when it was already too late for him to carry the warning back to the camp. The warrior—a brave man who had fought alongside Cochise for many years—begin shouting and shooting. The White Eyes turned their fire on him, hitting him in the thigh and in the chest. The warrior fell to the ground, but as the Whites came toward him, he took two pistols out of his belt and shot at the oncoming soldiers, all the while singing his death song in a strong loud voice. The warrior shot the White Eyes' *nantan* through the chest just as a rifle bullet tore out the back of his head, ending his death song abruptly. The White *nantan* sank to the ground and opened up his shirt to look curiously at the wound, then died without making a sound. The White Eyes continued their attack and killed fourteen—but most of the band escaped thanks to the courage of the sentry. One of the dead was Salvadora, a son of Mangas Coloradas who had left Cañada Alamosa with the Chokonen—so both Cochise and Dos-teh-seh mourned the death of a kinsman and a warrior and a connection to the time when the People had been masters in their own land.

Knowing the soldiers were scouring the mountains, Cochise kept his band moving constantly. They raided cautiously when hunger hunted them harder than the soldiers. One raiding party, returning without much plunder, ran off two mules from Fort Bowie, but the soldiers chased them, guided by several White Mountain men. The soldiers hit a Chokonen ranchero near Stein's Peak, killing three people before the band could scatter. Continuing on the trail with the help of the warriors turned like dogs on their own people, soldiers hit another Chokonen group led by a subchief long loyal to Cochise, killing fifteen people before they could scatter.

Shaken by all of these losses, some of the Chokonen bands
returned to Cañada Alamosa, hoping the White Eyes would let them
live there with the Chihenne instead of making them all move to
the ill-favored land near Fort Stanton. But Cochise remained aloof,
staying in the most remote camps, moving constantly, and consulting
his Power in long prayers every night. He moved down into Mexico
for a time when the soldiers grew too numerous, like wolves circling
the elk herds in the deep snow. But the Sonorans were hunting the
People as well and the country was infested with scalp hunters, so
Cochise moved back north to the Dragoons. He gathered a hundred
warriors from the allied bands and ran cattle and horses off ranches
along the San Pedro. Five foolish cowboys chased them, not realizing they were trailing a full war party headed by Cochise. Cochise
turned on them, killing three and letting two others escape wounded.
The next day, the warriors killed a mail rider, and the relatives of
women and children killed in the recent attacks on their camp cut
his body into pieces, as a lesson to the White Eyes and a release for
their grief and rage.

Soldiers led by Merejildo picked up the trail of the war party the
next day and pursued them into the Dragoons. Cochise moved his
men—half on foot—to the high point of the Dragoons, where they
could watch as the soldiers started up the canyon after them. Then
he backtracked along his own trail, until he came to a good place to
surprise the soldiers. He waited until the soldiers following Merejildo were surrounded on three sides, then rose up and gave the signal to fire. They might have done great damage to the soldiers if
they'd had enough guns and bullets, but they relied on arrows and
lances and so lacked the firepower to take advantage of the surprise
they achieved. However, it gave Cochise satisfaction to have picked
a place for the ambush Merejildo had not spotted. The troops kept
their discipline, even though they were nearly surrounded. They dismounted and sought good cover and returned fire with their limit-
less bullets and good guns. But Cochise had selected the positions
for his warriors with his customary skill, so the soldiers could do them
no harm. This was one reason the *nantans* hated to chase Cochise,
for he was the only leader of the People who often ambushed the
soldiers chasing him—so they always had to move with great care.
After twenty minutes, the soldiers retreated back down the canyon,
seeing they could do nothing against the entrenched warriors.

Cochise set scouts to keep track of the soldiers, then led his warriors through the mountain and down into the San Pedro Valley on the other side—splitting his force to frustrate the pursuit, sending some to the Whetstones and some to the Huachucas. When the soldiers gave up the chase, Cochise circled back to the Dragoons, where he knew every place-name. The Dragoons were a wild landscape of giant pinkish and yellowish boulders that glowed like a campfire in the sacred last light and first light. They lay tumbled in every shape and arrangement on the steep slopes, offering an unlimited number of places to hide—their surfaces mottled with brightly colored lichen, gay as songbirds. All the world of plants grew along the flanks of the mountain—from the mesquites with their hot season beans at the bottom to the pines covering the rocky summits rising to eight thousand feet. Along the way, the People could change the season by simply climbing or descending a few thousand feet. This enabled them to find food in any time of the year. Cochise now understood why his father had taught him the names of every place, and why Tipping Beetle listened for the Mountain Spirits, and why Child-of-the-Water had given the People to this place—as surely as he had given the elk to the forest and the antelope to the grass. For the rocks offered them hiding places and canyons and overlooks—and so their enemies could not strike them there unless they neglected their prayers and forgot their great debt of gratitude to the dreaming rocks of the Dragoons.

Even so, the soldiers pressed the Chokonen, forcing them to move constantly so they could not gather and roast mescal and store food for the Ghost Season. Cochise resolved to go south into Sonora, hoping the scalp hunters had tired and the Mexican soldiers had gone back to their towns. They raided Mexico, although the country seemed poor and picked over. They captured one of the leading men of Santa Cruz, then made him write a letter saying they would trade him for goods at Fronteras if the soldiers did not pursue them.[15]

Then they moved north and hit several ranches, mostly trying to take horses because cattle moved too slowly to be safe plunder when the war party was pursued so closely. They raided three ranches along the border, killing four men and wounding two others. But the cowboys and ranch owners fought back as most of the ranches had well-fortified buildings of stone. One rancher wounded Cochise slightly. But his warriors now had such confidence in his Power that

Dragoons. Cochise once said that sometimes the rocks of the Dragoons were his only friends. *(Peter Aleshire)*

his wounding only increased their confidence, for they knew any other leader would surely have been killed. And because his Power protected him, Cochise moved fearlessly in the forefront of the warriors in every attack, inspiring them with his courage and shaming them in their fear.

After months of raiding through Sonora and along the border, Cochise returned with his horses and his plunder to the camps of the Chokonen in the Dragoons. There, he received disturbing news. First, José María Trujillo—the justice of the peace from Cañada Alamosa who had often fostered trade with the Chokonen—had come to the Dragoons with some Chihenne and urged anyone he found there to return to Cañada Alamosa, for Agent Piper had promised them a reservation. About a hundred people left the Dragoons to go to Cañada Alamosa, including many relatives of the warriors who had been raiding with him. Dos-teh-seh had heaped disdain on the blandishments of Trujillo and the family and personal following of Cochise had remained to await his return, but he was disturbed by how many people had yielded to the longing for peace when they had not his Power to stiffen their courage.

Cochise also soon learned some better news from a warrior from Juh's band. Juh had killed one of the worst of the *nantans*, a fierce and determined officer named Lieutenant Howard Cushing. That *nantan* had been hunting Cochise a long time, relying on White Mountain warriors to guide him. Cushing and his men stayed in the saddle on the trail of raiders for months at a time, covering a thousand miles on a patrol and pushing on without pause. Cochise heard Cushing wanted to hunt him down, so Cochise had kept his Chokonen out of his path. But Cushing wiped out a camp and killed some relatives of Juh, so Juh vowed vengeance. Juh stalked Cushing, shadowing his patrols and trying to trick him into a trap. In this he had the help of Cushing's arrogance and blood lust. Finally Juh lured Cushing into a narrow canyon in the Huachuca Mountains near the Sonoita Valley, leading him in with the footprints of a woman. Juh had trapped the advance guard of the soldiers, holding them in place until Cushing came up to rescue them. Then the warriors directed their fire at the *nantan*, killing him quickly. After that, Juh let the rest of the soldiers retreat, for he had killed the man he set out after. Cochise thought this killing might make more trouble, but was glad to be rid of Cushing.[16]

Then a man with relatives among the Chokonen from the Arivaipa band brought terrible news. He was a follower of Eskiminzin, a hard-fighting chief who had once cast a long shadow of Power but who had shrunken down with death and loss so he had been willing to do almost anything for peace with the White Eyes. His people had lived in Arivaipa Canyon, with its many trees, year-round water, and deep crevasses. But Whites had harried and depleted them, until they were hiding in the high places and starving slowly to death. Eskiminzin made peace with the *nantan* at Camp Grant at the junction of the San Pedro River and Arivaipa Creek, agreeing to camp close to the soldier fort—mostly for protection from the settlers. The *nantan*—a man named Lieutenant Royal Whitman—seemed friendly and trustworthy, a true man with a good heart. But then some Pima, Mexicans, and White Eyes from Tucson attacked Eskiminzin's camp when most of the warriors were off hunting. They struck at dawn and moved through the camp with clubs, bashing in the brains of the sleeping women and children, who had trusted the protection of the soldiers. They killed perhaps 150 people—almost all of them women and children—which nearly destroyed the Arivaipa band. Whitman hurried to them, pleading with Eskiminzin not to seek his revenge and to trust in him and continue to work for peace. But Eskiminzin took the remnants of his band back into the mountains, broken with grief and sorrow.[17]

Cochise wondered how these two events would change the height of the ridge over which the Chokonen must pass if they were to survive. He could not guess the effect—for the White Eyes were as demented as a careless Ga'an dancer who dropped his stick. Maybe they would be shamed by the massacre—or perhaps they would have a dance of celebration and resolve to do the same everywhere. Maybe they would be discouraged by the death of Cushing—or perhaps they would redouble their efforts to obtain revenge. He could not tell, but the rumors of peace negotiations among the Chihenne and the White Mountain bands convinced him to risk talking to the White Eyes, despite what had happened to Eskiminzin.

Cochise felt caught in the midst of his enemies, like the deer who hears the echo of the wolves ahead and behind. Still recovering from his wound, he sent warriors to Cañada Alamosa to see how things stood there. Not long afterward, his sentries ran to him to say that Red Beard was coming with a Mexican and two warriors—one a Chihenne and one a Chokonen. Cochise sent warriors out to guide them to the camp, warning the warriors to watch Red Beard for a time before they talked to him to be sure soldiers were not following him. Cochise considered Red Beard his friend, but he was, after all, still a White man. Everyone he knew who had trusted a White man was already dead. But Red Beard came into camp with his customary courage and good humor, greeting Cochise affectionately. Red Beard said Nathaniel Pope, the chief of all of the Indian agents, asked him to find Cochise and urge him to move his band to Cañada Alamosa, where they would receive rations. Cochise told him to return to Pope and say that Cochise also desired peace, but would not risk leading the women and children back to Cañada Alamosa through the midst of so many soldiers, all seeking their blood.

Red Beard tried to convince him to come, showing Cochise a talking paper he said was a letter of safe conduct so the soldiers would not bother them. But Cochise only asked him if he thought the Arivaipa near Camp Grant had such a talking paper. Cochise thought then about the boy who had tamed the eagle—and wondered whether he had tamed Red Beard, or whether Red Beard had tamed him. He remembered the story about how Child-of-the-Water had killed the eagles—the advice of the stories in this matter seemed contradictory. He felt weary sometimes with the effort of under-standing what the stories wanted him to know. But in truth, Cochise had other reasons for not going to Cañada Alamosa. His Power warned him against it, and the rocks of the Dragoons warned him against it. He could sense the weariness among even his strong war-riors and the yearning for peace among the women, fearful their children would not live out another year. But if he yielded to this mirage of peace now, their will to fight might topple into the river of the White Eyes like a sandy bank. Then they must settle in the land of the Chihenne, shut away from the places that knew them. Cochise sent back a cautious answer and resolved to wait in the Dragoons until his Power directed him.[18] In the meantime, Cochise continued to exert his influence to keep the warriors from raiding the Ameri-cans. He hoped Red Beard had spoken truthfully, and that the Americans now wanted peace. But he was still unwilling to give up his own country as the price of that peace—and unwilling to trust the promise of the soldiers and make the dangerous journey to Cañada Alamosa. He waited and prayed, gathering up any scrap of information filtering to his secret camps.

The years now lay heavy on him—like a late snow on early flow-ers—for he had fought all of his life without pause and the People seemed more in danger now than ever. What was the point of all his fighting, if they must all die—a whole people whose name would be forgotten and spoken no more?

Still—even now—he could not yield. He could only wait as a man who has already sung his death song, to see what Power intended.

14

Mid-1871

Power Takes a Hand

The Ga'an Who Fought the Mexican Soldiers

This happened at the foot of the Cuchillo Mountains near the place where the woman was killed by the bear. A war party was going back to the mountain. They were on the plains near the mountain. Mexican cavalry came after them. The Indians had no guns; they had nothing but bows and arrows and spears. They couldn't hurt anyone from a distance with these, but the soldiers had guns and could kill from a distance.

One man and a few women got away though the soldiers surrounded the Indians. The man prayed to the Ga'an of the mountain as he ran. Then Ga'an came out from the mountain, many of them. They surrounded the soldiers. They opened a cave in the rocks and with their swords drove the soldiers into the cave. Then they shut the door again and not one of the soldiers ever got out. They say there are shoes piled up at the mouth of the cave yet to show where the soldiers were driven in.

All the Ga'an have real swords like the ones soldiers have. They had them at this time, and every time the Indians see the Ga'an, they have real swords, they say.

Soon worrisome news filtered back to Cochise, who remained quietly in the Dragoons trying to make the food stretch out so the warriors would not go raiding and stir up the soldiers. The soldiers had a new *nantan*—General George Crook—a strange, bearded, hard-fighting man who seemed a dangerous enemy. He arrived in the season of Many Leaves[1] and immediately traveled all through the territory in a way none of the other great *nantan*s had done. People said he was a hard but fair man. He talked to the White Mountain chiefs, hearing everything they had to say. He promised he would protect them if they lived quietly on the reservation—but would hunt them

236

down and kill them if they made trouble. He also said any warriors who wanted to live quietly with their families and keep the peace with the soldiers must help him hunt down the "bad" Indians who ran around like Coyote. This seemed ominous news, for Cochise knew that soldiers led by warriors posed a far greater threat to the survival of the free People than did any number of soldiers alone. The Americans could send a thousand soldiers against him with two hundred cannons and he would just look down from the high places and laugh. But forty soldiers with thirty warriors as scouts was as death riding over the hill, for they could hang onto his trail and hit him by surprise or seek out the hidden camps of the women and children when the warriors went raiding. Many of the *nantans* were arrogant and foolish, sneering at the warriors and sure of their own war power. These men Cochise did not fear—they could always be lured into the snare of their pride. But this General Crook was another matter, for he did not underestimate the People and so could turn their own strengths against them. The news seemed especially grim when he later learned that General Crook—whom people called the Gray Fox—had encountered Loco and the Cañada Alamosa justice of the peace Trujillo, who were coming to find Cochise. Gray Fox had nearly seized Loco and made him a prisoner, but then decided to send him back to Cañada Alamosa. Gray Fox said he was hunting Cochise, who was the worst of chiefs. Cochise heard this as the cottonwood feels the first frost of the season of the Ghost Dance.

Seeing the hunger in his camp, Cochise reluctantly agreed to let some of the younger warriors go out raiding. He admonished them to avoid attacking mail riders, which always stirred up the soldiers, and to move quickly and bring back only horses and mules. They went down into northern Sonora and brought back forty horses and mules taken from a Papago village. But those Papago followed the war party back to the Chokonen camp in the Santa Rita Mountains. They barely had a warning when the Papago struck, killing five warriors in the rear guard who traded their lives for time enough for the rest to run up the mountain, leaving behind their desperately needed supplies. The triumphant Papago cut off the ears of the people they killed, so they could collect the bounty—then they went down into Sonora. Cochise let them go, his band scattered and himself sick.

Cochise had felt the stirrings of something dark inside him in recent months. Sometimes he felt a pain in his stomach, like an old wound pulling open. He prayed and sought the advice of shamans in divining what this meant—but the feeling came and went, so he paid it little attention.[2] He had suffered many wounds in his life from the bullets Power had barely turned aside. He had ridden and fought and given out death in all its forms for more than sixty rounds of the seasons, so it seemed natural that time should wear on him now, like moccasins at the end of a long journey. But more than the physical pain that beset him, he sometimes suffered a weariness of spirit.

True enough, he had lived a full and admirable life. Dos-teh-seh still shared his bed, the great companion of his spirit throughout all of his long life, protecting him with her counsel and her love and her courage. She was loved and respected by everyone in the band, including his other wives, whom he had mostly taken into his protection to form alliances with other band leaders or to protect after the deaths of their husbands. Some had died. Others kept their wickiups close to his, but did not often expect visits from him. He stayed mostly with Dos-teh-seh and with Steps on Water,[3] a beautiful young woman with a fiery temper who helped keep Cochise from feeling the chill of his years in the darkness. He had fine sons, the pride of his heart. Taza had taken his place in the forefront of the warriors, demonstrating a growing Power in war. He was completely fearless and listened carefully to his father, who put all of his effort into teaching Taza the prayers and songs and stratagems necessary to leadership, hoping the other band leaders would turn to him when Cochise was gone. Naiche was still a boy, ready now for his warrior training and devoted to his older brother. Naiche loved to play and loll about and make clever things with his finely shaped hands, although he was cheerful and uncomplaining in the face of any hardship and of his training. He was graceful and quick and strong, but so far showed no sign of the Power that would distinguish a chief or even a war leader. Cochise was content that this should be so, for he did not want the loyalty of his followers to be divided between Taza and Naiche when he died. The People were already too fragmented without further division among the Chokonen. He hoped that Naiche would serve Taza as Juan had served him, in these long, hard years since the death of Coyuntura. So in all of these ways, Cochise had reason for happiness and satisfaction, for he had kept his family safe when so many others sat keening before the pyre of the wickiups of their loved ones. Cochise believed that this had been the reward of Power for the faithfulness with which he had followed the urgings of Power.

And yet, he could not escape the questions and doubts that beset him sometimes when his body faltered and his spirit quailed. He remembered the story about how the Ga'an had come out of the mountain to kill the Mexicans, drawn to the fight by the prayers of the people who had escaped the trap. That story had ridden alongside him in all the years since he had heard it, whispering to him so he could keep his courage up. Often enough, he had seen evidence of the protection of the Ga'an. He had been awakened in the middle of the night with the warning whispered in his ear, quiet as the song of Tipping Beetle. He had turned aside at just the right moment to avoid a party of soldiers coming toward him. He had many times seen soldiers with their guns leveled at him and seen the puffs of smoke from the muzzles, but never felt the bullet. He had felt strength come into his legs from somewhere else when he had none of his own. He had seen and blessed and given thanks to Power in its myriad forms and had no doubt that Power had protected the People and his warriors and his children. But he had never seen the Ga'an come out of the earth with their swords when their enemies had pressed them roundabout. And for all of the blessings of Power, the People dwindled and their enemies multiplied. Once, a thousand Chokonen would gather joyfully for feasts and ceremonies, and his father had led three hundred or more warriors on great sweeps through Mexico, so everyone fled their coming. Once the People had laughed and camped quietly in the Dragoons all through the season of the Ghost Dance, scarcely moving their camps. How had they come to this? And if the Ga'an had it in their power to come out of the earth and drive off the enemies of the People, why did they tarry so long now? Was it still a long and subtle test of his prayers? Or did the White Eyes come wielding a stronger Power—with their metal and guns and the gifts of Killer-of-Enemies? Were the People simply caught in a war between the Powers, as though the animals had renewed their contest with the birds to take back the light? Sometimes Cochise wrestled with these questions until his heart ached. Then he let them go. After all, who could account for the ways of Power? Death knew every man's trail and had memorized the rendezvous point long before he knew it himself. Every man must suffer; he had learned this as a boy watching the twig of sage burning on his arm held motionless. You could only accept suffering and learn its lessons, just as you let the stories work on you—not knowing what those stories intended until you turned the corner and saw what had been hidden. Then he would pray and let the beauty and the Power of the world make his mind smooth, and steady, and resilient.

As though to reward his faith, confusing but hopeful news came now from the east. Some Chihenne with relatives in the Chokonen camp brought news that the Great Father had sent out a new *nan-tan* who was not a soldier but seemed to have command over soldiers. This man was called Vincent Colyer, and people said he was a strange old man who was fond of praying and who treated the People with warmth, compassion, and no small measure of condescension. He went to Cañada Alamosa in the season of Large Leaves[4] and found most of the Chihenne had fled after learning of the massacre of the Arivaipa at Camp Grant. Colyer and Agent Piper sent out word for the Chihenne to come in to meet with him, promising rations and safe conduct. Loco and Victorio came in cautiously to meet with him. Colyer said the Great Father had learned of the Camp Grant Massacre, which grieved him deeply.[5] Colyer promised to establish a reservation where they could live, with ample rations and protection from the settlers and soldiers. He urged them to send word to Cochise, so the Chokonen would come in as well.

Cochise wondered if this was the response of Power to his prayers. But his band had lost nearly all its horses in the attack on his camp and had been forced to eat those that remained. Now they could not hope to cross the dangerous distance to Cañada Alamosa with the women and children on foot. Moreover, he did not understand the difference between the news he had of General Crook and this new information about Colyer. Perhaps it was like Chihuahua and Sonora, and Arizona and New Mexico had divided so he might play one against the other. Maybe New Mexico wanted peace while Arizona pursued war. In any case, he resolved to test the possibility of peace with New Mexico, now more willing to consider living among his brothers the Chihenne—for Cañada Alamosa was not so bad a place.

He summoned his subchiefs and they talked a long while until the consensus emerged, as the rocks are revealed as the snow melts. They decided to send out raiding parties to get horses for the journey to Cañada Alamosa and Cochise felt his heart rising up and his body strengthening as he planned the raid, by which he knew Power had approved of the decision. They divided the warriors, sending half down to Fronteras and the other thirty-five warriors under Cochise to raid to Camp Crittenden in the season when the Earth Is Reddish Brown.[6] Cochise carefully studied the movements of the horse herd guards, looking for the weakness in their pattern as a warrior would note that a knife fighter steps always to the right in retreating. He saw that some Papago worked in a meadow nearby and brought the hay into the camp in wagons every morning. He drove off the Papago and took their wagons. Then he dressed his men so they would look like the Papago, knowing the White Eyes never looked closely at Indians. Cochise himself climbed into the wagon with seven or eight warriors and rode boldly through the parade ground to the horse herd just at dawn, laughing to himself and thinking what heart it would give the people when the warriors told this story. When they had reached the herd, Cochise gave a great war whoop and warriors hidden in the trees dashed for the herd. The warriors in the wagon pulled out their hidden guns and bows and chased off the eight guards, who were taken completely by surprise. The warriors from the wagons each jumped onto the back of a horse and ran the herd off toward the rest of the war party, making off with fifty-four horses and seven mules, and leaving the soldiers so completely afoot that they could not even give chase. They rode quickly back to where the women and children remained hidden, then shifted their camp until they were sure the soldiers were not on their trail. Then they moved to the arranged rendezvous until the raiding party from Fronteras returned, driving eighty horses along ahead of them.

Now with enough horses to make the journey, the entire band left the Dragoons and pushed along in a series of night marches toward Cañada Alamosa. They arrived to find that Colyer had left, but not before he had established a reservation for the Chihenne there. Cochise sent a runner to find Red Beard, saying he was willing to settle with his Chokonen at Cañada Alamosa with the Chihenne. Red Beard gave this good news to Agent Piper, who asked Red Beard to go and meet with Cochise and bring him in for talks. Red Beard carried that message to Cochise, who was camped in a well-defended place with two hundred warriors. Cochise greeted his old friend with hugs, sure that Power had sent Red Beard to him in the hour of the People's need. They smoked and talked for an hour, passing along news of people they both knew in the unhurried courtesy of a meeting between friends.

Cochise, with his most trusted bodyguards, drew close to Agent Piper's camp to meet.[7] The agent invited Cochise to come and talk in his quarters, but Cochise would never walk willingly into such a trap again. "No," he said quietly, without either discourtesy or uncertainty. "We talk out here." He gestured to his warriors, who spread a blanket on the ground on which Cochise and Agent Piper could sit. They exchanged friendly remarks, and Agent Piper said the Great Father had bid him give them rations for agreeing to this talk in double the usual amount. He spoke with respect and courtesy. Cochise thanked Agent Piper for his gifts and his courtesy, saying he spoke fairly like a true man. "We want peace now," said Cochise quietly, "for my people are nearly all killed off." Cochise agreed to camp near Cañada Alamosa. He also promised to send out runners to other Chokonen bands to urge them to come to Cañada Alamosa. However, he warned Agent Piper that he could not be held responsible for the actions of other bands. He understood this only too well—for his Chokonen had often frustrated the efforts of other bands to make peace with Fronteras or Janos. But there was no help for it, because every warrior made his own decisions. How could it be otherwise for a true man? Still, he made this point carefully, repeating it several times, for the White Eyes understood cattle and camp dogs but not warriors.

Cochise talked with dignity and confidence, sitting as though unconcerned. But his warriors stood close by, fully armed, watching every White Eye. His most trusted warriors went everywhere with him, cast out from his feet as a shadow. And everywhere he went—and for however long he sat to talk—a warrior stood nearby with his horse fully saddled should he need once again to escape the treachery of the Whites.

After the conference, Cochise moved to Cuchillo Negro with thirty warriors and two hundred women and children to wait further word. The camp was easy to defend, and Cochise kept his sentries on alert and his scouts spread out so soldiers could not surprise them. At night, in his camp, he lay down to sleep with the lead rope of his horse in his hand and his weapons at his side. The White Eyes might kill him, but not because he forgot their nature.

Cochise camped for a time along the Cuchillo Negro River, then moved further off into the Black Mountains, never relaxing his guard. He did not understand why the White Eyes were waiting so long to act on Colyer's promises to the Chihenne. Loco and Red Beard brought in rumors the Whites might put the reservation in Tularosa, with its hard winters, short growing season, bad grass, unhealthful water, and malevolent Power.

As he had feared, raids by other bands caused trouble while the weeks dragged by with no clear decision. In the season when Earth Is Reddish Brown[8] Juh's Nednhis burned a ranch near Fort Bowie, killing one man. Soldiers chased him, but Juh set an ambush and killed one soldier in a four-hour fight, escaping with no losses even though the soldiers fired more than two thousand bullets. Many people blamed Cochise for the raid, because Juh was the only war leader who fought in the same style, with skillful ambushes, great control over springing the trap, good escape routes for the warriors, and skillful direction of the battle with cries and hand signals. The *nantan* from Fort Bowie who had fought Cochise in Horseshoe Canyon said Cochise was in the fight, but when some people came out from Cañada Alamosa they found Cochise waiting quietly in his camp. Agent Piper brought with him both a man from the *Las Cruces Borderer* and Charles Coleman, who had known Cochise when he had worked long ago at the stage station in Apache Pass. The chief agreed to meet with them and was curious to see one of the talking paper men. Red Beard often complained about these talking papers, saying they were often full of lies about Cochise and the People, but he also said the talking papers had great influence. Red Beard said the talking papers were a way Cochise could talk to the Americans in many places all at once.

Hearing Agent Piper's voice, Cochise came out of his wickiup and greeted the three White men with courtesy.

"Do you know me, Cochise?" asked Coleman, who had not seen him in fifteen years.

"Yes, Charlie. Apache Pass," returned Cochise. "A long time ago. You put on mule shoes."[9]

The newspaper man was impressed to see Cochise, who had a reputation as the most savage and bloodthirsty of Indians. Instead, he found a tall, almost ageless man with long black hair threaded with gray and smooth features accented by streaks of yellow ocher, with a sensitive, well-formed mouth, a prominent nose, and pleasant, thoughtful features touched by melancholy.

The reporter asked Cochise why he had left Arizona and come to Cañada Alamosa.

"We have been allowed no rest in the past year," said Cochise openly, "and the people of Arizona would give us no peace so that

the country was bad and everything there pinched us." He reminded
the White man the Chokonen had not sought this war; the Americans had forced it on them. "Tell the people that I have come here
to make peace, a good peace, that I like this country and wish to
spend the remainder of my life here at peace with all men."[10]
Cochise talked a long while with the newspaper man, remembering
the advice of Red Beard. He reminded the White Eyes that although
he had resolved to live quietly and keep the peace, other bands continued to raid. He thought he could convince all of the Chokonen
bands to make peace, but feared the Nednhis would fight until the
last one was dead—for Juh was tight in the grip of his Power and
Geronimo would never surrender. Cochise also said he and Victorio
and Loco and the other Chihenne would be happy to live out their
lives at Cañada Alamosa, but could not convince their people to live
in Tularosa, where the winters were cold, the summers swampy, the
grass bad, and the water unhealthy. He did not add that he did not
want to settle so far from the traders at Cañada Alamosa and therefore become completely dependent on the thin rations of the army.
Cochise hoped to influence Agent Piper, who was trying already to
convince Loco and Victorio to remove their people to Tularosa, a
hundred miles to the northwest. Cochise said if the soldiers tried to
make them move to Tularosa, two-thirds of the Chokonen would
resume raiding—even if he urged them to stay.

But the White Eyes did not listen to the warning Cochise tried
to convey. Both Colyer and Agent Piper insisted the Chihenne move
to Tularosa, and the Chokonen with them. Cochise tried to smooth
the ruffled feathers. He did not refuse to go to Tularosa, but said
only he would support the decision of Loco and Victorio, giving
them the warriors of his support in the raid of the argument. But
privately Cochise decided the odd insistence of the White Eyes on
Tularosa was the brush pulled over the mouth of the bear pit. Some
of the Mexican traders at Cañada Alamosa had warned Victorio the
soldiers would slaughter them all if they moved to Tularosa, as they
had done to the Arivaipa at Camp Grant.[11] Nonetheless, Cochise
waited, as the White Eyes shifted back and forth like a crazy man in
an argument with himself. Finally, Agent Piper insisted that all the
Chihenne and the Chokonen move to Tularosa in six months.

Still Cochise held back his warriors and his subchiefs, as a man
balanced on the ledge of a cliff face. Plagued by idleness and uncertainty, many warriors traded their rations for whiskey from the

traders at Cañada Alamosa, becoming violently quarrelsome. And so bad blood began to accumulate between the bands. Then Agent Piper got in a fight with the traders, just as Agent Drew had done. Once the people at Cañada Alamosa even had Piper arrested, which unsettled the warriors. Cochise remained far from the agency, sending Dos-teh-seh and others to collect the rations. But the longer he remained hobbled near Cañada Alamoso, the weaker grew his hold on the warriors. Some warriors would slip away from camp and come back later with horses—sometimes even army horses. Some warriors attacked mail riders, although Cochise did not know their band or whether they might have been Americans or Mexicans dressed as warriors to throw the dust of suspicion in the eyes of the soldiers. Cochise tried to discourage raiding, but the warriors had grown increasingly restive. Besides, a wave of illness and stomach pain went through the Chokonen camps, with several deaths. Cochise wondered if the White Eyes had poisoned the rations and stopped eating them. But his stomach had been bad before he started eating the Whites' rations and continued to pain him afterward, so he could not tell whether the rations were bad.

Cochise rarely went to the agency and avoided contact with the White Eyes as much as possible except for Red Beard, who came and went freely in his camp. Once Agent Piper came and asked Cochise to go to Washington to meet with the Great Father to settle the issue of the reservation. But Cochise would not go, for it would mean placing himself entirely in the hands of the Whites. Cochise said he had no need to go there and would rather talk on top of a mountain. Besides, he said, if he were gone, some of his warriors might steal things or make trouble, which would make him seem like a liar when he talked to the Great Father and promised to live in peace.[12]

Agent Piper and the other *nantan*s called a conference, trying once again to make the Chokonen move to Tularosa, which was said to be a place where foolish people had angered the Ga'an and the Thunder People. A *nantan* named Gordon Granger said the Great Father wanted the People to move to Tularosa. He gave Cochise a talking paper from the Great Father, but Cochise saw that it was bound with a red string. He tore it off in anger. "The red is not good," he explained, for red attracted lightning and was also an insult to wear in the presence of anyone who was grieving. Cochise quickly controlled his flare of anger and worry as the *nantan* made

little of the ribbon. You could never tell with the White Eyes, who
were both shrewd and ignorant. Perhaps they did not know anything
about Power and did not know anything about red, which they wore
freely. Or perhaps they were witching him even now, or merely
showing disrespect to unsettle him in the negotiations. So he put the
red ribbon on the talking paper out of his mind and explained to
the *nantan* that even if he were willing to live at Tularosa himself,
many of his warriors and headmen would not go. "This must look
strange to you," said Cochise across the impossible gulf separating
him from the soldiers, "but these are not all my people. I would like
to go to them and tell them what you have said." He said this seeing that the White Eyes were not reasonable people, but as stubborn
as a mule so thirsty it won't keep walking to reach water. He had
already decided that if the White Eyes would not relent, he would
find some excuse to leave the reservation so he would have a head
start in racing back to the Chiricahuas.[13]

Even so, he rose to the full height of his eloquence to make the
White Eyes see why the Chokonen wanted to remain at Cañada
Alamosa.

"The sun has been very hot on my head, and made me as in a
fire, but now I have come into this valley and drunk of these waters
and washed myself in them and they have cooled me. Now that I am
cool I have come with my hands open to you to live in peace with
you. I speak straight and do not wish to deceive or be deceived. I
want a good, strong and lasting peace.

"When God made the world he gave one part to the white man
and another to the Apache. Why was it? Why did they come together?
Now that I am to speak, the sun, the moon, the earth, the air, the
waters, the birds and beasts, even the children unborn shall rejoice
at my words.

"The white people have looked for me long. I am here! What do
they want? Why am I worth so much? If I am worth so much, why
not mark when I set my foot and look when I spit. I am not God. I
am no longer chief of all the Apaches. I am no longer rich; I am but
a poor man. I came here because God told me to do so. He said it
was good to be at peace—so I came! God spoke to my thought and
told me to come here and be at peace with all.

"When I was young, I walked all over this country, east and west,
and saw no other people than the Apaches. After many summers I
walked again and found another race of people had come to take it.

Chiricahua rocks. Cochise constantly shifted his operations from one mountain range to another, but one of his most secure and bountiful sanctuaries was the Chiricahuas, today a national monument. *(Peter Aleshire)*

How is it? The Apaches were once a great nation; they are now but few. I have no father or mother. I am alone in the world. No one cares for Cochise; that is why I do not care to live, and wish the rocks to fall on me and cover me up. How is it? Why is it that the Apaches wait to die—that they carry their lives on their fingernails.

"I want to live in these mountains. I do not want to go to Tularosa. That is a long ways off. The flies on those mountains eat out the eyes of the horses. The bad spirits live there. I have drunk these waters and they have cooled me. I do not want to leave here."[14]

But the White Eyes would not listen, clamped down on their own idea like a gila monster with his jaw locked on your hand. Perhaps they simply did not believe he would keep the peace unless he was removed to Tularosa. He tried to explain the world to them. "I have fought long and as best I could against you," said Cochise. "I have destroyed many of your people. But where I have destroyed one white man many have come in his place; but where an Indian has been killed there has been none to come in his place so that a great people that welcomed you with acts of kindness to this land are now but a feeble band that fly before your soldiers as the deer before the hunter. I am the last of my family, a family that for very many years have been the leaders of his people, and now on me depends their future—whether they shall utterly vanish from the land or that a small remnant remain for a few years to see the sun rise over the mountains, their home."[15]

Hearing him, the listening warriors uttered the Ho of assent. The sky heard him and the wind and the trees leaned over him to listen and the rocks attended to him, carrying his words to the Ga'an dancing off far away inside the earth. But the White Eyes could not hear him, for they knew not how to listen to the wind or the rocks or the words of a true man. They were like a man trying so hard to remember his own words that he can hear nothing else. They nodded and pretended to hear, and then said the Great Father said they must live in Tularosa and so that was all there was to say. And perhaps it was true. Perhaps they were ants, following the trail of their fellows without deviation. Perhaps when the Great Father had a thought, then they all must have the same thought—like their wagon horses wearing blinders so they could only see straight ahead. Maybe the White Eyes thought it was enough to repeat that the Great Father had given this order and they must follow along like the last ox in the team. But the Whites could not yoke Cochise to the words of the Great Father, who was only a man like himself. Seeing they were deaf and blind, Cochise gave up arguing with them.

When the *nantan* said Cochise must go to Washington, D.C., to meet with the Great Father, Cochise answered him by saying, "I am not a child. I would rather talk to you in this country. I would much rather live here in the mountains where the grass dies, for when I lie down, if it gets in my hair, I can get it out. I know that all things are right here."

But he asked permission to go out and gather up the Chokonen. In their arrogance and foolishness, they gave their assent. Later, Red Beard urged him to go to Washington to talk to the Great Father. But Cochise again declined, saying, "You believe these White men. I trusted them once; I went to their camp—my brother and two nephews were hanged; no, I will not go."[16]

Ten days after the conference in the season of Little Eagles[17] Cochise slipped away from Cañada Alamosa with his people, attending once more to the advice of his Power. And such was the confidence of his people in Cochise that three hundred went with him, although they knew they would once again be hunted like deer in deep snow. Knowing the soldiers would be angry that he had tricked them, Cochise went down to Janos. He tried to remain there as quietly as possible, but the movements of the troops near their camps eventually spooked the subchiefs. Cochise sent a runner back to Red Beard, saying they would be leaving Janos and inviting him to join them—for Red Beard had been much in his dreams lately. He sensed that Red Beard was the slender thread by which their hopes for peace with the White Eyes hung suspended. But Red Beard sent back word that he had fallen from a horse and broken several ribs and so could not travel for a time. The Chokonen moved back up into the mountains along the border. From there, some of the warriors raided to the north, bringing back livestock to feed their relatives.

Cochise sent runners to other groups, seeking any opportunity to hunt down a peace he could accept. He soon learned the Americans had forced the Chihenne to move to Tularosa after all. About 350 Chihenne under Victorio and Loco had finally assented to the move, partly at the urging of Red Beard and another white man the people trusted named Zebina Nathaniel Streeter. He was a trader and a onetime beaver hunter who had married a woman of the People and lived with some Nednhi and Chihenne bands. He had happily fought with them against the Mexicans, learning their language better than any other White. He seemed to have put his heart into becoming a warrior. He even joined them to fight the Whites, raiding and ambushing the soldiers. Other White Eyes had fought with the People—men like Kirker. But Streeter seemed the only man who had truly become a warrior and so earned great trust among the Chihenne and the Nednhis—now also his kinsmen. Loco and Victorio had yielded finally to the advice of Streeter and Red Beard, who said soldiers would hunt them without pause if they did not go to Tularosa. But most of the Chihenne had still refused to go to Tularosa. More than a thousand simply scattered into Mexico.

The different Chiricahua and Chihenne bands would camp together and the leading men would debate what to do. Cochise found himself divided even from old comrades and allies, especially among the Chihenne. One of his most trusted allies was Ponce, the son of a great warrior who had followed first Pisago Cabezón and then Cochise. Ponce had even married a daughter of Cochise, but now he said the People should come to terms with the White Eyes. Ponce and several other Chihenne subchiefs led three hundred people to Fort Stanton, hoping they could settle on the Mescalero Reservation. The agent there gave them rations, but the *nantan* at the fort said they could not stay. He warned them he would attack their camps if they didn't settle at Tularosa.

Cochise remained aloof, determined not to go to Tularosa, for his Power had warned him the People would dwindle and die there. He held back from raiding, but could not prevent the younger warriors from slipping away in small parties. Some warriors tried to run off the Fort Bowie horse herd, but it was too well guarded. They killed a mail rider near Stein's Peak. Soldiers led by Merejildo followed them back to the Burro Mountains before they scattered to confuse their trail.

The Sonorans had also become more active, sending soldiers to seek out the camps of the People. Many of the Chokonen, Nednhi, and Chihenne bands had moved down near Janos to seek peace and trade for goods taken on the raids, and the Sonorans feared a return of the old days when warriors lived safely in Janos and raided in Sonora. But the pressure of the Sonorans only convinced Cochise and even Juh to send emissaries to Janos. Cochise camped near Janos for several months, living quietly. Then runners brought news that a strong force of Sonorans had surprised Juh's camp in the Sierra Madre, killing many people and destroying his hoard of food and supplies. Seeing the Sonorans were raiding freely in Chihuahua, Cochise moved north again into the Chiricahuas, hoping the soldiers would have grown less vigilant because the Chokonen had remained away from their own country for several seasons.

They moved safely into the Chiricahuas under cover of darkness, having nearly exhausted their food in the journey. They camped in high and secret places, where they could see the soldiers coming a long way off. The women went out in small groups to gather acorns and mescal and berries and fruit. Some of the warriors went out to see if they could get some cattle. Cochise remained behind to guard the camp, for the pain in his stomach was frequent now. Taza, who had risen in Power and respect among the band, led a war party to watch the road to Tucson. Cochise felt a surge of pride in seeing Taza leading the warriors, although he also felt a pang of fear that Taza's desire for acclaim would lead him to take reckless chances when the People had such need of stealth. As Cochise had feared, Taza waited along the road until he saw an arrogant *nantan* with only one soldier in a buckboard pushing quickly out ahead of the rest of the soldiers. The warriors were waiting in Davidson Canyon and shot the *nantan* through the head. They tied the other man to a tree and killed him as well, mutilating his body to break his spirit and scare off his Chindi.[18] Then the war party raided through the

Sonoita Valley, killing seven Mexicans and running off some stock. The raid was a great success and the returning warriors were greeted with the cry of applause of White-Painted Woman. But when Cochise learned they had killed a *nantan* and left the body with their marks upon it, he knew the soldiers would seek them hard even in high places—so he shifted the camp and redoubled the sentries.

Cochise felt stronger here in the Dragoons than in any other place, although the soldier forts surrounded these mountains. Nonetheless, his heart always rose up as he returned to the familiar places— old friends who had taught him wisdom throughout his life. He felt Power greet him, the voice now as strong as it had been faint at Cañada Alamosa. As he thought about this, he decided he was fortunate the White Eyes had proven so adamant about Tularosa. He would have stayed in the Chihenne country if they had let him live at Cañada Alamosa and so would have given up the places that knew him. Feeling the need to smooth and steady his mind, Cochise went alone to the place of his birth. Reaching it, he lay down and rolled in the four directions, in respect and joy. Then he sat a long while praying and singing, for he felt Power strong in him. He remembered his Moccasin Ceremony, when he had walked in the four footprints painted onto the buckskin by the shaman as he became an aspect of Child-of-the-Water and promised to walk in that path. At first Cochise sang an old man's song, the tears glittering in his eyes and rolling like the last warrior down his cheek:

When I was young, I took no heed;
Old, old I have become!
Because I knew that age
Would come to me,
I took no heed.[19]

He saw his life as a lookout from a high place, all of his losses and triumphs shrunk to bumps and traceries of arroyos. He saw that the ambitions of his youth had been arrogant and foolish. He had dreamed of rising above even Mangas Coloradas and uniting all of the bands of the People to drive out the Mexicans and kill all the White Eyes. Perhaps he thought even Child-of-the-Water would look back in pride and speak the name of Cochise. He had danced out into the light of the fire when everyone called his name, seeming modest and leaving many of his strongest deeds unclaimed—but in

truth he had been swollen with pride. For a long time when the
world had turned against the People and the White Eyes returned in
their relentless numbers, he had scourged himself. He prayed to
know what offense he had committed: what prayer he had mumbled, what track he had stepped over, what enemy had witched him.
But sitting in the place of his birth as Power enfolded him, he could
see even those questions had been vanity. For he was only a man,
with his life measured in seasons. The strength of his youth must
give way to the steady smoothness of his old age, as inexorably as
the green glory of the cottonwood yields first to a marvel of gold and
then the stark silhouette of the season of the Ghost Dance. Now he
saw that all his life had been the journey to this place and the real-
ization he must save this land for his People. That was why his
father had so carefully taught him the names of each of the places
in the Dragoons and Chiricahuas. At first he thought his father had
taught him those stories so he would never get lost in his own land.
Then he had realized his father wanted the places to teach him how
to keep on the path of Child-of-the-Water. Now he realized these
places had also been given into his keeping, so he would not suffer
to let the People be taken from them. The People could not remain
the People in some other place; the Chokonen must hold on to the
Dragoons and the Chiricahuas just as the Chihenne must hold onto
Cañada Alamosa and Ojo Caliente. Of course, he still did not know
how they could do that, for the Mexicans must multiply and the
White Eyes would not turn back. Still, in the embrace of the place
of his birth he felt a great surge of faith and confidence that Power
would place into his hands the weapons he needed. So in joy—as
though Power had already shown him what to do—he sang:

> At the place called "Home in the Center of the Sky,"
> Inside is the home's holiness.
> The door to the home is of white clouds.
> They are all the Gray Mountain Spirits
> Rejoicing over me
> Kneel in the four directions with me.
>
> When first my Power was created,
> Pollen's body, speaking my words,
> Brought my Power into being,
> So I have come here.[20]

Cochise prayed and fasted for four days, seeking a vision and guidance. He came away smoothed and steadied, his mind resilient and full of joy and gratitude. He knew not what he must do, but he had released his grip on the question as he had let go of fear and vanity and pride.

Perhaps when next he painted the Mountain Spirit Dancers, the Ga'an themselves would come up out of the earth as when they had driven all the Mexicans into the cave. But it did not matter. Something would happen if he held himself in readiness for the workings of Power.

15

October 1872

The One-Armed General
and the Last War Won

How Antelope Got His Name

One time a man fell in a battle. He was seriously wounded, was
between life and death. When he was between life and death he
started to go to "the place of reddish ground," the afterworld.
The man was already in that place, for he was more dead than
alive. Unless he got out at once he would be there permanently, he
knew; he would be dead. All at once he saw himself as this animal.
He saw himself put on the nature of that animal, saw himself, his
ghost, look as that animal looks today.

    Then this animal dashed out of that place and got out on the
plains. And this man, when this animal got out, came back to his
senses, recovered, and did not die. Ever since then this animal has
been called "He Who Is Becoming," meaning that the man was
becoming that animal.

A runner came to Cochise as he rested in his camp in the Dragoons, which was in a hollow beneath an oak tree beside a great flat
rock on which he could hold council. The warrior was scarcely
breathing hard after his long run, and his message was memorized
exactly. He had come down from the small band posted on the high
ridge with the view of all the land to the east across the Sulphur
Springs Valley—all the way to the entrance to Apache Pass, forty
miles distant. The lookouts said a strange party was approaching
from the east. Leading them were the Chihenne chief Ponce, who
was Cochise's son-in-law, and Chie, the son of Coyuntura and the
nephew of Cochise. Red Beard also rode with them. Cochise knew
these men as kinsmen and friends. But they brought with them two
other men—a one-armed *nantan* and a younger, bearded *nantan*

254

who seemed like his *segundo,* his right hand. They had come from the east through the Chiricahua Mountains, avoiding Fort Bowie by coming down along back trails unknown to the soldiers. At first they had a large party—well armed with supplies packed on mules. They had camped near the soldiers who guarded the water at Dragoon Springs, which seemed suspicious and strange—for Chie and Ponce would not be safe going so close to the soldiers. After that, they had sent most of their number back to Fort Bowie, coming on with just Chie and Ponce and the two *nantans* toward the Dragoons. Chie and Ponce had been careful along the way to put up smoke signals indicating they came peacefully and warning the people up ahead as to the number of the party.

Cochise considered what he should do. Initially, he felt anger at Chie and Ponce and Red Beard for bringing these two strangers by the secret trails through the Chiricahuas and toward the Dragoons. He wondered whether his friends and relatives had betrayed him, as many others had done—so desperate to protect their families they would live as the whipped dogs of the White Eyes. If Red Beard brought a message from the Indian agent or the Great Father, why did he not bring it himself instead of showing these strangers the way to the best camps of the Chokonen? But he trusted these men and did not want to believe they would turn against him or become the tools of the soldiers, even though they had camped with the soldiers at Dragoon Springs. Cochise prayed and consulted his Power, striving to keep his mind smooth and steady so fear and anger would not betray him. After that, he set out warriors to watch the approaching party carefully, doing nothing until their intentions were clear. In the meantime, he alerted the bands camped nearby and sent out scouts to look for soldiers approaching from another direction while his gaze was focused on these *nantans* riding so boldly into his hands.

The *nantans* approached the Dragoons from the east, then climbed over the pass to approach the West Stronghold, where Cochise was camped. Warriors watched them all the while, although the *nantans* had no suspicion they were observed. The scouts brought back interesting information about the *nantans.* One of them was a young man who seemed nervous, looking about and keeping his weapons close at hand. He was clearly the *segundo,* as attentive to the older man as though he was his son. The scouts said the great *nantan* had only one arm, for his sleeve hung empty. He seemed completely fearless, looking about with eager eyes and great curiosity. He had a beard in the repulsive manner of many of the White Eyes, but his bearing was dignified and confident, as a man accustomed to command. The most remarkable thing about him was the way in which he often fell to his knees, closing his eyes and praying in a strong voice. The scout said he would be very easy to kill at such a time, for he talked to himself a long while with his eyes closed. Sometimes his *segundo* knelt with him, but mostly he drew away at these times as if in respect. Cochise paid close attention to this detail, for it seemed the behavior of a man who was talking to his Power. He had often wondered that the White Eyes paid so little attention to Power. They went to talk to Power as they did everything else—in large groups at regimented times. And then they did not each consult their own Power, but sat listening to the one or two men who could talk to Power. This seemed consistent with the bizarre ways of the White Eyes in which only a few could make decisions. Perhaps this man was a great *nantan* who could talk to Power and give the orders of Power to the others, who had no ceremonies of their own.

When the *nantan*s had reached the Dragoons, Ponce and Chie made camp, all the while using birdcalls and coyote cries to maintain contact with the watching warriors. Then Chie left the camp and rode into the Dragoons, where one of the warriors appeared to conduct him to the camp of Cochise. Chie rode up to his uncle, who waited for him on the council rock. He dismounted and came respectfully into the presence of the chief, waiting out of courtesy until Cochise should ask for his information. Chie was as handsome and strong and reliable as his father, with his regular, proud features, skin like burnished copper, a hard, lean body, and air of poised dignity. Now Chie explained why he had brought the *nantan*s into the camp of Cochise, straight into the Dragoons by the secret trails of the warriors.

The Great Father had sent the one-armed *nantan*, whose name was General Oliver Otis Howard,[1] bidding him to make peace with the People and giving him the complete authority to establish reservations. They said he was a good man, strong and kind and reverent—for he prayed openly to his Power as no other White man they had seen. At first, this had frightened Loco and the other Chihenne when Howard met with them, for they feared he was trying to witch them. But gradually they saw he was fearless and honest and treated

General Oliver Otis Howard. The pious, high-minded, one-armed Civil War general and hero rode fearlessly into the Dragoons to meet with Cochise and negotiate the end to years of warfare that cost thousands of lives. *(National Archives)*

the People with respect, although sometimes he also spoke to grown warriors as though they were children. Howard—whom they called called Tatti Grande, or Great Father—had lost his arm in the war between the Whites. This impressed Cochise, who thought Tatti Grande must have strong Power to have survived such a wound.

Tatti Grande traveled always with another *nantan* named Joseph Sladen, whom they called Teniente—for he was the lieutenant of Tatti Grande. He was also a brave and intelligent man, friendly, generous, and curious. He seemed genuinely interested in the People and treated them as human beings, so respectful and interested that he had even begun to learn their language. He also had fought with Tatti Grande in the war between the White Eyes and then had trained to become a healer in the way of the Whites, who relied more on potions and charms than on prayers.[2] He was of average height, with light hair and hazel eyes sparkling with intelligence, and he seemed interested in everything—especially the stars in the sky.

Tatti Grande had gone first to Red Beard, asking how he might meet with Cochise to make peace between the Americans and the People. Red Beard said only a man willing to go alone without soldiers into the Dragoons could talk to Cochise—and was surprised when Tatti Grande immediately asked Red Beard to take him there. At the first, Chie and Ponce agreed to go along as guides only because they trusted Red Beard. But they had come to admire both of the *nantans* on the journey. Outside Silver City some White Eyes had come riding up, well armed, to confront the party. One of the Whites was a bitter, hard-fighting man thirsty for revenge against the People, for a war party had killed his brother. Seeing Ponce and Chie, the White Eyes wanted to kill them. Chie told the story just as it happened, for it revealed important things about Tatti Grande.

"How do you do?"[3] Tatti Grande said to the Whites. "I am General Howard of the United States Army, going out with a party to look up some hostile Indians. Have you seen any Indians at all?"

"No. No by . . ." said the white man, his eyes blazing with hatred as he looked at Chie and Ponce. "We wish we had. We would have made it hot for them. And we would like to kill the two you have with you."

Tatti Grande was a strong man, but kindly. Now his eyes flashed with anger. "I accosted you, sir, as a gentleman and you reply by trying to insult me. I am a soldier, sir, and not to be intimidated by threats. You mean by 'killing' these Indians that you would like to murder them. You don't dare attempt to kill them. But if you want to try that, I will let them go off at a distance, to give them a fair show, and then you and your whole party can go in and try it on them, if you would like the opportunity, and we will see who it is that will be killed."

Ponce and Chie watched the exchange without expression, having placed themselves close to good cover as soon as the White Eyes rode up. Now they sat calmly on their horses with their hands near their guns, ready to start killing the Whites. But the Whites shrank back before the Power of Tatti Grande and so they turned aside with many dark looks. Ponce and Chie later asked Red Beard what the men had said and laughed so hard when they heard they had trouble staying on their horses. Hearing the story from Chie, Cochise laughed out loud himself, appreciating how Tatti Grande had shamed the White Eyes and protected the dignity of his friends. Chie broke into laughter again in telling it, seeming well pleased with the effect of his storytelling.

Now Cochise felt hope rising in him, like ashes on the heat of the fire. Perhaps this was the opening for which Power had bid him wait. Cochise told Chie to bring the *nantan*s to his camp, sending Naiche back with him to Tatti Grande. Cochise decided that Naiche, who was fifteen, might go safely into their camp and out again, bringing away good information. Naiche took with him another boy who was his constant companion.

They returned to Tatti Grande's camp with Chie, each wearing a red handband, buckskin moccasins nearly to their knees, shirts, and breechcloths. They carried their bows with a few arrows, riding on small ponies gaunt with hunger—their ribs etched—using no saddle and only a rope tied around the jaw to control them. The White Eyes dismounted to greet them in a friendly manner, so the boys were put immediately at ease. Naiche walked up to the two *nantan*s and touched their faces hesitantly, for he had never been so close to White Eyes except for Red Beard—who did not seem like other Whites. The two *nantan*s smiled, so Naiche felt reassured and patted them on the arms in the open and expressive manner of the People. The *nantan*s sat down and brought out food for the boys, who had not eaten in a long while—although the requirements of courtesy would have prevented them from asking for food not freely offered. The *nantan*s soon relaxed—smiling and laughing. Emboldened, Naiche took the good pistol out of the belt of the younger *nantan*. He made no move to stop Naiche, but watched closely as the boy turned it over in his hands, admiring its balance and the fine grain of the wood in the handle. Ponce and Chie smiled and laughed happily, for they knew Cochise had welcomed them to the Dragoons in sending his son to them. During the long journey with the *nantan*s, they had wondered how Cochise would greet them. A warrior could not be certain when dealing with Cochise, for he had a temper as sudden as lightning and attended to the demands of his Power. The warrior did not know if he would be embraced or run through with a lance if Cochise's Power required it. That was one reason the warriors so feared and respected him and walked quietly past his wickiup. But Naiche was now a guarantee of safe conduct, so they knew Cochise was willing to meet with the *nantan*. The boys stayed in the camp that night, delighted to satisfy their curiosity about White

people. The one-armed *nantan* was friendly, like a mother's uncle—
giving them small presents and talking to them in a kindly way. That
night, the one-armed *nantan* pulled back his blanket and made
space for the boys, who had nothing to ward off the chill of the
night. They snuggled up against him under the blanket and slept
more warmly than they had in weeks.

The next day, Chie led them on into a valley surrounded by the
silently watching rocks, rising up straight on every side to remind
them the life of man was short and frail as the grass. They camped
with the band of Tygee, one of Cochise's most trusted subchiefs.
Cochise wanted others to watch Tatti Grande a little longer so he
would have all of the advantage of information, prayer, and preparation when they talked, for he suspected the fate of the People hung
on this meeting. Tatti Grande and his *segundo* proved themselves
just as respectful and kind as Chie had said. They greeted Tygee
with respect. They invited the hungry people in his camp to share
their food, although they had nearly used up their supplies in the
journey to the Dragoons. They played with the children, letting them
crawl all over them and fishing all manner of curious objects out of
their pockets. That night, the *nantans* spread out their blankets so
the naked children could crawl underneath and gain some protection from the season when Earth Is Reddish Brown.

Tatti Grande and his *segundo* waited the next morning, hoping
Cochise would come to them. Now Cochise sent word ahead. His
brother Juan rode in, dashing down a ravine at breakneck speed, his
face vividly painted with vermilion and black. He rode up to Red
Beard, jerking his charging horse to a halt with nonchalant skill.
"This is his brother, Juan," said Red Beard quietly, for few people
spoke the name of Cochise openly. Whenever someone said "he" or
"his," most people knew they referred to Cochise. Red Beard indicated they should all take seats on the ground around a blanket.

Now came Cochise himself, straight as an arrow, with high cheek-
bones, keen clear eyes, a handsome face with a strong Roman nose,
his long, silver-threaded black hair bound with a yellow silk hand-
kerchief. He bore himself with the dignity of the trust Power had put
in him and the *nantans* could feel the mingling of respect and fear
that passed through all the other warriors who rose to greet him.
With him now were Naiche and Dos-teh-seh and his sister, riding
alongside him as equals and counselors, for he relied heavily on

Dragoons. Cochise often retreated into the Dragoons to rest between raids, posting lookouts on the high places to give warnings of approaching army patrols.
(Peter Aleshire)

their advice and insight. Cochise dismounted with the grace of an eagle turning and came toward Tatti Grande.

"This is he," said Red Beard.

Tatti Grande extended his hand in the way of the White Eyes and Cochise took it warmly, feeling the Power behind this man. "Buenos dias," said Cochise quietly.

Now he greeted Red Beard, hugging him and looking into his face warmly. He also embraced Ponce, who was his son-in-law and the son of his old companion who had raided with him in the days when Cochise and Mangas Coloradas thought they might kill every White Eye in the world. Ponce was a fearless daredevil of a warrior, indolent and indestructible, lazy and yet able to run for two days without slackening his pace. He loved practical jokes and story-telling, and people vied for a position around the fire when he told Coyote stories, with his many voices and gestures and sly jokes and double meanings. But he was fearless in raiding, laughed at hardship as though it was just a Coyote story, and was fiercely loyal. The others in the party also greeted Chie and Ponce, gathering the news of their relatives among the Chihenne. The sister of Cochise took Ponce aside to ask about a dear friend among the Chihenne, but broke into bitter tears when she learned her friend had died. Her grief cast its shadow over them all, reminding Cochise of the danger pressing down on them like rocks piled on their chest.

Cochise took Red Beard by the shoulders and in his own tongue asked him whether Tatti Grande was a true man who would keep his word. Red Beard answered, "Well, I don't know. I think he will, but I will see that they don't promise too much."

Then Cochise turned back to Tatti Grande. "Will the general tell me why he has come to me?"

"The President has sent me to make peace between you and the Whites."

"Nobody wants peace more than I do. I have done no mischief since I came from Cañada Alamosa, but I am poor, my horses are poor and I have but few. I might have got more by raiding on the Tucson road, but I did not do it," said Cochise, speaking truthfully—although he knew some warriors from his subchiefs had been raiding.

"Then as I have full power, we can make peace," said Tatti Grande.[4]

Now they sat to talk. Tatti Grande said he had talked to Loco and Victorio and agreed they should have a reservation at Cañada Alamosa. Now he urged the Chokonen to settle there as well. Cochise saw this opening, like a gap in the circle of his enemies. Months before, he would have gone through that gap quickly. But he had come back now into the places that knew him and had listened to them these past months. Now he hesitated. "I have been there and I like the country," he said. But then he surprised Tatti Grande, saying, "Give me Apache Pass, for my people and I will protect the road to Tucson. I will see that the Indians do no harm."

"But Cañada Alamosa is a better country for you," replied Tatti Grande. "It has five rivers; it has plenty of grass; plenty of mescal and nuts, and antelope and other game in the mountains."

But Cochise had resolved to win for the Chokonen their own land, for the war had been long and costly and must bring some great prize. Thinking of this, the bitterness of his loss escaped his lips. "The worst place of all is Apache Pass," he said. "There six Indians—one my brother—were murdered. Their bodies were hung up and kept there until they were skeletons. Now Americans and

Mexicans kill an Apache on sight. I have retaliated with all my might. My people have killed Americans and Mexicans and taken their property. Their losses have been greater than mine. I have killed ten white men for every Indian slain, but I know that the Whites are many and the Indians are few. So why shut me up on a reservation? We will make peace. We will keep it faithfully. But let us go around free as Americans do. Let us go wherever we please."[5]

Tatti Grande listened, but again urged them to settle with the Chihenne at Cañada Alamosa. Cochise shook his head gently, not willing now to confront Tatti Grande directly and make him dig down into his position like Badger. "How long will you stay?" he asked. "My people are scattered. Many of my captains are away. I must consult with them. They must know. It will take some time to find them and get them here. Will you wait until they come and have a talk with them?"

Sladen looked nervous at this suggestion, but Tatti Grande agreed. "The President has sent me a long distance to see you and your people and talk with you. I have been a long time traveling to get here. I must stay with you until I have talked with your people. I will stay until they come."

"Then I will send out runners for my captains," said Cochise, satisfied at the way Tatti Grande made his decisions quickly and firmly, instead of always saying he must ask permission. He seemed a man used to command, so perhaps his word would mean something. "I can't tell you where they are," Cochise continued. "They may take ten or twelve days to find them. My people have to separate into small bands and live a long way apart because the soldiers are hunting us all the time and the food is scarce. I want the soldiers to stop their operations so that my people can come here," he added, again testing the influence of Tatti Grande.

"I will send Captain Sladen here to Fort Bowie to carry orders for all the soldiers to be called back to their posts and to cease all hostilities," said Tatti Grande.

Cochise sensed danger in this. "Captain Sladen is only a *teniente*; the soldiers will not obey him. They will hear you, for you are a *grande*."

"Well, then, I will go with him," said Tatti Grande. "The Captain and I will go to Fort Bowie and I will issue the necessary orders and then we will come back."

But Cochise did not want to let them go entirely, for even if Tatti Grande spoke truthfully, other soldiers might be hunting them. Some raiding parties were still out, including Taza's. Cochise did not know what mischief they might have caused and so worried that soldiers might already be seeking revenge against the camps of the Chokonen. Keeping Captain Sladen with him would offer some protection. Besides, it would be another test of Tatti Grande's intentions. "Leave Captain Sladen. I will take care of him. Then you can come back. One of these Indians will go with you," he added, gesturing toward Chie with his chin. He knew Tatti Grande trusted Chie and had already protected him once. He knew also Chie would keep his eyes open and report back—for he did not know whether Tatti Grande could command the soldiers here, as he had come from Washington, D.C., without soldiers of his own. Cochise knew it would be hard for Chie to go with Tatti Grande to Fort Bowie, for it would mean passing by the place the soldiers had hung his father and his brother all those years ago. Even so, he knew Chie would do as he directed and the People had need of Chie now.

The conference broke up and they all rode to the camp of Cochise some four miles away, an easily defended place in the embrace of the rocks with a good year-round stream lined with great friendly oaks that spread their shade out like a prayer. Tatti Grande and Chie prepared immediately to leave, which pleased Cochise for Tatti Grande seemed a man of great fortitude and decision. Cochise also sent out runners to the scattered camps of the dozen subchiefs who owed their allegiance to him. The camp offered a long view out over the valley, so Cochise sat with Red Beard and Sladen for a long while as the mounted figures of Tatti Grande and Chie dwindled into the distance. They smoked quietly, Cochise and Red Beard exchanging languid observations in Spanish. Sladen seemed to sag down a little as Tatti Grande disappeared finally from sight.

Seeing this, Cochise turned to Red Beard, laughing. "Captain Triste (sad)."[6]

Sladen understood Spanish and replied, "No. Tell him that I am not blue at all, that I was only thinking."

"Sí," laughed Cochise, not fooled. "Sí. Captain Triste! Tell him not to feel triste," he said to Red Beard. "He can make himself comfortable here. He can leave his saddle in one place, his blanket in another, and his pistol in another, nothing will be lost; this is my camp; I command it."

Sladen smiled as Red Beard translated, so Cochise added, "Tell the captain that I will send off and get some tizwin and we will all get drunk and have a good time tonight," laughing again in his full-hearted way when he saw the cloud of concern pass over the open and friendly face of the *nantan*. They sat talking through the afternoon, Cochise curious and eager for this opportunity to understand how the soldiers thought. He had long ago stopped thinking of Red Beard as truly a White man, for he seemed more like a warrior and a friend. But he had always met the soldiers as enemies, wary as a circling knife fighter. Now it seemed this good man might help him understand the mystery of the soldiers, who had always seemed like men who had eaten too much loco weed. Cochise put Sladen to the test.

"What would you do if soldiers came to us now to fight us?" he asked.

"I would go out and meet them and tell them that we have made peace with you and they would listen to me and would not fight," said Sladen, with the confidence of a young man.

"But perhaps they would not listen to you. They might say you were a teniente, and not hear you," continued Cochise, watching Sladen carefully. "Would you fight them, or would you join them and fight us?"

"But they would not fight when I told them my message," protested Sladen. "General Howard is a Tatti Grande and they would not dare to disobey him."

"But if they would not hear you, would you fight against them?"

"No," said Sladen reluctantly. "I would not fight my own people, but I am sure they would not dare to fight after I had given them the General's orders."

Cochise laughed, glad of Sladen's reply. He had known Sladen would not fight his own people, but wondered if Sladen would lie to avoid angering Cochise. But he was not yet finished with the young *nantan*. "What would you do if the Mexican soldiers came to fight us?" asked Cochise.

"I would go and meet them and tell them that I was an officer of the United States Army and that the Indians and our people were making peace and that they must go back to Mexico," said Sladen promptly.

"But if they would not listen to you and would fight us, would you fight against us?"

"No. In that case I would fight with you against them, for they are not my people."

Now Cochise laughed out loud, delighted with this response. Sladen had spoken as carefully and truthfully as if he were one of the People, whose lives hung by their word.

That afternoon, Cochise took Sladen to visit one of his lookout posts on a peak of the Dragoons, so Sladen would understand things more fully. The lookout party was camped in a faint hollow at a place from which they could see to Tucson by looking west and to Apache Pass by looking east. When they arrived, the lookouts were watching something down in the valley. Cochise glanced at the sun to note the time of day, then peered down into the valley. He saw a tiny wagon which he pronounced to be Buckskin Alec, the mail rider between Fort Bowie and Tucson. Sladen strained to make out the moving dot, but quickly learned the lesson Cochise meant to impart. Now Sladen would report back to Tatti Grande how easily the warriors could have laid a trap for the mail wagon if they had decided to do so. They decided to spend the night with the lookouts, drinking some sweet tizwin and eating a small dinner of mescal. They drank and sang and danced all through the night, everyone laughing and teasing one another in the joyful and openhearted way of the People—into which Sladen entered with good spirit. Naiche attached himself to the *nantan*, constantly pointing out things and pronouncing their proper names—then struggling with the equivalent words in English. He applauded Sladen's every attempt, stroking him affectionately on the arm and saying "Bueno amigo"—good friend.

They returned to the camp near the foot of the mountain the next day, Cochise showing by his manner it was nothing to climb or descend six thousand feet on precipitous trails in a morning. Arriving in his camp, Cochise directed one of the younger warriors to bring back an antelope—He Who Is Becoming—for his guests, for Cochise did not want Sladen to judge him a poor man or a neglectful host. The warrior returned shamefaced some hours later, presenting himself to Cochise empty-handed. Cochise looked at the cringing warrior, conscious of Sladen's eyes on him and the eyes of the other warriors who had all stopped and turned to see what Cochise would do, smelling his anger like thunder in the air. Feeling shamed in front of his guest, Cochise surged to his feet with a burst of anger, his black eyes flashing. He whipped the warrior with the lash of his voice, standing flushed in the center of all of their eyes as the warrior slunk away. Then Cochise called Dos-teh-seh to bring his horse. Seizing his rifle with the inlaid handle, Cochise vaulted into the saddle and rode out of camp, not looking back.

He rode alone out into the grasslands of the San Pedro Valley, calming somewhat. He took a risk going alone out into the grass where the antelope lived, for everyone in this country yearned for his death. But he was spurred by pride now, for everyone had seen him ride out after humiliating the unsuccessful hunter—so he must not come back without an antelope. At one time, this would have been easy enough, for Usen had set many antelope to live among the People. But the herds had dwindled and grown even more wary as the Whites moved into their territory. Now many of the antelope had gone off someplace, perhaps following the buffalo into the earth to live with the Mountain Spirits. As Cochise rode, he smoothed his mind, using the story of the man who had become as the antelope and so had escaped from the land of the dead. Antelope was sacred, for he wore the ghost face and could become many things—even going back and forth from the Land of the Dead. The warriors prayed to Antelope Power so they could run quickly and eagerly sought antelope fat to rub on their legs. Cochise prayed to Antelope and gave thanks for the many blessings Antelope had bestowed on the people. Hunting was a prayerful and sacred act, as were most of the things the People did. The hunter could not have any success without luck and without Antelope Power's willingness and cooperation. So a warrior had to first approach hunting in a prayerful and reverential way or his skills would be useless. This was the thing young warriors did not understand, as they still believed most of all in their muscles and their bows.

Cochise rode to a place other people had seen a herd, a place he knew from the experience of years that antelope favored. He left his horse, which would frighten the antelope from a long ways off, and moved carefully through the tall grass in a prayerful way. When he finally saw the antelope grazing at a distance, he went down on his belly and approached them with great care. When he had gotten close enough, he tied a bit of red cloth to his bow and raised the cloth so the antelope could see it over the grass. Then he flicked the cloth back and forth in a certain unpredictable manner, not so violently that it would frighten the antelope, but in so odd and unpredictable a manner that it would make them curious—for antelope were as vulnerable to curiosity as Coyote. The antelope noticed the movement of the spot of red and tried to ignore it for a long while, but Cochise persisted with great patience, so finally some of the antelope came over to him. He shot one when he was sure of the distance.[7] He approached the antelope in a reverential manner, repeating the prayers of gratitude to Antelope Power for allowing this kill that he might feed those who depended on him. He carried the antelope back to his horse, remembering the story of the man who had become an aspect of the antelope. Cochise decided this had perhaps been a message sent by Power, which had denied the first warrior an antelope so Cochise would come out to the grassland and remember the story. It strengthened his resolve to trust in General Howard, who might perhaps lead the Chiricahua out of the land of twilight death in which they lived now and back to the land of the living—as Antelope had done for the man in the story.

Cochise rode back into camp and turned the body of the antelope over to Dos-teh-seh, who quickly divided it up. She saved the choice pieces to provide dinner for Sladen and Red Beard, but set aside much of the rest for women who had children but no husbands—for Cochise always shared food with those most in need. For his part, Cochise sat down again, rolled a cigarette, and continued the conversation he had left off just as if nothing had ever happened.

The scattered bands trickled in, each headman making a respectful report to Cochise as he sat with Sladen and Red Beard on the council rock. Cochise greeted each of them warmly, for they had shared many dangers and the leaders knew they all held the fate of the People in their hands.

Then a warrior from Taza's raiding party came in, approaching Cochise with nervous respect. He reported that the war party had killed the *nantan* and his driver along the Tucson road, mutilating the bodies and leaving them behind. Cochise was seized by a violent fear, for this one killing might now spoil everything. Perhaps it might even turn Tatti Grande against them when he heard about it from the soldiers at Fort Bowie. Cochise rose up in his anger and struck the warrior so violent a blow he was sent sprawling on the ground.[8] The warrior lay there stunned and submissive, and everyone watching held their breaths, wondering whether Cochise would drive his lance through the body of the unprotesting warrior. But the rage passed quickly. Cochise gathered his blanket around him and turned back to the rock, as the warrior slunk away. Cochise rolled a cigarette and smoked it to recover his calm, then gave orders to strike camp. If the soldiers did set out after the raiding party as a result of the death of the *nantan*, he must move to a safer place. Within moments, everyone was packing up essential supplies, and within an hour the camp was on the move. They continued up the steepest hillsides along nearly invisible trails, to the astonishment of Sladen, who could not believe riders could go safely along such cliff edges—especially as darkness overtook them. They traveled most of the night before stopping on a sheer slope below the ridgeline and lay down to rest on the faintest suggestion of a ledge or a level spot, each man holding the lead rope of his horse in his sleep. Cochise had picked the spot with care, knowing no one could approach them undetected and that they could easily disappear over the ridge if pursued.

The next day the lookouts reported a large party with a wagon leaving Apache Pass and heading out across Sulphur Springs Valley toward the Dragoons. Cochise breathed a sigh of relief, for soldiers on the trail of the raiding party would have come from Fort Lowell near Tucson to the west. Now Cochise led his people back down off the mountain, moving to meet Tatti Grande and coming along slowly toward the Dragoons.

Cochise waited for General Howard, who had brought his full party and a wagon pulled by four mules loaded with supplies for the People: two thousand pounds of corn, coffee, sugar, flour, and cloth. Cochise regarded the additional Whites with a wary eye, but growing confidence in both Sladen and Howard steadied him. Several warriors rode up to the wagon with presents, whooping and showing off their riding. They climbed onto the wagon—excited to see the fat mules in four-mule team—while the driver looked on dubiously. One of the warriors took the reins and whipped up the mules to a run, so the wagon bounded wildly over the rough ground, shedding boxes and bundles. The other warriors rode alongside, laughing uproariously. Some of them bet on whether the wagon would turn over or the warrior who was standing up holding the reins might fall off, for the People would bet on anything—even which beetle would be the first to cross an open space. But the white driver grew frightened and pushed the warrior aside to take back the reins. The warrior— a proud young man still trying to prove himself before the older warriors—made as if to pull out his knife, but a sharp word from Cochise stopped him. It seemed everything still hung by a twist of sinew, swaying with every breeze. Cochise resolved not to let some careless or unlucky moment snap the frayed cord that bound him to this last chance for peace. He had decided General Howard must pray to Power—perhaps the same Power as the People—and so was the only *nantan* he had ever met who might keep his word.

They all camped together where Cochise had first met General Howard, resting on the banks of the small stream and letting the horses graze in the good grass nearby. Cochise questioned Chie closely about his journey to Fort Bowie. He was reassured to learn that General Howard commanded the soldiers, who did everything he bid. Chie also reported that on the trip back from the fort, General Howard had lain down under a bearskin robe, inviting Chie to lie there as well with the robe as protection against the cold. Naturally Chie had refused, for anything having to do with bears touched on Power. None of the People would harm a bear, unless it was to preserve their own lives. Some said the spirits of dead warriors sometimes took the form of bears, so a warrior must always speak respectfully to Bear as though to his brother. Others said that only warriors who had behaved badly would come back as bears—which was another reason to be careful of them. Victorio had once told Cochise about a man who had shamed himself by remaining silent and letting another warrior take the blame for something that he had done. Shame had worked on that man so hard that he had finally left the band to live as an exile. Some said that he turned into a bear, because afterward the warriors often found bear tracks around his wife's wickiup. Several years later, that man came in out of the darkness to Juh's campfire—wearing bearskins—and said he had been wandering a long time alone, except for the bears that followed him about.[9] Whites were always doing things like this—using a bearskin in a disrespectful manner—so you never knew whether they intended offense or simply knew no better. But when Chie explained that the bearskin was bad medicine, General Howard immediately discarded it and used it no more. Cochise took comfort in this story, seeing that General Howard was different from the other *nantans*—a true man with a good heart like Red Beard.

On the first night, Cochise retired with the darkness to his wickiup, so no one else would see him struggle with the gnawing pain in his stomach. This wound with no mark now seemed to stalk him. He did not fear it for his own sake, for he had prepared himself to meet death a long time ago. But he could not afford weakness now, when everything depended on him. He remained in his wickiup, drinking tizwin to blunt the pain. The tizwin dulled both his pain and his mind. His wives kept fussing with him, coming into the wickiup and forcing him to cover up the pain. Finally he snapped when his sister came in to bother him as well. They shouted at each other and he scolded her and drove her out of the wickiup with blows. Fear of his temper had been an important tool of his leadership, but when the pain and the tizwin joined forces against him, he sometimes lost control, turning his anger on those who loved him. Everyone else drew away from his wickiup, not venturing to even look toward it. But he mastered himself until he fell finally into a troubled tizwin sleep.

The White Eyes and the People mingled in a friendly way. The children quickly got over their shyness and hung about continually in the camp of the Americans, holding their hands when they walked about, climbing into their laps when they sat down, and touching their lips when they talked in their strange manner. This was natural for children, for they were spoiled by everyone in the band—touched and patted and held. Children younger than ten went about naked and the older children wore not much more—breechcloths and moccasins for the boys and skirts and shirts for the girls. The People treasured their children, who were gifts in the midst of great trouble, carrying in their small hands the fate of the People. Most of them had never seen White people up close, except Red Beard. The White Eyes wandered freely about the camp, which resounded with the musical sound of the women singing their household songs and the high, clear laughter of children. They were a joyful and heartfelt people, to whom laughter came easily. The men especially were quick to anger—for they were both impulsive and proud—but their quarrels passed quickly and left no trace, like thunderstorms in the season of Large Fruit.

Everyone spent hours by the stream, enjoying the luxury of such a long camp near running water—for when they were hunted they camped well away from water. The children splashed and shouted for hours at a time. Both women and men spent hours sitting contentedly in the shade dressing one another's long black hair, combing it with their fingers until it shone like obsidian. The White Eyes were objects of endless curiosity and people were constantly in their camps, fascinated with the great mystery and variety of their things. But no one took anything not offered as a gift, for the People despised a thief, and no theft could go undetected among people who lived with their relatives and shared their lives under the open sky. Of course, none of these rules applied to the White Eyes or the Mexicans, who had no honor themselves.

The Whites in their turn seemed bemused by the People, whom they had thought were like wild animals. Some of the men looked openly and hungrily at the women, who were modest and chaste but not so careful about hiding their bodies as the white women. One man courted a young woman who had been captured in Mexico and raised as one of the people. He gave her gifts—even vermilion paint the women prized above cloth and beads and ornaments. But when he tried to touch her, she pushed him aside and explained that this was "not their custom." But she said perhaps she would go to Fort Bowie with him and marry him there—for the People were proper and chaste, and no one respected a woman who lay down with a man who was not her husband. Nor did they respect a man who would say improper things to a woman or push her to have sex with him when it would ruin her reputation.

Every night they held social dances, for the White Eyes had brought gifts of food, and it had been a long time since so many of the bands had gathered in one place and dared to light fires and dance through the night. One bold young woman with a great reputation for jokes urged Sladen to dance with her, flirting with him in the firelight until his eyes were full of her. Then she tried to maneuver him into a certain hole at the edge of the firelight while everyone watched, ready to laugh when he fell over his feet. But she was so amused by his awkward dancing that she forgot her own plan and fell in the hole instead. Now everyone who had been waiting for Sladen to fall down laughed twice as hard at the woman, many people howling with delight until tears ran down their faces. She scrambled to her feet, flushed with embarrassment. But a moment later she realized the joke and laughed herself. After that, she grew nearly helpless with laughter every time they danced near that hole. Everyone watching caught it from her, so the laughter spread around the circle like the joyful singing of a mockingbird.

Despite the good feeling in camp, Cochise kept his sentries spread out, watching every possible approach. The subchiefs continued to come in slowly, so the number of people camped continued to grow. One of the band leaders came in with fresh horses bearing an army brand and reported with a note of arrogance that he had raided a soldier camp, killing four men and making off with their horses. One warrior had been wounded in the attack and they had brought him to the camp. In a cold fury, Cochise rose from his seat on the council rock and struck the warrior a blow in the face, knocking him down to his knees. Cochise stood over the warrior— who was a brave and reckless man—conscious of the eyes of the others on them. His eyes glittered and he stood poised lest the man he had struck should come up off his knees with his knife in his hand. Cochise knew he must dominate his People so that even the wildest and most unruly of warriors would not dare to chase away the chance of peace, which stood now at the edge of camp, nervous as a deer. But the warrior saw the blaze of Power surrounding Cochise and backed away from him, not meeting his eye. Cochise looked around as though inviting a challenge, but everyone's eyes fell away. All except Juan, who grinned as though they shared a great joke. Cochise directed the warriors to hide the wounded man in the rocks, so the Whites would not ask questions.

Later, Sladen heard about that wounded man, hidden in the rocks. He took Cochise aside privately and explained he had been trained as a healer. He offered to go and treat the wounded man. But Cochise advised him against it. He observed that the man was hurt badly and would probably die. "If he did die, my people would think that the capitan had given him bad medicine and they would want to kill him," said Cochise diplomatically. Sladen quickly agreed.

Two weeks after he had sent out word, most of the subchiefs had gathered, although Taza was still raiding in Mexico. They decided to convene the peace conference nonetheless, for Cochise felt the risk of waiting grew with the days. They gathered beneath the shade of a great oak whose leaves had gathered news from the wind for longer than any man there had lived. Cochise sometimes wondered what wisdom he might have gathered had he the patience to sit as long and still as that oak, smoothed and steadied by the passage of the years. Cochise sat in the center of the circle of warriors along with Howard and Red Beard and El Cautivo, who served as his translator—although Cochise's command of Spanish was very good. El Cautivo watched the *nantans* with dour suspicion, for he believed Tatti Grande could just as well be witching them with his prayers as talking to his Power about peace. Cochise found his suspicion and insight useful. El Cautivo had insisted on wearing the shirt of the dead *nantan*, for the man who had killed him was from El Cautivo's band. Cochise did not prevent him, for El Cautivo was a man of Power and pride and not subject to the command of Cochise—only his counsel and advice.[10]

Tatti Grande, who had prayed with great intensity to his Power before they started, returned to the idea of Cañada Alamosa, saying the Great Father wanted all of his children to gather there. But Cochise had also consulted his Power—and the other leaders—and would not consider leaving his own country now. They went back and forth on this point for a time, each of the other band leaders saying they would not live at Cañada Alamosa, but would keep the peace in their own country. Their words wore away Tatti Grande's objection, as a knifepoint will wear away sandstone. After a talk of some hours that gave each of the subchiefs his rightful chance to speak, Tatti Grande agreed to establish a reservation that embraced both the Dragoons and Chiricahuas, with the agency for dispensing rations to be located near Fort Bowie.

Now Cochise's heart leaped up in his chest, like an eagle lunging against a tether. It seemed suddenly that everything he had fought for his whole life had come to this: a *nantan* he could trust who understood that the People and the land were aspects of one another, which was why they could not live peacefully anyplace else. But even in the moment of his great joy, Power whispered to Cochise, reminding him that keeping the peace would be as difficult as winning it. He feared Tatti Grande would go back to the Great Father. Who then would restrain the soldiers and be sure the People were not cheated? Instead of embracing the great gift of Tatti Grande's words, Cochise made one more condition. Tatti Grande must make Red Beard the agent in charge of the rations and everything happening inside the reservation. Red Beard seemed reluctant to accept this responsibility. But Tatti Grande assented readily, as though his Power had warned him about this condition ahead of time. For his part, Cochise promised to prevent all raiding against the Americans and to protect the road through Apache Pass to Tucson.

By the time Tatti Grande had agreed to all of these conditions, the day had slipped away. The council broke up for the night. The next day, the leaders all went aside to meet separately. Red Beard wisely told Tatti Grande and Sladen to go off alone and let the leaders talk, for each subchief must agree freely with the decision, and each warrior must agree freely with his band leader. Cochise had bound himself to Tatti Grande, saying he would control all raiding against the Americans on the part of all the bands living on the reservation, and he could only do that if each subchief agreed to the same conditions. Most of the band leaders followed quickly after Cochise, who was strongly supported by Juan and by Nahilzay, the most influential of the subchiefs. They reasoned in the varied and endlessly patient manner of the People, leaving each man free in his own mind. Some charged straight at the issue like a warrior with a lance. Others stalked agreement with stories or dreams, like a man investigating the camp of his enemy in the darkness. Everyone spoke as long as he pleased, careful never to interrupt anyone else, wary of directly disagreeing so that someone must lose face. Cochise spoke eloquently in the beginning in favor of the peace, his words creating the hillside down which the water of their talk would run. He was convinced they would never again have such an opportunity, and that Power had sent Tatti Grande in their time of great need. Even so, he could not command even a single warrior, only persuade them to his side for the good of their People.

However, El Cautivo expressed brooding doubts, reminding them the White Eyes were treacherous by nature. Poinsenay—an ambitious band leader with strong Power in war and a nature as wild as a horse that won't be ridden—also initially spoke against the peace, saying the Whites would tether them and then starve them. He said they would seem friendly and honest in the beginning, but would keep taking in the lead rope a little at a time. Eventually they would prevent the warriors from going down into Mexico, and the warriors would sit uselessly on the reservation, subsisting on dwindling rations with their dwindling spirits. In this argument, Poinsenay was supported by his brother Eskinya, one of the most influential medicine men. The opposition of these three men threatened the peace. Cochise understood their argument and remembered when he had stalked Mangas Coloradas with the story of Dog and Coyote. But now he argued the other side, matching his great Power and influence against theirs. The council went on for hours, the consensus growing slowly, as the sun of Little Eagles melts the last frost. In the end, every leader agreed with Cochise, and they resolved to accept the offer of peace and war no more with the Americans. Even El Cautivo and Poinsenay smothered their doubts, for although every man must make his own decision, the People also valued consensus and social harmony and did not often stand alone against the group.

Cochise returned to give General Howard and Captain Sladen this good news. But Sladen took Cochise aside privately and said he had seen one of the subchiefs wearing a shirt belonging to Lieutenant Cushing. Sladen said he did not want this to create a problem, but they could not ignore the killing of Lieutenant Cushing. Cochise listened carefully, then said he would investigate this matter carefully, but he thought none of his men had killed Lieutenant Cushing, so they must have obtained this shirt through trading. And this was true, for Juh had killed Cushing. But Cochise thought perhaps Sladen had confused Cushing with the other *nantan* in the buckboard—and was glad of the confusion.[11]

The council gathered again, this time with Tatti Grande and Sladen and Red Beard to render the decision of the leaders.

Cochise spoke eloquently, hopeful now for the first time in years. "Hereafter, the white man and the Indians are to drink the same water, eat of the same bread, and be at peace," he said.[12]

Now Cochise asked Tatti Grande to bring the *nantans* from the fort to be sure they agreed to the terms of the treaty. Tatti Grande readily agreed and sent word to Fort Bowie ordering the soldiers to meet him at Dragoon Springs.[13]

Cochise rode to the meeting alongside Tatti Grande, passing among the rocks that had sheltered and shaped him all his life. He could hear their long, slow song as he rode, feeling the assent of Power and the thrumming of the Ga'an through the earth carried up through the legs of his horse and vibrating in his bones. He said the place-names to himself as they passed, each calling out to him in a friendly way as with his father's voice: Water Flows Inward Under a Cottonwood Tree and Coarse-Textured Rocks Lie above in a Compact Cluster, and Water Flows Down on a Succession of Flat Rocks. Each offered its lesson and story as wise and loving as a mother in the darkness.

Coming to a place that offered a view to the horizon in two directions, shaded by the oaks, embraced by the rocks, Cochise turned to General Howard. "My home," said Cochise, gesturing with his chin to take in the rocks and trees and sky. "These rocks have protected me," he said, making one last effort to help General Howard understand why he had fought so long that he might die here—and his children after him. "Sometimes, they have been my only friends," he added, wondering if General Howard's Power might enable him to understand this statement, which seemed so incom-

Dragoons. The rocks of the Dragoons sheltered the Chiricahua and figured prominently in their myths. *(Peter Aleshire)*

prehensible to the White Eyes, to whom all places were alike because they had never belonged to any one place.

Cochise and all of his band leaders and a force of fifty warriors met the soldiers at Dragoon Springs in the season when Earth Is Reddish Brown.[14] The warriors came in their finest clothes and painted as for war, proud and unconquered. Cochise spoke proudly to the soldiers, for he had won this war and made them give him the thing he had most wanted. He did not cringe or fawn, but reminded them all of the things the soldiers had done to start this war and stretch it out. They listened respectfully, feeling the Power behind him and seeing for the first time in the open the warrior they had hunted so.[15] The officers responded respectfully, saying they were also willing to live at peace.

"I am getting old and would like to live at peace from this time on," said Cochise, his Power cast out from him as a shadow at sunset. "But if the white man will not let me do it, I will go away from here and fight him."[16] He spoke in a voice so strong and certain not one man listening doubted him—nor could any of them keep from shuddering to think how many more deaths he still had in him if pushed to it.

Finally, even the White Eyes surrendered to the Power of Cochise, who had fought all of his life, never forsaking his duty to his people or the prayers to his Power. He had walked in the footsteps of

Child-of-the-Water, and attended to the wisdom of places, and remembered his father's admonitions—so that now even the Giant must fall back from him.

For the Americans, it was the last war lost.

And in a final mercy, Cochise's Power rode silently with him back to the rocks of the Dragoons—never saying that this great gift of peace would scarcely outlive the already dying chief.

16

The Frail Peace—
the Dying Chief

The Origin of Old Age

Power talked to a man. It said, "I'm going to tell you something that is hard to do. If you try you can do it though. You are getting to middle age now, but I can show you how you can become like a young boy again."

This man listened. The Power said, "Start from here. Go back to the place where you first began to walk as a child. Then trail yourself through all the places you have been since you were a child. If you do not miss a place, the day you finish you will be young again and stay that way always."

The man tried, but he didn't get very far. He couldn't remember all the places where he had been. He didn't go halfway. So he did not get youth for us, either.

Now, for the first time in a generation, the Chokonen gathered in joy and thanksgiving in their own land—going openly in the daylight, camping again in the best places, and gathering to dance and celebrate. Cochise sent out runners to the scattered bands, saying they could come and camp safely near Fort Bowie and draw rations from Red Beard, the only White man they fully trusted. He sent runners to Cañada Alamosa to tell the Chokonen bands there they might come home. He even sent runners down to Juh in the Sierra Madre, inviting him onto the reservation as well. He did this after long thought, for Juh and Geronimo were wild spirits who might make trouble on the reservation. If they were on the reservation, he could insist they not raid among the Americans. But if they remained in the Sierra Madre, the Chokonen would be blamed when they raided north across the border. Therefore, it seemed worth the risk to bring the Nednhis inside his wickiup instead of waiting for them to cast stones from outside. All along the Tucson road, Cochise posted white flags so no one would bother any White Eyes on that road. The flags warned everyone that the road was under the protection of Cochise, who would hunt down anyone who broke the word he had given to General Howard.

Soon some 450 people were camped near Fort Bowie. Of course, Cochise did not relax the caution that had become the habit of a lifetime. He understood how frail was the peace, and although he trusted Red Beard and Tatti Grande, he did not trust any of the soldiers. Moreover, he knew that men like Poinsenay had come to peace reluctantly and could still make trouble unless Cochise kept them hobbled. Cochise usually traveled with a bodyguard of warriors and camped a mile or more from the agency, with its constant traffic of Whites and soldiers. He kept sentries posted on his camps and kept a close watch on any soldiers or strange White Eyes who came onto the reservation, determined his enemies should not use peace like a hunter's brush blind. He implored Tatti Grande to stay with them, for General Howard's will and word were the best guarantee of peace they had. But Tatti Grande said he must go back to Washington, D.C., at the bidding of the Great Father, and so Cochise was compelled to let him go. But Red Beard remained with him. Red Beard did not act like other agents, giving orders and running things to suit himself. He let the bands camp anywhere they wanted on the reservation, even loading up wagons to distribute rations at several different places so everyone would not have to come and camp near the agency. He understood the bands must scatter out over a wide area to hunt and harvest the gifts of the earth, so they would not become completely dependent on the inadequate rations. Moreover, Red Beard did not require people to wear tags like cattle, as General Crook had done in the White Mountains.

Red Beard also did nothing to stop the warriors from going down into Mexico to provide for their families. He agreed with Cochise that the Mexicans had been so treacherous for so long that they had earned the revenge the People continued to extract from them. Besides, if the Mexicans wanted peace, let them seek it from Cochise as the Americans had done.

Once, when Cochise did go to the agency to confer with Red Beard, he saw Merejildo Grijalva standing very still, watching him ride up alongside one of the *nantans*. Merejildo kept his face expressionless and his hands away from the gun in his belt, watching Cochise come toward him with an expression of casual interest— although he must have wondered whether Cochise might kill him where he stood. Cochise reined in his horse close beside Merejildo, who looked up at him with a mild, friendly expression and extended his hand, in the manner of the Whites. Cochise admired his composure, though in a flash of memory of all the love and hate between them. "I will not shake hands with this man until I have whipped him," said Cochise, jumping lightly from his horse. He came close up against Merejildo and struck him three times hard with his riding whip. Merejildo did not flinch, but continued to regard Cochise with the same mild and friendly expression. Then they embraced as old friends—for Merejildo had made his apology in standing without flinching, and Cochise had saved face before his warriors so he would not have to kill Merejildo. Then the two of them sat and talked a while, each showing the other the other side of the battles they had fought one against the other. Soon they were laughing and teasing each other—for both understood everything about the other and both respected that a warrior must follow the trail of his conscience, though it lead through the catclaw along the cliff edge.

But after only a few months of happiness and security, small things began to go wrong, like the sound of rocks tumbling down the slope above. Red Beard had to fight constantly to get the rations General Howard had promised. Months went by without the delivery of new rations, and when the supplies finally came they were only half of what had been promised. Sometimes Red Beard had to use his own money to buy extra cattle.[1]

Even so, many White Eyes bitterly criticized Red Beard for taking the part of the People and for remaining loyal to Cochise. General Crook repeatedly threatened to take over the reservation and maybe shut it down and force the Chokonen to live on the pestilent San Carlos Reservation, where everyone went around with tags. General Crook sent his *segundo*—a *nantan* named John Bourke—to investigate the Chiricahua Reservation. He proved an intelligent, fair-minded man who already spoke a little bit of the language of the People. He talked to Cochise in a respectful and friendly way— even noticing scars on both hands. Bourke asked about those scars and learned the chief's younger wife had bitten him badly during a fight, for she was perhaps the only person among all the Chokonen who did not fear his anger. She was a beautiful, resourceful, and fearless woman, fully alive—like an antelope in the moment of its greatest speed. After talking to Cochise, the *nantan* decided he had abided by the terms of his agreement with General Howard and so had given General Crook no pretext to close the reservation. Cochise explained he had promised to stop raiding the Americans and to let soldiers and people pass freely across the reservation, so long as they did not settle there. The *nantan* questioned Cochise closely on the matter of raiding in Mexico—a topic Cochise tried to avoid. But when the *nantan* persisted, Cochise said the Mexicans had killed many people whose relatives were bound to want revenge and so would go down there from time to time. "I don't want to lie about this thing," he said. "They go, but I don't send them."[2]

Sometime after that another White Eye came to meet with Cochise. Red Beard said his name was Governor Anson P. Safford and that he was the head of all of the people in Arizona besides the soldiers. They had an interesting talk in which Safford finally explained about the war between the White Eyes. Safford said that on account of this war the soldiers had all left the forts for awhile— not because of the war with the People. Cochise did not know whether to believe this or not. Safford said they had fought the war because some of the White Eyes didn't want the others to hold as slaves the dark-skinned men like the Buffalo Soldiers. Cochise listened carefully to this explanation, although it was confusing. Governor Safford said that the North had won that war and forced the South to release all of its slaves, and that was why the People could no longer keep as slaves women and children they had cap- tured down in Mexico. Cochise listened dubiously to this infor- mation as well, noting that the White Eyes had done nothing to make the Mexicans stop keeping people they had captured as slaves. But he ultimately concluded that this was just one more contra- dictory and unfair thing about the White Eyes and agreed to release slaves the warriors still held. Perhaps if he sent a few of these back to Mexico, then the White Eyes would do something to recover the many people held as slaves in Mexico. He had long ago given up thinking that the White Eyes would ever make much sense to him.[3]

But in the meantime, General Crook started a war with the Tonto and Yavapai bands living around Prescott and the Verde Valley. Those people had been driven off their lands by settlers, who killed them freely and even gave them poisoned rations. When the warriors finally fought back, General Crook hunted them down without pause, using mostly White Mountain warriors against them. They finally surrendered to him and settled along the Verde River. But soon greedy White Eyes saw the Tonto had good farmland and large herds, so they took the land away and sent the Tonto and Yavapai to live on the San Carlos Reservation alongside bands that had been their enemies. Cochise gathered news of all these things through his many sources, hearing it with foreboding.

He began to pay more attention to the raiding into Mexico carried out by the younger warriors, who were still anxious to make a name for themselves and not yet wise enough to look far ahead to see the consequences of their actions. Raiding parties from the reservation killed perhaps a hundred people in Sonora in the first half year after the establishment of the Chiricahua Reservation—but they touched nothing that belonged to the Americans. The other White Eyes and the Mexicans themselves sent many complaints to Red Beard, which he answered as best he could—saying much of the raiding was done by other bands.

Finally, the Mexicans even sent a delegation to the agency to complain. The Mexicans found several things in the camps of the warriors that belonged to people who had been killed in Mexico— but the warriors responded that the Mexicans had done their fair share of the killing. The discussion grew so heated that one warrior started to go after the Mexican commander until Cochise restrained him. Cochise then turned to the Mexican and said he could take his life and return to Mexico, but if the Mexicans came again onto the reservation his warriors would kill them all.[4]

The situation grew steadily worse. Perhaps three hundred Chihenne got tired of the restrictions on them at Tularosa—which was far from the Mexican border—and moved to the Chokonen Reservation. Red Beard provided them rations without complaint. This made problems between Red Beard and the officers at Tularosa, who complained he should send the Chihenne back, and insisted Red Beard only wanted the money and the rations so he could sell the supplies and pocket the money. Red Beard's enemies among the Whites circled around him like warriors who have trapped a wagon train. General Howard heard about these troubles and sent out his representative to help Red Beard fight off his critics. Still, the constant struggle and criticism wearied Red Beard, who began to think about quitting and living peacefully.[5]

Geronimo and Naiche. Naiche and Geronimo posed on horseback for this shot shortly before surrendering to General George Crook in one of the few photographs of Apache warriors in the field ever taken. *(Arizona Historical Society)*

Moreover, now these Chihenne started raiding in Mexico as well, along with Juh's Nednhis and Geronimo, who was as always the unquenched flame. Traders also came quietly onto the reservation and exchanged whiskey and guns for the goods brought back from Mexico. The whiskey made fresh problems, and soon fights and feuds broke out among the various bands, pitting the Chokonen against the Chihenne and the Nednhis against them all.

Cochise met with Red Beard, although the chief was weaker now and in pain from his stomach all the time. They decided they must stop the raiding into Mexico, which required gaining control of the Chihenne and Nednhis living on the reservation. Cochise called a council of all of the headmen, praying a long time for the strength to convince them they must stop going down into Mexico, even though the Americans had not provided enough rations and even though the Mexicans deserved killing. The Chokonen leaders all stood strongly behind Cochise, and most of the Chihenne and Nednhis agreed reluctantly. Some of the more warlike spirits only listened, looking stubborn and unhappy. In the end, Cochise rose up to the full stature of his Power and said the survival of the People now depended as heavily on the restraint of the warriors as it had once rested on their success at war. He said anyone who wished to remain alive on the reservation of the Chokonen must heed his words and give up raiding the Mexicans, leaving the threat of his anger unspoken but heavy in the air.

In the weeks that followed, Cochise sent out runners and scouts to locate all of the Nednhis and Chihenne bands still raiding. He and Red Beard worked together in this. Red Beard warned the bands with war parties out they would receive no more rations, and Chokonen raiding parties came by their camps to say that anyone who continued to raid must leave the Chokonen Reservation. Juh and Geronimo left, for they were both strong spirits who could not be governed by any will other than their own. Juh left angry and disdainful, saying he would remain in the Sierra Madre and live as a free man—even if he must fight every day of his life. He went back down into Mexico and played the deadly old game of hide-and-seek with the Mexicans. Before the season of the Ghost Dance had finished, Cochise had curtailed almost all raiding from the Chokonen Reservation.[6]

Cochise could only hope he had acted in time, for he could scarcely ride his horse anymore for the constant pain. Dos-teh-seh and his other wives tended him constantly and tenderly, grieved to see the way he had subsided into himself, like a great tree gnawed by termites. Sometimes he sat quietly by the fire, remembering his life, silently recalling all the names he could no longer speak. He would sing the songs of an old man, taking comfort in knowing these songs had been sung through all the rounds of life by all those who had gone on before him.

> When I was young, I took no heed;
> Old, old I have become!
> Because I knew that age would come
> To me, I took no heed.[7]

Cochise could feel the end approaching, as he could sometimes feel the presence of his enemies. He was in the box canyon of his many years and so could not run any longer from this premonition. Now he must prepare himself for the death that had all his life ridden alongside, more companion than foe. He called Taza to him and spoke a long while, although it wearied him to talk now. Taza fought against the death he saw gathered in the hollows of his father's face, saying someone must have witched him and vowing to seek out the witch so his father might recover. Cochise soothed him, seeing that Taza fought grief with anger—as befit a warrior. Cochise talked quietly to him, then called in Naiche as well. He asked them both to keep the peace he had made with the Whites, saying the time they could fight the Whites was long past. They had won their war and gained the only thing worth having: the land that knew them and protected them and heard their prayers. Fighting the White Eyes now could do no good; it would only give them the excuse they sought to break the promise of General Howard. Resolving to protect the People as their father had done, Taza and Naiche promised to keep the peace—and Naiche promised to serve as the strong right hand of his brother, as Juan had done for Cochise. Then Cochise called the other headmen to him, both the trusted companions of his youth and the new men who had stepped forward through the holes in the ranks of those who had gone on before. He urged them to follow Taza, who had learned all of Cochise's ceremonies and who had the ear of Power. Nahilzay and Eskinya promised to follow Taza, although both had perhaps their own, stronger claim to leadership. The other leaders also promised, although Poinsenay remained aloof—so that a small fear for the future nagged at Cochise even as his strength faltered.

The new superintendent of Indian affairs, a man named Levi Edwin Dudley, came to Cochise's camp when he had already begun to turn his back on the land of the living to prepare for his journey. Cochise was in constant pain now and at first did not want to talk to this new White man, although this man had charge over Red Beard and the reservation. But Dudley brought a picture of himself with General Howard, so Cochise's heart softened. They talked for an hour, which nearly exhausted his strength. Dudley gave Cochise the picture as a gift and the chief put it close by his bed. He looked at it affectionately, sometimes touching this aspect of the great friend of the People—the only White man who understood the nature of Power. The talk was friendly, but Cochise was surprised when Dudley said some people wanted to move the Chokonen to New Mexico to live with the Chihenne.[8] Cochise by then was too weak to fight that idea, saying only it must fall to Taza to decide. He had fought all his life with all his strength, but knew the struggle must pass into other hands. He had been the leading man among the Chokonen for eighteen years, suffering the many wounds and the countless fights and the burden of deaths to win their war and regain their land. But now he understood why Child-of-the-Water had continued on his journey and left the People behind. Each life had its seasons, and he could no more change their progression than he could hold back the snow.

Clenched with grief, Taza left his father's camp with several warriors to seek the witch who was killing Cochise. Power was just like people, working both good and evil. Sometimes greedy and foolish people twisted Power to do bad deeds. And sometimes Power twisted the people who sought it. Cochise had his enemies among the People, for he had bruised the pride of many men and by his commands caused many deaths. And so, the relatives of some people talked against him. Taza had heard that one such person had witched Cochise, bringing on his long illness. The warriors found the witch and seized him. They were determined to burn him, which was the best thing to do with witches, although they were hard to burn and took a long time to die. But Red Beard came quickly at the rumor of the burning and convinced Taza to spare the man's life. Taza did this reluctantly and only because he promised his father he would follow the advice of Red Beard, who was their best protection against the treachery and greed of the White Eyes.

In the season of Little Eagles,[9] Red Beard hurried to the camp of Cochise so he would not miss saying good-bye to his old friend. He found Cochise drifting in and out of consciousness, crossing and recrossing the boundary between the living and the dead. When Cochise heard the voice of his old friend, he revived somewhat and they talked a while. Seeing how the talk used up the last of his friend's strength, Red Beard made ready to leave.

"Do you think you will ever see me alive again?" asked Cochise, his voice faint, but without fear.

"No," said Red Beard, for they had never lied to each other. "I do not think I will. I think that by tomorrow night you will be dead."

"Yes, I think so too—about ten o'clock tomorrow," said Cochise, who knew this already from his Power. He did not fear it, for he was weary. "Do you think we will ever meet again?" he repeated, for he had often wondered whether the White Eyes would follow them to the Happy Place. He hoped they would not—except for Red Beard, who was dear to his heart.

Red Beard seemed surprised by this question, but he thought about it carefully before he answered. "I don't know," he said at length. "What is your opinion?"

"I have been thinking a good deal about it while I have been sick here," said Cochise with a trace of his old animation, "and I believe we will. Old friends will meet again—up there," he concluded, gesturing to the listening sky with his chin.[10]

Red Beard went sorrowfully on his way, knowing the world would be a smaller place when Cochise had passed from it.

Cochise died quietly the next morning. The word went out over the People black as a dust storm. Everywhere people stopped and turned toward the place where he had died and wailed in the despair of their grief—for who would protect them now that he had gone? The White Eyes passing by the camps of the Chokonen listened fearfully, for it seemed the cries and the keening would never stop. The sounds of the People's grief continued through the night and into the next day. Everywhere people hacked off their hair and threw away their clothing. And when they heaped together his things for burning, all the people of his band came grieving to the fire, throwing their own clothes into it until they stood naked and inconsolable.

Then Dos-teh-seh and his sister took his body and prepared him for burial. They washed him and combed his hair until it shone and painted his face. They dressed him in his best things, together with all of his charms and the contents of his ceremonial pouch. Then they wrapped him in a heavy woolen blanket and put him on his favorite horse, so he could ride as a chief to his burial. They conveyed him to a deep fissure in the heart of the Dragoons, among the rocks that had been waiting patiently for him to return to them since his parents had first rolled him to the four directions on the earth. Then they killed his horse and lowered him into the deep crack in the rock, so Cochise could ride in the afterlife. They put with him also his favorite dog, together with his bow and the beautiful rifle with the silver inlaid stock and the pearl handled pistols. Finally they lowered Cochise into the earth, crying out his true name for the last time.

So passed Cochise from the land of the living, where his shadow had been long.

He had kept his word—the promise made as his father and his mother and all of his people and Power itself had stood watching as he took his first unsteady steps in the footprints of Child-of-the-Water painted on the unblemished buckskin. He had protected his family and served his People and terrified his enemies. And although he could not shatter the arrows of the Giant with his breath, he had nonetheless walked in the Giant's shadow unafraid, and so won his fight.

What more could a true man do?

Epilogue

The death of Cochise effectively doomed his people, for with his passing none of the leaders had the stature to maintain the frail peace with the White Eyes. Beset by his critics and discouraged by Cochise's death, Jeffords soon quit his job as agent. The unruly elements among the Chokonen agitated for a resumption of raiding into Mexico, spearheaded by Poinsenay and abetted by Juh and Geronimo, who returned to the reservation periodically. Although Taza struggled to fulfill his promise to his father, he had neither the stature nor the political skills to dominate men like these. The final trigger came when Poinsenay and his brother—who had returned from raiding in Mexico—killed two station agents who sold them bad whiskey. Taza and Naiche led a band of warriors that fought a pitched battle with the renegades, but the incident gave the government the excuse it had been seeking to close the reservation.

Taza and Naiche obeyed their promise to their father and agreed to move their band to the San Carlos Reservation less than two years after Cochise's death. But Jeffords's prediction was borne out and about half of the Chokonen vanished—many going back down into Mexico with Juh and Geronimo. These roaming and restive bands driven off the reservation destabilized the tenuous peace General Howard had secured with his compassion and insight. Raiders showed up on the Chihenne Reservation in New Mexico with horse herds stolen from Mexico, which gave the government the pretext sought for the disastrous closure of the reservation.

Acting from a blend of greed and bureaucratic stupidity, the government sought to concentrate all the Apache bands on the hot, disease-ridden San Carlos Reservation, which led to the inevitable explosion and another ten years of tragic warfare in the Southwest and northern Mexico. First the Chihenne under Victorio fought a doomed war to regain their homeland, resulting in the deaths of thousands of Americans and Mexicans and the devastation of the

Chihenne. This was followed by the Geronimo wars, which involved mostly Chokonen bands that repeatedly left the reservation and spread death and destruction throughout the Southwest. At one point, one-quarter of the U.S. Army was chasing Geronimo and eighteen warriors. The war finally ended in 1886, when Geronimo surrendered. The government then loaded hundreds of Chiricahua— mostly people who had been living peacefully on the reservation and including many warriors who had scouted for the army against the hostiles—onto cattle cars. The Chiricahua remained prisoners of war for the next twenty-eight years in Florida, Alabama, and then Oklahoma—one of the most shameful chapters in the long, dispiriting chronicle of the conflict between the Americans and the native peoples.

Much of this might have been averted had Cochise lived long enough to stabilize the Chiricahua Reservation with Jeffords's assistance.

That makes the death of Cochise a tragedy for his enemies no less than for his people—and his life a lesson for us all. The lessons of his life are as persistent and profound as the voice of the Ga'an humming through the rocks of the Dragoons for those whose minds are steady and smooth and resilient.

The Journey of Cochise to the Happy Place

Cochise found himself walking along in a strange place, dressed in his finest clothes, with his rifle with the silver inlaid stock and his good pistols and his medicine pouch. First he came to a mulberry tree growing out from a cave in the ground. Before this cave a guard was stationed, but when Cochise approached without fear the guard let him pass. He descended into the cave, and a little way back the path widened and ended in a cliff many hundreds of feet wide and equal in height.

There was not much light, but by peering directly beneath him he discovered a pile of sand reaching from the depths below to within twenty feet of the top of the rock where he stood. Holding to a bush, he swung off from the edge of the rock and dropped onto the sand, sliding rapidly down its steep side into the darkness. He went unafraid, for he had always taken the risks allotted to him, trusting in Power.

He landed in a narrow passage running westward through a canyon that gradually grew lighter and lighter until he could see as well as if it had been daylight; but there was no sun. Finally he came to a section of this passage that was wider for a short distance and then closed abruptly and continued in a narrower path. Just where this section narrowed, two huge serpents were coiled. Rearing their heads, they hissed at him as he approached.

But once more—as in all of his life—Cochise showed no fear. As soon as he came close to them, they withdrew quietly and let him pass.

At the next place, where the passage opened to a wider section, were two grizzly bears prepared to attack him. But when he approached and spoke to them in a kind, strong, respectful voice, as he had always spoken to Power, they stood aside and he passed unharmed.

He continued to follow the narrow passage and for the third time it widened. This time two mountain lions crouched in the way. But when he had approached them without fear and had spoken to them, they also withdrew.

He again entered the narrow passage. For some time he followed this, emerging into a fourth section beyond which he could see nothing: the farther walls of this section were clashing together at regular intervals with tremendous sounds. But he recognized the rocks there, seeing they were but the rocks of the Dragoons which had spoken to him all his life and whose dreams he had known. So when he approached them they stood apart until he had passed.

After this he seemed to be in a forest, and following the natural draws, which led westward, he soon came into a green valley where there were many Indians camped and plenty of game. Antelope saw him coming; he looked up with his ghost face and nodded. Cochise realized that he knew already the names of each place here— and the stories to go with them—so he would never be lost again. Those places were happy to see him, too, for they had been thinking of him for a long time. Here he could feel the Life Force all around him—in everything, present as the sound of the wind in the trees.

He saw some men coming toward him, talking and laughing. He quickly recognized them. Coyuntura was coming on in the lead, grinning in that way Cochise had nearly forgotten. Behind him came Pisago Cabezón and Mangas Coloradas, talking seriously together—no doubt talking in places. Their names nearly caught in his throat, until he remembered he could speak them freely now.

Cochise went all the way past the guards and the lions and the bears and the rocks to the Happy Place, for he had walked in the path of Child-of-the-Water and shown no fear.

Now he broke into a glad run, having gone past fear and fatigue and pain.

He ran on toward Coyuntura, with only one question left.

He hoped there were no White Eyes here.

Notes

Preface

1. Many of these myths and stories are in the form of titled epigraphs located at the start of each chapter. The sources of these epigraphs—and, in some cases, additional commentary on this material—can be found in unnumbered notes for each chapter in the notes section.

For example, the source of the epigraph titled "The End of the World," which precedes the contents page, is Morris Edward Opler's *Myths and Tales of the Chiricahua Apache Indians* (Lincoln: University of Nebraska Press, 1942), 100. Today, many of the springs the Apache used in southern Arizona and New Mexico have dried up, although the spring at Apache Pass still flows year-round. Dams, diversions, and overgrazing have destroyed or severely degraded more than 90 percent of the riparian areas in Arizona and New Mexico—and the San Pedro remains the only undammed river. The water table has dropped hundreds of feet in most areas because of groundwater pumping—mostly to grow water-thirsty, federally subsidized cash crops like cotton. Throughout the Southwest, streams that once wandered back and forth across their floodplains to spawn forests of cottonwoods and willows have become entrenched for reasons still poorly understood, and the weedlike tamarisk has displaced the cottonwood/willow habitat biologists say is the most productive ecosystem in North America.

Chapter 1: He Turns to Fight (October 1869)

The story titled "The Destruction of the Earth" is taken from Morris Edward Opler, *Myths and Tales of the Chiricahua Apache Indians* (Lincoln: University of Nebraska Press, 1942), 1–2. This myth shows a possible Christian influence but may nonetheless have been told in the time of Cochise, as the Apache had been in contact with the missionaries for more than a century before his birth.

1. This describes the battle of Tex Canyon in the Chiricahua Mountains on October 19, 1869—although the memoirs of Captain Frederick Elisha Phelps indicated the fight took place in nearby Horseshoe Canyon. Phelps probably confused the location of this battle with an earlier fight.

2. Captain Reuben Bernard.

3. The wounded man was Lieutenant John Lafferty. Captain Bernard broke off the fight after a daylong engagement, concluding he had not enough men to breach Cochise's defenses. Captain Bernard claimed to have killed eighteen warriors, but that was probably an overestimate. He reported that the Apache warriors were recklessly brave and that Cochise was "one of the most intelligent Indians on the continent."

Chapter 2: In the Beginning

The tale "Two Women Play Dead and Escape from the Giant" is described by Morris Edward Opler in *Myths and Tales of the Chiricahua Apache Indians* (Lincoln: University of Nebraska Press, 1942), 21.

1. Geronimo started his autobiography with the story of Child-of-the-Water, saying that every warrior's life should follow in the footsteps of this pivotal cultural hero. Therefore, in deference to Apache conventions, I am using the myth here. *Geronimo, His Own Story*, as told to S(tephen) M(elvil) Barrett (New York: Duffield, 1906), 1.

2. This recounting of the birth of Child-of-the-Water comes from Opler, *Myths and Tales of the Chiricahua Apache Indians*, 1–14. I have mixed paraphrases with direct quotes from Opler, who recorded the myths precisely from Chiricahua Apache informants. Opler collected many variants of the key myths, but I have settled here on the version in which Child-of-the-Water and Killer-of-Enemies were twin brothers.

3. From here to the end of the myth it is taken from Opler, *Myths and Tales of the Chiricahua Apache Indians*, 12–14.

4. Ibid., 7.

5. Although estimates vary, Cochise was probably born in about 1810, but perhaps as early as 1800.

6. The Chihenne, or Eastern Chiricahua, have been referred to as the Mimbres, Coppermine, Warm Springs, Mogollon, and Gila Apache. I am accepting Chihenne here as the term most often used by Eve Ball's informants for their people in her excellent *Indeh: An Apache Odyssey* (Provo, Utah: Brigham Young University Press, 1980) and also in *In the Days of Victorio: Recollections of a Warm Springs Apache* (Tucson: University of Arizona Press, 1970).

7. Western and southern New Mexico, and northern Mexico.

8. The Southern Chiricahuas, referred to also as the Janero, Carrizaleno, and Pinery Apache.

9. The Navajo and the Apache both speak an Athabascan language and migrated down from Canada and Alaska, probably arriving in the southwest in the 1400s, just ahead of the Spanish.

10. Spanish accounts indicate six hundred warriors attacked Tucson on May 1, 1782.

11. In fact, the Spanish adopted an explicit policy of using cheap liquor and inferior guns to make the Apache dependent and to spread dissension among bands.

12. The Spanish adopted a peace policy in 1786, after nearly a century of warfare, and issued rations to about six thousand Apaches at a cost of two thousand pesos a year. The peace policy proved much more effective, and cheaper, than the decades of warfare that preceded it.

13. It is now unknown what name Cochise was given at birth. Typically, people acquired new names throughout their lives, depending on their accomplishments or characteristics. As a young man, Cochise was called Goci, a reference to the handsome prominence of his "Roman" nose. As a mature warrior, he acquired the name Cochise, which probably suggests certain hard, durable qualities of oak, according to Morris Opler, an anthropologist and linguist. Moreover, it's likely Cochise had another, purely Apache name, throughout his life—which would have been rude and perhaps dangerous for others to use. Names had a great significance to the Apache. For instance, if one warrior called another by his true name it invoked a heavy burden—either to join a raid, or to stand and fight even in the face of near certain death. Therefore, people rarely used one another's "real" name—and never spoke that name after death. To avoid confusion here and because the childhood name is now lost to history, I'm using Cochise throughout.

14. The birth of Cochise roughly coincided with the onset of the Mexican revolution, which would eventually drive out the Spanish and shatter the peace policy that had prevailed on the frontier for thirty years.

15. "Chiricahua" probably derives from the Opata word *Chiguicagui*, meaning "Mountain of the Wild Turkeys," and was not the name that the Apache used for the dramatic mountain range that runs north-south as it rises abruptly from the surrounding plains. It is not certain that Cochise was born in the Chiricahuas, although this was the core territory for the Chokonens. His band also spent a lot of time in Sonora, Mexico, especially during this peaceful interlude. Frank Lockwood, the first careful historian of the Apache, maintains that Cochise was born in the Chiricahuas, and I am here accepting his speculation.

16. The identity of the father of Cochise remains a matter of some debate. I am here agreeing with Edwin R. Sweeney, who wrote the masterfully documented historical biography of Cochise. James Henry Tevis, who knew Cochise in the 1850s, wrote that the father of Cochise was the "leader of all the Apaches" who was killed treacherously by Mexicans at a feast—a description that fits Pisago Cabezón. However, it might also fit Relles, another prominent Chokonen leader killed treacherously at the same time. I agree with Sweeney, however, that records show a closer association between Cochise and Pisago Cabezón than with Relles. Ace Daklugie, the

son of noted Nednhi chief Juh, told historian Eve Ball that Cochise's father was Juan José Compá—also killed treacherously in the manner Tevis described. However, Juan José Compá was Chihenne, and there's no other supporting evidence to suggest Cochise was born Chihenne rather than Chokonen.

17. This description of the training of the child of a leading man comes from Morris Edward Opler's *An Apache Life-Way: The Economic, Social, and Religious Institutions of the Chiricahua Indians* (1941; reprint, Chicago: University of Chicago Press, 1996), 12.

18. Sotol stalks for a boy, yucca stalks for a girl. This description of the making of a cradleboard and the description of the Moccasin Ceremony that follows comes from ibid., 12–17.

19. The Moccasin Ceremony was held between the ages of one and two, as described in ibid., 17.

20. This recounting of the myth is taken directly from Opler, *Myths and Tales of the Chiricahua Apache Indians*, 9.

21. I am once again using the adult names of the brothers of Cochise from the beginning. These are the names commonly used in the historical record, and are really just the bastardization of the Apache names, or nicknames used by the Mexicans or Americans, and not their actual Apache names. They each undoubtedly had different Apache nicknames as children, young warriors, and adult warriors.

22. This is speculation on my part. No Apache accounts give a clear listing of Pisago Cabezón's wives and children—which is why it is speculative even to assume Cochise was his son along with Coyuntura and Juan, who were clearly brothers of Cochise. Several other sons of Pisago Cabezón are mentioned in the historical record, presumably also brothers of Cochise.

23. The name of the fourth son of Pisago Cabezón is not known, so I have given him a name. He was killed in an attack on Pisago Cabezón's camp when still young, and the Apache habit of never again mentioning the name of the dead helped obliterate his name from the historical record. Note also that I am assuming Pisago Cabezón was the father of Cochise.

24. This is actually from Opler, *Apache Life-Way*, 27, which describes the rules of behavior related by one of Opler's Chiricahua Apache informants. I have here attributed it to Pisago Cabezón, on the assumption it represents a common Chiricahua social consensus and because it seems consistent with Cochise's dignified and principled behavior.

25. This is taken from Opler, *Myths and Tales of the Chiricahua Apache Indians*, 35.

26. This explanation of Apache place naming practices comes from Keith H. Basso's absorbing *Wisdom Sits in Places* (Albuquerque: University of New Mexico Press, 1996), based on his twentieth-century research among the White Mountain Apache. I have not seen a discussion of the practice

among the Chiricahua Apache, but have made the assumption that the parables and ethical stories connected to specific place names held sway among the Chiricahua as well.

27. Ibid., 53. The following story is about a place-name among the White Mountain Apache, but I have applied it here to the Chiricahua.

28. This speech is taken from ibid., 126–127, but I have attributed it to Pisago Cabezón. This assumes the philosophy of twentieth-century White Mountain Apache can be applied to Chiricahua Apache living a century earlier. Basso's informant for this statement was Dudley, a White Mountain Apache cowboy.

29. This practice was described by Opler in *Apache Life-Way*. I am here attributing it to Cochise.

30. Ibid., 315. This is generalized advice I'm attributing to Pisago Cabezón.

31. Ibid., 317.

32. Ibid., 138.

33. Ibid., 136. This is general advice to a novice; I have attributed it to Pisago Cabezón.

Chapter 3: The Peace Unravels (1824)

The source of the story titled "Usen Gives Corn to Killer-of-Enemies" is Morris Edward Opler's *Myths and Tales of the Chiricahua Apache Indians* (Lincoln: University of Nebraska Press, 1942), 14.

1. The Apache often made a sharp distinction between different Mexican towns and states, reasoning that they were each like independent bands—capable of making a separate peace. Often a particular band would consider itself at peace with one Mexican town, but free to raid other settlements.

2. The Spanish reduced the garrisons of the presidios sharply with the outbreak of the Mexican revolution in 1821.

3. Pisago Cabezón's Chokonens resumed raiding in about 1831.

4. This description of the imperatives of leadership comes from Morris Edward Opler, *An Apache Life-Way: The Economic, Social, and Religious Institutions of the Chiricahua Indians* (1941; reprint, Chicago: University of Chicago Press, 1996), 466.

5. Mangas Coloradas in this period was probably the warrior known as "Fuerte" in Mexican records, according to Edwin R. Sweeney, Mangas Coloradas's biographer.

6. There is no documentation that Cochise was present at this battle, but it appears likely given Pisago Cabezón's involvement.

7. The May 23, 1832, battle was a decisive victory for the Mexicans, who were commanded by Captain José Ignacio Ronquillo. He reported killing 22 warriors and wounding another 50, with the loss of only 3 killed

and 12 wounded. However, Mexican reports of battles with the Apache routinely exaggerated their gains and understated their own losses.

8. The treaty was signed on August 21, 1832, involving mostly Nednhi and Chihenne bands.

9. Spring 1834.

10. I am generally using American place-names throughout, for the sake of clarity. Actually, this pivotal place in Chiricahua history had many different names—the Mexicans called it Puerto del Dado. I considered using Apache place-names, but decided that would mostly confuse modern readers trying to place these events geographically.

11. October 24, 1834.

12. Most Apache leaders were believed to have Power, a relationship with a supernatural force that would help them in battle. Several historical sources indicate that Cochise had Power, but none of those sources provide details as to what sort of Power he had acquired. In fact, the Apache respect strong cultural prohibitions against any discussion of Power held by individuals. I am therefore speculating about his source and relationship to Power, based mostly on discussions of Power by Opler and others.

13. Opler, *Apache Life-Way*, 200.

14. Ibid. This is an example of a conversation with Power offered by one of Opler's informants.

15. This account of witchcraft and the burning of the woman comes from ibid., 243–254.

16. I am speculating here as to the specific gifts of Power that Cochise received.

17. Sonora began offering the bounty in September 1835.

18. October 27, 1835.

19. Reports of the death of the son of Pisago Cabezón are sketchy. Note that the name of the son who was killed was not recorded, so I have used the name Chirumpe. Also note that Chirumpe was the brother of Cochise only if Pisago Cabezón was his father, which is likely but speculative.

20. June 1886.

21. April 20, 1837.

22. The Apache leaders probably didn't know Sonora had, in the previous March, resumed a "War to the Death" against the Apache and reinstated the bounty on Apache scalps.

23. Johnson's main goal was to collect the scalp bounty. He had raised a band of cutthroats to cash in on the bounty and picked up the trail of Juan José's band at Fronteras, whose commander, the capable Antonio Narbona, first tried to discourage the expedition, but then supplied the cannon. The massacre of a band mostly friendly to Chihuahua, although still raiding in Sonora, only widened and embittered the conflict. Indignant Chihuahua officials later criticized Sonoran commander José María Elías González for allowing armed expeditions into the neighboring province.

Chapter 4: The Death of Pisago Cabezón and the Rise of Cochise (1838)

The tale "Horned Toad Saves a Woman and a Boy from the Giant" is described by Morris Edward Opler in *Myths and Tales of the Chiricahua Apache Indians* (Lincoln: University of Nebraska Press, 1942), 22.

1. Mexican accounts say that Chato, a son of Pisago Cabezón, negotiated. This may have been an earlier name for Coyuntura or Juan, or it may have been another son.

2. John Carey Cremony, in *Life Among the Apaches* (1868; reprint, Glorieta, N.Mex.: Rio Grande Press, 1969), came to the southwest shortly after these events and reported that in avenging the treacherous death of Juan José Compá, Mangas Coloradas exterminated nearly everyone at Santa Rita del Cobre. According to Cremony's account, a united force of Apaches first cut off supplies to the settlement. When the residents tried to leave, the waiting Apaches slaughtered nearly everyone before they could reach the safety of Janos. However, Mexican records describing the abandonment of the mines describe no such wholesale slaughter. I am here agreeing with Edwin R. Sweeney in *Cochise: Chiricahua Apache Chief* (Norman: University of Oklahoma Press, 1991), 37, whose study of Mexican documents convinced him that most of the people simply abandoned the settlement and that Cremony exaggerated the casualties.

3. Sonora's defenses faltered in 1838 and 1839 as a result of internal dissension, as rival groups battled for control of the province.

4. James Kirker was one of the leading scalp hunters, although the leading Apache chiefs did not realize this until later. In 1839, Kirker was offered 100,000 pesos to raise a private army to exterminate the Apache by Stephen Courcier, who hoped to reopen the copper mines at Santa Rita del Cobre. Kirker recruited a band of trappers, traders, and Delaware and Shawnee Indians and started hunting Apaches throughout most of 1840. He remained a bitterly controversial figure in Mexico, and Chihuahua governor Francisco García Conde canceled Kirker's state contract and refused to pay a 30,000-peso bounty, which suggests a high death toll on behalf of Kirker's scalp hunters. The ruthless Kirker then stole six hundred of the governor's horses by way of payment.

5. Morris Edward Opler, *An Apache Life-Way: The Economic, Social, and Religious Institutions of the Chiricahua Indians* (1941; reprint, Chicago: University of Chicago Press, 1996), 128. I am assuming that Cochise would have heard songs very much like these Chiricahua Apache songs recorded by Opler at the turn of the century.

6. Mangas Coloradas met with Chihuahuan peace commissioner Vicente Sanchez Vegara in late January or February 1843.

7. April 1844.

8. August 1844.

9. Chihuahua officials bitterly protested González's invasion, which shattered the peace that province had maintained for more than a year with the Apache. Janos officials insisted González had no justification for the attack and that the Indians living near Janos had not been raiding in Sonora. However, González produced substantial evidence the Janos bands had been actively raiding—evidence the federal government accepted in later backing the invasion.

10. I am here speculating Mangas Coloradas might have used that story to work on the minds of his warriors. Orators and storytellers often used these stories to make their points.

Chapter 5: War to the Death: Cochise He Rises (1846)

The source of the story titled "Coyote Causes Death" is Morris Edward Opler's *Myths and Tales of the Chiricahua Apache Indians* (Lincoln: University of Nebraska Press, 1942), 124.

1. Late fall 1846.

2. The United States declared war against Mexico in May of 1846. Brigadier General Stephen Watts Kearny and the Army of the West occupied Santa Fe on August 18. Kearny sent three hundred men to take California, but two-thirds of the command returned to Santa Fe after receiving word the California Volunteers under John C. Frémont had already taken California. That news proved premature.

3. The 340-man Mormon Battalion, commanded by Captain Philip St. George Cooke, set out on September 19 from Santa Fe, guided by Pauline Weaver and Antoine Leroux, and laid out the wagon road through Apache Pass and southern Arizona that would eventually connect California to New Mexico. The Mormons in Utah had raised the volunteer force to help the United States fight the Mexicans in hopes that if they earned the gratitude of the federal government they would head off a campaign against themselves in Utah.

4. March 1847.

5. Mexican records give the prisoner's name as Cucchisle. I am here agreeing with Edwin R. Sweeney's speculation that "Cucchisle" was Cochise. See *Cochise: Chiricahua Apache Chief* (Norman: University of Oklahoma Press, 1991), 30.

6. This recounting of the thoughts of Cochise in prison is speculative, but based on statements by Eve Ball's Apache informants that imprisonment in a small space was considered a terrible punishment by the Apache, who lived their entire lives under the open sky.

7. This description of storytelling and the antics of the storytellers comes from Morris Edward Opler, *An Apache Life-Way: The Economic, Social, and Religious Institutions of the Chiricahua Indians* (1941; reprint, Chicago: University of Chicago Press, 1996).

8. This story comes directly from Opler's *Myths and Tales of the Chiricahua Apache Indians*, 36.

9. Ibid., 53–54.

10. Ibid., 70.

11. Ibid., 58.

12. Spring 1849.

13. John Carey Cremony, in *Life Among the Apaches* (1868; reprint, Glorieta, N.Mex.: Rio Grande Press, 1969), reported that the brothers-in-law of Mangas Coloradas were so offended when Mangas Coloradas took a Mexican wife they challenged him to a knife fight in which he killed them both. But one must take Cremony with a dose of salt, as he was not above embellishments in his otherwise invaluable first-person descriptions of the Apache in the 1850s. I suspect this particular story is an exaggeration, as such a killing would involve grave social complications among the Apache and would undercut the reputation of a leader like Mangas Coloradas, who was as careful about using marriage relationships to gain allies as European royalty. Any social disgrace or lack of piety would quickly erode a war leader's following.

14. March 1850.

15. It is not certain that Cochise was at the battle of Pozo Hediondo. However, Merejildo Grijalva said a battle that sounds very much like Pozo Hediondo added considerably to the reputation of Cochise, so I am assuming Cochise played a prominent role in the battle.

16. The Mexican commander reported killing or wounding seventy warriors, which would have made the battle a disaster for the Apache forces. However, the battle was remembered as a victory by the Apache, so the Mexican estimates of their casualties was probably too high.

17. Sonora and Chihuahua engaged in a protracted angry correspondence after the battle. Sonoran commander José María Carrasco, who had replaced the popular Elías González, insisted with some justice that Janos was providing a safe haven for the raiders who were devastating neighboring Sonora—even providing a market for their plunder.

18. March 5, 1851.

19. Commissioner John Bartlett was sent out in 1851 to survey the new border between Mexico and the United States as a result of the end of the Mexican War and the purchase of what would become southern New Mexico and Arizona, the core of Chihenne and Chokonen territory.

20. Summer 1853.

21. Early American records lump all of the Apache bands in this region together as Gila or Mogollon Apache. Dr. Michael Steck, the first agent appointed to the Apache bands in New Mexico, seemingly misidentified Cochise ("Cochil") as a Coyotero (White Mountain) or Pinal subchief. The Americans did not begin to recognize Chiricahua Apache as a category until the late 1850s, after they established a stagecoach station in Apache Pass and came into regular contact with the Chokonen.

22. Late April 1856.

23. This description of the negotiation between a war shaman and his Power comes from Opler, *Apache Life-Way*, 158.

24. Narbona disappears from the record in 1856, with little detail as to his fate. I have here assumed he vanished while raiding with a small group.

Chapter 6: Storm from the East: The White Eyes Arrive (1856)

The tale titled "It Happened at Tuzhj Yaahigaiye (Whiteness Spreads Out Descending)" is taken from Keith H. Basso, *Wisdom Sits in Places* (Albuquerque: University of New Mexico Press, 1996), 28.

1. The Americans launched the halting and mostly ineffectual 1857 Bonneville campaign in response to minor raiding by Apache bands in New Mexico. The poorly conceived and executed campaign brought little result, although it did prompt many Chihenne, Bedonkohe, and Mescalero groups to take refuge in northern Mexico while the search for their campsites ran its course in southern and central New Mexico.

2. Records from this period remain unreliable concerning numbers. Some reports suggest a thousand Apache were camped near Janos at this time in the summer of 1857. But Mexican officials sometimes inflated the count in order to get more supplies from the central government, a practice later common among the people running the reservations in the United States as well.

3. The Mexican government was in an agony of indecision as to how to deal with the possibility of peace with the Apache. Some officials warned it was only a ruse by the Apache to buy time to harvest acorns, agave, and other seasonal food, while replenishing their supplies with rations—a probably accurate surmise. Meanwhile, both federal and provincial governments were divided by intense factionalism and maneuvering. One measure of the ambiguity was the appointment as peace commissioner of Rafael Angel Corella, who had been wounded in the Pozo Hediondo fight and hated the Apache. The resulting treaty, signed mostly by minor Chokonen, Chihenne, and Nednhi leaders, was rife with unenforceable conditions and dubious assumptions.

4. Michael Steck, the agent for the Chihenne in New Mexico, reported that the Chiricahua believed they had been poisoned at Janos in November 1857, and reported that many of the Chihenne families who returned to the vicinity of his agency were suffering from symptoms consistent with such poisoning. He reported about sixty people died in the epidemic. "They believe they have been poisoned and I have little doubt that many of them have as reports have reached here from the citizens of Janos that many of them have been poisoned and the symptoms described by the Indians resemble those of poisoning by arsenic—probably administered to them in

their rations." Edwin R. Sweeney, *Cochise: Chiricahua Apache Chief* (Norman: University of Oklahoma Press, 1991), 47.

5. The winter of 1857–1858.

6. May 1858.

7. Sonoran reports put the death toll at three hundred, although the figure seems high. I'm using it here to suggest the scale and devastation of the revenge raid, even if the specific numbers remain subject to debate or exaggeration.

8. September 16, 1858.

9. Lieutenant Colonel José Juan Elías had plans to bolster the defenses by 500 soldiers, including 150 at Fronteras, and raised money among the citizens to launch a campaign against the Apache. Beset by internal divisions and infighting, the defenses of Sonora rose and ebbed year by year, helping feed the cycle of action/reaction, massacre, and revenge that dominated Apache-Mexican relations for decades.

10. The Butterfield Stage Line by 1858 had 141 stations between St. Louis and San Francisco, one every 20 miles on a roughly 2,800-mile route. Each well-fortified station had three or four attendants and a set of fresh horses, with a peak payroll of about 1,000 men. The Mesilla-Tucson run was the most dangerous part of the line, with 9 stations and 100 employees—including a total of 5 in Chokonen territory.

11. James Tevis wrote later of the meeting that Cochise was "as fine a looking Indian as one ever saw. He was about six feet tall and straight as an arrow, built, from the ground up, as perfect as any man could be. He had only one peer in physique, Francisco, head of the Coyotero. I don't suppose that Cochise ever met his equal with a lance." James Henry Tevis, *Arizona in the Fifties* (Albuquerque: University of New Mexico Press, 1854), 149.

12. On December 30, 1858, Steck made the journey from New Mexico to Apache Pass in his ongoing attempt to bring the Chokonen into the fold and settled on a reservation where he could issue rations and control their raiding. He had already settled most of the Chihenne near Cañada Alamosa, Santa Rita del Cobre, and Agua Caliente, issuing rations and largely eliminating raiding north of the border.

13. The legend of Cochise holds he supplied the stage station with wood and grass. It might be true. Clearly, he could have led ambushes and raids that would have made it nearly impossible for the stage line to operate without a prohibitively expensive military escort. John Bourke (*On the Border with Crook*) reported in 1891 that old hands on the frontier told him Cochise used to supply wood under contract to the stage station. In the 1915 *History of Arizona*, it was reported the Cochise had a contract. One account even suggested Cochise killed four warriors at different times for raiding the stages or local ranches—which isn't impossible, but seems unlikely given the political consequences involved whenever one warrior killed another. However, Sweeney, the most careful and thorough writer

about Cochise, could find no evidence of such a contract with the stage company—nor any evidence Cochise had killed warriors for violating his orders, a story first reported by John Clum, the energetic but controversial agent to the Apache in the late 1870s (Sweeney, *Cochise*, 128). Sorting through the possibilities, I have here assumed Cochise had no objection to band leaders selling wood to the station keepers and that he threatened and intimidated his warriors to keep the peace, but didn't enter into a formal agreement to supply the station.

14. April 27, 1859.

15. Tevis left a fascinating series of letters about his time at Apache Pass, when he was one of the few Americans with any significant contact with Cochise. Although he feared and admired Cochise for his bearing and his authority, he viewed him as a bloodthirsty savage. He noted, "Cochise was a very deceptive Indian. At first appearance, a man would think he was inclined to be peaceable to Americans but he is far from it. For eight months I have watched him, and have come to the conclusion that he is the biggest liar in the territory! And would kill an American for any trifle, provided he thought he wouldn't be found out." *Weekly Arizonan*, June 9, 1859.

16. Grijalva reported this incident years later, saying that Cochise had killed a warrior who objected when he ordered the return of the stolen horses. Grijalva did not recount the actual knife fight, which is my speculation. Grijalva also said Cochise issued strict orders to the Chiricahuas to disturb nothing and no one in the United States during the 1850s. See Sweeney, *Cochise*, 215.

17. The original treaty between the United States and Mexico ending the Mexican War obligated the Americans to curtail Apache raiding into Mexico, which was one reason the Mexicans were willing to cede so large an area to the United States—most of it was empty and unsettled due to the constant threat of the Apaches. Therefore, the long war between the Apache and the Mexicans may have been the crucial factor in the Southwest ending up part of the United States. Later treaty agreements between the United States and Mexico dropped that specific provision, but the Americans still made sporadic attempts to stop Apache raiding.

18. Grijalva left the camp of Cochise in late 1859 or early 1860 and offered his services to Steck as a translator. One story said the Apache had killed five of his brothers, perhaps in continued raids. Another story claimed the girl he loved had been killed. Perhaps he merely decided to take advantage of his ability to move from the side that seemed ultimately doomed to the side with brighter prospects.

19. The name of the second wife of Cochise is unknown. She was later killed and disappeared from the records as a result of the Apache custom of not mentioning the names of the dead. It is uncertain precisely when his two daughters were born to this second wife—perhaps in the late 1850s, but perhaps in the early 1860s.

20. Deadly fights under the influence of whiskey obtained from the traders became increasingly common on the reservation, and each death spurred a sequence of revenge killings—which was why social harmony was such a crucial value among the Apache and why the enforced idleness and crowding of the reservation combined with the availability of cheap whiskey proved so terribly destructive to the fabric of Apache life.

21. David Roberts, *Once They Moved Like the Wind: Cochise, Geronimo and the Apache Wars* (New York: Simon & Schuster, 1993), 33. Tevis later recounted this story, in an effort to demonstrate Cochise was a proud man with a volcanic temper. Tevis left a vivid description of Cochise and probably had more personal contact with him than any other white that left an account in the early years. Tevis depicted Cochise as a vain and autocratic man with a sensitivity to insult, a terrible temper, and an instinctual sadism.

22. Late winter 1860.

23. Allegations that the Apache tortured their victims remain difficult and controversial. Many of the bodies of the victims of Apache raids were extensively mutilated—especially in the later years, when the Apache fury and need for revenge had accumulated. Eve Ball's Apache informants insist that the Apache almost never took scalps, except after the Mexican scalp hunters provoked a need to retaliate (see *Indeh: An Apache Odyssey* [Provo, Utah: Brigham Young University Press, 1980], 23). They also maintain that warriors rarely tortured living prisoners, but that most of the reported mutilation was inflicted on the bodies of the dead in retaliation for the slaughter and mutilation of their own women and children. The evidence suggests warriors did often mutilate the bodies of their enemies—probably after death in most cases. However, some accounts suggest the warriors sometimes did torture living prisoners in terrible ways. Mexican accounts indicate the Apache after this fight tortured one prisoner to death, and I'm accepting this account. However, the details of the torture don't appear in the record. I'm speculating they might have done to this prisoner as another band did to a settler captured years later near Wickenburg, whose body was found bristling with arrows that obviously had been placed to avoid killing him too quickly.

24. Ewell, who later became a prominent and effective general for the South, came under intense criticism for not attacking the Apache.

Chapter 7: "Cut the Tent"–Driven to War (1861)

The story titled "It Happened at Ma'Tehilizhe (Coyote Pisses in the Water)" is taken from Keith H. Basso, *Wisdom Sits in Places* (Albuquerque: University of New Mexico Press, 1996), 136–137.

1. This description of dream significance and the signs of Power comes from Morris Edward Opler, *An Apache Life-Way: The Economic, Social, and*

Religious Institutions of the Chiricahua Indians (1941; reprint, Chicago: University of Chicago Press, 1996), 186–196.

2. February 3, 1861.

3. It is unclear how much Cochise knew about Bascom's mission or the kidnapping of the adopted half-Mexican, half-Apache son of John Ward before he walked into the lieutenant's tent. Cochise did camp nearby and wait for most of a day before meeting with the lieutenant, so he was probably gathering information during that time. In one of history's bitter ironies, that boy grew up to become an Apache warrior turned scout and manhunter for the army named Mickey Free, who played a key role in the later Geronimo wars.

4. Cochise did not realize that Lieutenant Colonel Pitcairn Morrison, the commander of Fort Buchanan, had ordered Lieutenant Bascom to "do whatever you think is proper" to recover the boy. That order, in part, stemmed from the public thumping Captain Ewell had taken some months previously when he forced Cochise to return some—but not all—of the horses he had stolen from the mines near Tucson. Most historians agree that a White Mountain band had already taken the boy back to the Black Mountains, but Bascom claimed to have followed the trail of the raiders to Apache Pass, which would suggest they were Chokonen.

5. This converts a paraphrase of what Cochise shouted into a direct quote. This is from the account of a policeman named Oberly, *Missouri Republican*, December 27, 1861. I have combined various accounts of these pivotal events from several sources, selecting those that seem the most credible. Lieutenant Bascom left a written report, which at critical junctures apparently misstates events and minimizes his considerable mistakes in judgment. Most of the other existing accounts—almost all by whites—were written years after the event. Three different whites not then present left accounts, including William Oury and Assistant Surgeon Bernard John Dowling Irwin, who came on the scene a week after the initial confrontation. Two eyewitnesses—Oberly and Sergeant Daniel Robinson—also later wrote their versions. Contemporary accounts were also provided by wagon drivers A. B. Culver and William Buckley. Geronimo—who was probably not present—recounted the Apache version in his autobiography. Jason Betzinez, an Apache, also provided a version to historian Eve Ball. I have sorted through these versions and am here presenting what I think is the most likely chain of events. For instance, I don't believe Bascom's claim he let Cochise go look for the Ward boy. All of the Apache accounts and five of the six other accounts by whites say Cochise escaped by cutting through the tent. The sixth white account says he ran through the doorway and past the guards. I will note significant clashes in these accounts in footnotes to come.

6. February 5, 1861.

7. Bascom claimed they were surrounded by five hundred warriors, which is not a credible number. Cochise could probably command no more than one or two hundred warriors unless supported by the Chihenne.

8. Some accounts suggest Sergeant Reuben F. Bernard tried to convince Bascom to make the trade with such vehemence Bascom threatened to have him court-martialed. Edwin R. Sweeney (*Cochise: Chiricahua Apache Chief* [Norman: University of Oklahoma Press, 1991], 153 n. 44) disputes several near myths that have grown up concerning the details of this confrontation. Some secondhand reports suggest Cochise dragged Wallace by the neck behind his horse—but Wallace appeared in good health later. Another account suggests Bascom refused to release the family of Cochise in return for four prisoners held by the Apache—but Cochise didn't get the additional prisoners until later. Sweeney, *Cochise*, 14.

9. It's not clear precisely when Bascom found the note revealing Cochise now had four prisoners—a fact that might have convinced even Bascom to relent. In his later written report, he implied he received the note that night. But at the time of the incident, he dispatched couriers with a written report that did not mention the additional prisoners. He probably didn't actually retrieve the note until two days later, by which time it was too late.

10. This is speculation on my part. One of the great mysteries of the confrontation is why Cochise didn't make a stronger effort to negotiate with Bascom once he had four prisoners to trade instead of just Wallace. He may have simply relied on the note, which Bascom apparently didn't find until too late. But given how hard Cochise tried to win the release of his brother, it seems likely he must have had some other problem that prevented him from seeking the exchange. I think it likely that one of his warriors killed one of the prisoners—perhaps with Cochise's permission, but more likely without. This would explain why Cochise didn't display his prisoners, as Bascom would then discover the warriors had murdered a white. Therefore, Cochise would simply have waited to see if Bascom responded to the note and exchanged prisoners before he realized one of the whites was already dead. On the other hand, several Apache accounts gathered by historian Eve Ball say the whites killed their prisoners first and Cochise only killed his prisoners in retaliation. In this history, I am accepting Apache versions of events whenever possible. But in this case, Geronimo said the Apache killed their prisoners first when Bascom ignored the note (see *Geronimo, His Own Story*, as told to S(tephen) M(elvil) Barrett [New York: Duffield, 1906], 62). Besides, other credible white accounts indicate Bascom's prisoners were killed after the soldiers discovered the mutilated bodies of Wallace and the other white prisoners.

11. Friday, February, 8 1861.

12. Mexican accounts indicate that some Chokonen bands appeared in Fronteras after the fight at Apache Pass to report that the Americans had taken Indian prisoners and bayoneted them.

13. I am here assuming Cochise would have compared his behavior to the stories connected to specific places, as suggested by Keith Basso's

masterful study of Apache place-names among the twentieth-century White Mountain Apache.

14. Surviving accounts conflict as to which officer proposed the execution and whether Bascom opposed the order.

15. Not surprisingly, this detail does not appear in any of the official reports, but was recounted later by Oberley, *Santa Fe New Mexican*, November 1, 1870.

16. Various accounts say one or two of the prisoners were nephews of Cochise, and I am making the assumption here one older boy was the son of Coyuntura. The account of Coyuntura's death comes from the *Mesilla Times* as cited by Sweeney in *Cochise*, 163.

17. Reconstructing the events at Apache Pass remains difficult. Bascom and Moore both wrote official reports, which left out crucial details. For instance, Bascom's report didn't mention Cochise's escape from the tent, didn't indicate soldiers mistakenly killed Welch, reported the death of only one of the station keepers, didn't mention the loss of all his mules, and implied he recovered Wallace's note two days before he actually stumbled across it—by which time Cochise had killed his prisoners. His misleading report may have been approved by his superiors, however, to avoid blame for the disastrously mishandled incident. Bascom appears from this incident to have been a brave and coolheaded commander, with poor judgment and an abiding ignorance of the Apache. In any case, he received a commendation for his actions at Apache Pass. Bascom was killed about a year later at the battle of Val Verde, near the New Mexico–Colorado border.

18. Not all historians assign so much significance to this incident in starting the decade of war between Cochise and the Americans that followed. For instance, historian Donald Worcester in *The Apaches, Eagles of the Southwest* (Norman: University of Oklahoma Press, 1979) criticizes the "myth" of cut-the-tent. He maintains this incident happened in 1858, a year before the full-scale outbreak of hostilities. Many of the details of the incident come from an account published by Raphael Plumpelly in 1870 and may represent embellishments, according to Worcester. Worcester suggests the incident was a factor, but not the cause of the deteriorating relationship between the Americans and the Apache. Most other historians, including Sweeney, have concluded the incident was crucial in driving Cochise to war.

Chapter 8: War of Extermination (1861)

The story titled "Coyote Tries to Catch Turkey by Chopping Down Trees" is taken from Morris Edward Opler, *Myths and Tales of the Chiricahua Apache Indians* (Lincoln: University of Nebraska Press, 1942), 40.

1. Despite doubts about the importance of confrontation at Apache Pass expressed by some historians, Cochise throughout his subsequent con-

tacts with the whites consistently attributed the outbreak of the war to that incident—including documented conversations with whites in 1869, 1870, and 1871.

2. April 1861.

3. This may have been one of the rare cases in which the Apache inflicted torture before death, instead of mutilating the bodies afterward.

4. Roberts, *Once They Moved Like the Wind: Cochise, Geronimo and the Apache Wars* (New York: Simon & Schuster, 1993), 38. Tevis recounted this story, one of the few first-person accounts of the torture of living prisoners by Cochise or his warriors. Tevis's account suggests that he was released by a sympathetic warrior without the consent of Cochise, but this seems unlikely—so I have here made the assumption that Cochise approved of Tevis's release. I am also a little dubious about accepting Tevis's unsupported account, as it seemed self-serving and harsh in its depiction of Cochise—but he offers one of the few first-person glimpses of Cochise during this period and so I have accepted his account.

5. Morris Edward Opler, *An Apache Life-Way: The Economic, Social, and Religious Institutions of the Chiricahua Indians* (1941; reprint, Chicago: University of Chicago Press, 1996), 196.

6. Roberts, *Once They Moved Like the Wind*, 35.

7. Opler, *Apache Life-Way*, 283. This is actually a song used in a healing ceremony by someone with lightning power, according to Opler. I have taken the liberty of attributing it here to Cochise in connection with gathering wood touched by Lightning Power.

8. August 3, 1861.

9. The Union forces ordered the abandonment of forts in Arizona and New Mexico shortly after the outbreak of the Civil War. The soldiers marched off mostly toward California, where the goldfields were strategically important. Both sides realized that if the South could seize California, they would obtain both an important source of hard currency and ports that would be harder to close through blockade. As the Union soldiers left, the residents of Tucson and Santa Fe declared their sympathy for the South. The outbreak of the Civil War, which forced the abandonment of the forts and the Butterfield Stage Line, coincided with the peak of Cochise's war against the Americans, so the Apache assumed they had driven out the Whites, just as they had at other times driven the Sonorans and the Chihuahuans out of large expanses of territory.

10. July 1861.

11. The Cook's Canyon fight involved a band of experienced frontiersmen led by Freeman Thomas who were making a mail run to California. Some accounts suggest Mangas Coloradas and his Chihenne pulled out of the fight, and I'm accepting that version—although almost all of the accounts of the Apache side of these fights remain fragmentary and secondhand. For instance, William Oury, who left one secondhand account of this fight,

claimed the Apache lost 175 warriors—clearly an absurd number. Mangas Coloradas himself later admitted to Jack Swilling, a sometime scout who later helped found Phoenix, that the Apache lost 25 warriors in this fight, a far more likely number but still a disaster for the Apache.

12. This generalized description of a curing ceremony comes from Opler, *Apache Life-Way*, 261. In fact, each shaman developed his own variations on this general pattern.

13. Ibid, 130.

14. This is based on a healing ceremony described by Opler in ibid., 263: "You'd hear it on the roof. Then it was before you, a plant. He wouldn't take it up at once. He'd sing over it and talk to it first. When P asked for it, it would come right through the crowd and land on the buckskin before him."

15. Anthropologists have found that the Apache used many plants with a medicinal effect, including natural antibiotics and herbs that constricted blood vessels and reduced bleeding, as well as herbal treatments for pregnancy, contractions, nausea, and other ailments.

16. The party led by Felix Grundy Ake, a Sonoita Creek farmer, left Tucson on August 15 guided by Moses Carson, half brother of Kit Carson. They had abandoned their farms and ranches when the soldiers abandoned Fort Buchanan and had hoped to make the trip east along with the retreating columns of soldiers, but had missed the departure. They decided to risk the trip anyway, believing the party was too large to attack—which would normally have been true. They heard rumors the Apache had killed nine Mexican teamsters in the canyon, but dismissed them as another wild Apache rumor and continued into Cook's Canyon.

17. Several men, including the nephew of Sam Houston, fled with the wagon, protecting the women and children but leaving the rest of the party to its fate.

18. Captain Thomas Mastin, Lieutenant Thomas Helm, and Lieutenant Jack Swilling got news of the ambush and set out from Mesilla in pursuit. By this time, the Confederates had assumed control of New Mexico after the Union troops left Santa Fe, but their main task was to keep the road open between Mesilla and Tucson. Instead of heading directly for the canyon, Mastin assumed the fight would have already ended and the Apache would be taking their plunder to the closest refuge—the Florida Mountains. The soldiers therefore set out to ambush the warriors. The ambush worked, partly because the warriors were herding livestock. It is unclear which group of warriors fell into the ambush, but I'm here making the assumption it was the Chokonen. Mastin was a fierce, competent, courageous Indian hater, eager to implement the orders of Confederate lieutenant colonel John Robert Baylor to kill any Apache he encountered by any method available—including making friends, getting them drunk, and then shooting or poisoning them. Baylor's infamous order countenancing a

war of extermination with the Apache was later rescinded by Confederate president Jefferson Davis. The Apache had little understanding of the complicated military and political situation in the Southwest at this time and probably didn't realize the whites were engaged in a war with one another until later.

19. Fall 1861.

Chapter 9: Cochise Triumphant (1861)

The story titled "It Happened at Tliish Bi Tu'e (Snake's Water)" is taken from Keith H. Basso, *Wisdom Sits in Places* (Albuquerque: University of New Mexico Press, 1996), 17.

1. I am here assuming Cochise would have learned these songs and the preparation of the dancers, for he was considered to have great Power and was always a defender of the traditional beliefs and ceremonies. However, I have found no specific descriptions of which songs and ceremonies he knew.

2. This description of the Masked Dancer ceremony, including the specific songs, comes from a long description by Morris Edward Opler in *An Apache Life-Way: The Economic, Social, and Religious Institutions of the Chiricahua Indians* (1941; reprint, Chicago: University of Chicago Press, 1996), starting on page 100.

3. The following speech of a father to a son preparing to become a dancer is taken from ibid., 103. I have here taken the liberty of attributing it to Cochise.

4. Ibid., 108.

5. Ibid., 114.

6. Ibid., 125.

7. The winter of 1861–1862.

8. The man's last name was Gardner and he recovered from his wounds. Edwin R. Sweeney, *Cochise: Chiricahua Apache Chief* (Norman: University of Oklahoma Press, 1991), 191.

9. This was a seventy-five-man contingent of Confederates commanded by Captain Sherod Hunter that occupied Tucson in February 1862—the vanguard of an invasion of New Mexico and Arizona by Confederate forces from Texas. They were greeted happily by Tucson's mostly Mexican population.

10. General John Baylor, commander of the Confederate forces in the Southwest, on March 20 issued an infamous order that read: "The Congress of the Confederate States has passed a law declaring extermination to all hostile Indians. You will therefore use all means to persuade the Apaches or any tribe to come in for the purpose of making peace and when you get them together kill all the grown Indians and take the children prisoners and sell them to defray the expense of killing the Indians. Buy whiskey and

such other goods as may be necessary for the Indians. I look to you for success against these cursed pests who have already murdered over 100 men in this territory." Confederate president Jefferson Davis later rescinded the order and replaced Baylor, but the Confederates essentially pursued a policy of extermination throughout their occupation of New Mexico.

11. The Confederates had gathered their forces for the battle of Val Verde, where they failed to turn back a column of Union troops from Colorado. After this defeat, the Confederates abandoned New Mexico and struggled across the desert back to Texas, ending the Confederate dream of a conquest of the goldfields of California.

12. The lead elements of the 2,350-man California Column skirmished briefly with a Confederate patrol near Picacho Peak and then occupied Tucson in May 1862. Brigadier General James Henry Carleton declared martial law, ordered the reoccupation of Forts Buchanan and Breckenridge, and sent messengers east to establish communications with Union forces closing in on the Confederates there.

13. June 18, 1862.

14. WOR Series, 50, pt. I., 120.

Chapter 10: Battle of Apache Pass: Return of the Americans (July 1862)

The story titled "Coyote Helps Lizard Hold up the Sky" is taken from Morris Edward Opler, *Myths and Tales of the Chiricahua Apache Indians* (Lincoln: University of Nebraska Press, 1942), 37.

1. Brigadier General James Henry Carleton sent 140 men of the First Cavalry under Lietenant Colonel Edward Eyre to establish contact with Union forces in New Mexico. They arrived in Apache Pass on June 25 with orders to avoid a fight with the Indians if possible.

2. Arizona State University Library, copy of Hubert Howe Bancroft, "Scraps," 193.

3. This advanced contingent consisted of 126 men commanded by Captain Thomas Roberts of the First Infantry, including 24 men of the Second Cavalry commanded by Captain John C. Cremony, 10 men manning two howitzers, and 22 wagon teams with 242 head of stock.

4. Estimates of Apache casualties are uncertain and speculative. The U.S. Army often reported ridiculously high body counts—a long-standing military habit. The Apache accounts of battles rarely list casualties, in part because of the prohibition against mentioning the names of the dead. But some surviving Apache oral accounts of this battle say they had no deaths.

5. Cremony reported some sixty-three warriors killed in the shelling, but this isn't a credible number. Apache accounts suggest few or no deaths, which seems more consistent with both Apache strategy and the effects

of roughly forty howitzer shells lobbed onto a rocky slope against well-prepared positions.

6. Construction on Fort Bowie began on July 28, 1862, and the wall was constructed by August 14. Cochise never attacked it, for an assault on a walled fort would have been so costly in warriors' lives that it would have squandered his authority. Fort Bowie served a valuable role in supplying and dispatching patrols and keeping the spring at Apache Pass safe for travelers, but its first commander recommended its abandonment because of heavy snows in the winter.

7. Carleton's survey of the devastation in Arizona and New Mexico aroused in him an almost pathological hatred of the Apache. The Confederates having fallen back to Texas, Carleton turned his considerable energies to killing the Apache in the fall of 1862. A devout, efficient, fanatical, and rigid disciplinarian, Carleton assumed nearly dictatorial control of the territory. In October 1862, he issued orders to reject all flags of truce and kill any adult male Apache.

Chapter 11: Death of Mangas Coloradas: The Shadow of the Giant (Late 1862)

The story titled "Coyote and Dog Argue" is taken from Morris Edward Opler, *Myths and Tales of the Chiricahua Apache Indians* (Lincoln: University of Nebraska Press, 1942), 64–65.

1. I am speculating here that Cochise used myths and talking in places to convince Mangas Coloradas not to seek peace with the whites. This illustrates the role these stories and places played in making it possible for people to argue with one another while avoiding direct criticism, as described by Keith H. Basso in *Wisdom Sits in Places* (Albuquerque: University of New Mexico Press, 1996). Geronimo's autobiography indicates other leaders tried to convince Mangas Coloradas not to put himself in the hands of the whites in his search for peace.

2. Geronimo's autobiography notes the murder of Mangas Coloradas on January 18, 1863, as the greatest wrong done to the Apache by the whites. Mangas Coloradas was seized under a flag of truce by a group of frontiersmen led by Joseph Walker, which included Daniel Conner—whose account of the murder of Mangas Coloradas is the most objective and reliable. Conner later wrote that Colonel Joseph R. West took charge of their prisoners and implied to the guards that he wanted the chief dead. He was acting well within orders, as General Carleton in October had ordered the soldiers to kill any adult male Apache who fell into their hands. Conner was walking guard that night near the place where the two soldiers tormented Mangas Coloradas with heated bayonets and then shot him when he protested. The offical army report indicated the chief was killed "trying

to escape" and was a "fabric of lies" according to historian Daniel Thrapp (*Victorio and the Mimbres Apaches* [Norman: University of Oklahoma Press, 1991], 85). Mangas Coloradas's skull was later shipped to the Smithsonian Institution, where a researcher noted that he had a greater cranial capacity than Daniel Webster. The skull was subsequently lost. In the meantime, Captain Edmond Shirland led a detachment to the place where the family of Mangas Coloradas was camped and attacked, killing nine.

3. Edwin R. Sweeney, *Cochise: Chiricahua Apache Chief* (Norman: University of Oklahoma Press, 1991), 204. The order was issued by General Carleton as he prepared for a war of extermination with the Apache, starting with the Mescalero in eastern New Mexico. Carleton intended to kill most of the Apache and herd the survivors onto barren, malarial flats on the banks of the Rio Grande called Bosque Redondo.

4. July 15, 1862.

5. Mexico was at this point staving off a French invasion of Sonora and so had stripped its defenses on the frontier.

6. July 11, 1963.

7. Fort Cummings was established on October 2, 1863. The government spent millions building and garrisoning forts in Arizona and New Mexico—far more than it had ever been willing to spend to provide rations for warriors and their families willing to settle on reservations.

8. A captive who escaped from Cochise's band reported in late 1863 that the Chokonen were near starvation, with not much ammunition left.

9. A Mexican woman who had been a captive for years and who was recaptured by the Americans in this raid revealed that "we have no dried meat; have nothing to live on except mescal . . . can occasionally kill a deer. We have no powder or guns. Our guns are nearly all worn out . . . we have no clothing. We have to live down in the valleys. We cannot live up in the mountains; it is too cold." Sweeney, *Cochise*, 217.

10. RB393, LR, DNM, 42B, 1865, Houston to Burkett, March 22, 1865.

Chapter 12: Cochise the Avenger (Late 1864)

The story titled "It Happened at Gizhyaa'itine (Trail Goes Down between Two Hills)" is taken from Keith H. Basso, *Wisdom Sits in Places* (Albuquerque: University of New Mexico Press, 1996), 113.

1. The army split New Mexico and Arizona into different commands, a military mistake that hobbled operations against the Apache for years to come. General Carleton remained in command in New Mexico, but Arizona now fell under the command of Major General Irvin McDowell, commander of the Division of the Pacific, with headquarters in San Francisco. Brigadier General John Sanford Mason was given charge of the campaign against the Apache in Arizona and faced considerable costs and daunting logistical problems. The army had begun to come under severe criticism from settlers, and

faced rising political pressure to break the Apache resistance as quickly as possible because the costs of the campaign had mounted alarmingly.

2. June 1864.

3. French invaders had reached Hermosillo and the provincial Sonoran government had taken flight, debilitating defenses against the Apache.

4. Desperately short of soldiers and terrified of the Chokonen, Fronteras officials struck a deal with the Arizona Volunteers, an eighty-man force led by Captain Hiram Storrs Washburn composed mostly of "border scum." Washburn resolved to use treachery, as Kirker and Johnson had before him. He wrote: "At first these warriors will be very suspicious and will only fall into the snare by the most careful and astute dissimulation, which with liberal portions of mescal will soon gentle them, so that by the most cautious and most careful concern on our part and that of the authorities at Fronteras we may almost safely calculate in getting nearly the whole of these Indians without the loss of a man." Hiram Storrs Washburn Collection, Hayden File, Arizona Historical Society, Tucson.

5. Major James Gorman met with Cochise on October 30, 1865.

6. Army records indicate only that several Apache women came into the fort. I am here making the assumption one of them was Dos-teh-seh, given the reliance Cochise placed on her judgment.

7. Morris Edward Opler, *Myths and Tales of the Chiricahua Apache Indians* (Lincoln: Univerisity of Nebraska Press, 1942), 96.

8. Spring 1866.

9. Captain Wiliam Harvey Brown, the commander of the seventy-two-man detachment at Camp Wallen, reported that sixteen of his men had no rifles, sixty had no cartridge boxes, and thirty-three had no sabers—a measure of the strain that the war was putting on the army's resources.

10. Sonora and Chihuahua now lapsed into their old pattern of accusations and counteraccusations, with Sonora accusing Chihuahua of harboring the Apache and profiteering off the proceeds of raids on Sonora. Debilitated by the struggle with the French invaders, the central government could do little but log in the letters.

11. August 1866.

12. A captive Mexican boy named Priciliano Rivera who escaped from Cochise's band in early 1867 reported that Cochise was raiding with fifty-five warriors along the border, aided by a man from Janos.

13. February 1867.

14. The expedition was led by Cayetano Ozeta in April 1867.

15. Winter of 1867–1868.

16. May 1867.

17. On November 11, 1868, the *Arizona Miner* reported the near-death experience of the group of six traders led by Solomon Barth, but offered scant sympathy for Barth's party, which was suspected of selling guns and ammunition to the Apache.

18. On January 25, 1869, Lieutenant Colonel Thomas C. Devin wrote: "Cochise, the boldest and most enterprising Apache in this territory, and who for the past seven years has been a terror in Southern Arizona, has sent me word that if I will allow him to return to his home and remain there, he will not only remain at peace but be responsible for the safety of the Overland road and the stock in its vicinity. All this he used to effect before the attempt to take him prisoner aroused him to make war." RG393, E13, LS, District of Arizona, January 25, 1869. The army would have saved hundreds of lives and millions of dollars if they had given Cochise what he asked for at that moment.

19. January 20, 1869.

20. Estimates of Cochise's height range from five feet ten inches to six feet two inches.

21. *Arizona Miner*, March 20, 1869. The dialogue is taken from Perry's report.

22. The army supported fourteen military posts with 2,100 troops in Arizona, mostly to protect the state's 9,000 white inhabitants. The cost of military operations dwarfed the cost of rationing the Apache on reservations, but the war had substantial political support because the military remained the largest single source of cash and employment in the territory.

23. October 6, 1869. Witnesses reported three whites riding with the warriors in the attack on the cattle herd and wagon train. The historical record holds no more information on who these men were and why they were riding with Cochise. I have therefore assumed they were several of the shadowy border traders who played a poorly documented but probably important role in arming the Apache during this period.

24. This fight represented one of Cochise's most serious setbacks and stemmed from his effort to hang onto the slow-moving cattle herd to alleviate the starvation and hardship among the women and children. The soldiers were commanded by Lieutenant William Henry Winters, who performed brilliantly despite exhaustion and the superior numbers of warriors. Winters noted that "many efforts were made to kill Cochise but without success, with his mounted warriors he several times charged the men in advance and although conspicuous and special attention directed to him and many shots fired at him, he escaped." Edwin R. Sweeney, *Cochise: Chiricahua Apache Chief* (Norman: University of Oklahoma Press, 1991), 273.

25. The total toll of the decade-long war between Cochise and the Americans will never be conclusively tallied. David Roberts, in *Once They Moved Like the Wind: Chochise, Geronimo and the Apache Wars* (New York: Simon & Schuster, 1993), quotes an estimate of 5,000 people in the course of twelve years. That included 250 people in the first sixty days of the conflict, when settlers were widely scattered and unprepared. That's probably high. But the death toll in Mexico was probably even greater. At one point,

Cochise said he had lost more than 1,000 people, and had inflicted more deaths than he suffered.

26. Drew was appointed agent in 1870 and treated the Chihenne leaders with such respect and integrity that he rapidly gained their confidence. However, Washington largely ignored his reports, which urged the establishment of a reservation for the Chihenne that included their core territory.

27. January 1870.

28. The June 1870 expedition was commanded by Fronteras presidio commander Adrian Maldañado, who attacked bravely with a relatively small force of fewer than thirty men. The ability of thirty men to attack Cochise in the Dragoons and escape with their lives is evidence of the depletion of his forces after a decade of unremitting war.

29. July 17, 1870.

Chapter 13: Turn toward Peace: Thomas Jeffords (Early 1871)

The story titled "The Boy Who Trained an Eagle and Taught It to Hunt" is taken from Morris Edward Opler, *Myths and Tales of the Chiricahua Apache Indians* (Lincoln: University of Nebraska Press, 1942), 92.

1. August 30, 1870.

2. Territorial newspapers reported three different versions of the talk between Cochise and Major Green, all with somewhat contradictory details. One account was published by the *Alta California* as a letter by an eyewitness on September 17, 1869. The *Alta California* also published a letter on November 14 with Green's account, as told to Silvester Mowry two weeks after the talks. I am accepting a combination of those accounts here. White Mountain Apache witnesses gave Mowry a different version, which also found its way into print. In that version, Cochise swaggered into the conference with gold-handled revolvers and a gold chain he had taken from the neck of a dead officer, and was "insolent to such a degree that the interpreter was afraid to translate," claiming "the troops were cowards and the Americans were liars . . . he would go on killing as long as he pleased." Edwin R. Sweeney, *Cochise: Chiricahua Apache Chief* (Norman: University of Oklahoma Press, 1991), 284. This contrasts with other accounts of his words and demeanor and therefore seems unlikely. Cochise was careful in all his documented talks with the whites, rarely admitting specific acts for which he might later be punished. He would have had no reason to make the long journey and risk the meeting to be needlessly provocative, especially by openly wearing a gold chain taken from an officer. The version offered by Green seems much more likely.

3. I am here rendering Green's paraphrase of Cochise's statement into a direct quote. *Weekly Arizonan*, September 17, 1870.

4. The newspapers heaped insult and criticism on Green for not tricking and killing or capturing Cochise, a common practice with any military
officer who negotiated in good faith with Apache leaders. One newspaper
account suggested Cochise actually surrounded and captured Green and his
party. In fact, Cochise arranged the conference in such a way that he could
not have been surprised or surrounded, having learned his bitter lesson in
Bascom's tent. The furor mounted in the ensuing months when the army
proposed cutting costs by closing five posts, including Fort Bowie. The Arizona commander, Colonel George Stoneman, favored a peace policy. The
press objected violently, and an irritated Stoneman threatened to pull the
troops out of Tucson. However, when he met with the White Mountain
chiefs who said Cochise wanted to settle on Bonita Creek, Stoneman vetoed
the idea. Stoneman's abortive effort to close down military posts in Arizona
engendered so much protest it contributed to his replacement by General
George Crook, one of America's most successful Indian fighters and a crucial figure in the ensuing events.

5. September and October of 1870.

6. Agent Drew engaged in an ongoing struggle to curtail trade between
the residents of Cañada Alamosa and the Apache, maintaining that the
trade encouraged raiding into Mexico. He seized contraband whiskey, using
troops to make raids in Cañada Alamosa. Civil authorities there retaliated
by arresting Drew. He was later exonerated and the ruling was upheld by
the courts on appeal; nevertheless, he conducted a running battle with the
top elected officials in Cañada Alamosa throughout his tenure.

7. The legend of the relationship between Cochise and Jeffords is
encrusted with lore and misconceptions, greatly intensified by the success
of Elliott Arnold's novel *Blood Brother* (1947), which was made into the
movie *Broken Arrow* (1950), starring the ever-so-Anglo Jeff Chandler as
Cochise. The popular myth holds that Jeffords was running the mail line
into Tucson at the height of the war with Cochise. Frustrated by the deaths
of his mail riders, Jeffords rode fearlessly into the Dragoons to convince
Cochise to stop attacking them. The legend has it that Cochise was so
impressed with Jeffords's personal courage that he not only spared his life
but stopped attacking the mail riders. Sweeney has done a good job of
debunking this myth, pointing out that attacks on the mail riders continued
unabated all the time Jeffords was the superintendent and after his departure. In addition, it appears unlikely Cochise would have allowed any
strange white to leave the Dragoons alive in this period, unless they were
traders. One of Jeffords's own accounts suggests he first met Cochise "after
having been an Indian trader under a commission from Mr. Parker, Secretary of the Interior." RG75, T21, R15, Orlando Piper to Nathaniel Pope,
February 7, 1871. Jeffords was licensed as an Indian trader in December
1870, when he operated chiefly among the Chihenne. Therefore, I am here
agreeing with Sweeney that Cochise would have first encountered Jeffords

in 1870, when Cochise was investigating the possibility of settling with the Chihenne if Agent Drew could win approval of a reservation near Cañada Alamosa.

8. Jeffords was born in 1832 at Chautauqua Lake, New York, but not much is known about his early life. He never wrote about his own remarkable life and had only a handful of conversations that have been reported–thus leaving a sometimes contradictory and confusing version of events that happened decades before the conversations took place.

9. Jeffords apparently was a "conductor" on the mail line for about a year and left in 1869, before he first met Cochise–despite the legend to the contrary. Ace Daklugie, Juh's son, later told historian Eve Ball in *Indeh: An Apache Odyssey* (Provo, Utah: Brigham Young University Press, 1980) that the Chokonen captured Jeffords and took him to Cochise, who was impressed with his courage. I have here presented a version that's consistent with both Jeffords's recollection of riding to Cochise's camp after he was a licensed agent and Daklugie's recollection that warriors "captured" Jeffords as he approached the camp. This seems more likely than the story that Jeffords rode alone into Cochise's camp to ask him to stop killing the mail riders.

10. Fred Hughes, Jeffords's assistant in the early 1870s, said Cochise and Jeffords first met at Cañada Alamosa in the fall of 1870. Sweeney, *Cochise*, 294. Before his death in 1914, Jeffords told a friend Cochise had killed twenty-one men, fourteen of them working as mail riders for Jeffords. "I made up my mind that I wanted to see him. I located one of his Indians and camp where he came personally. I went into his camp alone, fully armed. I spent two or three days with him, discussing affairs and sizing him up. This was the commencement of my friendship with Cochise and although I was frequently compelled to guide troops against him and his band, it never interfered with our friendship." O(liver) O(tis) Howard, *My Life and Experiences among Our Hostile Indians* (Hartford, Conn.: A. D. Worthington, 1907), 187–88. This quote gave rise to the myth that Jeffords rode into the camp of Cochise when he was directing the mail line, as Jeffords or his listener combined those two periods nearly forty years after the events in question.

11. October 1870.

12. RG 75, T21, R12, Argalus Hennisee to William Clinton, October 31, 1870, Appendix A, Council held with Arny and Cochise.

13. Jeffords was an intensely controversial figure among the whites and widely distrusted. It is hard to judge the validity of the charges that he traded contraband whiskey and ammunition for horses and mules that raiding parties brought back from Mexico. He was charged with trading whiskey for a mule at this point, and another white claimed to have seen him trade guns. Given Jeffords's later expressed disdain for the Mexicans, he probably had few qualms about profiting from the Chokonen raids into Mexico. Given

his strong relationship with Cochise, it also seems likely that he provided goods the Chokonen most needed.

14. January 1871.

15. The prisoner was Antonio Ochoa, but the historical record leaves no word of his fate.

16. Cochise was widely credited at the time for leading the ambush that killed Cushing on May 5, 1871. However, historian Dan Trapp argues convincingly that Juh was the likely leader of the band based on the description of a stocky chief directing the battle on a small brown horse. In addition, Juh's son, Ace Daklugie, told historian Eve Ball in *Indeh* that his father had stalked and killed Cushing. The death of Cushing made national headlines and helped convince President Ulysses S. Grant that he should consider pursuing a peace policy to bring the long, costly, inconclusive Apache Wars to a halt.

17. The Camp Grant Massacre garnered national headlines, sharing space with news of the death of Cushing. These two events spurred President Grant to turn to mostly church-based advocates of a negotiated peace, ushering in a new phase in the relationship between the Apache and the whites.

18. Jeffords's claim he had met with Cochise provoked some controversy. Superintendent Piper refused to pay him the promised $1,000, partly as a result of rumors that Jeffords had turned back before reaching the Dragoons. General Otis Howard, who went with Jeffords to meet with Cochise, later verified Jeffords's claim.

Chapter 14: Power Takes a Hand (Mid-1871)

The story titled "The Ga'an Who Fought the Mexican Soldiers" is taken from Morris Edward Opler, *Myths and Tales of the Chiricahua Apache Indians* (Lincoln: University of Nebraska Press, 1942), 78.

1. When General George Crook took command of Arizona in May 1871, he was already recognized as the best Indian fighter in the U.S. Army. He had subjugated Indian tribes in California and the Pacific Northwest before serving as a successful cavalry commander in the Civil War. He returned to Indian fighting after the Civil War and was to enjoy more success against the Apache than any other military commander, mostly because he admired their culture and abilities in war and therefore relied heavily on Apache scouts, turning bands against one another. Not only did this make it possible for his troops to remain in the field on the trail of hostile bands for months at a time, it also helped fragment the various bands politically and culturally. For full details of his remarkable life, see my dual biography of Crook and Geronimo, *The Fox and the Whirlwind: General George Crook and Geronimo, a Paired Biography* (New York: John Wiley & Sons, 2000), or Crook's own absorbing autobiography (edited by

Martin F. Schmitt and published by the University of Oklahoma Press in 1960).

2. No one is sure what ailment Cochise suffered that increasingly debilitated him in the last few years of his life. It may have been cancer, given the reports of growing pain.

3. The domestic relations of Cochise remain unclear and speculative. Lieutenant John Bourke, who met with Cochise later, said he had a young, hot-tempered wife who seemed the only person in the band who was not afraid of him. I have here given her the name Steps on Water, a woman's name mentioned by Morris Edward Opler in *An Apache Life-Way: The Economic, Social, and Religious Institutions of the Chiricahua Indians* (1941; reprint, Chicago: University of Chicago Press, 1996). Other records suggest that Cochise also took on the support of Yones, Coyuntura's widow. He probably supported the wives of other warriors who had been killed, as losses among the warriors left many widows and few men to remarry them. The only wife who appears clearly and repeatedly in the records over a long stretch of time was Dos-teh-seh, the daughter of Mangas Coloradas and the companion of his life.

4. August 1871.

5. After the Camp Grant Massacre and the death of Lieutenant Cushing, President Grant appointed as Indian agents a host of reformers, many of them Quakers from a coalition of religious groups originally formed in the crusade against slavery before the Civil War. He appointed Colyer as a special agent with extraordinary powers to establish reservations for the Apache. Colyer was greeted with deep suspicion by General Crook, who believed that only a complete military defeat would convince war leaders like Cochise to live on the reservation. The territorial press was outraged by Colyer's mission and heaped vilification on him. One editor observed Arizonans should "dump the old devil into the shaft of some mine and pile rocks upon him until he is dead." Edwin R. Sweeney, *Cochise: Chiricahua Apache Chief* (Norman: University of Oklahoma Press, 1991), 321.

6. September 4, 1871.

7. The meeting took place on September 28, 1871. Details of this encounter are drawn from Sweeney, *Cochise*, 328.

8. October 21, 1871. The press and the military were deeply suspicious of Cochise during this time, with frequent reports that he or his warriors were continuing to raid. Several of the reports of Cochise raiding could not have been true; others might have been. I am here making the assumption that this raid was directed by Juh, whose Nednhis had not joined in the peace talks. Given the effort Cochise had made to move his band to Cañada Alamosa, it seems unlikely he would have risked squandering the chance for peace to ride hundreds of miles to go raiding.

9. *Las Cruces Borderer*, November 1, 1871. Cochise generally spoke to the whites in Spanish or through a translator, as he knew only a little

English. I have taken the liberty here of changing this slightly from the newspaper account, which indicated he said, "Much time ago. Put on mule shoes." The ungrammatical rendering of quotes by Indian leaders either struggling with English or with the whims of a translator gives a misleading impression of their intelligence and eloquence. Cochise was a masterful orator in his own language, but only a few of the direct translations of his remarks capture that quality.

10. Ibid.

11. The government's insistence on the Tularosa Reservation remains one of the most baffling examples of bureaucratic stupidity in the long, tragic history of the Apache Wars. The primary motivation appears to have been an effort to move the Apache as far from settlements as possible, partly to avoid the cost of buying out the squatters and partly to remove the Apache from the influence of the Cañada Alamosa traders. However, none of those factors seems sufficient to account for the persistence of the American effort to force the Chihenne and the Chokonen to settle in an area they so adamantly disliked for an array of practical and spiritual reasons. Had the government established an adequate reservation at Cañada Alamosa and spent up-front money to buy out the squatters, it would have avoided the Victorio wars and probably the subsequent Geronimo wars, which cost thousands of lives and millions of dollars.

12. The *Santa Fe Daily New Mexican* published an account in 1870 in which Cochise provided this rationale.

13. Several whites left excellent firsthand accounts of this conference, including the best rendering of Cochise's spellbinding oratory. Assistant Surgeon Henry Stuart Turrill wrote that Cochise "impressed me as a wonderfully strong man, of much endurance, accustomed to command and to expect instant implicit obedience," concluding that Cochise was "the greatest Indian that I have ever met." Sweeney, *Cochise*, 338.

14. Anderson Nelson Ellis, "Recollections of an Interview with Cochise, Chief of the Apaches," *Kansas State Historical Society Collections* 13 (1913–1914): 391–92; David Roberts, *Once They Moved Like the Wind: Cochise, Geronimo and the Apache Wars* (New York: Simon & Schuster, 1993), 68.

15. Roberts, *Once They Moved Like the Wind*, 92.

16. Ibid., 93.

17. March 30, 1872.

18. A Chiricahua war party ambushed Lieutenant Reid T. Stewart on his way to Tucson to preside over a court-martial on August 27, 1872. I have here assumed the war party was led by Taza. Stewart pushed on ahead of his escort over the protests of his driver, Corporal Joseph Black. Lieutenant Stewart had said, "I am not afraid of these Apaches. I can lick a whole regiment of them." Charles T. Connell, "The Apaches Past and Present," manuscript, Hayden Files, Arizona Historical Society, Tucson. The rest of the escort came upon the bodies a short time later and indicated that Black

was tied to a tree and tortured to death. As with most accounts of Apache torture, it is unclear whether the mutilations were inflicted before or after death. It is possible Black wounded or killed one of the warriors before he was captured, in which case relatives of the dead or injured man in the war party might have sought revenge through torture.

19. Opler, *Apache Life-Way*, 468. I am speculating this is a song Cochise would have sung.

20. Ibid., 114. This is actually a free-step song out of the Sunrise Ceremony, which I have taken the liberty of attributing to Cochise here.

Chapter 15: The One-Armed General and the Last War Won (October 1872)

The story titled "How Antelope Got His Name" is taken from Morris Edward Opler, *Myths and Tales of the Chiricahua Apache Indians* (Lincoln: University of Nebraska Press, 1942), 82.

1. President Ulysses S. Grant dispatched the devout Brigadier General Oliver Otis Howard to revive the peace initiatives squandered by the wrongheaded attempt to force the Chihenne to live at Tularosa. Howard had finished fourth in his class at West Point in 1846 and served with distinction in the Civil War, losing his arm in the battle of Fair Oaks but continuing to command throughout the war. After the conflict ended, Howard, a man of deep religious conviction, headed the Freedmen's Bureau, which was intended to help former slaves adjust to freedom. His naive faith in the goodness of man helped blind him to the political realities of that post, as the Freedmen's Bureau was rife with corruption and inefficiency. But President Grant turned to the fearless and humanitarian Howard to revive his floundering peace initiative to the Apache. Howard won the confidence of the White Mountain and Chihenne bands, but quickly realized Cochise remained the key to peace. At Cañada Alamosa he heard of a treacherous and unreliable gunrunner and whiskey seller who was the only white man who could take him to Cochise. But General Howard and Thomas Jeffords struck an immediate chord with each other, and when Jeffords dared Howard to go alone into the Dragoons to meet with Cochise, Howard accepted immediately. He took with him the insightful and courageous Captain Joseph Alton Sladen, a doctor and a decorated officer who fought alongside Howard through the Civil War and for years afterward. Sladen left a remarkable journal of this journey recently published under the title *Making Peace with Cochise* (Norman: University of Oklahoma Press, 1997). The details of this journey and the negotiation are taken from this journal, which remains one of the most remarkable first-person accounts of the free-living Apache culture by a man of rare insight, tolerance, compassion, and observation.

2. Sladen was born in England in 1841 and emigrated at the age of five to settle in Massachusetts. He served in the Army of the Potomac in the

Civil War, performing with courage at Chancellorsville, Gettysburg, and Sherman's March to the Sea through Georgia, and winning the Congressional Medal of Honor for gallantry at Resaca. He joined Howard's staff during the war and provided devoted service to Howard for most of the rest of his career. Sladen attended Georgetown Medical College, graduating in 1871.

3. The following dialogue is taken from Sladen's *Making Peace with Cochise*, 23. Chie undoubtedly told Cochise that General Howard had intervened to protect them, but may not have been able to report the exchange so precisely because he did not understand English. However, he probably got the gist of the confrontation later from Jeffords.

4. This dialogue comes from ibid., 4.

5. David Roberts, *Once They Moved Like the Wind: Cochise, Geronimo and the Apache Wars* (New York: Simon & Schuster, 1993), 96.

6. These direct quotations come from Sladen, *Making Peace with Cochise*, 44.

7. Sladen reported that Cochise went out in a rage to kill an antelope, but I have taken the liberty here of assuming he hunted the antelope in the manner described by John Carey Cremony in *Life Among the Apaches* (1868; reprint, Glorieta, N.Mex.: Rio Grande Press, 1969). Cremony went along with a Chiricahua warrior who demonstrated this technique.

8. I am here assuming the violent reaction of Cochise was related to news the raiding party had killed Lieutenant Stewart. Sladen did not understand the reason for Cochise's reaction at the time, but it seems reasonable that Cochise was concerned about retaliation, given his decision to move the camp.

9. Ace Daklugie, Juh's son, recounted this story to historian Eve Ball, who recorded it in *Indeh: An Apache Odyssey* (Provo, Utah: Brigham Young University Press, 1980). I am assuming Cochise might have heard this story as well.

10. Sladen mistook El Cautivo for Geronimo, who was probably not present as he had by now aligned himself strongly with Juh's Nednhis. In this I am guided by Edwin R. Sweeney's reasoning (see *Cochise: Chiricahua Apache Chief* [Norman: University of Oklahoma Press, 1991], 365), as Sladen wrote that Cochise's crafty and cruel-looking translator had lived with the Mexicans as a child, a description that fits El Cautivo but not Geronimo. Sladen did note that El Cautivo was wearing an officer's shirt with eastern cut and detail and concluded it belonged to Lieutenant Cushing. In fact, it was probably Lieutenant Stewart's shirt.

11. I am here making a series of assumptions, guided by the research of both Dan Thrapp and Sweeney. Thrapp concluded Juh directed the ambush of Cushing, although it was widely attributed to Cochise at the time. And Sweeney concluded that Sladen saw Stewart's shirt and that one of the Chokonen raiding parties loyal to Cochise had killed the lieutenant. I am here suggesting that raiding party was led by Taza.

12. Letter from Howard to Commissioner of Indian Affairs, September 23, 1873.

13. General Howard's compassionate, insightful, and fair-minded offer of peace to Cochise was met with skepticism and derision by both the press and other officers. General Crook, itching to launch a campaign against the Chiricahua and "iron the wrinkles" out of Cochise's band, disliked the higher-ranking Howard and considered him a naive Bible-thumper who had been hoodwinked by Cochise. But President Grant had given Howard extraordinary powers, and the peace he made with Cochise would probably have endured and prevented another decade of bloodshed and tragedy had men of similiar vision and authority abided by it—and had Cochise lived longer. Howard did make several crucial mistakes in the negotiations. Like an Apache, he trusted so strongly in the personal integrity of the men who accepted the agreement that he put nothing in writing—a bureaucratic blunder. More importantly, he did not directly address the issue of contin- ued raiding into Mexico—the issue that would ultimately lead to the closure of the reservation.

14. October 12, 1872.

15. Captain Joseph Theodore Haskell wrote: "The reports that we have had of Cochise have always given us to understand that he is old, used up, crippled from wounds and exposure and of no account whatever as a leader or a chief. How mistaken we were. We met Cochise and thirteen of his cap- tains and Cochise is as different from the others of his tribe, as far as we saw, as black is from white. When standing straight he is said to be exactly six feet tall. I took a good look at him and made up my mind that he was only five feet ten inches. He is powerful, exceedingly well built, bright, intelligent countenance, and as fine an Indian as I ever laid my eyes on. He was clean from head to foot. I looked at his scalp, his hair, his face (painted fresh), neck, body, arms, and legs and he was clean. Most of the others were so filthy that you could scrape enough dirt off them to start a potato patch." Sweeney, *Cochise*, 365.

16. RG75, T21, R17, Oliver Otis Howard to Nathaniel Pope, Septem- ber 19, 1872.

Chapter 16: The Frail Peace—the Dying Chief (1873)

The story titled "The Origin of Old Age" is taken from Morris Edward Opler, *Myths and Tales of the Chiricahua Apache Indians* (Lincoln: Univer- sity of Nebraska Press, 1942), 98.

1. Thomas Jeffords remained an intensely controversial figure for the persistence with which he championed the cause of the Apache. He was repeatedly accused of graft and corruption, with critics suggesting he inflated the count of Indians on the reservation so he could draw extra sup- plies and sell the surplus—a common practice among Indian agents at the

time. Moreover, he was bitterly criticized for not curtailing raiding into Mexico. The Mexican government lodged protests, maintaining that General Howard had actually encouraged raiding into Mexico, to the profit of traders on the reservation. The evidence suggests Howard discouraged raiding, but didn't make that prohibition explicit in his talks with Cochise. The evidence also suggests that Jeffords was more likely to supplement the rations with his own funds than to profiteer, although he was harshly critical of the Mexicans and probably did little initially to discourage raiding. Given his background as a trader, it's also possible he profited from trading for goods brought back by raiding parties from Mexico.

2. Bourke Diary, February 3, 1873, Hayden Files, Arizona Historical Society, Tucson.

3. Governor Safford concluded that Cochise agreed to release captives held by his bands. "My impression is that he is now in good earnest and that he desires peace, but he and his followers are wild men, and that despite the best efforts on our part some real or imaginary cause might at any moment set him again upon the warpath." David Roberts, *Once They Moved Like the Wind: Cochise, Geronimo and the Apache Wars* (New York: Simon & Schuster, 1993), 136.

4. Jeffords's failure to impress on Cochise the importance of curtailing raiding into Mexico was his single greatest lapse in judgment, and was fueled by his own disdain for the Mexicans. He was injudicious enough to tell a newspaper reporter for the *Tucson Citizen* that he "did not care how many Mexicans his people killed. For acts of past treachery with those Indians, the Mexicans deserved killing."

5. General Crook and other officers complained that Jeffords encouraged raiding and had treated emissaries from Sonora with disrespect. Acting Indian Commissioner H. R. Clum investigated and concluded Cochise had kept his promise to refrain from raiding, but the government had not provided the rations it had promised. On September 16, 1873, Indian Commissioner Edward P. Smith wrote to Sonora that the agreement between Howard and Cochise was not a formal treaty, but that Howard had not approved raiding nor provided guns and ammunition as the Sonorans claimed.

6. Cochise and Jeffords ended most raiding by January 1874. Jeffords reported: "I am happy to inform the department that it has been more than two months since any complaints whatever have been made against these Indians either by the citizens of this territory or by the people living on the other side of the Mexican line and I have strong hopes that we have heard the end of this raiding in Sonora. . . . The Indians here have also appeared more settled and satisfied during the last two months than at any other time since peace was made." *Arizona Citizen*, October 11, 1873. Unfortu-

nately, the crackdown on raiding came too late, and forces had already gathered to force the eventual closure of the Chiricahua Reservation.

7. Morris Edward Opler, *An Apache Life-Way: The Economic, Social, and Religious Institutions of the Chiricahua Indians* (1941; reprint, Chicago: University of Chicago Press, 1996), 471.

8. Jeffords managed to beat back the foolish notion of closing the Chiricahua Reservation and moving the Chokonen to Tularosa, insisting that no more than half of the Chokonen would willingly go. The rest would go down into Mexico to join the Nednhis and resume raiding—a prediction that proved tragically accurate.

9. June 7, 1874.

10. Frank Lockwood, *The Apache Indians* (Lincoln: University of Nebraska Press, 1938), 128–129.

Epilogue

I have taken the bulk of "The Journey of Cochise to the Happy Place," the story that concludes the Epilogue, from *Geronimo, His Own Story*, as told to S(tephen) M(elvil) Barrett (New York: Duffield, 1906), 167. Geronimo said in his autobiography that a warrior who had lain near death on the battlefield had recovered and then told him this story. I have added the ending and the details specific to Cochise.

Bibliography

Acuna, Rodolfo F. *Sonoran Strongman: Ignacio Pesqueira and His Times.* Tucson: University of Arizona Press, 1874.

Adams, Alexander B. *Geronimo: A Biography.* New York: Da Capo Press, 1971.

Aleshire, Peter. *The Fox and the Whirlwind: General George Crook and Geronimo, a Paired Biography.* New York: John Wiley & Sons, 2000.

————. *Reaping the Whirlwind: The Apache Wars.* New York: Facts on File, 1998.

Altshuler, Constance Wynn. *Starting with Defiance: Nineteenth Century Arizona Military Posts.* Tucson: Arizona Historical Society, 1983.

Ambrose, Stephen. *Crazy Horse and Custer: The Parallel Lives of Two American Warriors.* New York: Meridian, 1975.

Annual Reports of the Secretary of the Interior, 1858–1869, 1881, 1913, 1914. Washington, D.C.: Government Printing Office.

Annual Reports of the Secretary of War, 1882–1887, 1890, 1892, 1894–1896. Washington, D.C.: Government Printing Office.

Arizona Historical Society, Tucson. Hayden Files or collections. Diary of John Bourke; Willima Buckley; Charles T. Connell manuscript, "The Apaches Past and Present"; Robert Humphre Forbes; William Fourr; Thomas Gardner; Charles Gatewood; Merejildo Grijalva; Diary of George Hand; Fred Hughes; Policeman Oberley's account of the Bascom affair; William Sanders Oury; John Ward; Hiram Storrs Washburn; Charles Wood.

Arizona State Library, Phoenix. Territorial Records of Arizona.

Arizona State University Library. Benjamin H. Sacks Collection; Sylvester Mowry File; Copy of Hubert Howe Bancroft, "Scraps," clipped from Arizona newspapers.

Ball, Eve. *Indeh: An Apache Odyssey.* Provo, Utah: Brigham Young University Press, 1980.

————. *In the Days of Victorio: Recollections of a Warm Springs Apache.* Tucson: University of Arizona Press, 1970.

Bancroft, Hubert Howe. *History of Arizona and New Mexico.* San Francisco: History Company, 1889.

Barnes, Will C. *Apaches and Longhorns: The Reminiscences of Will C. Barnes.* Tucson: University of Arizona Press, 1941.

Basso, Keith H. *The Cibecue Apache*. Prospect Heights, Ill.: Waveland Press. 1973.

———. *Wisdom Sits in Places*. Albuquerque: University of New Mexico Press, 1996.

———, ed. *Western Apache Raiding and Warfare: From the Notes of Grenville Goodwin*. Tucson: University of Arizona Press, 1971.

Betzinez, Jason. *I Fought with Geronimo*. Edited and annotated by Wilbur Sturtevant Nye. Harrisburg, Pa.: Stackpole, 1959.

Bigelow, John. *On the Bloody Trail of Geronimo*. Edited by Arthur Woodward. Tucson: Westernlore Press, 1986.

Bourke, John G. *An Apache Campaign in the Sierra Madre*. New York: Charles Scribner's Sons, 1958.

———. *Apache Medicine-Men*. 1892. Reprint, New York: Dover, 1993.

———. *On the Border with Crook*. New York: Charles Scribner's Sons, 1891.

———. *With General Crook in the Indian Wars*. Palo Alto, Calif.: Lewis Osborne, 1968.

Bowman, John S., ed. *The Civil War Almanac*. New York: Facts on File, 1983.

Brown, Dee. *Bury My Heart at Wounded Knee*. New York: Holt Rinehart & Winson, 1970.

Browning, Sinclair. *Enju: The Life and Struggle of an Apache Chief from the Little Running Water*. Flagstaff, Ariz.: Northland Press, 1982.

Carr, Camillo Casatti Cadmus. *A Cavalryman in Indian Country*. N.p.: n.d.

Clum, Woodworth. *Apache Agent: The Story of John P. Clum*. Boston: Houghton Mifflin, 1936.

Colyer, Vincent. *Peace with the Apaches of New Mexico and Arizona*. Washington, D.C: Government Printing Office, 1872.

Connell, Evan. *Son of the Morning Star: Custer and the Little Big Horn*. San Francisco: North Point, 1984.

Conner, Daniel Ellis. *Joseph Reddeford Walker and the Arizona Adventure*. Edited and annotated by Donald J. Berthrong and Odessa Davenport. Norman: University of Oklahoma Press, 1956.

Corle, Edwin. *The Gila, River of the Southwest*. Lincoln: University of Nebraska Press, 1951.

Cortes, Jose. *Views from the Apache Frontier: Report on the Northern Provinces of New Spain*. Edited by Elizabeth John. New York: Macmillan, 1938.

Cozzens, Samuel Woodworth. *The Marvellous Country, or Three Years in Arizona and New Mexico*. Boston: Lee and Shepard, 1876.

Cremony, John Carey. *Life Among the Apaches*. 1868. Reprint, Glorieta, N.Mex.: Rio Grande Press, 1969.

Crook, George. *Address of General George Crook, U.S. Army at the Reunion of the Army of West Virginia at Cumberland, Maryland*. September 1884. N.p.: 1884.

————. *Address to the Graduates of the United States Military Academy, West Point, New York, Class 1884.* West Point, N.Y.: n.p., 1884.

————. *General George Crook: His Autobiography.* Edited by Martin F. Schmitt. Norman: University of Oklahoma Press, 1960.

Cruse, Thomas. *Apache Days and After.* 1941. Reprint, Lincoln: University of Nebraska Press, 1987.

Davis, Britton. *The Truth about Geronimo.* 1929. Reprint, Lincoln: University of Nebraska Press, 1976.

Debo, Angie. *Geronimo: The Man, His Time, His Place.* Norman: University of Oklahoma Press, 1976.

————. *A History of the Indians of the United States.* Norman: University of Oklahoma Press, 1970.

Du Pont, Henry A. *The Campaign of 1864 in the Valley of Virginia and the Expedition to Lynchburg.* New York: n.p., 1925.

Ellis, Anderson Nelson. "Recollections of an Interview with Cochise, Chief of the Apaches." *Kansas State Historical Society Collections* 13 (1913–1914): 387–392.

Ellis, Richard N. *General Pope and U.S. Indian Policy.* Albuquerque: University of New Mexico Press, 1870.

Farish, Thomas Edwin. *History of Arizona.* 8 vols. San Francisco: Filmer Brothers Electrotype, 1915–1918.

Faulk, Odie B. *The Geronimo Campaign.* New York: Oxford University Press, 1969.

Forbes, Jack D. *Apache, Navaho, and Spaniard.* Norman: University of Oklahoma Press, 1960.

Gerald, Rex E. *Spanish Presidios of the Late Eighteenth Century in Northern New Spain.* Santa Fe: Museum of New Mexico Press, 1868.

Geronimo, His Own Story. As told to S(tephen) M(elvil) Barrett. New York: Duffield, 1906.

Goodwin, Grenville. "Experiences of an Indian Scout." Parts 1 and 2. *Arizona Historical Review* 7, no. 1 (January 1936), no. 2 (April 1936).

————. *The Myths and Tales of the White Mountain Apache.* Tucson: University of Arizona Press, 1996.

Griffen, William B. *Apaches at War and Peace: The Janos Presidio, 1750–1858.* Albuquerque: University of New Mexico Press, 1988.

Haley, James L. *Apaches: A History and Cultural Portrait.* New York: Doubleday, 1981.

Hand, George. *The Civil War in Apacheland.* Edited by Neil B. Carmony Books. Silver City, N.Mex.: High-Lonesome, 1996.

Horn, Tom. *Life of Tom Horn.* Norman: University of Oklahoma Press, 1964.

Howard, O(liver) O(tis). *Famous Indian Chiefs I Have Known.* New York: Century, 1907.

————. *My Life and Experiences among Our Hostile Indians.* Hartford, Conn.: A. D. Worthington, 1907.

Johnson, Barry. *Crook's Resume of Operations against Apache Indians, 1882–1886.* London: n.p., 1971.

Josephy, Alvin M. *The Civil War in the American West.* New York: Random House, 1991.

Knight, Oliver. *Following the Indian Wars: The Story of the Newspaper Correspondents among the Indian Campaigners.* Norman: University of Oklahoma Press, 1960.

Leermakers, J. A. *Great Western Indian Fights.* Lincoln: University of Nebraska Press, 1960.

Lockwood, Frank. *The Apache Indians.* Lincoln: University of Nebraska Press, 1938.

———. *Pioneer Portraits.* Tucson: University of Arizona Press, 1968.

Lummis, Charles. *General Crook and the Apache Wars.* Flagstaff, Ariz.: Northland Press, 1966.

Mails, Thomas. *The People Called Apache.* New York: BDD Illustrated Books, 1993.

McGaw, Willima Cochran. *Savage Scene: The Life and Times of James Kirker, Frontier King.* New York: Hastings House, 1972.

Miles, Nelson A. *Personal Recollections.* Chicago: Werner, 1897.

———. *Serving the Republic.* Freeport, N.Y.: Books for Libraries, 1971.

Miller, Darlis M. *The California Column in New Mexico.* Albuquerque: University of New Mexico Press, 1982.

Miller, David Humphreys. *Custer's Fall: The Native American Side of the Story.* New York: Meridian, 1957.

Miller, Joseph, ed. *Arizona Cavalcade: The Turbulent Times.* New York: Hastings House, 1862.

Moody, Ralph. *Geronimo, Wolf of the Warpath.* New York: H. Wolf, 1958.

Moorehead, Max L. *The Apache Frontier: Jacobo Ugarte and Spanish-Indian Relations in Northern New Spain, 1769–1791.* Norman: University of Okahoma Press, 1968.

Murphy, Lawrence R. *Frontier Crusader—William F. M. Arny.* Tucson: University of Arizona Press, 1972.

Olge, Ralph Hedrick. *Federal Control of the Western Apaches, 1848–1886.* Albuquerque: University of New Mexico Press, 1970.

Opler, Morris Edward. *An Apache Life-Way: The Economic, Social, and Religious Institutions of the Chiricahua Indians.* 1941. Reprint, Chicago: University of Chicago Press, 1996.

———. "A Chiricahua Apache's Account of the Geronimo Campaign of 1886." *New Mexico Historical Review* 13, no. 4 (October 1938).

———. "Mountain Spirits of the Chiricahua Apache," *The Masterkey* 20, no. 4 (July 1946).

———. *Myths and Tales of the Chiricahua Apache Indians.* Lincoln: University of Nebraska Press, 1942.

———. *Myths and Tales of the Jicarilla Apache Indians.* New York: Dover, 1994.

Pattie, James O. *Personal Narrative of James O. Pattie of Kentucky.* Edited by Timothy Flint. Chicago: Donnelley and Sons, 1930.

Perry, Richard. *Western Apache Heritage, People of the Mountain Corridor.* Austin: University of Texas Press, 1991.

Pumpelly, Raphael. *Travels and Adventures of Raphael Pumpelly.* New York: Henry Holt, 1920.

Redstorm, Lisle. *Apache Wars: An Illustrated Battle History.* New York: Barnes and Noble, 1990.

Rickey, Don. *Forty Miles a Day on Beans and Hay: The Enlisted Soldier Fighting the Indian Wars.* Norman: University of Oklahoma Press, 1963.

Roberts, David. *Once They Moved Like the Wind: Cochise, Geronimo and the Apache Wars.* New York: Simon & Schuster, 1993.

Sandoz, Mari. *Cheyenne Autumn.* New York: Avon, 1953.

Santee, Ross. *Apache Land.* New York: Charles Scribner's Sons, 1947.

Schellie, Don. *Vast Domain of Blood: The Story of the Camp Grant Massacre.* Los Angeles: Westernlore Press, 1968.

Sheridan, Philip H. *Personal Memoirs of P. H. Sheridan.* 2 vols. New York: n.p., 1888.

Simmons, Marc. *Witchcraft in the Southwest.* Lincoln: University of Nebraska Press, 1994.

Sladen, Joseph Alton. *Making Peace with Cochise.* Norman: University of Oklahoma Press, 1997.

Smith, Cornelius C. *Fort Huachuca: The Story of a Frontier Post.* Washington, D.C.: U.S. Government Printing Office, 1981.

Smith, Sherry. *The View from Officer's Row: Army Perceptions of Western Indians.* Tucson: University of Arizona Press, 1990.

Sonnichsen, C. L. *Geronimo and the End of the Apache Wars.* Lincoln: University of Nebraska Press, 1986.

———. *The Mescalero Apaches.* Norman: University of Oklahoma Press, 1958.

Stockel, Henrietta. *Women of the Apache Nation: Voices of Truth.* Reno: University of Nevada Press, 1991.

Sutherland, Edwin Van Valkenburg. "The Diaries of John Gregory Bourke: Their Anthropological and Folklore Content." Ph.D. diss., University of Pennsylvania, 1964.

Sweeney, Edwin R. *Cochise: Chiricahua Apache Chief.* Norman: University of Oklahoma Press, 1991.

———. *Mangas Coloradas.* Norman: University of Oklahoma Press, 1998.

Terrell, John Upton. *Apache Chronicle.* New York: Thomas Y. Crowell, 1974.

Tevis, James Henry. *Arizona in the Fifties.* Albuquerque: University of New Mexico Press, 1854.

Thrapp, Dan L. *Al Sieber, Chief of Scouts*. Norman: University of Oklahoma Press, 1964.

———. *The Conquest of Apacheria*. Norman: University of Oklahoma Press, 1967.

———. *General Crook and the Sierra Madre Adventure*. Norman: University of Oklahoma Press, 1972.

———. *Juh: An Incredible Indian*. Southwest Studies, monograph no. 39. El Paso: Texas Western Press, 1973.

———. *Victorio and the Mimbres Apaches*. Norman: University of Oklahoma Press, 1974.

Tiller, Veronica E. Velarde. *The Jicarilla Apache Tribe: A History*. Lincoln: University of Nebraska Press, 1992.

U.S. Congress. Senate Executive Documents. 49th Cong. S. Doc. 73, 117.

U.S. Congressional Record, Vol. VIII (1879).

U.S. Department of War. Reports of the Secretary of War, 1866–1867.

United States Government, National Archives and Records Center. Record Group 94. Records of the Adjutant General's Office (AGO), 1870s–1917: AGO Microcopy 619, Roll 737, Report of Bvt. Col. Reuben F. Bernard relating to the engagement at Chiricahua Pass, Arizona, on October 20, 1869; AGO, Microcopy 666 Roll 24, correspondence relating to Vincent Colyer's mission to the Apache; AGO, Microcopy 666, Roll 123, correspondence relating to the agreement with Cochise negotiated by General Oliver Otis Howard; AGO, File titled "General Howard correspondence relating to peace with Cochise"; AGO, Letters Received, 1850–1876, Miscellaneous Letters Received concerning Indian affairs in Arizona and New Mexico.

    Record Group 75 (RG75), Records of the Bureau of Indian Affairs; Microcopy 234, Letters Received, 1824–1880, Arizona Superintendency, 1863–1880, Rolls 3–12; Microcopy 234, Letters Received, 1824–1880, New Mexico Superintendency, 1849–1880, Rolls 546–64; Microcopy 734, Records of the Arizona Superintendency of Indian Affairs, 1863–1873, 8 rolls; Microcopy T21, Records of the New Mexico Superintendency of Indian Affairs, 1849–1880, Rolls 1–18; Miscellaneous Divison, Traders' Licenses; Report Books of the Office of Indian Affairs, 1838–1885.

    Record Group 393, Records of United States Army Continental Commands, 1821–1920. Arizona: Letters Received, Department of Arizona, 1871–1874; Letters Sent, Department of Arizona, 1871–1874; Letters Received, District of Arizona, 1862-71; Unregistered Letters and Orders Received, District of Arizona, 1862–1871; Book of Scouts, District of Arizona; Brief of Affairs at San Carlos, 1871; Letters Sent, District of Arizona, 1862–1871. Letter Received, Southern Subdistrict of the Gila; Letter Received, Subdistrict of Tucson; Letters Sent, Subdistrict of Tucson; Letters Sent, Department of New Mexico, 1849–1865; Letters Sent, District of New Mexico, 1866–1874.

Utley, Robert. *A Clash of Cultures: Fort Bowie and the Chiricahua Apaches.* Washington, D.C.: National Park Service, 1977.

———. *Frontiersmen in Blue: The United States Army and the Indian, 1848–1865.* Lincoln: University of Nebraska Press, 1967.

Wellman, Paul I. *The Indian Wars of the West.* Garden City, N.Y.: Doubleday, 1947.

Worcester, Donald. *The Apaches, Eagles of the Southwest.* Norman: University of Oklahoma Press, 1979.

Index

American Civil War, 171–72, 257,
282, 311n.9, 312–13n.18,
313n.9, 313–14n.10, 314nn.1,
11, 12
Americans (White Eyes), ix, 3–7,
40–41, 51–63, 66–68, 85, 89,
93, 101–18, 210–17
Apache Pass confrontation with,
120–35, 136, 146, 151, 210,
223
Apache Pass fort built by, 179–80
Apache war parties against,
51–63
atrocities by, 185, 203
attacks by, 191–92, 229, 282
at Cañada Alamosa, 103
Chihenne treaties with, 87
Chokonens' first contacts with,
40–41, 101
Cochise's ambivalence about, 118
Cochise's hospitality and, 270–72
Cochise's revenge war on, 136–59
Cochises's initial reactions to, 62,
67–68, 108–9
cooperation with Mexicans, 202,
205
critics of Jeffords, 281, 283, 291
decision-making style of, 220
and Geronimo wars, 292
Indian agents, 220–27, 240–45,
286. See also Jeffords, Thomas;
Steck, Michael
Killer-of-Enemies favoring, 4
legend on origin of, 1
Mangas Coloradas's initial
reaction to, 84–85
move into Chihenne territory by,
66–67, 81, 84–86, 89

peace moves by, 210, 217–33,
240, 242, 256–61
and Power, 256
return to Apache Pass by, 175–81
return to Tucson by, 172–73
supply-dependence of, 147–48
surrender to Cochise's Power by,
277–78
treachery of, 49–50, 51, 61–62,
185–86
war with Mexicans, 67, 72, 81,
85, 86, 302nn.2, 3, 306n.17
See also specific individuals
Animas Mountains, 49, 157, 192,
197
antelope hunt, 266–68
Antelope Power, 267–68
Antelope stories, 12, 20, 254, 293
anthropology, x, 312n.15
Apache (the People)
anthropological accounts of, x,
312n.15
atrocities by, 114, 127, 133,
140–41, 142, 148, 207,
307n.23
attack by Navajos on, 190
band divisions, 13, 15–16, 36
beliefs and rituals of, 17–35, 153,
270, 161
betting by, 269
ceremonial dances, 161–68
Child-of-the-Water gifts to, 4, 19,
154, 195, 231
child rearing practices, 17–22,
271
code of, 15, 17
contact with Spaniards, 13–17
courtship customs, 55–56